AMERICANS IMPORT MERIT:

Origins of the United States Civil Service and the Influence of the British Model

Richard E. Titlow

University Press of America™

TOVE

Gave love, encouragement and invaluable support.

CHRISTIAN AND KAREN

Christian, chairman of my "fan club," and Karen, always
available when needed, grew strong and tall waiting for
the typewriter to stop.

ISABEL

Never thought she would live to see the final chapter.

TABLE OF CONTENTS

Page

PREFACE   vii

CHAPTER I   INTRODUCTION   1

    Objective
    General Developments
    Chinese Civil Service
    German (Prussian) Civil Service
    French Civil Service
    The First Review by the United States of the
        French Civil Service
    Common Elements of Chinese, German, and
        French Systems

CHAPTER II   BRITISH ADMINISTRATION BEFORE 1850   23

    The Practice of Patronage
    Corrupt Administrative Practices
    Administrative Features of Parliamentary
        Supremacy Struggle
    Reform Activity from 1820 to 1850
    The Concept of Patronage as Applied in
        England Before 1850
    Efforts to Reform the Civil Service Before 1850
    Civil Service Reformers
            Thomas Babington Macaulay
            Benjamin Jowett
            Charles Edward Trevelyan
            Stafford Northcote
            Robert Lowe
            William Ewart Gladstone
    Reform Movement of the Indian Civil Service
    Reform Movement in the Universities
    Reform Movement in the Home Civil Service
    Unified Reform Campaign

CHAPTER III   BRITISH CIVIL SERVICE REFORM   55

    Civil Service Reform in India
    Northcote-Trevelyan Report
    Campaign for Reform
    Order in Council of 1855
    University Reform
    Civil Service Commission
    Northcote Select Committee of 1860

iii

Treasury Control of the Civil Service
    Commission
Struggle for Open Competition
Order in Council of 1870
Application of the OIC of 1870
Role of the Treasury in Civil Service
    Functions
Classification of Government Employees
Playfair Commission of 1873
Foreign Influence in the United States

CHAPTER IV   UNITED STATES FEDERAL SERVICE TO 1865   101

Search for a System
Establishing Precedent
Alexander Hamilton, Secretary of Treasury
Congress
Development of Political Parties
Jefferson-Hamilton Conflict
President John Adams' Policies
Removals for Party Purposes
Selection by Examination
Office Seekers Deportment
Tenure of Office Act, 1820
Increased Congressional Interest
State and Local Governments
Changes Ensue
Manifestations of Change
Application of the System of Rotation
Selective Factors
Congressional Action
Corruption-Customhouses
Growth of the Spoils System
Personnel Management

CHAPTER V   INTRODUCTION OF CIVIL SERVICE REFORM: 141
               1864-1868

Seward and Sumner Ponder
Thomas A. Jenckes
The Legislative War on the Executive Branch
Civil Service Reform Attracts Attention
Campaign for Reform
Congressional Campaign
Expectations of General Grant
Grant Alienates Reformers

CHAPTER VI   RELUCTANT REFORM: 1869-1871   171

    Climax of Reform Campaign
    Spoilsmen Counterattack
    Jenckes' Bill Changes Again
    New Leaders Join the Campaign
        George William Curtis
        Henry Adams
        Carl Schurz
    Jenckes' Last Speech
    Political Events of 1870
    Grant's Endorsement

CHAPTER VII   BRITISH INFLUENCE DURING THE JENCKES   191
               ERA: 1864-1871

    Jenckes and the British Precedent
    Report Number 47
    Foreign Influence Attacked
    Direct Contact with Reformers in England
    Response to Logan and Woodward
    British Example -- Curtis and Adams
    Familiar Arguments Persist
    British Developments Reported
    Use of British Influence in Reform Campaign

CHAPTER VIII   ABORTIVE EFFORT: 1871-1880   211

    Political Atmosphere Surrounding the
        Commission's Deliberations
    Dorman Bridgeman Eaton
    Hayes Arrests the Decline
    New York Stalwarts -- Attempts to Weaken
    Hayes Fails

CHAPTER IX   REFORMERS GO TO ENGLAND   233

    Grant Commission Looks to Britain for
        Inspiration
    British Influence Under the New Chairman
    Congressional Debate
    Reformers Made Infrequent Use of British
        Example
    Dorman Eaton to England
    Trevelyan Writes Eaton
    Eaton Reports
    Content of the Report
    Impact of the Report
    Curtis Introduction and Hayes' Last Message

CHAPTER X   VOTERS DEMAND REFORM: 1881-1883   257

    Civil Service Reform League
    Garfield Administration
    Garfield and Civil Service Reform
    Star Route Frauds
    Congress and Civil Service Reform Activities
    Assassination of President Garfield
    Impact of Assassination
    Exploiting Garfield's Illness
    Chester Alan Arthur
    Arthur on Civil Service Reform
    Congress Changes Tactics
    Political Assessments
    Second Annual Meeting of Reform League
    Election of 1882
    The Pendleton Bill
    President Chester Arthur Signs

CHAPTER XI   BRITISH INFLUENCE ON THE PENDLETON ACT: 289
          1880-1883

    Continued Use of British Example
    Eaton's Book Motivates Reformers
    Committee Hearings on the Pendleton Bill, 1881
    President Arthur Attacks the "English System"
    Senator George Pendleton's Speech
    Committee Hearings on the Pendleton Bill, 1882
    Congressional Debate on the Pendleton Bill

CHAPTER XII   BRITISH LEGACY   305

    Examinations
    Promotions
    Aristocratic Classes
    Government Stability
    Ridley Commission
    Similarities in the British and American Systems
    Anglo-American Movement
    Decline of British Influence

BIBLIOGRAPHY   321

INDEX   345

PREFACE

Reformers acknowledged that they modeled the present
civil service system after Great Britain. This study set
out to examine the influence of Great Britain on the
American civil service system, but it soon became obvious
that the study required a good understanding of the government service and its historical developments in both countries. Because of this, the study expanded into three
major categories covering the history of administrative
developments in Great Britain to 1875, the history of administrative developments in the United States before 1865,
and the influence of the British reform movement on the
United States. The complete study includes a history of
the British and American public administrations and the
civil service reform movements in both countries.

I could not have completed this work without the un-
usual support extended to me by the staff of the Civil
Service Commission Library. They acquired sources from
many locations, found pertinent information, lent me
valuable records beyond a reasonable due date, made arrangements with other libraries for me to see important sources
and purchased material from distant locations so that I
could use them. I owe a special tribute to Rachael Raisin
and Elizabeth Dance on the CSC Library staff for their
support. Violet Dee Swisher, the Head Librarian, offered
continuous encouragement and gave me valuable editorial
assistance on her own time.

Several of my friends generously gave me professional,
technical and editorial assistance to elevate the level of
writing and scholarship. I wish to thank Saul Kruger for
his editorial assistance. I owe a special vote of thanks
to Professor Robert Beiser for his professional assistance.
Professor Janet Minnihan was particularly helpful in reviewing the British segments while my long time friend and
advisor, Jean T. Joughin, extended valuable assistance in
analyzing the complete work. John F. Scott, one of the most
knowledgeable experts at the U. S. Civil Service Commission,
rendered important technical assistance.

vii

CHAPTER I

INTRODUCTION

Objective

The personnel management system presently operating in the United States Federal Service came into being in 1883 after a monumental political struggle lasting almost twenty years. It required the combined efforts of some of the most respected minds in the country to effect the change. Before 1883, the personnel management practices of the United States Government were strongly character- ized by patronage manifested in the unique American version known as the "Spoils System." Briefly, patronage is the right of a government official to nominate individuals to political office as a favor. The Spoils System augmented the patronage principle by regarding government office as the peculiar property of a successful political party to be used for its own advantage.

The patronage system led to a number of undesirable consequences. It produced a very inefficient government administration, since officials seldom chose individuals for their ability to perform the work required of them. The system often led to corruption, incompetence, graft, blackmail, and many other forms of distasteful conduct, including political assassination. Even the victors had reason to question the advantage, since they devoted enormous amounts of time to dispensing patronage. Con- sequently, the time left to carry out their official duties was seriously diminished.

Gradually, the defects of the patronage system became so intolerable that important intellectual and political leaders led a concerted effort to overthrow it. United in opposing the patronage system, they made many proposals for a better system to replace it. During this formative period, reformers studied the practices of other countries to see how they handled their personnel management systems. They studied these systems to determine if they could adapt them to the United States, in whole or in part. The re- formers found four highly developed administrative systems that merited careful consideration. They reviewed the Chinese, German, French, and British civil service systems. In the end, that of the British proved to be the most in- fluential with the Americans. This book attempts to

1

describe British influence on the development of the
United States civil service system. The system, which
began with the passage of the Pendleton Act of 1883,
owes much to social influences in America including
that of the business community. Great Britain, however,
exerted the most extensive and identifiable influence on
the United States.[1]

General Developments

Efforts in the United States to bring about administrative reform were not the result of conditions peculiar
to the United States alone. Important administrative
changes took place here, in Great Britain, Europe, and the
rest of the world in general during the last half of the
nineteenth century. Some of the major factors that contributed to these changes include the great expansion of
business interests as a result of the industrial revolution, imperialism, the growth of labor, and the growth of
social services.

The period experienced a tremendous growth in the
size of government bureaucracies that outstripped a
simultaneous growth in populations. Accompanying this
growth was the decline in acceptance of the eighteenth
century concepts of "laissez faire" and "free trade."[2]
At the same time a very important struggle was undertaken
between the legislative and executive branches of government that eventually resulted in a reduction of the power
of the legislative bodies.[3]

A profound shift began to take place in the relative
strengths of the large powers. The United States, Germany,
and Japan challenged such traditional "great powers" as
France, China, and Russia.

----

[1]This topic has attracted little scholarly attention primarily because the documents on the subject, which should
be most valuable, apparently no longer exist. Pertinent
correspondence between English officials and American reformers cannot be located on either side of the Atlantic.
Most of the letters in American files disappeared after
the collapse of the Grant Civil Service Commission in 1875.
Several scholars, including the author, attempted to find
related papers in Great Britain with equal disappointment.

[2]Samuel Edward Finer, A Primer of Public Administration
(London: Frederick Muller, Ltd., 1950), pp. 10-12.

[3]Ibid., pp. 19-25.

All of these general trends exercised significant influence on the administrative structure of many countries.

In the first half of the nineteenth century, China, Prussia, and France had worldwide reputations for efficient bureaucracies. Most nations desirous of modernizing their administrative systems looked to one of these countries for inspiration.

Chinese Civil Service

The Chinese had the oldest civil service system in the world. Scholars generally trace the origin of the Chinese system of examinations to the ancient Emperors Yao and Shun, who reigned over China, 2357-2255 B.C.[4] The idea that the ruler should be surrounded by advisers who were known for their moral integrity and wisdom has deep roots in Chinese history. Many attribute the long enduring strength of the concept to Confucius' teaching[5] that "the essence of righteous rule is moral guidance." Civil service examinations became integrated with the educational system during the Chow Dynasty (1122 B.C.). Few officials, however, were chosen by this method, as most government positions were given to members of eminent families on a hereditary basis.[6] When the Han Dynasty (206 B.C.-221 A.D.) ruled in China, the examination system was given additional importance as Confucian ideas began to affect public policy. The first active recruitment of civil servants on the basis of merit took place when local officials were asked to recommend the most talented men they could find to fill official positions. Examinations were then added to supplement these recommendations. The earliest link between an education in the Confucian classics and a government career began when Confucian scholars were hired by government officials to teach in the national university.

---

[4]Korch Huang Lo, The Civil Service System of China (Taipei: China Cultural Service, 1957), p. 1.

[5]Johanna M. Menzel, The Chinese Civil Service, Career Open to Talent? (Boston: D.C. Heath & Co., 1963), p. vii.

[6]Lo, p. 1.

During the Sui Dynasty (589-618) and the T'ang Dynasty (618-906), the civil service examination system became a weapon in the government's struggle to overcome the powers of regionalism and the hereditary aristocracy. The government recruited most government officials from among examination graduates. By the end of the T'ang Dynasty the examination system was firmly in place and lasted virtually unchanged until 1905.[7]

The scholar-official rose to the highest position in the Chinese social ladder. The dynasty freed itself from dependence on the older, hereditary aristocracy.[8] The civil service system became interwoven into the country's education system. All education in China looked to the ultimate goal of taking and passing the civil service examinations. Standards and practices of the examination system shaped traditional Chinese thought and learning. All educated people competed for examinations. In fact, most educated people studied for the examinations all of their lives. The civil service system became a valuable tool of the ruling dynasty because it gave the rulers considerable control over intellectuals. Arduous and time-consuming preparations for the examinations created an "examination life" for the educated which stifled originality and fostered conformity. It drew intellectual energies of generations into the orbit of the state.[9]

The Chinese system consisted of three major levels of examinations. At level one, aspirants competed for the Sheng yuan degree (government student) which was held in the local prefecture. Graduates received a number of coveted privileges. They qualified for certain grants and subsidies to continue their studies. This gave them the privilege of unlimited access to all educational facilities in the district, prefecture or province. Graduates were exempt from taxes. "The greatest of their privileges was that as soon as they were admitted to the district college,

---

[7]Ibid., pp. 2-5; Wolfgang Franke, The Reform and Abolition of the Traditional Chinese Examination System (Cambridge: Center for East Asian Studies, Harvard University Press, 1960), pp. 1-4.

[8]Menzel, p. viii; E.A. Kracke, Jr., Civil Service in Early Sung China--960-1067: With Particular Emphasis on the Development of Controlled Sponsorship to Foster Administrative Responsibility (Cambridge: Harvard University Press, 1953), pp. 68-70.

[9]Menzel, p. viii.

they became members of the gentry."[10] As members of the
gentry they acquired many unofficial responsibilities.
They were included in discussions of all local affairs.
The government did not require them either to bow before
magistrates or other government officials or to submit to
corporal punishment. Other benefits came their way,
but the degree did not award them an official government job.[11]

Success at level one awarded each candidate the right
and responsibility to sit for the second degree examination. The central government administered this examination
in each provincial capital. Graduates received the Chu-jen
(provisional graduate) degree. They qualified for government jobs but had no right to ask for one. However, the
imperial government appointed the most successful candidates in the provisional examination directly to various
government posts.[12] All graduates of the second level exam
were admitted to the Palace Examination supervised by the
Emperor himself.[13]

The Palace Examination, given by the Department of
Rites in Peking, capped the civil service system. It took
place one month after the provisional examination. Successful graduates received the prestigious Chin-shih (metro-
politan) degree. Students entered the Palace examination
as equals, but successful candidates emerged divided into
three grades. Class 1 consisted of the three highest men,
Class 2 was composed of about 25 per cent of the graduates,
while Class 3 contained the rest of those who passed. This
rating system entitled the graduates to certain jobs.
First and second class graduates became editors and compilers
at the Academy of Letters. Third grade scholars filled
secretarial jobs in the departments. The government awarded
each graduate a large sum of money, invited him to a ban-
quet given by the Emperor, and engraved his name upon a
tablet in the Imperial College.[14]

---

[10]Pao Chao Hsieh, The Government of China (1644-1911)
(Baltimore: The Johns Hopkins Press, 1925), p. 151.

[11]Ibid., pp. 140-185; T'ung-Tsu Ch'u, Local Government in
China Under the Ch'ing (Cambridge: Harvard University
Press, 1962), pp. 173-177, 180-185.

[12]Hsieh, p. 164.

[13]Lo, p. 5.

[14]Hsieh, p. 166.

5

At first civil service examinations covered a wide
variety of topics, but by 1644 the examination covered
a narrow range and had largely become standardized. It
consisted chiefly of the Confucian classics (Four Books
of Confucius) and the orthodox interpretation defined by
philosopher Chu Hsi in his Five Classics.[15] Examiners
selected topics from the Confucian Four Books and gave
them to the candidates. They wrote an essay on these
topics in the "Eight Legged" literary style of less than
700 words, using references to the "Five Classics" in the
essay. This essay had to be completed in four paragraphs
consisting of two parts of an equal number of sentences
and words. "The writer was to express no opinions of his
own but simply to put the few words of Confucius . . .
given in the theme into an essay following the prescribed
rules."[16]

Students took their examination in a building specifically built to service this need. In most American
and European towns and villages the most prominent archi-
tecture is often the church or cathedral. The Examination
Hall held similar prominence in Chinese towns and villages.
The buildings occupied considerable land; the one in Canton
was located on sixteen acres. Inside the exterior wall of
a main entrance led to a broad street lined on one side
with buildings used by examiners and other official staff
employees. Narrow lanes on the other side of the street
led to almost nine thousand cells.

These cells are five feet nine inches by three
feet eight inches wide, their height being a
trifle over that of a man. There are two
grooves in the wall for two planks; one forms
a table, the other a seat for the solitary student shut up in each cell. The examiners
searched each student before he entered to protect against cheating. The students were allowed to bring food, bedding, writing material,
and candles for light.[17]

---

[15]Menzel, pp. vii-viii; Franke, pp. 10-11.

[16]Mary A. Nourse, A Short History of the Chinese (New
York: Bobbs-Merrill Co., 1943), pp. 162-163.

[17]J. Dyer Ball, Things Chinese (London: Sampson Low,
Marston and Company, Limited, 1893), pp. 168-169.

A typical test might consist of two questions: write a poem on the theme "The sound of the oars, and the green of the hills and water"; write an essay on the following topic: "Tsang Tsze said, 'To possess ability, and yet ask of those who do not; to know much, and yet inquire of those who know little; to possess, and yet appear not to possess; to be full, and yet appear empty.'" The examiners never inserted questions pertaining to science, business, or industry. Judges did not seek knowledge; instead they looked for judgment and character.[18]

A considerable amount of research and attention has been devoted by Western scholars to prove that the Chinese examination system was corrupt. Representative Thomas A. Jenckes of Rhode Island, father of the civil service system reform movement in the United States, wrote an essay on the Chinese civil service emphasizing the corrupt aspects of the system. Jenckes probably wanted to lead the reader to conclude that while the Chinese had a good system,[19] America's adoption of it would not eliminate corruption. The subject is still a lively topic among historians. They have ample evidence that on rare occasions some individuals could purchase the lowest degree. By the nineteenth century the purchase of appointments became frequent and flagrant, and all along members of the Manchu ruling caste did not have to compete for office by taking the examinations. Nonetheless, historians have generally found the Chinese examination system one free of corruption and permitting a high degree of social mobility among officials in the government.[20] Scholars from all social strata could rise to prominence by passing the civil service examinations.

However, the Chinese system of recruitment did not produce efficient officials. Chinese dynasties used the civil service system pragmatically -- to control intellectuals by keeping them too busy to revolt. The Emperor

---

[18]Will Durant, Our Oriental Heritage (New York: Simon and Schuster, 1935), pp. 800-801.

[19]U.S. Congress, Joint Select Committee on Retrenchment, Civil Service of the United States, H. Rept. 47 to accompany H.R. 948, 40th Cong., 2d Sess., 1868, pp. 110-122.

[20]Francis L.K. Hsu, "Social Mobility in China," American Sociological Review 14 (1949):764-71; E.A. Kracke, Jr., "Family vs. Merit in the Chinese Civil Service Examinations During the Empire," Harvard Journal of Asiatic Studies 10 (1947):103-105 and 108-123.

intended that educated classes would spend time studying, studying, and studying. Unsuccessful candidates simply returned to their studies and prepared for another exam. In this way, many scholars spent a lifetime unsuccessfully trying to pass the civil service examinations. Government officials, selected under the Chinese civil service system, found it difficult to cope with the challenge of foreign countries in the mid- and late-nineteenth century. China simply did not have enough efficient, effective, and specialized employees to help it respond to western encroachments.[21]

German (Prussian) Civil Service

The rulers of Prussia recognized the need for an efficient and effective civil service. In the late eighteenth century a "subtle conversion [took place from] bureaucratic monarchial autocracy [to] government by an oligarchical bureaucracy."[22] The Hohenzollerns were blessed with three outstanding administrative rulers in Frederick William the Great Elector (1640-1688), Frederick William I (1713-1740), and Frederick the Great (1740-1786).

Destruction of Germany by the Thirty Years' War (1618-1648) caused "widespread suspension of authority and civil disobedience. . . which came close to anarchy."[23] Before the Thirty Years' War a landowning aristocracy, known as the Junkers, came to dominate economic, social and legal foundations of most eastern German principalities. They functioned as a selfish, highly productive economic leadership group, once they gained control of the agrarian economy and the government. The "ruler of an east German principality was scarcely more than a super-Junker."[24]

---

[21]Kenneth Scott Latourette, A Short History of the Far East (New York: The Macmillan Co., 1951), pp. 155-56; Franke, pp. 16-27.

[22]Hans Rosenberg, Bureaucracy, Aristocracy and Autocracy: The Prussian Experience: 1660-1815 (Cambridge: Harvard University Press, 1958), pp. 15-16.

[23]Fritz Morstein Marx, "Monograph 5, Civil Service in Germany," Leonard D. White et al., Civil Service Abroad, Great Britain, Canada, France, Germany (New York: McGraw-Hill Book Co., Inc., 1935), pp. 167-68.

[24]Rosenberg, pp. 28-29 and 31-32.

8

The Thirty Years' War changed all this. The Junkers emerged from the war impoverished and in need of state help. Frederick William, the Great Elector (1640-1688), chose to capitalize on the situation and built up a strong central government. The key can be seen in the Great Elector's use of the army, the base upon which he built his empire.[25] He defied the Estates by illegally maintaining unauthorized troops and using them to collect unauthorized taxes. Frederick William based his strength on establishing three illegal political monopolies: "the making of foreign policy without consent, and introduction of permanent taxation, and the maintenance of a standing army."[26] Eventually the King created a new public administration outside the old administration controlled by the Estates. By the end of his reign the new public service controlled all revenue collections, postal administration, and public education.[27]

The civil service Frederick William created adopted entrance qualifications by 1700. The government expected each candidate to have a university education in "cameralism." Cameralism consisted of courses in economics, politics, social studies, agriculture, and general state policy. Recruiters required candidates to take written and oral tests as a requirement for entrance into the civil service.[28] This system opened up the civil service to commoners, bourgeoisie, and, unlike France, to the nobility. Prussian administration absorbed some French civil servants, but eventually the Junkers and other nobles came to establish a near-monopoly of offices in the government, the army, local government, and justice. Frederick the Great made a concerted effort to draw the sons of his and his father's officials into the executive career.[29]

[25]Sir Ernest Barker, The Development of Public Services in Western Europe: 1600-1930 (Hamden, Connecticut: Archon Books, 1966), p. 19.

[26]Rosenberg, p. 35.

[27]Marx, pp. 170-71; Reinhold August Dorwart, The Administrative Reforms of Frederick William I of Prussia (Cambridge: Harvard University Press, 1953), pp. 18-25; Herman Gerlach James, Principles of Prussian Administration (New York: The Macmillan Co., 1913), pp. 20-26.

[28]A. Dunsire, Administration: The Word and the Science (New York: John Wiley & Sons, 1973), p. 53; Marx, p. 174; and Finer, p. 412.

[29]Marx, p. 175.

The Prussian administration was personally under the centralized control of the king. He worked through the Military Cabinet, consisting of military and civilian officials. The king directed the activities of the departments of ordinance, recruitment, supply, and transportation. He surrounded himself with the commanding generals, military thinkers, and the twelve highest yearly graduates from the Academie des Nobles. This centralized, authoritarian pattern remained substantially in operation until 1919 in spite of later adaptations.[30]

Prussian military disaster at the hands of Napoleon led the way for reformers in the army and civil service. The order created under the three great Hohenzollern rulers was a personal absolutism governed by two instruments -- a nobility-dominated army and a civilian bureaucracy that had absorbed the old privileges and liberties of the provincial estates. Gerhard J.D. von Scharnhorst designed the reforms initiated in the army. "He desired that the army serve the nation, not solely the king."[31] Strenuously opposed by the Junkers who feared a loss of status and power, Scharnhorst managed to expand the ranks of the army by initiating a form of universal military service. Karl Freiherr vom Stein (1757-1831) became the prime mover in other areas of reform. Stein abolished serfdom, inaugurated peasant proprietorship, and in 1808 passed a system of municipal reform. He abolished hereditary distinctions and class qualifications for the pursuit of various occupations. Stein had a poor opinion of the civil service. He saw it, although administratively efficient, as stagnant and unresponsive to "potent social undercurrents." Therefore, he liberalized entry into the government. Military officers and civil servants helped Stein and Scharnhorst achieve these reforms. The reforms left absolutism intact but increased the efficiency of government.[32]

In Prussia the best brains went into literature, the professional life, the civil service, and the officers' corps. All of Prussia's great politicians came from one of

---

[30]Finer, p. 414;   Dorwart, pp. 182-196.

[31]Finer, p. 414.

[32]Barker, p. 22;   Marx, p. 189;   Walter M. Simon, The Failure of The Prussian Reform Movement, 1807-1819 (Ithaca, New York: Cornell University Press, 1955), pp. 41-196.

these groups and were either Junker aristocrats or emulators of Junker aristocrats.

Prussia's liberal and democratic elements made an important attempt to modify the authoritarian government of Prussia in particular and Germany as a whole. The Revolution of 1848 resulted in electing a liberal German National Assembly at Frankfort. The entire experiment collapsed when the King of Prussia refused to accept the crown offered by the Assembly. Civil disorder forced the Assembly to ask the Prussian King for troops to restore order.[33]

Otto von Bismarck dominated political activity in Germany at the time of the struggle for civil service reform in the United States. From 1862 to 1890 he governed Prussia and then Germany under the authoritarian principles laid down by the early Hohenzollerns. His government was based on the Prussian Crown, the Junkers, the army, and the civil service. He fought three wars which resulted in the unification of Germany, and then had the good sense to consolidate his power while championing peace abroad.

The National Civil Service Act of 1873 extended the Prussian system of civil service to the entire German Reich. It made the principle of life tenure a general rule in order to strengthen the administrative independence of the service.[34]

Civil servants served the Reich efficiently. They needed to acquire a law degree, sit for "stiff examinations," and serve a three or four year apprenticeship before securing a career appointment. The government excluded "socialists, liberals, and Jews." The largely conservative civilian employees were "extremely efficient," paid close attention to administrative details, and were very loyal to the government. Department heads generally came from the career civil service, and politicians seldom held these positions. Most civil servants came from the nobility or aristocracy with the Junkers securing the largest block of jobs. Ministers seldom belonged to a political party but often

---

[33] John R. Gillis, The Prussian Bureaucracy In Crisis: 1840-1860; Origin of an Administrative Ethos (Stanford: Stanford University Press, 1971), pp. 89-188.

[34] Marx, p. 193.

followed the parties of the right and center. The same
civil service examinations were used to select regular
army officers and judges. The civil service frequently
accepted these officials for civilian positions. "Prussia
provided 60 per cent of the ministers for the Reich."
The central departments of each state controlled the local
government system.[35]

European and American administrators and politicians
respected the Prussian civil service for its efficiency.
The government required civil service candidates to pass
a number of examinations and to meet several specific
entrance prerequisites. All candidates must have served
some time in the army.

All candidates graduated from certain educational
institutions. Recruiters required the candidate to pass
his graduation examinations as the first civil service
test. Finally, entrance requirements demanded that each
candidate present evidence of his ability to support himself for three years without salary.

Government regulations permitted candidates with proper prerequisites to be examined after presentation of
evidence of their "good address, quick understanding and
innate intelligence." Designated officials conducted
examinations both verbally and in writing. Officials
evaluated candidates at the end of one year. If progress
was good enough, they could be admitted to a salaried job
without further examination. If, however, their progress
was poor, evaluators dismissed them. Officials subjected
those candidates whose performance was not good enough for
immediate appointment or not bad enough for dismissal to
another examination. In case of failure, examiners dismissed them immediately. If successful, a candidate was
granted another trial period without salary.

The Prussian government awarded a number of benefits
to employees in the permanent civil service. Should a
reduction-in-force become necessary, the departments
granted the released employees a reduced salary. Ill
health and old age entitled employees to a pension for retirement. The German population held permanent government
employees in great respect and high esteem.[36]

---

[35]Finer, p. 427.

[36]House Report No. 47, Civil Service of the United States,
1868, pp. 122-129.

Representative Thomas A. Jenckes attributed the
success of the Prussian civil service to ten factors:
Prussian common law; quality of the Prussian education
system; a stringent system of examinations; oath of
office; spirit of military discipline; superior moral
and mental culture of the German people; benefits granted
permanent civil servants; civil servants' contentment
with their jobs; the impartiality of the appointing power;
and the almost total absence of fraud in the Prussian
service.[37]

French Civil Service

As in Prussia, the primary reason for establishing
what has become the foundation of the French administrative
system was the central monarchy's struggle to control the
aristocracy. The system which developed lasted from about
1614 to 1789.

France based its administrative system on the principle of "Divine Right of Kings." The principle came to
be identified with "absolutism" throughout Europe and was
the basic principle upon which centralization was based.
Administratively, the king achieved and exercised centralization through the royal ministers. He organized his
royal ministers into various councils. The most important
of these was the Council of State (Conseil d'Etat), an
advisory body composed of only four or five members who
met with the king to consider such supreme matters as
international treaties and war. Council members often
participated in decisions but the king held the final
authority. The Council of Despatches (Conseil des Depeches)
considered questions affecting internal administration.
The Council of Finance (Conseil des Finances) concerned
itself with tax questions. The king directed the deliberations of this council which held its meeting in the royal
departments. The Privy Council (Conseil Prive) met without
the king and usually acted as the highest judicial court
in France. The lines of responsibility were not clear
among the various councils which caused considerable confusion.

The ministers served the king who named and dismissed
them. By the seventeenth century French kings dropped
members of nobility from the council, having found commoners
more pliable.

Some thirty intendants closely linked the country to
the central government. Cardinal Richelieu assigned one

---

[37]Ibid.

13

intendant to each administrative district in France.
Intendants dominated the local representative bodies
(provincial estates) and held the power of taxation and
control over public works. The three orders in rural
France (nobles, church, and third estate) cooperated
well on local matters, but the intendants stifled their
work and weakened their strength by awarding individuals
of their own choice various offices in municipalities.

In 1683 the government gave intendants the power of
final approval of all budgets and personnel appointments
within their districts. This power provided them strength
enough to destroy self-government of small local oligarchies
that manned the municipal and city councils. The final
step in bringing the local government completely under the
control of Paris came in 1764 when the local mayors became royal appointees.

Certain characteristics of the administrative system
carried themselves down to the nineteenth century. To
achieve strong centralized authority the French demanded
complete loyalty as the first indispensable requirement
for the new type of high official. The government
achieved it by recruiting men not tied to the existing
quasi-feudal elite. As a result, recruiters drew predom-
inantly from the lower elements of the nobility, the bourgeoisie, and from foreign ethnic elements to fill the first
generation of high administrators. Louis XIV intentionally
tried to separate status and power, reserving the former
for his noble cousins but allocating the latter to those
who depended on him for status.[38] Time greatly diminished
these distinctions. The royal power became helpless in
preventing this integration because to stop assimilation
would mean undermining one of the crown's major supports.

Ancien regime administration developed an official
esprit de corps. Officials came to see themselves as
guardians of the royal or state interest. French royalty
encouraged this concept of state supremacy as a barrier to
feudal and particularist tendencies. Hereditary recruitment became one result. Sons, nephews, and sons-in-law of
high administrators regularly entered official careers.
Nepotism became an important principle of government recruitment. Mazarin, Prime Minister from 1642 to 1661,

---

[38]J.A. Armstrong, "Old-Regime Administrative Elites:
Prelude to Modernization in France, Prussia and Russia,"
International Review of Administrative Sciences 38 (1972):23.

tried to mute the most obvious defects of such a tendency
by restricting intendants to terms of two or three years,
but subsequent ministers frequently violated and soon
forgot the restriction.

French administrators perpetuated themselves by
using examinations and education requirements to insure
that relatives of officials received preference in recruiting. The government demanded that all have degrees
in law. The law course was neither intensive nor demanding. A degree from the Sorbonne became the only formal qualification for most officials but the crown encouraged applicants to purchase positions. The high cost
of an education gave wealthy candidates more opportunity
to acquire a government position. Relatives of government
officials composed a very large majority of the French
students.

Once recruited, new employees were systematically
indoctrinated in the proper way to function. Trainers
stressed priority of the king's interest, firm conduct of
royal business, close supervision of private individuals
as well as public officials, and promotion of commerce
and industry.[39]

The administrative system functioned relatively unchanged until Napoleon Bonaparte introduced a new administrative reform. Woodrow Wilson wrote that the French
Revolution "removed all the foundations of French politics,
but scarcely any of the foundations of French administration."[40]
Napoleon built a bridge which united democracy and bureaucracy. At one end of the bridge rested the foundation of
national will granted to Napoleon by votes of the people.
At the other end rested controlled and centralized administration under effective control by its reformer, Napoleon.

Napoleon began by creating a centralized tax system.
He entrusted to agents appointed by central government
the apportionment and collection of taxes. This act resulted in the elimination of much corruption, a fairer
apportionment of taxes, and a more certain income to the
government. The Emperor retained the administrative divisions which had previously been set up. Four ministers,
those of Finance, Foreign Affairs, War, and Justice,

---

[39]Ibid., pp. 25-26; 29-30; 35.

[40]Barker, p. 14.

15

formed the "national and general" services. The Ministry
of Interior looked after the "local and special" services.
Each Ministry consisted of divisions and sections.
Throughout, the government held each official responsible,
not only to his superiors, but to the law, for the correct
discharge of his appointed tasks. Napoleon had inherited
the Ecole Polytechnique, the training school for engineering and other specialists, from which came an elite
corps of expert civil servants and army officers; he extended the system, creating the basis of the present
higher civil service, the "Grand Corps" entry to which
was based on intellectual merit and conferred on graduates
high prestige. Through this device he established the
principles of "the career open to talent." Napoleon personally chose and directed the top five hundred men.
Through them he managed the various departments on his
own principles.[41]

Napoleon strengthened the centralized authority of
the government. A prefet governed each department. The
prefect, appointed by the central government, was the
chief administrative officer of the department. The
central government appointed administrators to the subdivisions of the department, now called arrondissements
instead of districts. Napoleon's central government even
appointed the mayors of the communes, who had formerly
been elected. These authorities had an administrative
council, locally elected through indirect ballot. The
appointed officials saw that the council assessed taxes,
voted their budget, and advised on local needs and
interests.[42]

The Napoleonic Conseil d'Etat acquired an element of
cardinal importance in the new administration. It dif-
fered entirely from the Conseil d'Etat of Louis XIV.
It consisted of some forty-five salaried councillors --
lawyers, administrators, and men of civil and military
experience. It became the great and trusted organ of the
regime, constantly at work and constantly consulted. The
Conseil d'Etat drew up ordinances relating to public administration. It arbitrated the settlement of administrative disputes and rendered judgment of cases which involved
officials or services of the State. It was, in other
words, the supreme organ in all cases of administrative law.[43]

---

[41]Dunsire, pp. 66-67; and Finer, p. 239.

[42]Finer, p. 239.

[43]Barker, pp. 14-15.

16

Napoleon designed the system to enhance his personal
rule. He created a strong hierarchical government dependent from beginning to end on his personal powers, exercised
in policy, appointments, discipline and dismissals. He
covered the land with police and spies. These agents im-
prisoned leading opponents of the government. The government censored the press, and controlled the number of newspapers through a system of licenses. The Emperor increased control of education by assuming responsibility
for appointing teachers. Napoleon appointed local judges
and justices of the peace. He even controlled juries by
requiring them to be chosen from a list of approved names.
He purged or abolished some legislative bodies.

The Napoleonic system was the natural child of the
Old Regime that Louis XIV had perfected. It was, in
essence, the system which governed France during the last
quarter of the nineteenth century, and for that matter
governs France today.[44]

The Napoleonic administrative system operated in
France during the years of civil service reform in the
United States (1865-1890). During this period French
governments made only two minor adjustments in this system. In 1871 the National Assembly passed a law permitting election of additional local deliberative bodies.
It extended the law in 1884. Administration, nonetheless,
remained centralized. The prefect continued to be an
official nominated and controlled by the central government.
The central authority continued to maintain its dominance
by placing strict controls on the elected bodies with
respect to their decisions and their expenditures.[45]

Five characteristics can be identified as underlying
the public administration of France. French government
institutions operate on the principle of "supremacy of the
state." The administration rests upon the authority of the
state and that authority determines the relations of the
administration with private individuals and the internal
structure of the administration itself. The French theory
of the divine right of kings and therefore the divine
right of government served as the foundation for the political and administrative system of absolute monarchy.

---

[44]Malcolm Anderson, Government in France: An Introduction
to the Executive Power (Oxford: Pargamon Press, 1970), 18-21.

[45]Walter Rice Sharp, The French Civil Service: Bureaucracy
in Transition (New York: The Macmillan Company, 1931), p.
83; Barker, p. 17.

After the French Revolution the People replaced God.
French law recognizes an inequity between the administration and the private citizen. Consequently, two categories
of law exist in France, administered by two sets of courts.
The rights of the individual form private law or civil law,
and the rights of the state form public law or administrative law.[46]

The second characteristic of administration in France
is the propensity for centralization. For this reason
local governments in France have never reached the same
development as those in Germany and Britain. Throughout
the nineteenth century the French government developed a
multiplicity of general rules applicable to the whole of
the civil service.

A third characteristic of administration is the
strong concern with permanence. French administration
has always known a high degree of permanence in its personnel.[47] Even the French Revolution did not result in
wholesale disruption of the civil service. Many officials
who started work between 1770 and 1785 did not retire
until after forty or even fifty years of uninterrupted
service. We have no evidence that the French civil service had more promotions or turnover of staff than usual
during the three political regimes between 1848 and 1851
or in the revolutionary years of 1870 and 1872.[48]

The fourth characteristic of administration in France
developed from the supremacy of the state characteristic.
The Administration, the embodiment of the State, consequently formed a separate social group with its own men-
tality, traditions, virtues, honor, and pride. Its members considered themselves to be the elite of French
society and were envied by most people. At least one son
in every important family trained to enter the civil service.

---

[46]Anderson, pp. 5-7.

[47]William A. Robson, ed., The Civil Service in Britain
and France (New York: The Macmillan Company, 1956), pp.
161-163; Anderson, pp. 15-17.

[48]Roger Gregoire, The French Civil Service (Brussels:
International Institute of Administrative Sciences,
1964), pp. 35-36.

A fifth characteristic called for delegation of
personnel management to each of the five major departments. Each developed its own rules and regulations
which had a considerable degree of variation. American
nineteenth century reformers noted this contradiction of
the French characteristic of centralization and opposed
the lack of a centralized personnel management organization.[49]

The First Review by the United States
of the French Civil Service

Reformers in the United States sought to use France,
so far as we know, as the first model of a foreign civil
service for possible application to this country. Secretary
of State William Henry Seward asked John Bigelow, United
States Consul in Paris, to provide him with information on
the civil service in France which might benefit the United
States. Bigelow responded to Seward's 1862 request by
transmitting a comprehensive study of the personnel management practices of the French Ministry of Finance.

Bigelow described the Ministry of Finance as a highly
centralized, hierarchical organization with an amazing
record of fraud-free service. He attributed this record
to the personnel management system. Bigelow considered
permanent tenure of service as its most important feature.
The Ministry of Finance appointed employees for life. It
provided each employee with a pension.[50]

The Ministry of Finance recruited all new employees
at the lowest level of clerk and filled all positions by
promotion from within. Entrance requirements were stiff
and strictly enforced. No employee could enter without
passing a competitive examination. The politics
of a candidate had no influence on his entrance or promotion. The recruit between the ages of eighteen and
twenty-five could apply for admission. He had to have no
medical defects, have good character references, be a
French citizen, and show his ability to support himself
without salary for one year. The Personnel Office asked

---

[49]Robson, pp. 164-169.

[50]A sixty-year-old employee with thirty years service could
retire with seventy-five per cent of his average salary for
the highest six years of service. United States Civil Service regulations today permit an employee to retire after
thirty years of service and fifty-five years of age at sixty
percent of his average salary for the highest three years of
service. He is entitled to not more than eighty per cent of
his average salary regardless of length of service.

each candidate to take an oral and written examination.
The Ministry created a register of successful candidates
for use in filling vacancies during the succeeding year.
Candidates selected from the register worked one year
on probation, without financial compensation. Bigelow
recognized that the system made it easier for children of
existing employees and veterans to enter the service.
Once in France, a civil servant found a very structured
hierarchical promotion system. Supervisors compiled performance evaluations on each employee for inclusion in a
permanent personnel folder. The department prepared promotion lists from these performance evaluation forms.
Promotion panels selected employees for promotion from the
list. The personnel system contained very detailed procedures for dealing with misconduct and poor work performance.

John Bigelow concluded in his 1863 report, "there is
much in the organization of the French revenue service
by which the United States might profit." He singled out
the permanent tenure of office, lack of corruption, and
potential use of civil servants for a loyal military reserve in time of grave national crisis as the most important aspects of the system. He acknowledged that the French
system required more employees than the United States system. However, French employees accepted lower salaries
than corresponding employees in the United States because
of the security and responsibility they acquired from the
civil service. He felt that the system of promotion secured the most competent and faithful men for the higher
and more responsible grades of service. By recruiting at
the lowest level the system insured that France would have
the service of these men during the best years of their
lives. The French system guaranteed her employees a constantly improving livelihood.

Bigelow was not optimistic about chances of adopting
the French system in the United States. He wrote,

Unhappily, I fear, none of these advantages can
be grafted upon our system of quadrennial changes
in the administration. The whole value of the
French system depends upon the permanent tenure
of the service. The moment that is rendered in-
secure the whole fabric crumbles to pieces; and
unless some method can be devised by which those
who enter the subordinate departments of the
United States government can be guaranteed a
similar permanence, we must pay much higher
salaries, get very inferior service, waste our
experience, and, withal, fall a prey to the
infinite brood of frauds which inevitably re-

20

sult from the constant conflict between
interest and duty which our execrable practice of mutation in office engenders.[51]

Common Elements of Chinese, German,
and French Systems

Government administration attracted high quality
candidates in China, Germany, and France. All three
countries used highly centralized personnel management
systems. This centralization extended down to the lowest
levels of government. Employees in the bureaucracy developed into an elite social group, separate from the
general public. Civil servants received certain privileges and commanded great respect from most citizens.
Consequently, many sought these coveted positions with
much enthusiasm. Intellectuals in China competed for
the relatively few government positions. Competition became a way of life for most. Junkers developed great
pride in Prussia's efficient administration, which they
dominated. France's great families considered the civil
service so prestigious that many trained at least one son
for entrance.

Civil servants from each country gave great loyalty
to the ruling king or emperor. They held little feeling
of service to the public and seldom considered themselves
protectors of the public interest. Each civil service
system became static. The governments responded slowly
to new ideas and initiated major changes only after times
of political disaster, and then they never undertook a
complete revision. Each of these three services had rather
severe education prerequisites which acted as a means of
preselection. Stringent educational requirements allowed
only a small portion of the population to meet the requirements. Thus, the civil service came to be dominated by a
single social class. Civil service requirements greatly
influenced educational institutions in each country.

Finally, all three countries required some sort of
competitive examination for entrance into its civil service system. However, these competitive examinations became rigid and did little to measure actual skills an

---

[51]John Bigelow to William H. Seward, Paris, August 25,
1863, quoted in House Report No. 4, Civil Service of the
United States, 1868, pp. 176-182.

21

employee needed on the job. Managers filled vacancies by promoting employees to higher positions exclusively from current civil servants. They permitted little, if any, new blood to enter the service at the higher grades.

CHAPTER II

BRITISH ADMINISTRATION BEFORE 1850

The English considered public service "a task for intelligent amateurs."[1] Many years of slow progress passed before public service became a task for professionals.

After the Wars of the Roses, the Tudors initiated important administrative changes. They frequently chose their public servants from the upper middle class -- the gentry -- the same men who controlled local government and promoted better local administration by expanding the duties of the justices of the peace. The Tudor rulers acted energetically to manage the Parliaments.

Administrative absolutism, begun by the Tudors, was firmly entrenched during the religious upheavals of the Reformation. It ended in 1689. Establishment of parliamentary supremacy eventually replaced that of the crown. The Bill of Rights of 1689 recognized the change. "Henceforth the theory of the English State is a theory not of the administrative absolutism of a king, but the legislative omnipotence of a parliament -- a parliament which, indeed, included the king as well as the lords and commons, as it moves again, from 1832 onwards, to the signification of the commons alone."[2]

The Practice of Patronage

Politicians acquiring high government and party positions gained powerful rights to dispense patronage. Generally, these politicians exercised this privilege in similar ways. Part of their patronage went to relatives and family members. Another segment went to friends and friends of important individuals. Current civil servants called upon politicians to appoint their sons to government jobs. The most important portion of a politician's patronage went for political purposes. Political patronage had to be dispensed carefully, with consideration given to all segments of the party, local patrons, and powerful in-

---

[1]Ernest Barker, The Development of Public Services in Western Europe: 1660-1930 (Hamden, Connecticut: Archon Books, 1966), p. 29.

[2]Ibid., p. 31.

23

dividuals in society. Not only was the politician expected to dispense jobs, but exercise influence on the advancement of officeholders who acquired their jobs through his influence.

Unfortunately, politicians found that their control of patronage absorbed enormous amounts of their time and resulted in diminishing benefits, since the demand steadily grew in proportion tc the number of positions available. Patrons soon found that every position given to satisfy one office seeker created two or more enemies of those who went home empty handed.[3]

Corrupt Administrative Practices

The English civil service at the end of the seventeenth century consisted of employees who gained their positions directly from the Crown. In general, various accepted forms of corruption characterized the public service. The Crown appointed officials who gave it their political support. Officials used their positions for personal and political gain. Corruption in the form of dishonesty, forgery, fraudulent accounting, misuses of public money or supplies, extortion, improper pressure to secure advantages, and bribery was common. Some forms of corruption characterized specific government branches more than others. Military pay machinery offered opportunities to practice forgery involving the issuance, by the War Treasurer's Office, of certificates or debentures in the amounts owing to the individuals and units concerned. Dishonest officials issued false or forged debentures in large numbers. Dishonest treasurers and accountants took advantage of their jobs to fill their own pockets. These officials made large illicit gains through fraudulent accounting practices. Everyone, including the Crown, Parliamentarians, advisors, noblemen, politicians, and government employees practiced one form of bribery and extortion or another. These techniques were so commonplace and effective that the first moves toward administrative reform attempted to eliminate them.[4]

---

[3]Henry Parris, Constitutional Bureaucracy: The Development of British Central Administration Since the Eighteenth Century (London: George Allen and Unwin, Ltd., 1969), pp. 50-72.

[4]G.E. Aylmer, The King's Servants: The Civil Service of Charles I: 1625-1642 (London: Routledge & Kegan Paul, 1974), pp. 176-182; G.E. Aylmer, The Civil Service of the English Republic 1649 to 1660 (London: Routledge & Kegan Paul, 1973), pp. 140-145 and 153-154.

Administrative Features of
Parliamentary Supremacy Struggle

Fearing that the king would circumvent the Bill of
Rights of 1689 by purchasing support with direct gifts
to civil officers, Parliament passed a series of laws to
prevent this likelihood. The first of these exclusion
acts came in 1694 when Parliament forbade members of the
newly created Revenue Board for Stamp Duties from holding
a seat in Parliament.[5] From then on, civil officers became
pawns in the struggle between Parliament and the King.
Eventually, Parliament excluded masses of officials from
sitting in Parliament.[6] In 1699 several excise officers
were included in the prohibition. The Act of Settlement,
1701, contained a sweeping exclusion clause. The Act provided that "no person who has an office or place of profit
under the King, or receives a pension from the Crown shall
be capable of service as a member of the House of Commons."
This proved too sweeping for politicians to accept and in
1706 Parliament greatly modified it. Thus began the principle which persists today that public officers consisted
of two groups, those who held office as temporary political
chiefs, allowed to win and hold a seat in Parliament, and
the great majority of permanent officials, forbidden to
sit in Parliament.[7]

Government officials helped partisan politicians
during elections. Parliament decided to extend the exemp-
tion principle to include barriers against participating
in elections by government employees. The first acts
came in 1712 when Queen Anne signed a law forbidding postal
officials from taking part in elections.[8] The next Parliamentary act came seventy years later as a result of Edmund
Burke's campaign for economic reform. The cost of the
American Revolution prompted Burke to say: "Neither the present, nor any other first lord of the Treasury, has ever

---

[5]Dorman B. Eaton, Civil Service in Great Britain: A History
of Abuses and Reforms and Their Bearing Upon American Politics (New York: Harper & Brothers, 1880), p. 72.

[6]Finer, p. 31.

[7]Robert Moses, The Civil Service of Great Britain (New York:
Columbia University, 1914), p. 21.

[8]Finer, pp. 32-33.

been able to make a survey, or make even a tolerable mess
of the expenses of government of any one year, so as to
enable him with the least degree of certainty, or even
probability, to bring his affairs into compass."[9]
Burke's charges led to the Act of 1782 which disfranchised
customs, excise, and postal officials, amounting to about
one-sixth of the total number of government employees.
Burke saw the problem of the civil service as one of lack
of efficiency. Far ahead of his time, his efficiency criteria never applied to the selection process for government employees. Instead, family and political influence
dominated appointments until the middle of the next century.[10]

The Burke Law of 1782 demonstrated the need for another technique to audit public offices. Parliament responded by establishing a series of official investigations.
Lord North created the first of such inquiries, a Commission on Public Accounts in 1780. The Commission completed its work seven years later. This committee's report
gave Parliament its first comprehensive information about
the operation of public business. The Commission helped
the then Prime Minister William Pitt (the Younger) introduce a number of administrative reforms, including a new
system for financial auditing. Between 1786 and 1788
the Commission on Fees produced ten reports on its investigation into the much abused system of paying public servants
with a salary supplemented by fees. They found that fee
payments increased, at times, to unreasonable heights, and
as the fee system increased the value of the patronage
available to the King increased. Pitt refused to release
the last report on the Post Office to the Postmaster Generals because it was so embarrassing. The Select Committee
of 1797 produced a comprehensive statement on the condition
of the nation's finance.

Burke's Civil Establishment Act of 1782 marks the
beginning of another administrative reform, pertaining to
sinecures.[11] This act abolished 134 sinecure offices.
Sir William Petty, First Marquis of Lansdowne and Second
Earl of Shelburne, abolished another 144 as First Lord of

---

[9]Parliamentary History (1780), Vol. 21, p. 29, quoted in
Emmeline W. Cohen, The Growth of the British Civil Service:
1780-1939 (London: George Allen & Unwin, Ltd., 1941), p. 22.

[10]Finer, pp. 32-33.

[11]Sinecures constitute a type of patronage where political
officials appoint a favorite to a salaried government office
or position which involved little or no responsibility or
active service.

the Treasury in the same year. Pitt ended 765 offices
in 1789 and another 196 in 1798. The Committee on Sinecure Offices issued a general attack on the practice in
1810-12, recommending abolition of each office after the
death of existing office holders. In 1817 another 313
were identified for abolition, and finally in 1832 some of
the most important sinecure offices were abolished with
the retirement of their incumbents. By 1833 another
Committee on Finance discovered only 55 sinecure posts
remaining. Anthony Trollope reflected the unpopularity
of sinecure positions when he told an audience of civil
servants: "But a sinecurist proper, a man who takes pay
and does not give or has given nothing for it, is a con-
temptible fellow."[12]

Burke's Act of 1782 also began the attack on the mis-
use of pension payments. The government paid pensions
through the use of the Civil list.[13] Burke's law limited
the payment of pensions from Civil list funds to a maximum
of 95,000 pounds. He incorporated into the law an abolition of the secrecy that had surrounded these payments.
The Scottish-Irish Civil lists, diplomatic and military
pensions, colonial pensions, and special exchequer revenue
pensions all came under attack. The sum paid out in Civil
list pensions steadily declined. The recommendations of
the Select Committee on the Civil List in 1831-33 resulted
in further reductions. Parliament settled the issue at
the start of Queen Victoria's reign (1837) by establishing
regulations to govern future awards. Parliament restricted
pensions to those who made important artistic or scientific
contributions, served the Crown, or made significant contributions in public service.[14]

The Civil list itself came under the reform movement.
In 1802 Parliament required that deficits in the Civil list
be reviewed each year. In the next fifteen years the government removed a number of expenditures from the Civil list
and assigned them to a separate Civil Establishment. Fin-

---

[12]Anthony Trollope, "The Civil Service as a Profession,"
Four Lectures, ed. Morris L. Parrish (London: Constable
& Co., Ltd., 1938), p. 11.

[13]The Civil list consisted of money granted by Parliament to
each king with which to defray the civil expenses of government. When the king overspent, the deficits accumulated until
he asked Parliament to provide funds to eliminate the debt.

[14]Peter G. Richards, Patronage in British Government (Toronto:
University of Toronto Press, 1963), p. 29.

ally, the Select Committee on the Civil List (1830-31) [15] restricted it further by defining specifically its use. Table 1 summarizes the British administrative reform activity from 1455 to 1820.

Reform Activity from 1820 to 1850

During the 1820's, 1830's, and 1840's the broader movements for parliamentary reform overshadowed interest in administrative reform, culminating in the great Reform Bill of 1832. Nevertheless, a number of developments took place in England which influenced civil service reform.

The great Utilitarian philosopher Jeremy Bentham made a contribution to patronage reform. In his book Official Aptitude Maximized, Expense Minimized (1830) he presented a "general basis for a reform of the corrupt officialdom and rank patronage of his time."[16] He developed a detailed code of official appointment and pay in his book Constitutional Code. Bentham even advocated oral examinations for civil servants which he thought would prevent examiners from accepting obviously incompetent applicants. [17]

Reform spread to many areas during this period. In 1833 the British abolished slavery in the colonies, terminated the trade monopoly of the East India Company, and initiated factory inspection and an educational grant-in-aid program. The government established the Committee on the Privy Council, a central administrative authority, to administer the grants. The Committee gave guidance on the terms which grants were to be made and authorized enforcement through inspectors. The Administration sponsored laws to reform the municipal system. In 1834 Parliament established a municipal and country police force and began the appointment of local Boards of Health. It expanded the franchise in 1832, and after a monumental Parliamentary struggle, terminated the corn law tariffs in 1846. Patronage reform was only one of a long series of reforms, just as far-reaching, adopted in this era.

---

[15] Ibid., p. 30.

[16] Finer, pp. 33-34.

[17] David Roberts, Victorian Origins of the British Welfare State (New Haven: Yale University Press, 1960), pp. 29-34.

TABLE 1

ADMINISTRATIVE REFORM ACTIVITY
FROM 1455 TO 1820

Date	Activity	Administrative Implications
1455-1485	Wars of the Roses	Tudor reforms. a. Selection from upper-middle class. b. Local administrative improvements. c. Creation of administrative absolutism.
1689	Bill of Rights	a. Ends administrative absolutism. b. Establishes Parliamentary supremacy.
1694	First Exclusion Act	Prevents government employees administering the Stamp Duties from sitting in Parliament.
1699	Excise Tax Officers in Exclusion Act	Bars excise officers from sitting in Parliament.
1701	Act of Settlement	Sweeping exclusion law--no one paid by the government could sit in Parliament.
1706	Modification of Act of Settlement	Prohibits career employees only from sitting in Parliament.
1712	First Prohibition Against Participating in Elections	Forbade postal officials from participating in elections.

Date	Activity	Administrative Implications
1782	Civil Establishment Act	a. Disfranchises customs, excise, and postal officials. b. Advocates new technique in auditing public offices. c. Abolishes first sinecure offices. d. Limits funds for Civil list.
1782	Lansdowne's Treasury Order on Sinecure Offices	Abolishes 144 sinecure offices.
1787	Commission on Public Accounts Report	Provides Parliament with first comprehensive look at public administration.
1786-88	Commission on Fees Report	Exposes financial abuses.
1789	Prime Minister Pitt Abolishes Sinecure Offices	Abolishes 765 sinecure offices.
1797	Select Committee of 1797	Comprehensive review of finances.
1798	Prime Minister Pitt Abolishes Sinecure Offices	Abolishes 196 sinecure offices.
1802	Parliamentary Law on Civil List	Requires annual review of Civil List deficits.

Date	Activity	Administrative Implications
1810-12	Committee on Sinecure Report	Recommends abolishing all sinecure offices.
1817	Government Identifies Sinecure Offices for Abolition	Abolishes 313 sinecure offices.

The relative strength of aristocrats occupying civil service posts declined during this period. Historian J. Donald Kingsley states that the Reform Act of 1832 had more effect on the civil service than on the Parliament. While the aristocracy continued to dominate the Parliament for many years after 1832, the middle class began to command a share in official spoils for support of the government. Although the public service remained aristocratic, the middle class share steadily increased.[18]

Herman Finer writes that the code of ethics of the British aristocracy made an important contribution to the movement leading toward civil service reform.

> . . . they had created among themselves
> standards of honourable service. There
> must be honesty and efficiency and public
> spirit in their own home. Their inherit-
> ance must not be wasted. Noblesse oblige.
> This tradition passed over to the newly
> risen middle class. . . .[19]

The Concept of Patronage as Applied
in England Before 1850

Historian Peter Richards outlines four basic methods of selecting officials for public office. Chance is the most democratic, but it assumes that all men are equally suitable. Heredity selects by birth. It has the advantage of providing continuity and certainty but the disadvantage of being undemocratic and unresponsive to public opinion. In essence, heredity provides no public accountability. Competition has two major subdivisions: some form of election, or some form of impersonal examination. Elections provide an opportunity for officials to test public opinion. It does a poor job of selecting individuals on the basis of personal suitability. Selection by examination enables officials to be chosen on the basis of ability. It is not good for responding to public opinion or political considerations and requires great

---

[18] J. Donald Kingsley, Representative Bureaucracy (Yellow Springs, Ohio: The Antioch Press, 1944), pp. 54-56; Roberts, pp. 137-138; W.J. Reader, Professional Men: The Rise of the Professional Classes in Nineteenth Century England (New York: Basic Books, Inc., Publishers, 1966), pp. 73-83.

[19] Finer, p. 38.

confidence in the test validity to work properly. The
fourth basic method of selecting government officials is
by the technique of _patronage_. This method places control
of appointments in the hands of certain individuals or
groups of people. It assists those in power to maintain
their position by providing them with a tool to offer others
for continued support. "Those who enjoy the favour of the
mighty enjoy place and prosperity; those who offend them
are jobless or worse." Patronage benefits an authoritarian
form of government best.[20]

Once a most powerful prerogative of the crown, patronage gradually came under the control of the ministry, and
eventually it fell to the majority party in Parliament.[21]
A few ministers, such as the First Lord of the Treasury and
the Home Secretary, had patronage power in departments outside their own. But most restricted their activities to
their own organizations.[22] The English applied no moral
restriction on the right of political leaders to confer
favors. They considered it one of the benefits of leadership. The degree of control exercised by political leaders
varied from place to place and from time to time. This
fluctuated with changing circumstances such as the death of
the head of a family or sale of property.[23] Each department
established its own rules for dispensing patronage and
numerous variations prevailed. At the Treasury the high
volume of business motivated the First Lord of the Treasury
to acquire a full-time assistant, the Patronage Secretary,
to dispense patronage on his behalf.

Patronage had a profound impact on politics. The
powerful denied favors to those who opposed them. Office
holders carried out their public duties in such a way as to
avoid offending their patrons. Before making a decision,
officials gave great consideration to the relative power of
patrons. They deliberated on such things as who had superior or equal power, or how far one's influence extended.

---

[20]Richards, pp. 11-16.

[21]Moses, p. 19.

[22]Maurice Wright, _Treasury Control of the Civil Service:
1854-1874_ (Oxford: Clarendon Press, 1969), p. xxiv.

[23]Richards, p. 20.

Government by patronage required a continuous flow of favors. Powerful men came under constant pressure to dispense favors among the influential. Relatives, friends, and constituents competed for positions. A minister might have so few appointments at his disposal that he often caused more animosity among competitors who failed to get positions than any benefit patronage gave him. Ministers devoted a staggering amount of time to patronage. The subject dominated their correspondence.

John Wood, Chairman of the Board of Inland Revenue in 1854, charged that patronage brought political corruption to voters, Parliament, and the government. He stated in 1854:

> Let any one who has had experience, reflect on the operation of patronage on Electors, Parliament, and the Government. Over each it exercises an evil influence. In the Electors it interferes with the honest exercise of the franchise; in Parliament it encourages subservience to the administration; it impedes the free action of a Government desirous of pursuing an honest and economical course, to their particular fitness. . . . It is bribery in its worst form.[24]

Patronage had profound effects on the civil service itself. For one thing, employees gave their loyalty to the patron to whom they looked for protection. Workers considered themselves part of an individual department or bureau, for no one felt part of a government service or profession. Civil servants seldom participated in the preparation or formation of policy. They primarily carried out decisions made by ministers. A job in a department was generally comfortable and secure and especially unexciting. Most spent their careers on routine and humdrum tasks which required no ability or energy and only part of their time. Civil servants copied most documents and papers by hand. Vast numbers of them spent their entire day reproducing these documents. Time weighed heavily on the hands of many civil servants. Anthony Trollope described times when employees spent hours for lunch, played cards, and held smoking parties to occupy their time.[25]

---

[24]Great Britain, Parliamentary Papers, Papers Relating to the Re-Organization of the Civil Service (London, Her Majesty's Stationery Office, 1855), p. 302.

[25]Anthony Trollope, An Autobiography of Anthony Trollope (New York: G. Munro, 1883), p. 53.

> . . . occasionally they would be joined at
> lunch-time by "equally bored" young Guards-
> men from neighbouring barracks and together
> played cricket in a large room at the top
> of the office. . . . One of the attic rooms
> was set aside. . . to pass away their spare
> time, a piano was provided. . .as well as
> foils, single-sticks, boxing gloves, and
> other sources of amusement.[26]

Many important literary figures took advantage of government positions to write much of their important works.
Anthony Trollope, Edmund Yates, Matthew Arnold, Arthur
Hugh Clough, and Henry Taylor, full time civil servants,
pursued successful literary careers in this period.
"Security and modest financial comfort were attractive
to the writer; the short official hours left time for
writing, and the flexibility of office procedure and
working conditions made it possible to pursue other activities without too much difficulty."[27]

In 1808 investigations inquired into the Stamp Office in the Post Office Department. They found that
clerks disliked going beyond their exact assignments.
Employees displayed a vast indifference toward the public
business. Many clerks amused themselves by "singing,
fencing, rioting, or in any other way most agreeable to
themselves." Some clerks, the inquiry found, had a habit
of bringing dogs to the office.[28]

Appointments by patronage took no account of ability
or energy and discouraged the most able men from making
government their career. Nevertheless, patronage in
England never produced a "spoils system"[29] similar to that
in the United States. A party coming into office did not

---

[26]Sir Edward Hertslet, Recollections of the Old Foreign
Office (London: J. Murray, 1901), p. 25.

[27]Wright, pp. xxxiv and xxxv.

[28]Wyn Griffith, The British Civil Service: 1854-1954
(London: His Majesty's Stationery Office, 1954), p. 11.

[29]See Chapter IV for a discussion of the "spoils system"
as applied in the United States. A good study on the subject is Leonard D. White, The Jacksonians (New York: Macmillan Co., 1954).

automatically eject the nominees of their predecessors. Patronage applied to vacancies and new positions with some pressure on promotions, although the seniority convention generally applied in the public service.[30] "On the other hand the partisan, or at any rate political appointee, who was utterly inefficient or hopelessly lazy, enjoyed the protection of a permanent tenure, which only death or voluntary resignation could interrupt."[31]

Once the British tried a purge. From 1763 to 1765 the administration evicted supporters of the Duke of Newcastle from public office. However, the new government did not act vindictively and remove the new employees when it returned. It simply reinstated those who had lost their jobs.[32]

The system of rotation in office probably did not come to Great Britain for a number of reasons. The British had a great respect for vested rights, in contrast to a genuine fear of the entrenched and arbitrary authority of permanent office holders that grew out of the colonial experience in the United States. Government changes in Britain often resulted from a change in a coalition of personal and political interests between the departing ministry and the new government and not because of a party defeat. The English system of government offered new administrators no guarantee of a tenure of four or eight years duration as the Constitution granted governments in the United States. The British considered public office as personal property and to eliminate the incumbent was almost as bad as stealing. In respect for this principle, the British eliminated an unnecessary office by writing it out of existence after the last incumbent died or resigned his post.[33]

Efforts to Reform the Civil Service Before 1850

Reform of the British Civil Service evolved over a period of twenty eventful years, from 1850 to 1870. A small group of far-sighted, energetic, and powerful individuals came together to act as a catalyst for the reform.

---

[30]Richards, p. 41.

[31]Moses, p. 24.

[32]Richards, p. 41.

[33]Ibid., pp. 41-2.

It took the combined efforts of three reform movements that merged to bring about the desired results: reform of the university system, reform of the Indian civil service, and reform of the home civil service.

Isolated attempts to mute the most offensive aspects of patronage can be found throughout the second quarter of the nineteenth century. After all, members of Parliament and departmental managers had a built-in conflict of interest. The member of Parliament wanted to satisfy his constituents for political reasons, but ministers needed a minimum amount of ability to perform the functions of the departments. When patronage appointments fell below minimum standards, ministers had to act. "By 1832 there was fairly widespread agreement that the efficiency of the public service should not suffer through the unfettered use of patronage."[34]

Prime Minister Robert Peel declined on several occasions to dispense government jobs to individuals without qualifications for the positions. In 1843 he refused to give the Member of Parliament for Evesham a diplomatic post. Again, he refused to appoint Captain Boyd, son of the Member of Parliament for Coleraine, to the new post of Register-General in Ireland.[35]

Probably the boldest attempt to incorporate an ability criterion into the patronage system came from Sir James Graham at the Admiralty. The First Lord of the Admiralty from 1830 to 1834, Graham was so disturbed by the adverse effects of patronage on the efficiency of his department that he decided to ignore the system and appoint competent officers irrespective of their political affiliations. His action caused a great uproar in Parliament and led to a reprimand from the Patronage Secretary. He defended himself skillfully against those who demanded a change of policy. Graham wrote one complaining Parliamentarian: "I care not what people may say, so long as my conscience tells me I have acted justly; and if I am swayed by other motives, in the difficult and odious task of distributing patronage, I should be altogether unworthy of the office which I hold."[36] To another he wrote: "All promotions in

---

[34]Richards, p. 38.

[35]Ibid., p. 39.

[36]C.S. Parker, Life and Letters of Sir James Graham: Second Baronet of Netherby, P.C., G.C.B.: 1792-1861 (London: J. Murray, 1907), p. 163.

the Dockyard will henceforth be given as the reward of merit, on the recommendation of the Admiral Superintendent. As [for] patronage I cease to exercise it, and I have made it over to the Board, with the intention of carefully watching its distribution."

The Whig Patronage Secretary reprimanded the First Lord by stating:

> I have undoubted authority that the Tories are at a loss to devise any other motive in your recent dispensation of the patronage at the Admiralty than a desire to conciliate and cultivate the Conservative party, it is quite time you should be made acquainted with the murmurs of your friends, and the jeers of the enemy.[37]

Graham responded by saying: "The officers have generally been selected by me for their efficiency, and not for their politics; and if professional merits be regarded by my successor he will have no reason to complain of my appointments."[38]

Parliamentary attacks or the rebuke from the Patronage Secretary failed to persuade Sir James to change his politics. When Graham's tenure expired, the hold of patronage in the Admiralty returned as strong as ever.[39] Graham's weakness was that he failed to systematize his policies on recruitment and appointment.

Treasury officials made several feeble attempts to put some restraints on the effects of patronage in the Treasury Department. In 1820 they prescribed age limits for appointees of the Customs office. In 1836 officials acknowledged that a revenue official who violated revenue laws should not be appointed. The Treasury Minute of 1831 suggested that appointees be required to serve a probational period in order to enable the department to eliminate inefficient nominees. The Treasury even experimented with

---

[37]C.S. Parker, p. 164.

[38]Ibid.

[39]Richards, p. 40; John Trevor Ward, Sir James Graham (London: Macmillan, 1967), pp. 128-129; Arvel B. Erickson, The Public Career of Sir James Graham (Oxford: Blackwell, 1952), pp. 105-107.

departmental examinations. From 1834 to 1841 Treasury officials prescribed that each vacancy should be filled from a choice of three nominations. Employers chose the successful candidate according to his test score. Such feeble attempts made no significant impact on the department's attempt to eliminate the unfit or select the most suitable candidates.[40]

Civil Service Reformers

Political influence remained supreme in the area of government appointments throughout the second quarter of the nineteenth century. The battle against these abuses began with a small group of influential reformers interested in administrative reform in the universities at Oxford and Cambridge and in the colonial administration of India.

The cast of characters who played the most prominent part in this reform began with the great British historian Thomas Babington Macaulay (1800-1859). Macaulay was born in Leicestershire, England, and educated at the University of Cambridge. He was admitted to the bar in 1826. Macaulay was a prolific writer who contributed numerous articles to the Edinburgh Review, including his famous one on Milton in 1825. He wrote a five-volume History of England covering the reigns of James II and William III and also a book entitled Lays of Ancient Rome. Macaulay's public career spanned most of his life from 1830. He was a Member of Parliament 1830-1834, 1839-1847, and 1852-1856. He served in the civil service as a member of the Supreme Council of India (1834-38), Secretary of War (1839-41), and Paymaster of the Forces (1846-47). The Queen raised him to the peerage in 1857 as First Baron Macaulay.[41] Macaulay developed the basic concepts of civil service reform and applied them to patronage reform in the Indian service.

Benjamin Jowett (1817-1893) devoted his entire life to education. A Greek scholar and educational administrator, the English theologian was born in London in 1817 and educated at St. Paul's School and Balliol, Oxford. He was ordained in 1842 and became a tutor in the college. In 1848 his attention turned to reform of the university system. He was keenly interested in the reform of the Indian

---

[40]Cohen, p. 77.

[41]George Otto Trevelyan, Life and Letters of Lord Macaulay, 2 vols. (London: Longmans, Green, 1876); John Clive, Macaulay: The Shaping of the Historian (New York: Alfred A. Knopf, 1973); Dictionary of National Biography, 1921-2 ed., s.v. "Thomas Babington Macaulay."

civil service sponsored by Macaulay. He contributed to
the Royal Commission on Oxford University (1850-52) in
its efforts to reform the university system. He became
intimately familiar with the examination system introduced
there. This interest led him to become a close associate
of Sir Charles Trevelyan and Robert Lowe, prominent civil
service reformers. Jowett came under severe attack in
1860 when his opponents accused him of heresy before the
vice-chancellor's court as a result of an essay he contributed to Essay and Reviews (1860). Charges were eventually dropped, but university officials nevertheless reduced his salary. His best known works were his transla-
tions of Plato (1871), Thucydides' History (1881), and
Aristotle's Politics (1885). He was elected Master of
Balliol in 1870 and served until 1893. He was also vice-
chancellor of Oxford from 1882 to 1886.

Jowett was a gifted classical scholar and one of the
great teachers of his time.

An insight into human nature, devotion to his
pupils, many of whom became life-long friends,
and a belief in the value of close contact between tutor and individual minds, combined in
inspiring scores of young men who were called
upon to take a leading part in the national
life. Jowett never failed in assisting men of
ability, whether of the poorer or more wealthy
classes. All he required was sincerity and promise of ability.[42]

Sir Charles Edward Trevelyan (1807-1886), unofficial
leader of this group of reformers, was born in 1807 into
an old, well-educated family in Cornwall. At fifteen he
enrolled at Haileybury prep school for service in India,
where he won prizes for classics, history, political
economy, and Sanskrit. Upon graduation, he began service
as a writer in the Bengal civil service where he served
from 1826 to 1838. Though only nineteen when he began
his Indian service, he brought with him certain characteristics which made him known throughout England and India
by the time he was twenty-one. He combined the qualities

---

[42]Encyclopedia Brittanica, 1962, s.v. "Benjamin Jowett,"
by Stanley J. Curtis; Evelyn Abbott and Lewis Campbell,
ed., The Life and Letters of Benjamin Jowett, 3 vols.,
(London: J. Murray, 1897).

of a tireless, efficient administrator with an overbearing conceit, rigid integrity, and conviction of the rightness of his own actions. Two years after going to India he publicly charged his popular and respected superior, Sir Edward Colebrook, of taking bribes from natives. The "establishment" closed ranks behind Sir Edward and hurled abuse on the brash "upstart." The young Trevelyan responded by collecting proof of his charges which he presented to a board of inquiry. In the end, colonial officials sent Sir Edward Colebrook home in disgrace and dismissed him from the service. Trevelyan received congratulations from the Indian Government and the Directors of the East India Company.

During his tour of duty in India, Trevelyan became a close friend of Macaulay. This relationship led to a marriage between Sir Charles and Macaulay's sister, Hannah More Macaulay. Macaulay described Trevelyan in a letter written in 1834.

> He has no small talk. His mind is full of schemes of moral and political improvement, and his zeal boils over in his talk. His topics, even in courtship, are steam navigation, the education of the natives, the equalization of the sugar duties, the substitution of the Roman for the Arabic alphabet in Oriental languages.[43]

This relationship between Trevelyan and Macaulay probably resulted in Trevelyan's devotion to civil service reform. The two discussed with great zeal various schemes for the reform of the Indian civil service. Trevelyan read Macaulay's draft of his report on recruitment by competitive examination before it was issued.

Trevelyan returned to England in 1838 with a reputation as a fearless opponent of corruption and outstanding administrator. He accepted appointment as Assistant Secretary to the Treasury in 1840 where he held office for nineteen years. Five years after his appointment Trevelyan became director of Irish relief during the devastating famine in Ireland. As usual, Trevelyan took up his task with great industry, but in time his overbearing nature made him unpopular in Ireland and a nuisance to his

---

[43]Macaulay to Mrs. Cropper, Calcutta, 7 December 1834, G. Otto Trevelyan, Life and Letters of Lord Macaulay, I:341.

subordinates. He could not refrain from interfering in
any area that he thought was managed improperly. He
even turned occasionally to indiscreet actions to make
his views known. Once the Prime Minister reprimanded
him for publishing two letters that undercut him. Toward the end of the Irish famine, he turned his attention
to the question of administrative reform, which absorbed
much of his energy until he left the ministry.

In 1859 Trevelyan resigned to return to India and
become Governor of Madras. Within months he was in
trouble again. This time he publicly attacked his former Treasury colleague James Wilson, now Finance Member
to the Governor-General's Council. Trevelyan charged
that Wilson's budget was too large and contained unnecessary additional taxes. The way Trevelyan pursued
the attack caused much embarrassment to the government
in India and in England. In the end, the bitter personal
struggle between the two men led to Trevelyan's recall
to England. Ironically, Wilson died soon after Trevelyan's
recall,and Sir Charles succeeded him as Finance Member.
Trevelyan devoted the last three years in India to an enthusiastic campaign which led to the abolition of the
purchase of army commissions. Trevelyan retired from
public life in 1865 and died in 1886. Sir Charles had
one more asset which served him well during his turbulent
career. He had the advantage of being independently
wealthy, a considerable asset for a boat-rocking reformer.[44]

Anthony Trollope used Sir Charles as one of his three
heroes in the novel The Three Clerks. Trollope gave him
the appropriate name of Sir Gregory Hardlines.[45]

Sir Stafford Northcote's position on reform vacillated
from reformer to reactionary. Yet, on several occasions,
he played a prominent role in the reform movement. Sir
Stafford was born in London on October 27, 1818, and educated at Eton and at Balliol, Oxford, where he took honors

---

[44]Moses, p. 35; Cohen, p. 84; Griffith, p. 13; Richards,
p. 42; Wright, pp. xvii-xxii; Jenifer Hart, "Sir Charles
Trevelyan at the Treasury," English Historical Review 65
(January 1960): 92-110; Dictionary of National Biography,
s.v. "Charles Trevelyan."

[45]Anthony Trollope, The Three Clerks: A Novel (New York:
Harper & Brothers, 1874); R.A.W. Rhodes, "Wilting in Limbo:
Anthony Trollope and the Nineteenth Century Civil Service,"
Public Administration 51 (1973): 207-219.

in humanities and mathematics. Students remember him
in school for his grace as an oarsman and his perfection
of the "Eaton Style." On leaving Oxford in 1843 he became private secretary to William Gladstone at the Board
of Trade. Eventually he became legal secretary to the
board. In this capacity he gained a reputation for hard
work and understanding for business, which earned him the
great respect of Gladstone and other influential Whig
ministers. He was recommended to Prince Albert as a
worthy adviser, and in 1850 appointed one of the secretaries of the Great Exhibition where he captured the
Prince's respect and attention. During his tenure at the
Board of Trade, Northcote obtained his first national attention when he wrote a much debated and highly respected
pamphlet on the Navigation Laws in which he supported free
trade. He unexpectedly resigned from the Board of Trade
on the death of his father in 1851. He succeeded his
father to become the 8th Baronet only to suffer a severe
illness which kept him inactive for a year. In December
1852 Northcote wrote Gladstone and requested appointment
to the Treasury Committee to inquire into the organization
of the Board of Trade. It was in this capacity that Northcote began his collaboration with Trevelyan. These two
men worked closely together during the early and middle
fifties.

In 1855 Sir Stafford entered Parliament as a Conservative M.P. for Dudley; in 1858 he represented Stamford
and, in 1866, North Devon. He consistently supported his
party and acquired the confidence of Disraeli. He became
President of the Board of Trade in 1866, Secretary of
State for India in 1867, and Chancellor of the Exchequer
in 1874. From 1871 to 1873 he represented his country in
Washington, D.C., as one of the Commissioners for the
settlement of the Alabama claims. He succeeded Disraeli
as leader of the Conservative party in the Commons after
Disraeli entered the House of Lords in 1876.

Sir Stafford was too gentle for many of his more
energetic party leaders. Consequently, Salisbury "kicked
him upstairs" in 1885 by engineering his move to the House
of Lords with the title of Earl of Iddesleigh and Viscount
St. Cyres. He was, however, included in the Cabinet as
First Lord of the Treasury. In 1886 Lord Salisbury appointed him Secretary of State for Foreign Affairs, but
the appointment did not satisfy the Administration. Again
Salisbury set to work to arrange his resignation, but Sir
Stafford obliged his opponents by suddenly dying in January 1887.

43

Northcote's gentle temperament made him unsuitable
as a party leader. Sir Stafford had a highly successful
but undistinguished and largely forgotten career. He
was eleven years younger than Trevelyan and certainly an
improbable choice to work with the highly respected
Treasury official. He complemented Trevelyan's rude and
brash behavior with his instinctive understanding of
balance and "simply perfect" temperament. Trevelyan considered him so indispensable to the reform movement that
he opposed his election to Parliament on the grounds that
he could not be replaced.[46]

Sir Robert Lowe, First Viscount Sherbrooke (1811-1892),
was born in Nottinghamshire. He was educated at Winchester
and at University College, Oxford, and elected fellow of
Magdalen College in 1835. Sir Robert acquired a reputation as an outstanding tutor and avid supporter of university reform. In 1842 he passed the bar and emigrated to
New South Wales, Australia, where he became a prominent
supporter of efficient, representative government. Sir
Robert returned to England in 1850 and became a writer for
the Times. Two years later he was elected to Parliament.
Lowe began a public career when Lord Aberdeen appointed
him Secretary of the Board of Control for India. In 1853
he became both Vice-President of the Board of Trade and
Vice-President of the Council for Education. In these
positions he helped establish competitive service in the
Indian civil service, facilitate the formation of joint-
stock companies by accepting the principle of limited
liability, and introduced the code of "payment by result"
in elementary education.

Lowe turned his attention to Parliamentary affairs.
In 1866 he deserted the Liberal Government to lead the
attack against Lord John Russell's Reform Bill. Despite
the mutiny of 1866, Gladstone appointed him Chancellor
of the Exchequer in 1868 where he led the final installment
of civil service reform in 1870. Lowe became a liability
for Gladstone, who transferred him to the Home Office in
1873. Lowe retired from public life because of ill health
when the administration fell in 1874. Gladstone paid him
a last compliment by raising him to the peerage as a
Viscount in 1880.

---

[46]Andrew Lang, Sir Stafford Northcote: First Earl of Iddes-
leigh, 2 vols. (Edinburgh: William Blackwood & Sons, 1890);
Encyclopedia Brittanica, 1962 ed., s.v. "Stafford Henry
Northcote, Iddesleigh"; Griffith, p. 18; Cohen, p. 85;
Wright, pp. xvii-xix; Hart, pp. 108-9; Dictionary of Nat-
ional Biography, 1921-2 ed., s.v. "Sir Stafford Henry
Northcote."

Sir Robert was an effective speaker and capable administrator. His style and manner were very similar to those of Trevelyan in that he was brazen, sarcastic, and offensive to many. He was an albino and nearly blind. Highly conceited, he had no doubts as to his intellectual capacity. He strongly advocated merit principles in admission to the civil service but regarded democracy as the enemy of good government. He thought government should be based upon a limited, informed electorate. Viscount Sherbrooke died in obscurity in 1892.[47]

The last of the great civil service reformers was William Ewart Gladstone (1809-1898). Gladstone was born in Liverpool in 1809 of Scottish parents. He was educated at Eton and later at Christ Church, Oxford, where he received recognition in the classics and mathematics. He was first elected to Parliament in 1832 with the support of the Duke of Newcastle. Peel appointed him to a minor office in the Treasury (1834-35), and then Lord Aberdeen elevated him to Undersecretary for Colonies. Gladstone began his career as a strong supporter of the Tory party and conservative policies but gradually he acquired more liberal views. His influence in the Conservative party increased by 1841 so that Peel appointed him Vice-President of the Board of Trade. With Peel's help, he set to work on a project to simplify the tariff laws. By 1843 Peel promoted him to President of the Board of Trade. In 1846 Gladstone accepted leadership of the Colonial Office, but his swing to a free trade position antagonized the Duke of Newcastle who asked him to resign his seat at Newark. Out of Parliament, Gladstone turned his interest to the plight of political prisoners in Naples, Italy. His efforts were not very successful. In 1852 he attacked Disraeli's budget and helped bring down Lord Derby's government. He then joined Aberdeen's coalition as Chancellor of the Exchequer. He devised a bold and comprehensive budget which he carried in Parliament. In 1853-54 Gladstone devoted much of his

---

[47]Arthur Patchett Martin, Life and Letters of Right Honourable Robert Lowe, Viscount Sherbrooke. . . with a Memoir of Sir John Coape Sherbrooke, G.C.B. (London: Longmans, Green & Co., 1893); D.W. Sylvester, Robert Lowe and Education (New York: Cambridge University Press, 1974); Encyclopedia Brittanica, 1962 ed., s.v. "Robert Lowe, Viscount Sherbrooke," by Arthur Frederick Thompson: Dictionary of National Biography, 1921-2 ed. s.v. "Robert Lowe"; J. Ewing Ritchie, British Senators: or, Political Sketches, Past and Present (London: Tinsley Brothers, 1869), pp. 61-68; James Winter, Robert Lowe (Buffalo: University of Toronto Press, 1976).

time and energy to civil service reform, university reform, and Indian administrative reform. He left the
government in 1855 over a disagreement with Palmerston,
who had succeeded Aberdeen. He did not reenter the
government until 1859 when he joined Palmerston and
Russell in helping secure the unification of Italy.

Gladstone remained in Lord Russell's government
until Robert Lowe helped defeat his Parliamentary Reform
Bill in 1866. Disraeli introduced another Reform Bill
in 1867, which passed Parliament after John Bright and
Gladstone strengthened its provisions in committee.
When Disraeli fell in 1868, Gladstone formed his first
administration, which lasted from 1868 to 1874. Designated the "Second Reform Era" by some historians, these
six years achieved considerable success. Gladstone expanded parliamentary reform, adopted administrative reform measures in the universities and civil service,
and sought solutions to the Irish Question.

In 1880 Gladstone returned to form another ministry
which continued until 1885. He managed to push through
a "Third Reform Act" in 1884, but foreign policy issues
in such areas as Egypt, Sudan, Russia, Greece and Turkey
dominated his time. Again the Irish Question plagued him.

He returned to the Prime Ministry in 1886 and, finally, from 1892-1894. Both terms were short, generally
unsuccessful, and preoccupied with the Irish Question.
In retirement he devoted time to editing the works of
Bishop Joseph Butler and denounced Turkish atrocities in
Armenia. He died of cancer on May 19, 1898, at the age
of eighty-nine.

The Great Liberal was addicted to hard work. He had
extraordinary vigor, self-control, and devotion to duty.
He entered politics because of a strong sense of duty.
He had great political courage and strength and was a
gifted administrator. His relations with people were
characterized by sincerity, delightful manners, and sympathy for others. Politically he was a formidable debater,
an adequate orator, and an inspiring leader.[48]

---

[48]Philip Magnus, Gladstone (New York: E.P. Dutton & Co.,
Inc., 1964); Encyclopedia Brittanica, 1962 ed., s.v.
"William Ewart Gladstone," by Michael Richard Daniell Foot;
John Morley, Life of William Ewart Gladstone, 3 vols. (Lon-
don: Macmillan & Co., Ltd., 1903).

Reform Movement of the
Indian Civil Service

Patronage, with its disregard for merit and ability, provided India with many unsatisfactory civil servants. Lord Richard Wellesley, Governor-General of India from 1797 to 1805, attempted to improve the abilities of civil servants sent to India after their recruitment on a patronage basis. In 1800 he wrote to the Court of Directors of the East India Company, who dispensed most of the patronage nominations in India, and recommended that he establish a college in India "for the purpose of enabling the servants of the Company to perfect themselves in those acquirements which form the necessary qualifications for the different lines of the service, in which they may choose to engage."[49]

Wellesley established Fort Williams College which provided training in law and Oriental languages to civil servants who spent from six months to four years studying upon their arrival from England.[50] In 1806 the Directors of the East India Company expanded the principle of training civil servants. They created Haileybury College in England to augment Fort Williams College. The company required a nominee to spend two years at Haileybury before proceeding to India. The college acquired immediate success and gradually increased its standards until it equaled the scholastic standards of Oxford and Cambridge. Qualifying entrance examinations for all candidates nominated by patronage was part of the system from the beginning. These examinations became progressively more difficult especially after 1836 when the company hired outside examiners to administer the entrance examinations. Many prominent men received their training at Haileybury, including Charles E. Trevelyan.[51]

Renewal of the East India Company's charter in 1833 offered another opportunity to make changes in the Indian administration. This time the chief protagonist was Thomas B. Macaulay. At the time, Macaulay was Secretary to the Board of Control. He outlined a plan to introduce a system

---

[49]Cohen, p. 79.

[50]Bernard S. Cohen, "Recruitment and Training of British Civil Servants in India, 1600-1860," in Asian Bureaucratic Systems Emergent From the British Imperial Tradition, ed. Ralph Braibanti (Durham, North Carolina: Duke University Press, 1966), pp. 111-116.

[51]Ibid., pp. 116-137.

of limited competition for civil service positions. His system required four candidates to compete for every vacancy, the winner to be determined by means of an examination. Defending the scheme in the House of Commons, Macaulay stated, "We conceive, that under this system, the persons sent out will be young men above par -- young men superior either in talents or diligence to the mass."[52] Parliament incorporated the Macaulay proposal into the India Act of 1833, but the Directors postponed and never carried out its implementation.[53]

The Indian Charter came before Parliament again for revision in 1853 and this time Macaulay had more success.

Reform Movement in the Universities

Education available at Cambridge and Oxford declined to "the nadir of lethargy" in the eighteenth century.[54] Agitation for reform of the Universities took place throughout the nineteenth century. Students sat for examinations at Cambridge for many years but they were little more than supplemental exercises until 1747 when the university began to publish examination results in "descending order of merit." By 1852 the examination system consisted of three parts and came to be known as the Tripos. The Tripos examined students in philosophy, mathematics, and classics. By 1825 the examination acquired a reputation of excellence.[55] The Tripos was not a requirement for graduation and relatively few students chose to sit for the examinations.[56] Oxford adopted the examination method with passage of the Examination Statute of 1800. Oxford's examinations, known as "Greats," were also administered to a narrow segment of the student population.

---

[52] A.B. Keith, ed., Speeches and Documents on Indian Policy (London: H. Milford, 1922), p. 251.

[53] Bernard S. Cohen, p. 138.

[54] Michael Sanderson, ed., The Universities in the Nineteenth Century (London: Routledge & Kegan Paul, 1975), p. 26.

[55] John Roach, Public Examinations in England: 1850-1900 (Cambridge: At the University Press, 1971), p. 13.

[56] Cohen, p. 81.

Utilitarians stimulated a controversy about the value of an education at Cambridge or Oxford. R.L. Edgeworth began the debate in 1809 when he published an "Essay on Professional Education." Edgeworth stated that the value of education depended on its usefulness. Reviewers took the opportunity to support or oppose an Oxford education on the basis of its utility. Sydney Smith wrote an article in the Edinburgh Review attacking the impracticality of an Oxford education.[57] Edward Copleston, Provost of Oriel, defended the classical education at the universities as useful in understanding civil government, helpful in training the mind to face real life problems, and intrinsically good in itself. William Whewell, prominent Cambridge teacher, supported the universities' emphasis on mathematics. He claimed that a mathematical education promoted "exact reasoning."[58]

Sir William Hamilton, professor at the University of Edinburgh, wrote a series of articles in the Edinburgh Review between 1831 and 1834 condemning the system at Oxford and Cambridge for its weak by-laws, educational methods, and programs. Bishop Copleston defended the universities against Hamilton's attacks but admitted the universities had weak examinations and that few students, if any, failed to graduate.

Both Oxford and Cambridge drew criticism for their close relations to the Anglican Church. These close ties resulted in the exclusion of Dissenters. The control of the universities by conservative professors, emphasis on the classics and mathematics, omission of practical education, and exclusion of Dissenters led to the creation of new universities. The Royal College of Chemistry, Royal School of Mines, and the University of Durham were typical examples. The University of London led the list of new universities founded in municipal and provincial locations. The University of London offered a professional education to Dissenters with training in the arts and sciences. Scottish universities offered an alternative to Cambridge and Oxford. Scottish universities accepted younger students, stressed philosophy, classics and science, and encouraged enrollment from students of all social classes.[59]

---

[57]Edinburgh Review, October 1809: 50-1.

[58]Sanderson, pp. 26-27.

[59]Ibid., pp. 28-33, 75.

By mid-nineteenth century the conservative universities contained a number of young scholars who recognized the need for change. These reform-minded scholars included Arthur P. Stanley and Goldwin Smith of University College, Henry H. Vaughan of Oxford, Benjamin Jowett of Balliol, and Francis Jeune, Master of Pembroke. Some limited changes were attempted by the leadership at Cambridge and Oxford. Cambridge introduced two new tripos examinations, moral sciences and natural sciences, in 1848. The Oxford Examination Institution of 1850 created schools of Natural Sciences, Law and Modern History, and Mathematics and Physics.[60]

Prime Minister Lord John Russell, who did not believe the universities could make sufficient reforms internally, appointed a Royal Commission in 1850 to inquire into the affairs of Oxford and Cambridge. The Prime Minister appointed members of the Royal Commission who were generally liberal and receptive to reform suggestions. The Oxford Commission was especially influenced by the radical reformer Henry H. Vaughan, Regius Professor of Modern History at Oxford. The ruling powers at the universities greeted the Commission with hostility and obstruction. The Commissioners took testimony on a number of subjects. They probed the relationship between the colleges and central university, quality of fellows, celibacy requirement for tutors, non-resident fellows who did not contribute to the teaching load, election of fellows, expensive coaching system, need for a wider curriculum, importance of professors, relationship between the church and the universities, secular relationships, large expense of a university education, need for new chairs, scientific teaching, scholarship restrictions, admission of Dissenters, need for reform of college statutes, use of competitive examinations, increase in secular studies, and the purpose of college endowments.[61]

The Commission investigating Oxford, appointed in 1850, submitted its report in 1852. The Commissioners found that the university now used examinations as a major device for testing the proficiency of students. Free competition produced high morale. The report recommended reform in the Oxford University government. It stressed the

---

[60]Sanderson, pp. 75-76; Roach, pp. 17-21; G.E.W. Bill, University Reform in Nineteenth-Century Oxford: A Study of Henry Halford Vaughan, 1811-1885 (Oxford: Oxford University Press, 1973), pp. 1-2.

[61]Sanderson, pp. 76-77; Bill, pp. 93-110.

importance of teaching professors and defined the relationship between professors and tutors. The report
recommended an increase in the number of chairs and
schools. It advised that the universities appoint non-
celibate professors. It made recommendations to free
scholarships from certain restrictions, introduce scientific subjects, and expand the curriculum.

William Gladstone had strongly opposed the appointment of the Royal Commissions in 1850. The report con-
verted him to the cause, and Lord John Russell appointed
him to prepare a bill to effect the needed changes[62] Benjamin Jowett assisted Gladstone in these efforts.

Reform Movement in the
Home Civil Service

The opening round of events which led to the reform
of the British civil service began in 1848. Concern over
the high cost of civil administration in Parliament led
the government to appoint an inquiry into the public service. The investigation concentrated on trying to reduce
expenditures which had risen rapidly because of increases
"in the scope and intensity of government activities and
the rise in the number of civil servants."[63] The committee
conducted a broad inquiry and invited many government departments to give evidence. Assistant Secretary to the
Treasury (Permanent Head of the Treasury) Sir Charles E.
Trevelyan testified on behalf of the Treasury.

Trevelyan supported the suspicion of Parliamentarians
who demanded the inquiry by agreeing that much of the work
pursued in government departments was superfluous and inefficient. He challenged the committee members to see for
themselves, but they failed to take the bait. He refused
to permit his testimony to become mired in small details
and took every opportunity to draw attention to the broader
questions. Sir Charles outlined a plan to reorganize the
Treasury. He began by describing the present system as
having a few, overworked officials who carried the major
burden of responsibility in the departments. He emphasized this with an explanation of what constituted his own
workday. He attributed his own overworked condition to the

---

[62]Bill, pp. 110-115; Cohen, pp. 82-83; Wright, pp. 55-56.

[63]Wright, p. xiii.

51

inefficient staff which came just under him and his
counterparts.[64]   The inefficient staff was the natural
result of the system of training and promoting civil
servants. All appointees started at the bottom and
worked up to senior positions in order of seniority.
Such a training, according to Trevelyan, did not fit
them for the important duties of the top positions.
Instead, an employee assigned to incessant copying
duties got the "feeling he is employed on work of an
inferior kind. . .regards his business as a tax upon
his time, and executes it as a task he must get through."[65]
To correct the defects, Trevelyan proposed a complete re-
organization of the Treasury. He suggested that the work
of a department be divided between intellectual work and
routine copying. He rejected the concept of filling
positions with those who worked up from the bottom. The
concept of promotion throughout the grades should be
abolished. He interposed here the concept of ability.
Trevelyan suggested that the most responsible positions
should be given to men who had never served at the bottom. Talented employees should be assigned "superior
duties" from the beginning of their employment so that
they would be qualified to give useful service when called
upon. The best source for such employees was those who
had completed a university education.

Charles Trevelyan realistically suggested that his
proposed changes not be adopted quickly. Instead he
suggested that the civil servants currently employed be
permitted to continue under the existing circumstances,
but future employees should enter under the new program.

The committee recognized the government-wide implications of Trevelyan's remarks and solicited opinions
from other officials. They generally condemned the proposals and none gave them unqualified support. The most
favorable comment came from J.G. Shaw Lefevre, Clerk of
the House of Lords, who later became one of the first
Civil Service Commissioners. Other than publish Trevelyan's

---

[64]Jenifer Hart, after analyzing Trevelyan's manuscript
books at the Bodleian Library, concluded that his overworked conditions were caused more by his own inefficient
use of his time than by the inefficient staff under him.
He was, according to Hart, "Bad at delegating work" and
"in many respects a bad organizer." Hart, p. 102.

[65]Great Britain, Parliament, Parliamentary Papers (Commons),
1847-1848, Vol. 18, "Minutes of Evidence of the Select
Committee on Miscellaneous Expenditures," pp. 177-178.

comments and reactions to them, the Select Committee expressed no views on these suggestions, since they did not
concern reductions in public expenditures.[66]

United Reform Campaign

Sir Charles Trevelyan's testimony made little impact
on the Members of Parliament who considered the report
of the Select Committee. The executive branch of government decided that something had to be done to improve conditions in the civil service. Gladstone asked Trevelyan
to participate in an inquiry at the Colonial Office in
1848. This initiated a long series of committees, select
committees, and commissions which followed in a continuous
succession from 1848 to 1857. Gladstone initiated most
of these inquiries, and his appointment of Sir Charles to
sit on all of them established the precedent of Treasury
supremacy in the area of civil service. From 1849 to
1854 Trevelyan participated in thirteen inquiries, and on
eight of them Gladstone's former private secretary, Sir
Stafford Northcote, assisted him. These inquiries produced a mass of details about the operations of the individual departments. They covered such departments as the
Treasury, Colonial Office, Irish Office, Board of Trade,
Department of Practical Science and Art, Poor Law Board,
Privy Council Office, Copyhold, Enclosure and Tithe
Commission, Colonial Land and Emigration Office, Office
of Works, and the Board of Ordnance.[67]

A number of dedicated reformers converged on the
government at the same time. From 1852 to 1854 Gladstone
was Chancellor of the Exchequer; Trevelyan, his chief
subordinate, was Assistant Secretary to the Treasury;
Northcote sat on a Treasury committee to inquire into the
organization of the Board of Trade; Macaulay, Trevelyan's
brother-in-law, pressed for reform of the Indian civil service in Parliament; Sir Charles Wood, greatly influenced

---

[66]Ibid.; Cohen, pp. 87-91; Richards, p. 43; Henry Roseveare, The Treasury: 1660-1870: The Foundations of Control
(London: George Allen & Unwin, Ltd., 1973), pp. 96-98,
201-204; Henry Roseveare, The Treasury: The Evolution of
a British Institution (New York: Columbia University Press,
1969), pp. 166-167.

[67]Hart, pp. 103-106; Roseveare, The Treasury: The Evolution,
pp. 167-168; William Joseph Reader, Professional Men: The
Rise of the Professional Classes in Nineteenth Century England
(London: Weidenfeld & Nicolson, 1966), p. 83.

by Trevelyan while serving as Chancellor of the Exchequer during the Irish famine, was now Secretary of State for India; Robert Lowe was Wood's Parliamentary Under-Secretary; and Benjamin Jowett, Fellow and Tutor of Balliol College, Oxford, saw reform of the Indian and British civil service as an influence in bringing about a reform of the universities.[68]

A series of intricate interpersonal relations between these men in 1853-54 connecting the three movements for reform of the universities and the two civil services produced significant results. Trevelyan collaborated with Macaulay in a new attempt to reform the Indian civil service. They spent many hours at home discussing the principles of civil service reform. Trevelyan threw his support behind the education reform movement because he thought it gave him greater strength and support for opening up the Indian and British civil services. Jowett recognized that Indian and British civil service reforms would benefit the universities. Gladstone backed Trevelyan at the Treasury and supported reform of Oxford after the 1850 Commission of Inquiry report. Prime Minister Aberdeen assigned him the task of writing a Parliamentary bill. In the meantime, Northcote closely worked with Trevelyan on the departmental inquiries. Trevelyan served as the common denominator and drew all the elements together into a potent force.[69]

---

[68]Cohen, pp. 90-93; Richards, p. 43; Wright, pp. xiii-xviii and 53-56.

[69]Wright, p. 56.

CHAPTER III

BRITISH CIVIL SERVICE REFORM

Civil Service Reform in India

The reform campaign opened in 1853 on the occasion
of the renewal of the East India Company's charter. Sir
Charles Wood, Secretary of State for India, drafted and
introduced a charter bill for India. On June 3, 1853,
Wood delivered a five-hour speech as he introduced the
bill in the House of Commons. The bill called for retention of the Company's rule in India, but that rule
was to be reduced in many ways. It empowered the government to nominate one-third of the directors and approve
nominations of members of the councils at Calcutta, Bom-
bay, and Madras. The Governor-General lost his position
as Governor of Bengal to a new Lieutenant-Governor.
From the standpoint of administrative reform, the most
important provision in the original bill was Clause 36,
which provided "that all powers, rights, and privileges
of the court of directors of the said India Company to
nominate or appoint persons to be admitted as students
. . . shall cease."[1] Patronage at Haileybury and Addis-
combe College was to end.

Trevelyan, accompanied by Northcote and Ralph Lingen,
visited Oxford in July 1853 to explain to Jowett the expected impact of the Wood bill on the future of Haileybury.
Trevelyan invited the Reverend Doctor Charles Vaughn, Headmaster of Harrow, to join the meeting with Jowett. The
two theologians grasped the importance of the bill immediately and decided to act swiftly. Jowett wrote to Gladstone urging him to support changes in the India Act which
would open the service to all university graduates. Doctor Vaughn opposed the proposed constitution of Haileybury
for it excluded university graduates from other schools
from entering the Indian service. He wrote a formal letter to Trevelyan objecting to the Haileybury constitution
and advocating instead the principle of open competition.
Jowett sent copies of the Vaughn letter to Gladstone,
Wood, and Dr. Henry Liddell,[2] Headmaster of Westminster.

---

[1]Eaton, pp. 178-179.

[2]Henry Liddell was a prominent member of the 1850 Royal Commission that investigated the affairs at Oxford.

Wood agreed to support the change while Gladstone assumed the responsibility of explaining the proposal to Prime Minister Aberdeen.

In the meantime, the House of Commons passed the original Wood India bill.[3] On Trevelyan's suggestion the Administration selected Earl Granville, another member of Aberdeen's cabinet, to introduce the amendment into the House of Lords. Dr. Liddell sent Granville a copy of Vaughn's letter and urged him to support its provisions. Granville inserted Clause 37 stating that "subject to such regulations as might be made, any person, being a natural born subject of His Majesty, who might be desirous of presenting himself, should be admitted to be examined as a candidate."[4] The formidable pressure group, mobilized by Jowett, was largely responsible for adoption of this provision.[5]

Macaulay made a masterly defense of the principle of competition in debate on the Wood India bill. He explained that withdrawing patronage powers from the Board of Directors of the East India Company solved nothing if the power were transferred to the Governor-General or Parliament or anyone else. The evil was not the Directors but the principle of patronage, no matter where employed. "Every Governor-General would take out with him, or would soon be followed by, a crowd of nephews, first and second cousins, friends, and political hangers-on; while every steamer arriving from the Red Sea would carry to India some adventurer bearing with him testimonials from people of influence in England."[6] Robert Lowe delivered an important speech in support of the India bill also.[7]

---

[3]See Chapter II.

[4]Eaton, p. 179.

[5]R.J. Moore, "The Abolition of Patronage in the Indian Civil Service and the Closure of Haileybury College," The Historical Journal 7 (1964):249-253; Wright, pp. 55 and 57; Winter, pp. 73-74.

[6]Trevelyan, pp. 588-590.

[7]Martin, pp. 78-79.

Trevelyan and Jowett vigorously pursued the advantage won in the House of Lords. Jowett drafted a proposed outline on such items as age, qualifications, content of examinations, and sent it to Sir Charles Wood. Wood acted by creating an advisory committee on the subject. Trevelyan exerted his influence to have his reform friends installed on the committee. Macaulay and Jowett joined Lord Ashburton; Dr. Melville, Principal of Haileybury College; and J.G. Shaw Lefevre. Using Jowett's outline and Macaulay's writing skills, the committee issued its report, which became famous for its defense of competitive examinations.[8]

> We think it most desirable that the examination should be of such a nature that no candidate who may fail shall, to whatever calling he may betake himself, have any reason to regret the time and labour which he spent in preparing himself to be examined. . . . We believe that men who have been engaged, up to one or two and twenty, in studies which have no immediate connection with the business of any profession, and of which the effect is merely to open, to invigorate, and to enrich the mind, will generally be found, in the business of every profession, superior to men who have, at eighteen or nineteen, devoted themselves to the special studies of their calling. . . . We therefore think that the intellectual test about to be established will be found in practice to be also the best moral test that can be devised. . . . He should have received the best, the most liberal, the most finished education that his native country affords. Such an education has been proved by experience to be the best preparation for every calling which requires the exercise of the higher powers of the mind.[9]

The heart of the plan stated that candidates for entrance to the Indian civil service be selected by open competition. The examinations would consist of liberal

---

[8]Moore, pp. 254-256; Macaulay gave Trevelyan the first opportunity to read and comment on it. Trevelyan, p. 314.

[9]Quoted in Moses, pp. 56-57.

arts topics taught at British universities. Most candidates should therefore acquire a degree from Oxford or Cambridge. The report recommended establishing the minimum age at eighteen, but the difficulty of the examination meant that entrance was unlikely before twenty-one. It also recommended that the examination include questions in classics, mathematics, French, German, Italian, Sanskrit and Persian, natural sciences, moral sciences, and literature. Macaulay wanted the examinations to demand that candidates have a deep knowledge of some subjects to prevent accepting those who had a superficial knowledge from entering. The committee developed a proposed grading system for examinations. Passing grades should be determined by the needs of the service. Successful applicants entered a probationary period of two to three years and confined their study to Indian subjects, such as history, geography, government, law, finance, economy, and languages. Completion of the probation period came with a final examination to determine the ranking for seniority selection for Indian positions.[10] Adoption of the report marked the end of Haileybury College. Following Wood's decision to close the school, it accepted the last students in January 1856 and closed its doors in December 1857.[11]

Trevelyan and Jowett were pleased at their success in introducing competition as a basis for appointment to the Indian civil service. Trevelyan, in particular, saw the success in the Indian civil service as a major step in bringing about the reform in the British civil service. He thought the time ripe to press for total success. Perhaps he overestimated the forces which led the members of Parliament to vote against patronage in the East India Company. Unhappiness with the East India Company and the privileges associated with the directors of that company motivated many politicians to vote with the reformers. Many interest groups and politicians pushed for abolition of the company and its incorporation into the government. When this failed, the opposition directed its attention to reducing the power of the directors. One of the most conspicuous privileges which the directors exercised was that of patronage. Many bitterly opposed to the introduction of open competition in England voted for it in India. The directors' patronage was very unpopular because only an exclusive few exercised it. The reform of the Indian civil

---

[10]Trevelyan, pp. 314-315.

[11]Cohen, p. 138; Moore, p. 243.

service was not based on attempts to eradicate widespread incompetence as was the case in the Home civil service.[12]

Northcote-Trevelyan Report

On April 12, 1853, Gladstone issued a Treasury Minute[13] summarizing the inquiries made by Trevelyan and Northcote into the different departments. He commissioned them to write a report on their general reflections and conclusions based on their experience. Gladstone stated in his Treasury Minute that:

> The general result of these inquiries and of the proceedings which will be taken on them, will, undoubtedly, be that the public service will be conducted in a more efficient manner by a smaller number of persons than is the case at present. The gain in point of econ-omy will probably be important. . . .[14]

Again, like the inquiries which came before, the stated objective was budgetary savings. Trevelyan made no pretense of economy, for he wanted to correct defects in the system. In 1875 he testified before the Playfair Commission:

> We found, as we went in, the same evils and circumstances pointing to the same remedies, with reference to every department; so that when we came to make our general report we had gone with such detail into the state of the different establishments, that the conclusions arrived at in our report were the necessary logical inference of what had preceded.[15]

In October 1853 Trevelyan and Northcote turned to drafting their report on the British civil service. To emphasize that it was a culmination of the inquiries con-

---

[12]Moses, p. 59; J.M. Compton, "Open Competition and the Indian Civil Service: 1854-1876," The English Historical Review 83 (April 1968):265.

[13]Treasury Minutes are official Treasury Department directives.

[14]Wright, p. xiv.

[15]Great Britain, Parliament, Parliamentary Papers (Commons), 1875, Vol. 33, "Second Report of the Civil Service Inquiry Commission," p. 100.

ducted since 1848 and not connected with the India bill,
they decided to publish it together with the other reports
from the separate department inquiries.[16] The report was [17]
not an analytical treatment designed to inform or persuade.
The authors wrote a blanket condemnation of the existing
civil service and flatly stated their conviction that the
evil of the patronage system was at fault. With equal
confidence the writers proposed a solution they were
certain would correct the deficiencies. The ideas it
contained were mostly Trevelyan's[18] developed over many
years of observation and thought.

The report began with a short statement on the importance of the permanent civil service.

> That the Permanent Civil Service, with all its
> defects, essentially contributes to the proper
> discharge of the functions of Government, has
> been repeatedly admitted by those who have suc-
> cessively been responsible for the conduct of
> our affairs.[19]

From there on, it delivered a devastating attack on
the permanent civil service. The report argued that although civil service jobs were in high demand, they did
not attract the ablest men.

> It would be natural to expect that so important
> a profession would attract into its ranks the
> ablest and most ambitious of the youth of the
> country; . . . Such, however, is by no means
> the case. Admission into the Civil Service is
> indeed eagerly sought after, but it is for the

---

[16]Several of the most controversial reports were never
published. Hart, pp. 103-106.

[17]The twenty-three page report, an important document on
administrative reform, exercised influence on Great Britain
far beyond the period of its publication and attracted wide
international influence as well.

[18]Hart, pp. 106-107.

[19]Great Britain, Parliament, Parliamentary Papers (Commons),
1854, Vol. 27, "Report on the Organization of the Permanent
Civil Service Together with a Letter from the Rev. B.
Jowett," p. 3.

unambitious, and the <u>indolent</u> or <u>incapable</u>,
<u>that it is chiefly</u> desired.[20]   (Italics mine.)

Trevelyan emphasized this point again in a letter
to the <u>Times</u> dated February 2, 1854.

> There can be no doubt that our high Aristo-
> cracy have been accustomed to employ the
> Civil Establishments as a means of providing
> for the Waifs and Strays of their Families --
> as a sort of Foundling Hospital where those
> who had no energy to make their way in the
> open professions, or whom it was not conven-
> ient to purchase one in the Army, might re-
> ceive a nominal office, but real Pension, for
> life, at the expense of the Public.[21]

The result, according to the Trevelyan-Northcote Report, "is that the public service suffers both in internal
efficiency and in public estimation."[22]

Trevelyan and Northcote attributed the difficulty
of securing high quality employees to two causes: (1)
The system of recruitment was based on patronage. The political chief controlled patronage, and he was likely to
"bestow the office upon the son or dependent of someone
having personal or political claims upon him, or perhaps
upon the son of some meritorious public servant, without
instituting any very minute inquiry into the merits of
the young man himself."[23] The report concluded that
"political considerations have led to the appointment of
men of very slender ability."[24] (2) Poor organization
of the civil service, which stifled initiative and encouraged
incompetency. The Government made no attempt to find and
promote men of talent according to their merit; instead
they promoted employees on the basis of seniority. This
insured that the "dull and inefficient" rise side by side
with the "able and energetic."

---

[20] <u>Parliamentary Papers</u>, p. 4.

[21] <u>The Times</u> (London), February 2, 1854.

[22] <u>Report on the Organization of the Permanent Civil Ser-
vice</u>, p. 4.

[23] <u>Ibid.</u>, p. 6.

[24] <u>Ibid.</u>, p. 7.

In the meantime his salary is gradually advanced
till he reaches, by seniority, the top of his
class, and on the occurrence of a vacancy in the
class above him he is promoted to fill it, as a
matter of course, and without any regard to his
previous service or his qualifications. Thus,
while no pains have been taken in the first instance to secure a good man for the office, nothing has been done after the clerk's appointment to turn his abilities, whatever they may
be, to the best account.[25]

Once accepted in the service, the employee is assured lifetime employment. "After a young man has been once appointed, the public have him for life. . . . The feeling
of security which this state of things necessarily engenders tends to encourage indolence."[26] One might think that
experience obtained from long service would be beneficial
to the public service. Not so, according to Northcote and
Trevelyan. Experience had no chance to work because:

The young man thus admitted is commonly employed upon duties of the merest routine.
Many of the first years of his service are
spent in copying papers, and other work of
an almost mechanical character. . . . The
remainder of his official life can only exercise a depressing influence on him, and
renders the work of the office distasteful
to him.[27]

The fragmentary character of the service was another detri-
mental feature of the public service.

Each man's experience, interests, hopes, and
fears are limited to the special branch of
service in which he is himself engaged. The
effect naturally is, to cramp the energies of
the whole body, to encourage the growth of
narrow views and departmental prejudices, to
limit the acquisition of experience, and to
repress and almost extinguish the spirit of

---

[25] Report on the Organization of the Permanent Civil Service, p. 6.

[26] Ibid., p. 5.

[27] Ibid.

emulation and competition; besides which,
considerable inconvenience results from the
want of facilities for transferring strength
from an office where the work is becoming
slack in one in which it is increasing, and
from the consequent necessity of sometimes
keeping up particular departments on a
scale beyond their actual requirements.[28]

The report identified age as another factor which influenced the character of the service. Most entered
"at an early age when there has been no opportunity of
trying their fitness for business, or forming a trustworthy estimate of their characters and abilities. . .
consequently [they] have but limited opportunities of
acquiring that varied experience of life which is so important to the development of character."[29] A person admitted into the service at a later age was usually "someone who has failed in other professions."

Because of the inefficient staff available to a chief,
he sometimes was obliged to go outside "to make an appointment of visible and immediate importance to the efficiency
of his department." Such actions resulted in perpetuating
a vicious circle.

This is necessarily discouraging to the Civil
Servants, and tends to strengthen in them the
injurious conviction, that their success does
not depend upon their own exertions, and that
if they work hard, it will not advance them, --
if they waste their time in idleness, it will
not keep them back.[30]

Thus, Trevelyan and Northcote concluded that the
civil service could improve by adherence to the general
principle that

the public service should be carried on by the
admission into its lower ranks of a carefully
selected body of young men, who should be employed from the first upon work suited to their

---

[28]Report on the Organization of the Permanent Civil Service, p. 8.

[29]Ibid., p. 5.

[30]Ibid., p. 7.

63

capacities and their education, and should
be made constantly to feel that their promotion and future prospects depend entirely
on the industry and ability with which they
discharge their duties, that with superior
powers they may rationally hope to obtain
to the highest prizes in the Service, while
if they prove decidedly incompetent, or in-
curably indolent, they must expect to be
removed from it.[31]

From this principle they developed their own specific recommendations to upgrade the government service.
They proposed that departments base recruitment on competitive literacy examinations at the level of the great
universities of Oxford and Cambridge. Examination would
be open to all and administered by an independent Board
of Examiners. Successful candidates would also have to
serve "a short period of probation." Having secured the
right men the government would have to make the best use
of their abilities. The civil service would be treated
as a unified whole, not as a number of separate departmental units. The report recommended that civil service
posts be graded into two distinct divisions of clerks.
The higher division would consist of university graduates
for employment on the intellectual work of the office.
The lower division would perform the more mechanical
clerical work. Mobility between levels was not encouraged
and would be possible only in exceptional instances.
Promotions by seniority would be eliminated. Merit promotions would apply only to all new recruits, the authors
recognizing that such a provision would be unpopular with
the existing civil servants. The government should not
abandon the right of appointing men of ability from outside the service to staff appointments in case of necessity. Merit would be determined on the basis of efficiency
ratings prepared by each superior and retained in a personnel
folder for use in preparing a register of eligible employees
for each vacancy. The Head of the Department could make
"a tolerably correct estimate of the merits of each individual" by reference to the personnel folder of those listed on the register. The report recommended that the government adopt a principle of mobility to train employees
for increasingly responsible positions, suggesting that
departments regularly transfer civil servants between

---

[31] Report on the Organization of the Permanent Civil Service, p. 9.

64

different branches so that they might acquire wide experience to fit them for senior posts. To mute the effects of inbred stagnation, the report recommended that senior posts be open to civil servants from all departments. Finally, Northcote and Trevelyan mentioned the problem of pensions. They suggested that pensions be awarded on a uniform and consistent basis according to service and character.

In summary, the writers stated their objectives were:

1. To provide, by a proper system of examination, for the supply of the public service with a thoroughly efficient class of men.
2. To encourage industry and foster merit, by teaching all public servants to look forward to promotion according to their deserts, and to expect the highest prizes in the service if they can qualify themselves for them.
3. To mitigate the evils which result from the fragmentary character of the service, and to introduce into it some element of unity.[32]

Trevelyan augmented the report with a letter from the Reverend Benjamin Jowett. In it Jowett outlined a plan which he considered suitable for recruitment to the superior offices. He proposed two examinations: a preliminary test to screen out those unfit for the civil service, and the selecting examination. Jowett advocated that the ideal examination should be based on a university education. He recommended that general topics include history, classics, philosophy, law, physical science, and foreign languages. "We must test a young man's ability by what he knows, not by what we wish him to know."[33] In other words, a candidate would have to be tested in the subjects in which he specialized at the universities. He even went so far as to suggest that examinations be held at London, Edinburgh, and Dublin, and that there should be eight examiners. For the lower grades Jowett recommended that the examination include material to test reading, writing and dictation, geography, and a general test of knowledge.[34] For Jowett

---

[32]Report on the Organization of the Permanent Civil Service, p. 22-23.

[33]Ibid., p. 27.

[34]Ibid., pp. 24, 31.

the success of the proposals depended to a large extent
on the adequacy of the examination system. Jowett selected intellectually oriented criteria for the upper
level examinations and task-oriented criteria for the
lower level.[35]

Once the reformers completed the report, they turned
to selling the product. In January 1854 Trevelyan and
Jowett prepared the ground for publication of the report.
Between them they knew many influential citizens in the
government, administration, education, and the press.
They carefully chose a few of these to test the probable
reaction to the report. In general, it met with mixed
reception. Trevelyan included their comments in the
final publication. Unhappy with the report, civil servants complained because of its critical nature. Many
questioned the validity of examinations, believing it
impossible to develop an adequate system of examination.
Supporters of the idea questioned the timing. Most of
them felt the time was not yet ready for its introduction.

For example, John G. Shaw Lefevre, Clerk Assistant
to the House of Peers, wrote:

I believe that the proposed measure, both as
to the character and intellectual qualifications of those whom it will introduce into the
public service, will fully realize the expectations of those who have proposed it to Her
Majesty's Government.[36]

John Wood, Chairman of the Board of Inland Revenue,
agreed with Lefevre but opposed the tone of the report:

In the general principle of that Report, and
in many of its detailed recommendations, I
entirely agree. But its tone has unfortunately
been supposed to imply an almost indiscriminate
censure of the Civil Service. This prevalent
impression has produced an effect injurious to
the scheme: the whole class considering itself
included in censure applicable only to a part.[37]

---

[35]See Edward Hughes, "Civil Service Reform 1853-5," History
27 (June 1942):66-67 for a shorter summary of the report.

[36]Great Britain, Parliament, Parliamentary Papers (Commons),
1854-55, Vol. 20, "Papers Relating to the Re-Organization
of the Civil Service," p. 4.

[37]Ibid., p. 301.

R.R.W. Lingen, Secretary to the Committee of Council for Education, particularly pleased Trevelyan and Northcote by his comments. Lingen wanted to correct several minor comments but thought the recommendations "would effect an immense change for the better."[38]

G. Arbuthnot, Auditor of the Civil List, considered the entire report incorrect. He indignantly refuted every charge.

> Such language, employed by gentlemen who had
> a solemn and responsible duty imposed on them
> by your Lordships, is calculated to convey a
> very unfavorable impression regarding the
> general characteristics of the civil service,
> and to create a very painful feeling in the
> minds of an honourable class of men, whose
> labours are little known, and who, from their
> position, have no opportunity of coming for-
> ward to justify themselves before the public.[39]

Sir Alexander Spearmen, Secretary and Comptroller General of the National Debt Office and Trevelyan's predecessor at the Treasury, unalterably opposed the reform. He did, reluctantly, agree with some of the findings.

> I do not mean to say that there are not to be
> found offices badly organized, into which un-
> qualified persons may have been received, and
> in which undeserved promotions may have been
> made, and where the efficiency of the service
> has consequently been injured; but wherever
> that has been the case, I think the evil more
> attributable to those at the head of the de-
> partment than to the system on which the Civil
> Service is really constituted.[40]

---

[38] Parliamentary Papers, p. 102.

[39] Ibid., p. 403.

[40] Ibid., p. 397.

Campaign for Reform

The comments taken as a whole were far from an enthusiastic endorsement of the proposals. Trevelyan tire-
lessly worked to secure its acceptance. He managed the
campaign enthusiastically, soliciting backers, consulting
with Jowett and Gladstone daily, and defending the report
against its detractors. Supported by Dr. Jeune, Master
of Pembroke, Jowett directed the campaign at Oxford.
Urged on by Trevelyan, the Regius Professor of Greek
managed the campaign at Cambridge and Dr. Jeff managed
it at King's College, London. Trevelyan kept posted on
the arguments against his proposal in discussions with
Sidney Herbert, Sir James Stephen, and John Wood. Sir
Charles bombarded the press with letters and editorial
material. According to Trevelyan, he secured the support
of seventy-five per cent of the newspapers in the country,
including The Times and the Morning Advertiser, the most
popular daily papers. Trevelyan tried to secure support
from every important segment of the community. He wrote
to Gladstone: "The classes interested in the maintenance
of Patronage are so powerful that unless we can get our
plan read and understood by the rest of the Community I
shall begin to fear for its success."[41] Both Jowett and
Trevelyan instructed their supporters on exactly what
contribution they should undertake. Trevelyan urged
Gladstone to write to France and find out how that country
applied competitive examinations.[42] Northcote wrote an
article on how government employees could acquire a university education. He responded to opinions received and
continually urged Gladstone to settle for nothing less than
open competition.[43]

Trevelyan's grasp of the issue and his intelligent
responses to criticism show through brilliantly in a
January 17, 1854 memorandum he sent to Gladstone entitled
Thoughts on Patronage. Trevelyan argued that patronage
reform was necessary to preserve the electoral system and
the popular form of government. Patronage brings "electoral corruption."

---

[41] Sir Charles Trevelyan to W.E. Gladstone, 1 March 1854,
British Museum, quoted in Wright, p. 60.

[42] Trevelyan to Gladstone, 9 March 1854, quoted in Wright,
p. 60.

[43] Wright, p. 58.

> . . . each member of the Party depends upon
> his Constituents; hence a tacit agreement
> to share the public Patronage and a perverted
> state of public feeling which prevents the
> matter from being seen in its true light. We
> do not appear to be aware of the portentous
> significance of the fact that a Functionary
> of high standing is attached to the central
> Department of the Government with the recog-
> nized official duty of <u>corrupting</u> Members
> of Parliament and Constituencies.[44]

Patronage should be eliminated because it had an adverse
effect upon "the public service." He argued that the
"efficiency of the Public Establishments is habitually
sacrificed" by patronage. Public opinion had made such
progress since the time of Walpole that "a Government
will gain more by a direct single-handed attention to
the public interests than by having any amount of Patronage at its disposal." Public morality of British
statesmen had outgrown the system of patronage, which
should be discontinued. If Britain adopted the proposed
plan, the

> Public Establishments would be recruited by
> the best of the rising generation. The tone
> of Parliament itself would be raised. In-
> terested motives would have less to do both
> with obtaining a seat in Parliament, and with
> the use made of it when obtained. Above all,
> the Government and the Governing class would
> cease to be on the side of corruption.

Finally, Trevelyan enlisted the patriotic element. "We
are apparently on the threshold of a new era pregnant
with great events, and England has to maintain in con-
cert with her allies the cause of right and liberty and
truth in every quarter of the world."[45]

The Northcote-Trevelyan Report motivated several
supporters to publish and distribute propaganda pamphlets favorable to the reform. Trevelyan's campaign

------

[44]Sir Charles E. Trevelyan to W.E. Gladstone, <u>Thoughts
on Patronage</u>, 17 January 1854, memorandum quoted in
Richards, p. 45.

[45]<u>Ibid</u>., pp. 45-47.

helped encourage wealthy merchants to organize the
Administrative Reform Association in May 1855 and publish its own Official Paper.[46]

Unfortunately, the small group of reformers had too
small a popular base to build on. Lord John Russell,
Foreign Minister and President of the Council in Lord
Aberdeen's government, a most influential opponent,
objected to open competition. Jowett and Trevelyan solicited the assistance of Dean Dawes of Hereford, a friend
of Russell, to help persuade him to support the Northcote-
Trevelyan Report. The two reformers could not decide how
best to use the Dean. Jowett urged the Dean to write a
letter to Russell "on the Organization of the Civil Service with reference to its bearing on the education of
the lower classes."[47] Trevelyan did not think such an
appeal would secure Lord Russell's support. Instead, he
urged the Dean to address a letter "to the Earl of Aberdeen and not to Lord John Russell."[48]

Gladstone assumed responsibility for persuading the
Queen and Prince Consort to support the proposal.

On February 17, 1854, Queen Victoria wrote to Gladstone about the proposed plan. She had doubts about the
plan and asked where "the application of the principle
of public competition is to stop." She wondered whether
it "would be necessary" for "candidates to compete for
employment" if "they should be otherwise eligible." The
Queen agreed with Disraeli that competitive examinations
may not necessarily select candidates with strength of
character, loyalty, and dependability. She suggested that
Gladstone devise some method for selecting candidates with
practical qualifications.[49]

---

[46]William Laurence Burn, The Age of Equipoise: A Study of
the Mid-Victorian Generation (New York: Norton, 1964), p. 143;
A Subordinate Therein, Administrative Reform, The Re-Organization of the Civil Service (London: Smith, Elder & Co., 1855).

[47]Rev. Benjamin Jowett to Dean of Hereford, 5 February 1854,
British Museum, quoted in Wright, p. 60.

[48]Sir Charles E. Trevelyan to Dean of Hereford, 6 February
1854, British Museum, quoted in Ibid., p. 61.

[49]Arthur Christopher Benson and Viscount Esher, ed., The Letters of Queen Victoria: A Selection from Her Majesty's Correspondence Between the Years 1837 and 1861, 3 vols. (New
York: Longmans, Green & Co., 1907), 3:13-14.

Gladstone replied on the same date with assurances that: "Experience at the universities and public schools of this country has shown that in a large majority of cases the test of open examination is also an effectual test of character. . . ." Hard work and "self denial" required of those who do well on competitive examinations "are rarely separated from general habits of virtue." He assured Victoria that "the securities for character" of those selected under this system "will be stronger and more trustworthy than any of which the present method of appointment is susceptible."[50] Queen Victoria reluctantly agreed, after discussing the question with the Prince Consort.[51]

The exchange between Gladstone and Queen Victoria suggested some of the social and cultural biases which may have contributed to the resistance which the Northcote-Trevelyan Report encountered. The Queen's comments indicate a concern over the spread of competitive examinations to other areas. This might lead to a decrease in the benefits of privilege, especially for the upper classes. She probably did not want to sanction a system which could threaten the prerogatives of the ruling classes. What of the members of the aristocracy who were unable to acquire a university education for one reason or another? Open competition was no guarantee that the privileged could maintain their position, even after attending Oxford or Cambridge, for they must compete with other citizens.

Gladstone seems to imply that a certain kind of education guaranteed a gentleman of strong moral character. These assumptions and biases that clung to the traditional public school and university education played an important part not only in the debate on civil service reform but also in the long and difficult struggle to modernize secondary school and university curricula in Great Britain.

Gladstone himself tried to gain Lord John Russell's support by suggesting that the new system represented no threat to the aristocracy, since the average aristocrat would "prove superior to the rest of the nation."[52] Trevelyan agreed, but Gladstone's assurances failed to get the support of Lord Russell.

---

[50] The Letters of Queen Victoria, op. cit.

[51] Philip Magnus, Gladstone (New York: E.P. Dutton & Co., Inc., 1964), p. 118; Roach, pp. 30-31.

[52] Ibid., p. 117.

Twice Gladstone had to reprimand Trevelyan for his press activities and once for releasing a confidential Treasury memorandum to other reformers. Arbuthnot, second in command at the Treasury, was particularly disturbed by Trevelyan's campaign. He complained to Gladstone that Trevelvan used the Treasury as a lobbying center for civil service reform. Many others questioned Trevelyan's dubious ethical conduct. A crescendo of opposition developed within the public service, in Parliament, and in the country. The forces were so strong that they threatened Trevelyan's career.[53] The Civil Service Gazette attacked the plan in its entirety, charging that it helped the universities more than it did the Service. Palmerston and Russell in the cabinet, and many members of Parliament, felt the report unfairly attacked the civil service and resented the "injustice done by that Report to the civil service of the country."[54] Sir James Graham, famous for his refusal to use the patronage system in the 1830's, told Gladstone that the plan sounded good but was probably impractical. "I am not certain that Parliamentary Government can be conducted on such principles of purity. Notwithstanding all our reforms, the experiment is to be tried non in republica Platonis sed in faece Romuli."[55]

In January 1854 Macaulay was optimistic. He wrote: "There is good public news. . . . The plan for appointing public servants by competition is to be adopted on a large scale, and is mentioned in the Queen's Speech. . . . If the thing succeeds, it will be of immense benefit to the country."[56]

Later his optimism turned to gloom. "I went to Brook's and found everybody open-mouthed, I am sorry to say, against Trevelyan's plans about the Civil Service. He has been too sanguine. The pear is not ripe. I always thought so. The time will come, but it has not come yet."[57]

---

[53]Wright, p. 61; Moses, p. 74.

[54]Wright, p. 63.

[55]Sir James Graham to W.E. Gladstone, January 1854, quoted in Cohen, p. 109.

[56]Macaulay's journal, quoted in Moses, p. 73 and Trevelyan, p. 378.

[57]Macaulay's journal, quoted in Moses, p. 74 and Trevelyan, p. 380.

The opposition advanced three major arguments against the Northcote-Trevelyan Report. First, they contended the established institutions were not as bad as the report stated. Many came forth to defend their civil servants as being faithful and diligent. The second argument questioned the desirability of recruiting on the basis of examination scores. Examinations, according to the critics, only benefited the universities and not the civil service. Further, they argued that the civil service demanded character and discretion, which could not be measured by means of an examination. Third, opponents objected to the principle of merit. Merit, they claimed, was a subjective assessment and prone to more abuses than patronage. According to them, the existing seniority system for promotions, and recruitment on the basis of recommendations from respected political personalities, was easily understood and certainly as reliable as merit.

Gladstone and Trevelyan could not silence the critics of the Northcote-Trevelyan Report nor could they ignore them any longer. In May, Gladstone informed the House of Commons that the Government would not submit any reform legislation that session. Trevelyan set to work drafting more limited proposals which he hoped would eventually lead to total reform. During the winter of 1854 he prepared a number of Order-in-Council drafts and submitted them to Gladstone, Northcote, W.H. Stephenson, and Gladstone's successor, Sir George Cornewall Lewis. Trevelyan gave up hope of acquiring the total package. He now tried to initiate as much reform as possible while preserving the authority of department heads to develop their own recruiting procedures. This, of course, meant a considerable softening of the Northcote-Trevelyan Report recommendations.[58]

Order-In-Council of 1855

In June 1854 the Treasury asked Department heads and other competent administrators to review the Northcote-Trevelyan Report. It published the responses in 1855. Most of the responses criticized the report for being too harsh on the quality and competence of the existing civil servants. No consensus was achieved on the abolition of patronage. Many strongly opposed competitive examinations but accepted an independent central examination system, as long as it preserved the power of the Department heads to make the final selection.

---

[58]Hughes, pp. 68-72.

The reform probably would have disappeared without any further action had events not taken a turn favorable to administrative reform. The Aberdeen government drifted into the Crimean War in 1854 and during the winter all organization for the war collapsed. The British Expeditionary Force in the Crimea found itself short of tents, huts, boots, knapsacks, food, medical supplies, and ammunition. Military disaster caused by incompetent organization resulted in widespread public criticism. The House of Commons voted "no confidence" because the Aberdeen Cabinet resisted demands for an inquiry into the conduct of the war. Sir George Cornewall Lewis was appointed to the new Palmerston Cabinet to replace Gladstone as Chancellor of the Exchequer.

The Administrative Reform Association pressed for administrative improvements. It organized meetings in most of the big towns and passed resolutions favorable to reform. It issued published summaries of other inquiries into public offices, including the Northcote-Trevelyan Report. It demanded civil service reform and managed to maintain the influential interest of The Times in the movement.

Cornewall Lewis inherited from Gladstone a complete draft Order-in-Council and negotiations concerning the appointment of Civil Service Commissioners. He took no action from February to May 1855. Revelations of mismanagement in the Crimean War augmented by formation of the Administrative Reform Association convinced the Palmerston Administration that it must take some action. Lewis, who had opposed the Northcote-Trevelyan Report because of its plan for open competitive examinations, accepted the draft Order-in-Council as accommodating his views. The Cabinet promulgated the Trevelyan Order-in-Council on May 21, 1855.[59]

A few days later the question of open competition was introduced in Parliament. The newly elected Member, Sir Stafford Northcote, and recently retired Chancellor of the Exchequer Gladstone, defended it in debate. Their words failed to influence sufficient votes and Parliament rejected it by a vote of 140 to 125. The vote gave the Government a free hand to implement the more limited Order-in-Council.[60]

---

[59]Wright, pp. 60-65;   Cohen, p. 111;   Moses, pp. 72-90; Richards, pp. 47-50;   Hughes, pp. 74-76.

[60]Moses, pp. 90-91;   Hughes, pp. 78-79.

The Order-in-Council of 1855 established the Civil Service Commission. Lewis appointed three Commissioners to carry out its functions: as Chairman, Sir Edward Ryan, a close friend of Macaulay, former Chief Justice of Bengal and Assistant Comptroller-General of the Exchequer; J.G. Shaw Lefevre, Clerk to the House of Lords, who had welcomed the Northcote-Trevelyan Report; and Edward Romilly, long time civil servant and current Chairman of the Audit Board. The Order made these three men responsible for examining every candidate for junior positions in the civil service to satisfy themselves as to their age, health, character, and abilities. The Order-in-Council expressly denied the Commissioners power to interfere with nominations. Heads of Departments retained the power to appoint men to certain posts without securing a Commission certificate. The Commissioners received power to establish what constituted "requisite knowledge" after consultation with the heads of departments. A six-month probation was established for all newly appointed officers.[61]

The Government made no attempt to introduce a general competitive system. Limited competition, though not mentioned, was expected. Practically, the Order assigned the Commission responsibility for conducting examinations and investigations, previously the responsibility of the departments. Appointments remained political gifts. The Order ignored Trevelyan's recommendation that the civil service be divided into an upper and lower level.[62]

University Reform

While the reformers devoted a considerable amount of time to administrative reform in India and England, they did not neglect university reform. The report of the Royal Commission induced considerable activity among the faculty and officials at Oxford. The Hebdomadal Board, the ruling body which represented the conservative elements, formed a committee to consider the report. The committee decided to take testimony on the report from various elements at the university. The working residents revised the Tutors' Association and began to hold meetings to prepare for their testimony before the Hebdomadal Board committee. The liberals began to meet for the same purpose.

---

[61]Great Britain, Parliament, Parliamentary Papers (Commons), 1860, "Select Committee on Civil Service Appointments, Report... together with the Proceedings of the Committee: Minutes of Evidence: Appendix and Index," p. v.

[62]Cohen, pp. 111-112; Roseveare, The Treasury: The Evolution, p. 170.

Dr. Francis Jeune, Master of Pembroke, led a majority of reformers to support the report, but a smaller group, led by Henry Halford Vaughn, broke away and demanded further reforms. This radical group had great influence on the Royal Commission but when their supporter, Lord John Russell, fell from office in February 1852 the moderate reformers and the Tutors' Association gained more influence on the government. The Tutors' Association publicized its views by issuing a series of reports on various topics covered by the Royal Commission. The Association no longer supported the Royal Report recommendations but advocated milder reforms.

A major controversy took place between the conservative elements and the reformers. The Hebdomadal Board published its report which was generally critical of the Royal Commission recommendations. The most important part of the committee report was a defense of the status quo by Edward Pusey. Pusey opposed increasing the strength of the university over the colleges and elevating the professors to a position of great influence, as had been recommended by the Royal Commission. Henry Vaughn answered Pusey with a masterful defense of the Commission recommendations. He added arguments for further reform proposals. The constitutional question was the key issue. The two sides basically argued over whether power would remain in its present location or shift toward one section or another at the university.

Gladstone, Parliamentary representative for the universities, wrote and received hundreds of letters from December 1853 to March 1854, when the bill was introduced. He soon realized that internal reform was impossible after publication of the committee report. He recognized that the government could not get sufficient support to implement the entire package of recommendations presented by the Royal Commission. Gladstone accepted advice from Jowett and Jeune, and largely followed the schemes favored by the moderate members of the Tutors' Association.

The Government bill contained provisions for eliminating religious oaths for enrollment and graduation. University expansion was encouraged by allowing the Vice-Chancellor to issue licenses for new halls and apply revenue from trusts to construct additional facilities. The bill opened most appointments to competition and abolished all undergraduate fellowships. Gladstone allowed the majority of fellows to take Orders, but colleges were authorized to fill twenty-five per cent of their fellowships with laymen. Fellows, tutors, office holders, and parish ministers were required to live within three miles of the university.

76

The bill gave pay raises to fellows and authorized the expansion of professional chairs. Funds for these came from money saved by abolishing fellowships and reallocating other college income. Colleges were required to revise their statutes, subject to the approval of a commission appointed by Parliament.

The most important and controversial provision of Gladstone's bill pertained to the governing council. Gladstone adopted essentially the scheme proposed by the moderate elements of the Tutors' Association. The bill adopted sectional representation in which the governing Hebdomadal Council of twenty-seven members would distribute its membership in three equal groups among the Heads, tutors, and other convocation members, and the professors and examiners. The proposal increased the participation of the professors, but did not give them the controlling strength which the Royal Commission recommended and the radical reformers desired.

Most segments of the university expressed their approval of the Chancellor of the Exchequer's bill, except for a small element on each side of the controversy. Radical reformers Vaughn and Liddell refused to accept the compromise and remained strong supporters of the Royal Commission recommendations. Conservative extremists gathered around Roundell Palmer in opposition to any changes. The extremists on both sides took their case to Parliament. The radical reformers lobbied in Parliament and convinced James Heywood, Edward Horseman, and J.F.B. Blackett to champion their cause. They were supported by the Dissenters. The Conservatives gained the support of Lord Derby in the House of Lords. The ensuing Parliamentary debate on the bill, supported by Gladstone with considerable energy, almost resulted in defeat for the Administration. By May, Gladstone realized he had to make some adjustments to his bill. He removed the clauses relating to the colleges and added powers to the Parliamentary commission. His move resulted in isolating the radical reformers. The Oxford bill passed Parliament after a debate over the composition of the University Parliamentary Commission.

The Oxford Act of 1854 set the stage for major changes in the universities and rapid expansion. The Government extended the important elements of the Oxford Act to Cambridge in 1856. The Cambridge Act of 1856 placed university power in a new council and appointed commissioners to draft new regulations governing the university and colleges. It also abolished religious tests for everyone except divinity degree students.

The reforms resulted in extensive building of class-
rooms and museums, increase in the use and importance of
examinations, and the establishment of new fellowships
and professorships. It eliminated ancient laws, opened
fellowships and scholarships to competition, transferred
the universities from clerical to academic hands, and
enlarged many studies.[63]

Civil Service Commission

Sir Charles Trevelyan expressed no disappointment
about his failure to effect the total reform package.
He wrote to Jowett that he was "quite satisfied with the
progress we are making. The institution established by
the Order-in-Council will, I think, develop naturally
without any new violent effort, into all we desire."[64]

The limited power of the Civil Service Commission
did not prevent it from making a significant contribution
to improving the quality of candidates entering the government. The three Commissioners took their job seriously,
and conscientiously attempted to carry out their responsibilities. The Commission developed realistic examination
questions and moderate standards, rejecting only the most
incompetent. Nevertheless, opponents severely attacked
the Commission, charging that it purposely developed complex examinations to keep down the number of candidates
certified. The Commission stood on firm ground in this
argument because it had arranged the standards with each
department head. Subjects covered by the examination
varied, depending upon the agreements reached with the
department heads. However, they all required candidates
to show proficiency in dictation, English composition,
arithmetic, and bookkeeping. Examiners incorporated one
foreign language, usually Latin, and English history into
many other examinations. The Colonial Office, for example,
selected for its optional subjects handwriting, spelling,
geography, two foreign languages, geology, and chemistry.[65]

---

[63]Bill, pp. 117-174; Magnus, p. 117; Sanderson, pp. 77-78;
Roach, pp. 31-32; Edward Geoffrey Wilson Ball and J.F.A.
Mason, Christ Church and Reform, 1850-1867 (Oxford: At the
Clarendon Press, 1970), pp. 33-37; W.R. Ward, Victorian Ox-
ford (London: Frank Cass & Co., Ltd., 1965), pp. 156-209.

[64]Charles Trevelyan to Benjamin Jowett, 6 June 1855, quoted
in Wright, p. 65.

[65]Moses, pp. 92-93.

The Commissioners pleasantly surprised the reformers by their vigor and determination. They managed to introduce uniform standards in recruiting procedures, and they advertised their achievements by publishing an annual report. The first report revealed spectacular consequences. Nearly one-third of all candidates examined were rejected on the grounds of gross ignorance.[66] Those who failed did so, not as a result of complex examination questions, but because of a complete lack of the most fundamental skills in spelling, arithmetic, and penmanship. The Commissioners observed that they expected failures to increase because Departments nominated more candidates for each vacancy, even though the number of vacancies remained constant. The Commissioners confirmed one of the major contentions of the Northcote-Trevelyan Report - that patronage nominations were made without regard to the ability of the individual candidate.

Members of Parliament and powerful members of the Administration exerted enormous pressure on the Commissioners to allow special favors to nominees with influential connections who failed the examinations. These efforts brought no relief, as the Civil Service Commission stood firm. Prime Minister Palmerston suffered the same fate as other influential individuals. One of his nominees failed the examination, and Palmerston asked the Commissioners to reconsider their declination. The Commission rejected Palmerston's appeal, and he angrily ordered that the papers of his candidate be sent to him immediately. The Commissioners firmly refused to comply with the demand and informed the Prime Minister that he had to review the papers in the Civil Service Commission office. Palmerston accepted the decision and never pursued the issue any further. Such examples demonstrated the determination of the Commissioners to elevate the principles of merit and efficiency over the demands of family, influence, or party.[67]

The Commissioners worked diligently to introduce a measure of uniformity into the civil service. Even though the Order-in-Council of 1855 confirmed the principle of departmental supremacy, the Commission began immediately to establish uniformity. In the next fifteen years they managed to set standardized requirements for health, moral fitness,[68] and age limits applicable to all government

---

[66]309 candidates failed out of 1,078 tested.

[67]Wright, p. 65.

[68]Standards for "moral fitness" included assurances against alcoholic use, a clean police record, and recommendations from prominent community leaders on the candidate's qualifications.

departments. They made much progress in developing
general standards for testing skills and abilities.
The departments, however, were insensitive to Commission
attempts to introduce some sort of competition into the
recruiting process. They knew that the Commission was
on weak legal ground and ignored their appeals to adopt
some form of competitive examination. Consequently, the
Commission held very few open or limited competitive
examinations before 1870.[69]

     The Civil Service Commission may have been unsuccess-
ful in getting government departments to accept competitive
examinations, but the idea began to grow in certain influential circles. Members of the House of Commons increasingly
introduced and debated a number of resolutions advocating
open competition. Support for these measures grew. Sir
Charles Trevelyan continued to advocate introduction of
open competition. Testifying before the Select Committee
on Civil Service Superannuation in 1856, Trevelyan blamed
patronage and fragmented organization for extravagant pension bills. The vertical organization structure confined
a man to the department he entered, and he could not transfer to another office when the wordload demanded. Sir
William Hayter, long time Patronage Secretary to the
Treasury, refuted the charges and launched a vigorous
personal attack on Trevelyan. Sir Charles easily defended himself by demonstrating how the reduction-in-force
necessitated by the decline in work at the Irish Poor Law
Office and Board of Works led to placing many capable
employees on the "redundant list," which retired them on
two-thirds pension.[70]

     The Superannuation Act of 1859 provided the Civil
Service Commission its first enforcement tool. According
to the Act, all persons appointed after April 19, 1859,
must have had a certificate from the Civil Service Commission in order to qualify for a pension. The Civil Service Commission now had power to deny a pension to employees
who failed to follow its rules and regulations.[71]

     Organizationally, the Order-in-Council of 1855 lo-
cated the new Civil Service Commission in the Treasury
Department. The Treasury came under constant pressure

---

[69]Wright, pp. 66-67; Moses, -p. 94-95.

[70]Cohen, pp. 114-115; Richards, p. 51.

[71]Marios Raphael, Pensions and Public Servants: A Study
of the British System (Paris: Mouton & Co., 1964), p. 160.

from supporters of patronage practices to interfere with the Commission's activities or intervene in individual cases. In general, the Treasury supported Civil Service Commission decisions when required, carefully avoiding any interference in its work. The Treasury Department protected the Civil Service Commission in three general areas. First, the department adopted all Civil Service Commission recommendations, thereby giving leadership to government acceptance of the Commission regulations. Second, the department consistently refused to interfere in decisions of the Commission and emphatically refused to act as a court of appeal. Third, the department insisted that all government employees obtain a certificate from the Civil Service Commission before qualifying for a pension, as required in the 1859 Superannuation Act.[72]

Northcote Select Committee of 1860

The Government was satisfied with the operation of the Civil Service Commission and the conditions now existing in the government service. Advocates of further reform in Parliament proposed in 1860 a resolution calling for the appointment of another Select Committee "to inquire into the present mode of Nominating and Examining CANDIDATES for JUNIOR APPOINTMENTS in the CIVIL SERVICE, with a view to ascertaining whether greater facility may not be afforded for the Admission of properly qualified Persons."[73] Opposition to the motion came from the Patronage Secretary, Sir William Hayter, and unexpectedly from Sir Stafford Northcote (no longer under the influence of Gladstone and Trevelyan) on the grounds that such an inquiry was premature. Nevertheless, the resolution carried and the Government agreed to appoint a committee.

The Inquiry Committee consisted of many prominent reformers and two former Patronage Secretaries. Sir Stafford Northcote, John Bright, and Robert Lowe were the most famous reformers, while Sir William Jolliffe and Sir William Hayter represented patronage interests.[74] The Committee confirmed the findings of the Northcote-Trevelyan

---

[72]Wright, p. 66.

[73]Great Britain, Parliament, Parliamentary Papers (Commons), 1860, "Report from the Select Committee on Civil Service Appointments; Together with the Proceedings of the Committee, Minutes of Evidence, Appendix, and Index," p. iii.

[74]Other members included John Arthur Roebuck; Richard Monckton Milnes; Lord Edward Stanley, Chairman of the Committee,

Report of 1855. They agreed that "the best mode of procuring competent persons to fill the junior clerkships"
was a system of open competition.[75] They made very
favorable comments on the work of the Civil Service Commission. CSC examinations had successfully excluded
many totally incompetent nominees from the service. Yet
the evidence given clearly showed that the quality of
nominees remained very low. Most agreed that Commission
examinations were much superior to those which formerly
had been conducted by the departments independently. The
Civil Service Commission introduced limited competitive
examinations, but its campaign to get broad acceptance
of this principle made little progress. The Commission
certified only nine per cent of the appointments to Government service from competitive examinations.[76] Even
when departments submitted to limited competition, some
used a variation of Sir William Hayter's practice, perfected before the foundation of the Civil Service Commission, of employing two "Treasury Dunces" to sit for
examinations.

The Committee found that "the best mode of obtaining
the most competent persons for these situations is by
general competitive examinations, open to all" but, ac-
ceding to the opinions of patronage advocates, they argued instead that since "sufficient time has not elapsed
to show to their full extent the results of the present
system, it may be the safer course to continue the system

---

who had experimented with competitive examinations for
clerkships in the London India Office; Lord Robert Arthur
Cecil, conservative opponent of democracy and radical ideas
of progress; John Francis Maguire; James Clay; William
Tite; and John Pope Hennessey, who introduced the resolution which had resulted in creation of the committee.

[75]Select Committee on Civil Service Appointments, p. 14.

[76]Ibid., p. 8.

[77]The Treasury Dunces or Treasury Idiot technique, attributed to Sir William Hayter, required that the Patronage
Secretary keep two totally ignorant candidates to compete
against those he wanted to qualify for a job. Their
stupidity assured the success of the favored candidate.
Roseveare, The Treasury: The Evolution, p. 172; Hughes,
p. 80.

of limited competition."[78] Therefore, they recommended
that all departments adopt a system of limited competition. They suggested that the Commission adopt a fixed
proportion of competitors required to take the examination. A single vacancy necessitated five competitors
while examining to fill seven vacancies required only a
ratio of three to one. To prevent use of the "Treasury
Idiot" technique, the Committee recommended that each
candidate sit for a preliminary examination to determine
his qualification for the position.[79]

The Civil Service Commissioners welcomed the Committee's recommendations. Even though the Committee made
mild recommendations designed to appeal to conservative
sentiment, the Government took no action on them. The
Commissioners had no power to implement any changes and,
therefore, the Pass/Fail Examination system continued to
dominate recruitment into the civil service for another
ten years.[80]

Treasury Control of the Civil Service Commission

Without power to coerce compliance with the 1860
Committee recommendations, the Civil Service Commission
chose to appeal to the Treasury to adopt them in order
to set an example for other departments. Gladstone was
back as Chancellor of the Exchequer in Palmerston's government. The Treasury willingly agreed to comply with
the general recommendations of the Civil Service Commission and issued a Minute of 1861 requiring nominees
to pass a qualifying examination before taking a limited
competition examination. The results were spectacular.
The Civil Service Commission rejected forty-five per cent
of the first 540 candidates tested as unfit to compete

---

[78] Select Committee on Civil Service Appointments, p. xxv.

[79] Ibid., pp. xix-xxix.

[80] Ibid.; Cohen, p. 119; Wright, p. 68; Richards, p. 53;
Gladden, p. 21; Roach, pp. 206-209; The Pass/Fail Examination system was not competitive. Pass/ Fail examinations
were designed to establish a standard below which a candidate
was not allowed to hold a government position. Those who
passed the examinations were certified to hold a civil
service job.

for any vacancy. Yet, no other government department
followed the Treasury's lead. The Treasury did its
best to support the Civil Service Commission over the
next ten years. Treasury officials were so eager to
avoid weakening the Commission's authority that they accepted recommendations and regulations made by the Civil
Service Commission which affected the Treasury alone.
For example, the Treasury wanted to increase the upper
age limit for some jobs. The Civil Service Commission
overruled them, so the Treasury withdrew the proposal.
On another occasion the Commission refused to certify a
nominee of the Patronage Secretary. Gladstone supported
them because he feared "our overruling them in our own
case must greatly weaken their authority."[81]

The same Treasury policy of accepting Civil Service
Commission decisions prevailed with respect to those affecting other departments. In 1862 the Treasury notified
the War Office that it would not interfere with the Commissioners' refusal to certify a temporary clerk and, fur-
thermore, it announced that it would not accept any other
requests from departments on future acts which would
place it in the position of acting as a court of appeals
for Civil Service Commission decisions. The decision
against the War Office was particularly important, since
Treasury officials thought the Commissioners' position
was unrealistically harsh and arbitrary.[82] The Treasury
was drawn into the controversy over enforcement of the
provisions of the 1859 Superannuation Act. Here again,
the Treasury consistently supported the Commission's decision not to issue certificates unless a candidate passed
a civil service examination. The Superannuation Act of
1859 required that government employees pass a civil service examination to qualify for a pension.[83]

The Commission consistently pointed out the limitations of pass examinations and limited examinations and
urged departments to adopt open competition. Nevertheless,
ministry after ministry refused to take additional measures
to strengthen the public service. Most argued that the
1855 decision worked well enough. In 1867-8 the Civil Service Commission reported that "the conditions which the
Select Committee regarded as indispensable, have been im-
perfectly realized in the practice of nominating departments."[84]

[81]Memorandum from W.E. Gladstone to Frederick Peel, 14
November 1861, quoted in Wright, p. 70.
[82]Ibid., p. 71.
[83]Ibid., p. 72.
[84]Great Britain, Civil Service Commission, Thirteenth Report of
the Civil Service Commissioners, 1867-8, p. xxii; Roach, pp. 205-9.

Struggle for Open Competition

Sir Charles Trevelyan's conviction that satisfaction with the Order-in-Council of 1855 would lead the country to adopt open competition within a few years did not stand up to the test of time. Some public organs agitated for further reform of the civil service but not strongly enough to command government attention. In fact, press attention declined. Maurice Wright surveyed ninety-seven of the most important journals, magazines, and periodicals but found only three contained articles on some aspect of the British Civil Service, and none supported the introduction of open competition.[85]

As before, it took the catalytic action of two strategically located reformers, Robert Lowe, Chancellor of the Exchequer, and W.E. Gladstone, Prime Minister, to complete realization of the proposals outlined by Trevelyan and Northcote fifteen years before. The most logical explanation for the surfacing of this civil service question in 1869 is that Robert Lowe had committed himself personally to the principle, and that in his powerful position he felt strong enough to advocate its adoption. He knew that his Prime Minister, Gladstone, would give the idea a favorable ear. No other explanation can withstand close scrutiny, even though most historians have attributed further reform to other reasons.[86] Maurice Wright systematically searched all available records and simply was unable to substantiate any of the claims advanced by other historians.[87]

---

[85]Wright, p. 76.

[86]Cohen attributes the proposal to a gradual change in the attitude of the press toward civil service from 1860 to 1870. Moses simply states that "Everyone was tired of the patronage system" (page 127). Richards thinks that the case of open competition was overwhelmingly evident, and that the open competition was a logical conclusion after the Second Reform Bill and the Liberal victory of 1868 (page 53). For Kingsly, the reason was the agitation of the middle class as expressed in the Liberal victory of 1868. For him, reform of the civil service was ideally suited to Gladstone's pledge of reform and strict economy (page 75). Dorman Eaton wrote: "The demand for the suppression of the official monopoly of patronage had become too strong for the administration to withstand" (page 228). For Griffith the reason was that it just took time to implement so important a reform (page 15). Sir Charles Trevelyan attributed the order to agitation from the "middle class" (page 100, Appendix F, Playfair Commission, 1874).

[87]Wright, p. 76.

Although there was no substantial agitation for further reform, public opinion and the political atmosphere
were much more favorable to recommendations on further
reform than in 1854. The timing was Lowe's but the subject was familiar to politicians, civil servants, the
press, and the public by 1869. Fifteen years of experience with pass examinations showed that civil service
reform improved the government without inflicting severe
harm on the politicians or aristocracy. Middle class
representation in the government service had improved as
a result of the reform. Few agitated for further reform,
but almost no one agitated for a return to the days of
unlimited political patronage. All that was needed was
a catalyst to take advantage of the favorable environment.

We know that Robert Lowe, on his own initiative, can-
vassed each member of the Gladstone Ministry to solicit
opinions on further civil service reform. He found sufficient support to write to Gladstone:

> As I have often tried in vain, will you bring
> the question of the civil service before the
> cabinet today? Something must be decided.
> We cannot keep matters in this discreditable
> state of abeyance. If the cabinet will not
> entertain the idea of open competition, might
> we not at any rate require a large number of
> competitors for each vacancy? Five, or seven,
> or ten?[88]

The cabinet met to discuss the issue for the first time
on June 5, 1869. It decided at that meeting to establish a
cabinet committee to consider competitive examinations.
George W. Villiers, Fourth Earl of Clarendon, venerable
foreign secretary, and, unexpectedly, John Bright, President
of the Board of Trade, opposed the principle of open competition. Outside the committee, Bruce and Fortescue supported them. Lowe counted on support from First Viscount
George J. Goschen, President of the Poor Law Board; John
Wodehouse, First Earl of Kimberly, Lord Privy Seal; Lieu-
tenant-General Charles Grey, the Queen's secretary; and
Hugh C.E. Childers, First Lord of the Admiralty. The committee proposed use of open competition in the civil service in a memorandum issued June 29, 1869. Opponents of
the memorandum persuaded Gladstone to circulate it around
the Cabinet again. On August 8, 1869, the memorandum came
under discussion again in Cabinet and the opposition
adamantly objected to it.

---

[88]Robert Lowe to W.E. Gladstone, quoted in Cohen, p. 121.

The initiative now shifted from Lowe to Gladstone.
Gladstone suggested an ingenious compromise. He proposed
that the new method of recruitment be adopted only by
those departments of the civil service where the minister
agreed. Lowe objected at first for fear no one would co-
operate. Instead he asked Gladstone: "Could you not
prevail on the Cabinet to leave the matter in our hands
[Treasury's] with the understanding that we do not go for
perfectly open competition?"[89] The Cabinet discussed
the memorandum again on December 7, 1869. In the meantime, Lowe had changed his mind and agreed to push for
the Gladstone compromise.[90] At the meeting Gladstone
further agreed to grant the ministers the right to withdraw from the scheme or to modify it at a later date.
Accepting the compromise, the Cabinet approved the plan
and instructed Lowe to circulate it among the departments
for their views.

Lowe moved quickly to retain the momentum he had
acquired. On December 8, 1869, he issued a Treasury
Minute on the subject and sent it to all departments.
All departments favored the introduction of open competition, except the Home and Foreign Offices. Several
of the departments requested a little flexibility in applying the concept. They, in essence, expressed the same
concerns as Arbuthnot who wrote to Hamilton in 1862,
"there ought to be a safety valve, permitting some relax-
ation of the strict rules of the Civil Service Commission
in special cases under Treasury sanction and approved by
the Commission."[91]

Robert Lowe and Baron Robert R. Wheeler Lingen, who
replaced Hamilton as Permanent Secretary to the Treasury,
drafted the Order-in-Council of June 4, 1870. Parliament
did not participate in the policy decision at any stage.
Once the Government promulgated the Order, Parliament,
the press, and the majority of civil servants welcomed
the system of open competition. Patronage supporters
did not accept defeat silently. G.G. Glyn, Gladstone's
Patronage Secretary, protested vigorously to the Prime

---

[89] Robert Lowe to W.E. Gladstone, 10 November 1869, quoted
in Wright, p. 81.

[90] Robert Lowe to W.E. Gladstone, 22 November 1869, quoted
in Ibid., p. 81.

[91] George Arbuthnot to George Alexander Hamilton, 5 April
1862, quoted in Ibid., p. 71.

Minister. "Your patronage at the Treasury which has been
left to me as 'Secretary' is entirely swept away. . . .
Without entering into the very debatable ground of the advantage or otherwise to the party of political patronage,
I will only say that I lose, without notice, and at once,
the great advantage of the daily correspondence and com-
munication with members of the party. . . to say nothing
of the power which it placed in my hands."[92]

Order-in-Council of 1870

The Order-in-Council of 1870 substituted the system
of merit for the system of patronage in recruiting civil
servants. Some of its most important features included:
(1) All future vacancies should be filled by open competitive examinations except in the Foreign Office and
Home Office; (2) The civil service would be divided into
two sections with separate examinations. Division I required university education and targeted candidates for
the higher positions. Division II examinations encompassed
all other offices; (3) Any person desirous of a civil
service job had to sit for a Civil Service Commission examination and receive a certificate of qualification before
appointment to a government job; (4) The Treasury accepted responsibility for approving all Civil Service
Commission decisions; and (5) To make an appointment
without submitting the certificate to a civil service
examination, a Department had to obtain the express approval
of the Treasury Department and Civil Service Commission.
This provision permitting hiring specialists with unique
qualifications of knowledge or ability. (6) Further,
Civil Service Commission examinations could be dispensed
with to facilitate transfer from the "Redundant List"
(displaced employees).[93]

The Order-in-Council completed the adoption of the
recommendations contained in the 1855 Northcote-Trevelyan
Report. It further reduced the discretionary powers of
the individual departments and established the Treasury as
the regulator of the entire process. It did not eliminate

---

[92]G.G. Glyn to W.E. Gladstone, quoted in Richards, pp. 53-54.

[93]Great Britain, Parliament, Parliamentary Papers (Commons),
1875, V. 33, Cmnd. 113, "First Report of the Civil Service
Inquiry Commission," pp. 6-8.

patronage altogether but instead inflicted on it a mortal wound from which the patronage'system withered and practically disappeared as time went on.

Application of the Order-in-Council of 1870

The Civil Service Commission acquired responsibility for implementing the Order-in-Council of 1855. The Treasury Department took its place following issuance of the Order-in-Council of 1870. Robert Lowe, Chancellor of the Exchequer, and his Permanent Secretary,[94] Ralph Robert W. Lingen, assumed responsibility for implementing the Order. Lowe had agreed with Gladstone's compromise that each minister could decide whether to adopt open competition or not; and if adopted, would determine how extensively it would be applied. Implicit in the compromise was the assumption that a minister could withdraw his decision to participate at any time. Robert Lowe reversed his position immediately and repudiated the compromise; once participation was elected, Lowe considered the decision irrevocable.

Chichester Samuel Fortescue, Gladstone's Chief Secretary for Ireland, attempted to withdraw the Irish Office from participation in open competition recruitment. Lowe applied considerable pressure on the minister and persuaded Gladstone to help prevent Fortescue from raising the issue at a Cabinet meeting. The Irish Office remained under Civil Service Commission jurisdiction.

Lowe and Lingen mustered all their power on a sustained attack against the Home Office and the Foreign Office. John Bruce, Home Secretary, finally agreed to fill a few of his positions by open competition. This did not satisfy Lowe who kept up the pressure. As long as Bruce remained, he granted no further concessions to the reformers. At the Foreign Office Lowe thought his chances greatly improved when George W.F. Villiers, Earl of Clarendon died and Granville George, Earl of Granville, replaced him. Gladstone reported that Granville was not opposed to open competition but did not want to reverse Clarendon's decision immediately. Consequently, the Treasury pair used more subtle tactics on the Foreign Office. "References by the Treasury to the application of open competition were more moderate in tone and altogether less insistent than those made to the Home Office in similar circumstances."[95] Granville had, after all,

---

[94] Known at the time as Secretary to the Treasury.

[95] Wright, p. 96.

89

supported open competition for the Colonial Office, but
civil servants at the Foreign Office insistently argued
that their work was unique and should not be compared to
other departments. By 1873 Lowe followed Lingen's advice
and began to increase pressure on Granville. He singled
out the Treaty Office and Library Departments for the
breakthrough. Unfortunately, scandal at the Post Office
forced Gladstone to make some important Cabinet changes.
He transferred Robert Lowe to the Home Office to replace
John Bruce. Immediately, Lowe directed the Home Office
to accept open competition for all its junior positions.
Gladstone assumed the position of Chancellor of the Exchequer as well as Prime Minister and discontinued efforts to apply open competition at the Foreign Office.
His inaction terminated the last opportunity for converting the Foreign Office to open competition until World
War I.[96]

Resistance to the Order-in-Council of 1870 came primarily from the civil service and not Parliament. The
Order permitted the listing of special circumstances such
as unique scientific knowledge. The Government published
these positions as "Schedule B." Each required Treasury
approval. Departments bombarded the Treasury with applications for inclusion on Schedule B. They argued that the
qualifications they wanted could not be tested under open
competition. Frequently the departments argued that positions should be placed on Schedule B because of their

---

[96]Gladstone's inaction in extending open competition to the
Foreign Office was probably caused by its relatively low
priority in his last year in office. Gladstone's problem
mounted as the year progressed taking his attention away from
administrative matters. Civil Service reform already applied
to the great majority of government jobs. The exclusion of
the Foreign Office from the civil service caused little harm
to the principles of reform. Gladstone's political strength
was severely weakened when he agreed to continue in office
following defeat of the Irish University Bill. His assumption
of the post of Chancellor of the Exchequer following the Post
Office scandal and problems with the First Commissioner of
Works confronted him with a constitutional crisis over the
legality of holding two offices. He backed into another problem by allowing his name to be used in sponsoring a public
memorial for John Stuart Mill only to withdraw after he found
out that Mill had once advocated birth control. These and
problems associated with the marriage of his eldest daughter,
Agnes, caused the Prime Minister to sink into a mood of de-
pression. Under such circumstances, it is no wonder that
placing the Foreign office under Civil Service Commission rules
did not get his attention. Magnus, pp. 224-228.

confidential or secret nature. Lingen and Lowe brushed
off these arguments with the contention that candidates
selected by merit were just as likely to be honest as
those selected by the patronage system.

Even if a department succeeded in getting a position
listed on Schedule B, the incumbent was denied a pension
under the Superannuation Act of 1859.

Gladstone prevented Lowe from converting all Treasury offices to open competition. He tried to soften
the blow of open competition on the Patronage Secretary
by agreeing to withdraw the Census Office, Custom House
offices, and Excise men from coverage.[97]

Role of the Treasury
in Civil Service Functions

Other departments objected to the government-wide
responsibilities assigned to the Treasury by the Order-
in-Council. The Treasury did all it could to get acceptance. When possible, the financial institution used
its power over the purse as a leverage to force acceptance of open competition. For instance, the British
Museum in 1872 wanted funds to expand, but the Treasury
refused to support the request unless it agreed to open
competition. When this did not work, the Treasury refused to grant Museum employees an authorized pay increase. Lowe won the day when the Museum agreed to follow Civil Service Commission rules and regulations.

The Treasury tools included persuasion, persistent
pressure, financial power, political pressure from Gladstone, power of the pension, and on occasion, the press.
Gradually, resistance subsided in all areas but the
Foreign Office.

The Treasury assumed an active part in preparing the
new regulations for competitive examinations. The Order-
in-Council gave the Treasury power to approve proposals
advanced by the Civil Service Commission. Lowe and Lingen went beyond this and assumed total control of the
development and approval of all examination regulations.
This evidently did not disturb the Commissioners for the
closest cooperation characterized their relationship with

---

[97]Wright, pp. 96-102.

the Treasury officials. The two organizations drafted
regulations for three types of examinations under the
major criteria of uniformity and economy. In essence,
the Treasury demonstrated its control of recruitment
by its preoccupation with standardization of examination
content and regulations, direct approval of detailed recruitment procedures, and subordination of the Civil Service Commission. Once the Treasury approved the regulations, it sent them to the various departments for comments. The departments purposely delayed sending any
reply so that the target date of August 1870 could not
be met. This put the Civil Service Commission under
undeserved criticism, and it responded by asking the
Treasury for permission to implement the draft regulations without the departments' approval. The Treasury
gave its permission with the understanding that the
Commission acquire Treasury approval for all unique
interpretations of the draft regulations. Treasury responses to these unique questions usually took the
force of new regulations.[98]

Classification of Government Employees

Trevelyan had made the first rudimentary attempts
to address the issue of classifying the Civil Service in
1848. Taking advantage of his testimony before a Select
Committee appointed by Parliament to seek a reduction in
the cost of civil administration, he proposed that the
civil establishment be separated into two divisions; the
mechanical forces and the intellectual group. Mechanical
forces consisted of those individuals, such as writers
and copyists, who carried out routine duties. The intellectual force constituted the leaders and policy makers
who directed the functions of the departments. The scheme
of a two-tiered civil service got little support from
other witnesses.

Trevelyan and Northcote had followed up the suggestion by including it in their famous report of 1855.[99]
They coupled the suggestion of a two-tiered service with
"the importance of transferring the clerks from one department of the office to another, so that each may have
an opportunity of making himself master of the whole of
the business before he is called upon, in due course of
time, to take a leading position."[100] Trevelyan or

[98]Ibid.; Winter, pp. 262-268.

[99]Papers Relating to the Re-Organization of the Civil
Service, p. 17.

[100]Ibid., p. 18.

Northcote held office in the Treasury until 1860 and used their position to further this proposition. The Colonial office was the first important department to adopt and implement the system. By 1860 most government departments and offices had introduced a two-tiered establishment, calling them the Superior and Supplementary Establishments.

Unfortunately, the system never worked well. Problems developed from the beginning. The departments found it almost impossible to keep the divisions apart. Some departments employed the lower level clerks in upper level work. Others used upper level clerks to carry out lower level tasks because they did not have enough lower level employees to do the jobs. To fill the gap left when lower level employees assumed upper level work, the departments hired "unestablished copyists and writers." This, in essence, created a third level of employees, and it resulted in dissatisfaction among the regular workers. Supplementary clerks doing upper level work objected that they did not receive the same salary as Superior clerks who did exactly the same work. Likewise, unestablished clerks complained about lower compensation while doing the same work as other Supplementary clerks. Even though the distinction between mechanical and intellectual work remained blurred, the Treasury continued to support the two-tiered establishment, arguing that it was the most efficient, economical, and practical organization.

The three separate examinations introduced in 1870 reinforced the general pattern.[101] No one questioned the basic principle. The only discussion centered on how best to implement the principle. "It was now generally accepted that the work could and should be divided, distinguishing that which had an intellectual content from that which was mainly mechanical and routine."[102] Classification problems continued to plague the Service for some fifty years.

The Treasury tried to cope with the problem by appointing a new committee of inquiry in 1860. Northcote and Ralph Lingen participated in the inquiry. They surprised the Treasury by abandoning the original system first devised by Trevelyan and Northcote and proposed a new approach. The Committee of Inquiry suggested abolishing the Supplementary Establishment (lower level) and returning to

---

[101] The Commission administered a preliminary examination to qualify candidates for Level one or two examinations.

[102] Wright, p. 143.

the old one-tiered establishment. They suggested the Government assign all mechanical work to a new "Central Copying Agency" consisting of unestablished and temporary clerks. The department would hire these clerks on a daily or weekly basis from the Central agency. Separating the mechanical workers from the department, the committee thought, would make it more difficult to use them for intellectual work. The proposal was never adopted because it met a chorus of hostile criticism. The departments opposed eliminating the Supplementary establishment and creating a central copying agency be-[103] cause it would restrict their management freedom.

The problem of classification resulted in opening up a new avenue of patronage in the civil service. Unestablished clerks, hired from the old "pass/fail" examinations, did not compete in competitive examinations required of the "establishment" civil servants. Consequently, departments with authorization to hire unestablished clerks promoted those clerks into the establishment positions. Lowe recognized the problem clearly and characterized it as "putting down patronage with one hand and setting it up with the other." He moved swiftly and issued the Order-in-Council of August 19, 1871. "By Order-in-Council temporary service was made strictly temporary by the abolition of progressive wages, sick-leave and holidays, and by forbidding appointment to the establishment." He introduced modifications in 1873 to accommodate certain inequities.[104]

Playfair Commission of 1873

Concern for the high cost of salaries resulted in the appointment of another Parliamentary inquiry into civil service expenditure in 1873. Once again the Government appointed Sir Stafford Northcote chairman of the committee consisting of seventeen members. The committee made an extensive inquiry and published a voluminous report but with disappointing results. The report gave no support for many of the reforms advocated in the Northcote-Trevelyan Report of 1854. It rejected proposals for improving efficiency and instead expressed the opinion that efficiency depended on the system of promotion. The report

---

[103] Wright, pp. 122-123.

[104] Ibid., pp. 139-140; Cohen, p. 127.

rejected classification proposals which applied government-wide, including the two-tiered approach. Instead
it advocated a return to vertical classification along
departmental lines. The recommendations "amounted to
little more than a tepid sanction of the Order-in-Council
of 1870, coupled with a refutation of the validity of the
principle of division of labor."[105]

The results were so unsatisfactory that Northcote,
now Chancellor of the Exchequer, felt compelled to appoint a new investigation into the entire conditions of
the civil service. He appointed Sir Lyon Playfair
chairman of a new Civil Service Inquiry Commission, composed of two Members of Parliament and six Heads of Departments. The Commission sat from 1874 to 1875, when
it issued three reports.

Northcote instructed the Commission to investigate
four specific subjects which particularly concerned him.
These dealt with (1) recruitment; (2) inter-office
transfers with emphasis on displaced employees; (3)
grading the civil service; and (4) employment of un-
classified temporary employees.[106]

This investigation marks the last time the reform
principles originally articulated by Trevelyan and Northcote in 1854 would be questioned in detail. The Commission examined in considerable depth almost every premise
they advocated. It heard a great number of witnesses
who represented the entire range of opinion. Everyone
sensed that this inquiry was the last stand for patronage. The Gladstone Administration fell in 1874, to the
great joy of the civil servants. Gladstone's cabinet
officials, as well as their civil service reform, were
extremely unpopular. Disraeli succeeded him and needed
to determine if the Conservatives wanted to adopt, reject, or modify the program initiated by the Liberals.
They had the ideal circumstances because their Chancellor
of the Exchequer was none other than Sir Stafford Northcote, co-author of the 1854 report. But Sir Stafford was
"no longer an eager enthusiast for free and open competition."[107] He questioned whether the new system was
the best method for the Conservative administration.
Northcote used the Playfair Commission as his decision-
making vehicle.[108]

---

[105]Cohen, pp. 128-129.

[106]First Report of the Civil Service Inquiry Commission, p. 3.

[107]Moses, pp. 137-138.

[108]Ibid.

The reasons for Northcote's apparent reversal of
position are not specifically known. His career suggests that he had been strongly influenced by Trevelyan
and Gladstone back in the 1850's and 60's. As that influence waned, he found it difficult to take and hold a
strong reform posture. Northcote's later career shows
signs of vacillation and inability to make firm decisions.
His position on civil service reform became more and more
ambivalent as he grew older.

The Playfair Commission, dominated by civil servants,
devoted much of its time to questioning officials closely
connected with the practical work of the government, including Robert Lowe and Sir Charles Trevelyan.[109] The
testimony depicted a civil service consisting of employees
recruited by patronage, ' pass/fail examinations,
limited examinations, and open competition. They
found a lack of consistency throughout the service in pay,
organization, classification, and promotions, resulting
in discontent among the employees. The Commission supported the use of competitive examinations as the best
method of recruitment. "As regards appointment by competition, there seems to be no doubt that both the limited competition which existed before the recent Order-
in-Council, and the open competition for Clerkships under
Regulation II, have produced good candidates."[110]

The Commission thought the confusion and inconsistency
in the government was caused by the lack of enforcement of
the two-tiered classification system originally proposed
by Trevelyan. The results were wasteful and generated discontent among employees. The Commission developed its own
version of the two-tiered classification system. It suggested an upper division composed of two groups -- an elite
group of Administrative Officers, chosen by merit, and a
small Higher Division, chosen from men of liberal education
after two competitive examinations. As before, the Lower
Division, assigned to clerical and mechanical work, would
be recruited by competitive examination "in subjects included in the range of an ordinary commercial education."[111]
The Commission created a fourth classification, below the
Lower Level, called "Boy Clerks." Boy Clerks would replace

---

[109]See the Playfair Commission Index to the Appendices.

[110]First Report of the Civil Service Inquiry Commission,
p. 7.

[111]Ibid., p. 10.

the old establishment writers and work on the most basic and repetitive duties in the government. The Commission recommended recruiting Boy Clerks between the ages of fifteen and seventeen "by a competitive examination of a very limited character."[112] It proposed advancement to the Lower Division after passing a more complex examination. Those who failed would be discharged at the age of nineteen. The Report also proposed restricting entrance to the Upper Division from the Lower Division. In all, it contained some thirty-five recommendations.[113]

The Playfair Commission satisfied very few. Many thought its report unconvincing and unclear. Northcote charged that the recommendations were reactionary. He objected particularly to the proposals for the Upper Division and thought the report's recommendations pertaining to transfers would discourage merit promotions. Sir Charles Trevelyan attacked the report for introducing special examinations for special positions. The press attacked the report for fear it would lead to the reintroduction of patronage. The Government decided to delay action and appointed a committee to advise the Treasury on how far it should go to introduce the Playfair proposals.[114]

The Conservatives eventually decided to implement the Playfair recommendations on a selective and very limited basis. The Order-in-Council of February 12, 1876, provided that the demarcation line between Upper and Lower Divisions should be increased and the number of clerks in the Upper Division reduced. The Order restricted movement from Lower to Upper Divisions. Lower Division employees became subject to transfer between departments. Finally, the Government agreed to create a new class of "Boy Clerks" along the lines recommended by the Playfair Commission. The Conservatives ignored the other recommendations including those pertaining to the Upper Division.[115]

Failing to significantly alter conditions in the civil service, the Playfair Commission did have some profound results. In regulations pertaining to the Lower Division, the Commissioners accepted the principle of uniform conditions throughout the

---

[112] First Report of the Civil Service Inquiry Commission, p. 10.

[113] Ibid., pp. 5-30.

[114] Moses, pp. 153-155.

[115] Ibid., p. 155.

government. This greatly weakened the Department's
argument about the uniqueness of their jobs. The system introduced by the Orders-in-Council of 1855 and 1870
remained in force and its principles were never seriously
challenged again. Patronage advocates received a death
blow as the Conservative Party committed itself to the
principles of civil service reform. This removed the
last political base in support of patronage.

The British Government continued to evaluate its
civil service establishment through the method of official
investigations. The Ridley Commission came next in 1886-
1890, followed by the MacDonnell Commission (1912-1915),
Haldane or Reorganization Committee (1919-1920), Tomlin
Commission (1929-1931), Prestley Commission (1953-1955),
and most recently the Fulton Committee (1966-1968).

The British Civil Service of the post-Playfair Com-
mission era exerted the most significant influence on the
United States, especially through the efforts of Dorman
Eaton who came to England in 1877 to research his book.
Ironically, the pendulum has reversed and the American
Civil Service System now influences the British, for many
of the Fulton Committee recommendations resulted from a
thorough study of the United States Civil Service Commission.

Foreign Influence in the United States

One can do little more than speculate why the system
in China, Germany, and France did not have much influence
on the civil service reform movement in the United States.
All three had strong, firmly established civil service
systems with years of experience. The British, on the
other hand, installed a new administrative system in 1855,
admittedly incomplete and experimental, with relatively
few years of operating experience. The international community held the Chinese, German, and French systems in
high regard and each attracted imitators. The British
commanded little attention among other countries. Perhaps
some of the reasons the United States looked to Britain
instead of China, Germany, or France were:

(1) Political and administrative conditions in the
United States more closely paralleled conditions in Britain
than any other foreign country.

(2) The recent administrative developments in Britain
were fresh in the minds of American reformers.

(3)   The background of the major United States reformers helped turn their attention to Great Britain.
Carl Schurz's unhappy experience in Germany during the
revolutions of 1848 did not encourage him to imitate the
administrative system of his native country.   Thomas A.
Jenckes, E.L. Godkin, Charles Sumner, George William
Curtis and Dorman B. Eaton descended from important
English families.   Each maintained extensive personal
contacts in England and had a wide knowledge of political events there.

(4)   Liberals in Great Britain and the United States
advocated and supported civil service reform.   They
corresponded frequently with each other and wrote about
mutual problems and political issues.

(5)   Political parties did not have significant influence in shaping civil service systems in China, Germany, or France.   In Great Britain and the United States
political parties benefited from the patronage system,
which in turn helped shape the direction of civil service reform movements.

(6)   The administrative systems of China, Germany,
and France offered little help in eradicating a number
of the most severe problems which faced the United States.
Corruption, nepotism, and elitism existed in all four
countries, but the new administrative system in Britain
made important improvements in these conditions.

On the other hand, strong anti-British sentiments
in the United States made imitation of the British administrative system subject to considerable criticism.
American reformers, early in the civil service reform
movement, frequently tried to mute this criticism by
using examples from all four countries to support their
arguments.

CHAPTER IV

UNITED STATES FEDERAL SERVICE
TO 1865

Search for a System

The American government, under the Constitution
established in 1789, found no acceptable model on which
to base its public administration system. The brief experience under the Articles of Confederation had given
no inspiration. The experience under Great Britain exerted a negative influence. Corrupt, inefficient, and
scandalous government, indelibly etched on the minds of
the Founding Fathers through the colonial experience,
characterized the British tradition. The English aristocracy controlled the appointing powers and used that
power to reward relatives and political friends. They
created and awarded sinecures and income from the sale
of public office. Skill and ability on the part of the
applicant were not qualifications for official positions.
The Government often appointed obvious incompetents to
colonial positions to satisfy the demands of powerful
families. Standards of performance were mediocre at
best, and generally downright poor. Americans wanted
to avoid the British example.

Few colonists knew enough about the French administration to emulate it. Thomas Jefferson, although acquainted
with France, displayed little in-depth knowledge of the
French administrative system. He would not have been
pleased with its reliance on tradition, disregard for
public opinion, and lack of local initiative. The Prussian and Chinese systems were practically unknown.[1]

Initially, Americans attributed the abuse of administrative power in the colonies to excessive centralization.
Consequently, the Articles of Confederation gave administrative authority to Congress. Discontent with this experiment
led to acceptance of the concept of political and administrative centralization.

The Constitutional Convention adopted Montesquieu's
doctrine of the separation of powers among the executive,

---

[1]Leonard D. White, The Federalists: A Study in Administrative History (New York: The Macmillan Co., 1948), p. 468.

101

legislative, and judicial branches of government. The
delegates established the structure for a strong independent executive responsible to the legislature through
the provision of impeachment. Delegates at the Convention assigned the Senate additional checks on the administrative powers of the executive. The Constitution
provides that the President

> . . . shall nominate, and by and with the
> Advice and Consent of the Senate, shall
> appoint Ambassadors, other public Minis-
> ters and Consuls, Judges of the Supreme
> Court, and all other Officers of the
> United States, whose Appointments are not
> herein otherwise provided for, and which
> shall be established by Law; but the Con-
> gress may by Law vest the Appointment of
> such inferior Officers, as they think
> proper, in the President alone, in the
> Courts of Law, or in the Heads of De-
> partments.[2]

Delegates augmented this provision with emergency Presidential powers of appointment should the Senate not be
sitting.[3]

Establishing Precedent

The Constitution provided the framework within which
the Government exercised its administrative powers.
Each individual office holder, however, applied standards
of performance according to his personal beliefs and those
of his superiors. President Washington set the tone,
which his chief advisors and political supporters largely
followed. Washington recognized from the beginning the
value of an efficient administration to the new government
and began immediately, upon taking office, to consult ad-

---

[2]U.S. Constitution, art. II, sec. 2, para. 2.

[3]U.S. Constitution, art. II, sec. 2, para. 3.

ministrative papers of the Confederation period.[4] He augmented this study with requests for information from former heads of departments.[5] The President developed his administrative principles from these studies, his military experience, and management of his estate at Mt. Vernon. Whatever the source, he established exceptionally high standards, far superior to those of most administrators of his day.[6]

General Washington recognized from the beginning the great difficulties he would encounter in selecting individuals to fill government jobs.

> I anticipate that one of the most difficult and delicate parts of the duty of my Office will be that which relates to nominations for appointments. . . . Though from a system which I have prescribed to myself I can say nothing decisive on particular appointments. . . .

Sixteen days later he answered James Kelso's application for appointment as Controller of Customs of Baltimore, Maryland.

> . . . I cannot undertake to make nominations for appointments, cr give indications of patronage in any instance, before offices are created. Nor will it be of any use, for any Candidate to remain in this place, for the sake of making personal applications to me. Facts and testimonials will alone be of avail, and I shall endeavor upon a general view of circumstances to act upon them accordingly.[8]

---

[4]George Washington to Edward Rutledge, May 5, 1789, printed in John C. Fitzpatrick, ed., The Writings of George Washington From The Original Manuscript Sources, 1745-1799, 39 vols. (Washington, D.C.: George Washington Bicentennial Commission, Government Printing Office, 1944), 30:309 (hereafter Writings).

[5]George Washington to Acting Secretary for Foreign Affairs, June 8, 1789, Writings, 30:343-344.

[6]White, Federalists, pp. 101-102, 257.

[7]George Washington to Edward Rutledge, New York, May 5, 1789, Writings, 30:309.

[8]George Washington to James Kelso, United States, May 21, 1789, Writings, 30:329.

Washington's deportment toward office seekers was exemplary. He made no commitments to office seekers and accepted no applications for vacant jobs. Office seekers never flocked to the Capital, because the President refused to communicate with them. He resolved "not to create an expectation, which thereafter might embarrass my own conduct."

> The truth is, I never reply to any application for offices by letter; nor verbally, . . . lest something might be drawn from a civil answer, that was not intended.[9]

Washington never permitted any one individual or group to influence him consistently on filling job vacancies.

The first President's criteria for selection matched his high standards toward office seekers. He conducted an independent investigation to acquire information on those under consideration, trying at all times to find the best qualified candidate available. Merit was his overriding selection factor. He wrote to Mary Wooster,

> I must be permitted, with the best lights I can obtain, and upon a general view of characters and circumstances, to nominate such persons alone to office, as, in my judgment, shall be the best qualified to discharge the functions of the departments to which they shall be appointed.[10]

He told Joseph Jones,

> In every nomination to office I have endeavored, as far as my own knowledge extended, or information could be obtained, to make fitness of character my primary object.[11]

Although merit dominated his selection, he gave weight to other criteria. Judicial appointments required demonstrated legal skills. Once he turned down his nephew for a

---

[9] George Washington to E. Pendleton, New York, March 17, 1794, _Writings_, 33:298.

[10] George Washington to Mary Wooster, New York, May 21, 1789, _Writings_, 30:327.

[11] George Washington to Joseph Jones, New York, November 30, 1789, _Writings_, 30:469.

position as Attorney to the Federal District Court because he felt he lacked sufficient knowledge of the law.[12]

Washington put great weight on a candidate's reputation in his local community. In this way he hoped to enhance the reputation of the new government. "I have thought it my duty," he wrote, "to nominate . . . such men as I conceived would give dignity and lustre to our National Character."[13]

The geographic location of a candidate influenced the President. He saw this not only as a means to secure a broad based government but also to help create bonds to meld the three great regional blocks of the United States into a single unit. He advocated "the distribution of appointments in as equal a proportion as might be to persons belonging to the different States in the Union. . . ."[14]

Washington tended to give little preference to veterans. He wrote the widow of Brigadier General Wooster,

> Sympathizing with you, as I do, in the great misfortunes, which have befallen your family in consequences of the War; my feelings as an individual would forcibly prompt me to do everything in my power to repair those misfortunes. But as a public man, acting only with a reference to the public good, I must be allowed to decide upon all points of my duty without consulting my private inclinations and wishes.[15]

Everything being equal, however, he asked that veterans be given preference for army appointments in 1791.[16] Again,

---

[12]George Washington to Bushrod Washington, New York, July 27, 1789, _Writings_, 30:366.

[13]George Washington to the Associate Justices of the Supreme Court, New York, September 30, 1789, _Writings_, 30:425.

[14]George Washington to Samuel Vaughn, Mt. Vernon, March 21, 1789, _Writings_, 30:238.

[15]George Washington to Mary Wooster, New York, May 21, 1789, _Writings_, 30:327-38.

[16]George Washington to William Drake, Mt. Vernon, April 4, 1791, _Writings_, 31:270.

he considered this preference in making his appointment
to the office of Collector of Annapolis.[17]

President Washington understood the political implications of the appointing power. Before he became President he wrote to Benjamin Harrison that "due regard shall
be had to the fitness of characters, the pretensions of
different candidates, and, so far as is proper, to political considerations."[18] It appears that the "political
considerations" most important to the First President
pertained to a candidate's loyalty to the new government.

President Washington's personnel selection factors
show that he tried to choose those with the best qualifications. In addition, Washington considered a candidate's political position, his geographic location, state
of residence, reputation in his local community, veterans'
status, and occasionally a candidate's financial condition.

Alexander Hamilton, Secretary of Treasury

Washington's chief advisors, Hamilton and Jefferson,
held similar views on the subject of appointments. Hamilton was particularly important for he articulated the
Federalist public administration platform in the Federalist Papers. Hamilton strongly supported the role of the
Senate in the appointment process. He thought this provision of the Constitution would prevent abuses by presidents who might have difficulty resisting the tendency
to appoint personal favorites and family members to important government positions. Hamilton agreed with
Washington that the major selection criterion for a
candidate should be his fitness for office. He determined fitness by the candidate's ability, character, and
political considerations. He also thought reliability
and firmness important qualities for a candidate. For
subordinate positions Secretary Hamilton thought that
concern for political reliability unnecessary when applied to military appointments. Hamilton acknowledged

---

[17]George Washington to John Eager Howard, Philadelphia,
August 25, 1793, Writings, 33:67.

[18]George Washington to Benjamin Harrison, Mt. Vernon,
March 7, 1789, Writings, 30:225.

the interest of individual states but thought that par-[19]
ticular influence should be reduced as much as possible.

Congress

The principle of separation of powers between the
executive and legislative branches accounts for the intense interest by the branch in public administration.
The Federalists, in general, and Hamilton, in particular,
recognized that the principle of separation of powers
could not be carried to absurd and rigid lengths. Such
rigidity would only lead to static government. "The
essential principle was that each major branch of government be allotted the functions it could best fulfill."[20]

The first major debate over the respective powers
of the two branches of government started within two
weeks of the first session of Congress. It took place
during the debate on establishment of the Department of
Foreign Affairs and centered around the administrative
powers of the executive branch. The debate began unob-
trusively enough when Congressman James Madison introduced
a provision granting the President the exclusive right to
remove the head of the Department of Foreign Affairs. A
general debate on the appointing and removing powers of
the President and Congress ensued. Some advocated the
impeachment procedure as the only way to remove a department head. Others argued that the executive powers implied unlimited rights of removal. The debate lasted
many days and at times became bitter as members reviewed
the old arguments originally debated in the Constitutional
Convention. Control of executive officials rested on the
outcome. Beneath the surface, legislators' confidence in
President Washington played an exceedingly important role.
The House of Representatives, by a vote of 31 to 19,
confirmed the power of the President to remove the Secretary of Foreign Affairs without the consent of the Senate.
The Senate reached a deadlock, necessitating the first use of
Vice-Presidential powers to cast a vote in case of a tie.
John Adams agreed that the President held both the ap-
pointing and removal powers, limited only by the provisions

---

[19]Lynton K. Caldwell, The Administrative Theories of Hamilton
& Jefferson: Their Contribution to Thought on Public Admini-
stration (Chicago: University of Chicago Press, Studies in
Public Administration, 1944), pp. 80-82.

[20]Ibid., p. 35.

for Senate confirmation. This decision remained unchallenged until 1868 when the impeachment of President
Andrew Johnson raised the same issue.[21]

The results of the great debate of 1789 did not
mean that Congress remained content with its role in
the administrative field. Congress initiated a precedent
in 1792 by requiring the executive departments to submit
information about their present and future programs.
Congress further established its right to directly intervene in administrative decisions. Five times Federalists
tried to persuade Congress to delegate to the President
and Postmaster General responsibility for establishing
post roads. From 1790 to 1792 Congress consistently determined the location of each post road in the country.
The legislative body quickly established its right and
responsibility to supervise administrative activities
through the power of investigation, which it exercised
without restriction. The basis for this action centered
on the appropriation responsibilities. In 1790 it investigated Robert Morris, Superintendent of Finance during the Confederation. In 1792 Congress established its
right formally to investigate the conduct of officers
under the control of the executive when it investigated
the defeat of General St. Clair. Washington decided
not to oppose the Congressional action after consulting
with his Cabinet.[22]

The most important precedent, in terms of the future
Federal civil service, came when Congress exerted influence
upon executive appointments. John Adams correctly predicted
that granting the right to advise and consent in executive

---

[21]William M. Goldsmith, The Growth of Presidential Power: A
Documented History, 3 vols. (New York: Chelsea House Pub-
lishers, 1974), 1:178-195; Paul P. Van Riper, History of the
United States Civil Service (Evanston, Ill.: Row, Peterson &
Co., 1958), pp. 14-16; M. Berris Taylor, U.S. Civil Service
Commission, History of the Federal Civil Service: 1789 to
the Present (Washington, D.C.: Government Printing Office, 1941),
pp. 2-3; and White, Federalists, pp. 20-25; James Hart, The
American Presidency in Action: 1789: A Study in Constitutional
History (New York: The Macmillan Company, 1943), pp. 155-214.

[22]Arthur M. Schlesinger, Jr. and Roger Bruns, Congress Investi-
gates: A Documented History: 1792-1974, 5 vols. (New York:
Chelsea House Publishers, 1975), 1:3-100; Marshall Edward
Dimock, Congressional Investigating Committees, Johns Hopkins
University Studies in Historical and Political Sciences, vol.
47 (Baltimore: Johns Hopkins University Press, 1929), pp. 72-84.

nominations to the Senate would develop into a real problem. Writing to Robert Sherman he argued that an ambi-
tious senator will

> . . . be under a temptation to use his in-
> fluence with the President as well as his bro-
> ther senators, to appoint persons to office
> in the several states, who will exert them-
> selves in elections, to get out his enemies
> or opposers, both in senate and house of
> representatives, and to get in his friends,
> perhaps his instruments? Will he not natur-
> ally be tempted to make use of his whole
> patronage, his whole influence, in advising
> to appointments. . . to increase his in-
> terest and promote his view?[23]

Washington consulted several legislators to advise
him on vacancies because he felt they were good sources
of information. Although freely consulting legislators
on nominations, the President promised them nothing. Unfortunately, few Presidents were able to maintain their
independence as well as Washington. Before the Federalists
left office in 1801, "the convention had become established
that Congressmen were normally consulted concerning nominations to federal office."[24]

Development of Political Parties

The development of political parties had a profound
effect on public administration. This development stimulated use of the appointment power for political reasons.
Political parties did not form immediately. One of the
most important antecedents to the first party affiliations
came over the issue of adopting the Constitution. The
faction supporting the new Constitution called themselves
Federalists, and those opposing became known as Anti-
Federalists. This distinction faded quickly after Washington's inauguration, and most legislators operated as individual members in the first years. This issue of fiscal

---

[23]John Adams, The Works of John Adams, Second President of
the United States: With a Life of the Author, by Charles
Francis Adams, ed. Charles Francis Adams, vol. 6: Works
on Government (Philadelphia: J.B. Lippincott & Co.,
1850-1856), 6:434.

[24]White, Federalists, p. 83.

policies and foreign affairs eventually created a new set
of affiliations that historians designate the beginning
of the American party system. Supporters of the Administration continued the designation of Federalists, and those
opposed adopted the name Republicans to underscore their
charge that Federalists were monarchists. Alexander Hamilton attracted the politicians supporting the Federalists'
cause, and Thomas Jefferson gravitated toward the politicians espousing Republican policies.[25]

Jefferson-Hamilton
Conflict

Basic policy decisions separated these politicians.
Jefferson favored an agricultural economic policy while
Hamilton advocated a balance between industry and agriculture. Hamilton supported a strong executive while
Jefferson talked of legislative prominence. Jefferson
supported strong relations with France and saw benefits
to the French Revolution while Hamilton felt it wise to
maintain good relations with Great Britain.

Personality conflicts exacerbated the policy issues.
Hamilton was not content to let the direction of foreign
policy rest exclusively in the hands of the Secretary of
State, Thomas Jefferson. He continually advised President
Washington on foreign issues and frequently disagreed with
Jefferson. Jefferson perpetuated the feud by attacking
Hamilton in hopes of reducing his influence. Jefferson
first tried to use the appointment power for political
purposes. In April 1791 he attempted to persuade Washington to appoint his political supporter, Tench Coxe,
as Assistant to the Secretary of the Treasury, the number
two job in the Treasury. He failed. Again, he tried to
get President Washington to appoint his supporter as Postmaster General in July 1791, but the President ignored
the recommendation and selected Hamilton's nominee instead.

Jefferson next tried to dismember Hamilton's Department after failing to induce Washington to appoint his
supporters to important Treasury positions. In February

---

[25]Ibid., p. 51: Noble E. Cunningham, Jr., ed., The Making
of the American Party System: 1789 to 1809 (Englewood Cliffs,
N.J.: Prentice-Hall, Inc., 1965), p. 1-2; Richard P. Mc-
Cormick, The Second American Party System: Party Formation
in the Jacksonian Era (Chapel Hill, N.C.: The University of
North Carolina Press, 1966), pp. 5-6, 19-31.

1792 he recommended that President Washington transfer the Post Office from the Treasury Department to the Department of State. Washington took no action on that recommendation, but six months later he accepted Jefferson's counsel to transfer the U.S. Mint from the Treasury to the State Department. Not content, Jefferson convinced Congressman Madison to make an attempt to split the Treasury between Internal Revenue and Customs. Federalist predominance in the Senate frustrated this attempt.

The feud moved into the open when Jefferson attacked Hamilton in the press, accusing him of being a monarchist. Soon the public witnessed a bitter newspaper attack by the two most powerful department heads in the government. Jefferson attacked Hamilton in the National Gazette, and Hamilton counterattacked Jefferson in the Gazette of the United States during the last half of 1792. Washington tried to intervene, but the two protagonists refused to compromise. Ultimately, Jefferson and Hamilton both left the government.[26]

The battle between these two stalwarts personified the movement toward political parties. The Federalists supported Hamilton's financial policies and ratification of the Jay Treaty with England. The opponents gravitated toward Jefferson and Madison and formed into the Republican Party. The feud had many ramifications but one of the most important, from the administrative standpoint, was Jefferson's attempt to use the appointing power of the executive for political purposes.

President John Adams' Policies

The political struggle between the Federalists and Republicans intensified under President Adams. Hamilton unnecessarily antagonized John Adams but maintained his own influence, because Adams unwisely retained many of Hamilton's political allies as cabinet officers. Adams continued Washington's policy of trying to select the best qualified people for public office. This meant the

---

[26]Caldwell, pp. 211-229; White, Federalists, pp. 222-236; Cunningham, American Party System, pp. 43-50, 88-90; and Noble E. Cunningham, Jr., The Jeffersonian Republicans: The Formation of Party Organizations, 1789-1801 (Chapel Hill, N.C.: The University of North Carolina Press, 1957), pp. 9-32.

college educated and therefore the upper class. Adams supported the principle of life tenure for those who received his appointment and may have accepted hereditary offices. Nevertheless, he made more politically oriented appointments and occasionally resorted to nepotism.[27]

John Adams did not have the opportunity to appoint large numbers of civil servants as Washington had done in establishing the federal administration. He confined his appointments to newly established jobs and those vacated by normal attrition. Adams removed only nineteen employees, most for incompetence; however, he removed a few for political purposes. Scholars point to his removals of Tench Coxe, Joshua Whipple, and William Gardner as prime examples. These and other removals were not party oriented actions but were designed to eliminate those who failed to support the President's policies.[28]

Adams accepted the general understanding with respect to the tenure of office for civil servants. "It was understood to be at the pleasure of the appointing agency. . . and almost universally permanence in lower offices was taken for granted."[29]

> On the whole, Adams seems to have developed no such systematic policy of appointments as Washington, but to have yielded more to influence, time, and circumstances; he was more moderate than some of his advisers, but more proscriptive than the first president; the line of division that he drew was not exactly between the Federalist and Republican parties, but rather between those with whom he agreed.[30]

---

[27] Sidney H. Aronson, Status and Kinship in the Higher Civil Service: Standards of Selection in the Administration of John Adams, Thomas Jefferson, and Andrew Jackson (Cambridge: Harvard University Press, 1964), pp. 3-7.

[28] Carl Russell Fish, The Civil Service and the Patronage (Cambridge: Harvard University Press, 1904; reprint ed., New York: Russell & Russell, Inc., 1963), pp. 16-21.

[29] White, Federalists, p. 257.

[30] Fish, p. 21.

President Adams maintained very high standards in appointing civil and military officials, though not as high as Washington. Unfortunately, his last appointments gravely tarnished his reputation and established a regrettable example. In February 1801 Congress increased the number of Federal courts. Lame duck President John Adams made a series of "midnight appointments" to fill the new positions with enemies of the newly elected President Jefferson. The largest number of positions involved were justices of the peace for the recently created District of Columbia. The staff of the Office of the Secretary of State worked under tremendous pressure to certify the appointments by preparing the signed commissions, affixing the seal of the United States, and delivering them to the new office holders before Adams' term expired. However, time ran out before they completed the process.

Jefferson, furious with Adams, felt the last minute appointments an affront to him. Jefferson and his Republican colleagues found that they had won the election only to face a hostile civil service and judiciary system consisting of their political rivals, the Federalists.[31]

Removals for Party Purposes

The question of patronage confronted Jefferson immediately upon assuming the Presidency. He articulated his intentions in letters to Colonel James Monroe, March 7, 1801, and Horatio Gates, March 8, 1801.[32] In these letters Jefferson rejected the principle of efficiency as the only consideration for service in public administration. He wanted to conciliate the Federalists and at the same time satisfy the legitimate demands of his own party. In order to accomplish this difficult task, the new President recognized that he must move slowly and carefully.

Jefferson declared his policy publicly after a demonstration against removal of the Collector of Customs in New Haven. He wrote on July 12, 1801, that the

---

[31]Thomas Jefferson to Mrs. John Adams, June 13, 1804, quoted in Lester J. Cappon, ed., The Adams-Jefferson Letters: The Complete Correspondence Between Thomas Jefferson and Abigail & John Adams, 2 vols. (Chapel Hill: University of North Carolina Press, 1959), 1:269-271.

[32]Thomas Jefferson, The Writings of Thomas Jefferson, Memorial ed., 9 vols. (Washington, D.C.: Andrew A. Lipscomb, 1853), 9:204-206.

total exclusion [of Republicans] calls for
prompter correctives. I shall correct the
procedure; but that done, disdain to follow it, shall return with joy to the state
of things, when the only questions concerning a candidate shall be, is he honest? Is
he capable? Is he faithful to the Constitution?[33]

Party considerations came first for Jefferson until
the civil service acquired a balanced mixture. The President,
of course, acted as the sole arbiter of when that balance
should be reached. In the meantime he wrote to Monroe,
"I have given, and will give only to republicans, under
existing circumstances."[34]

The "midnight appointments" offered him an ideal issue with which to begin the battle. He ordered Secretary
of State James Madison to withhold issuing all incomplete
"midnight appointments." Madison refused to deliver the
commission to a number of individuals, even though Adams'
Secretary of State had signed and sealed them. One of
these individuals, William Marbury, refused to accept
Jefferson's action. He applied to the Supreme Court for
a writ of mandamus, under section 13 of the Judiciary
Act of 1789.[35] Chief Justice John Marshall, another
late appointment of President Adams, delivered the opinion of the court in the famous Marbury v. Madison case in
February 1803. The court agreed with Marbury but refused
to issue a writ of mandamus to force the government to
carry out its duty, because it declared section 13 of the
Judiciary Act of 1789 unconstitutional. Section 13
authorized filing such suits with the Supreme Court instead of a lower court. According to Justice Marshall,
this provision violated Article III of the Constitution.[36]

---

[33]The Writings of Thomas Jefferson, pp. 273-274.

[34]Ibid., p. 204.

[35]Writ of mandamus is a court order to enforce the performance of some public duty; in this case to force the Secretary of State to do his duty and deliver the signed and
sealed commission.

[36]Albert J. Beveridge, The Life of John Marshall, 4 vols.
(Boston: Houghton-Mifflin Co., 1919), vol 3: Conflict &
Construction: 1800-1815, pp. 101-156.

Even though the court agreed with Marbury, the net result of the decision supported Madison, whose Republican nominee replaced Marbury. The Republicans did not confine themselves to positions with undelivered commissions. Jefferson selected three categories of government employees for special attention; declared all of Adams' appointments after December, including the "midnight appointments" subject to removal;[37] encouraged officials to remove civil servants for misconduct;[38] and, unable to gain control of the judiciary after the Republicans failed in removing ardent Federalist Samuel Chase by impeachment, singled out government attorneys and marshalls for removal.[39] Party considerations dominated removals in all three categories but not exclusively. A few of the "midnight" appointees retained their positions. The executive occasionally removed Republicans for misconduct and some particularly competent Federalist attorneys and marshalls were retained.

By 1803, removals ceased to be an important consideration as Republicans reverted to the principles practiced by Federalists under Washington and Adams.

The net result of all this activity in removing office holders was quite modest indeed.[40] During Jefferson's entire eight years in office he removed no more than 109 employees. These included 40 "midnight appointments," 11 attorneys, and 26 collectors of customs; most of which came during the first two years of his term. His Republican successors confined

---

[37]Jefferson, Writings (Memorial ed.), 9:237 (March 27, 1801).

[38]Jefferson, Writings, 9:390-391 (August 28, 1802).

[39]Ibid., p. 223 (March 3, 1801).

[40]Most historians agree with this assessment. For example see: Noble E. Cunningham, Jr., The Jeffersonian Republicans in Power, Party Operations, 1801-1809 (Chapel Hill: The University of North Carolina Press, 1963), pp. 69-70; Dumas Malone, Jefferson the President: The First Term: 1801-1805 (Boston: Little Brown, Inc., 1970). Carl E. Prince disagrees. He concluded that Jefferson "was not the moderate party leader in power that historians have depicted him." Jefferson, according to Prince, "moved decisively in ridding his administration of Federalists. . . ." Carl E. Prince, "The Passing of the Aristocracy: Jefferson's Removal of the Federalists, 1801-1805," Journal of American History 57 (June 1970-March 1971): 575-575.

their removals to "legitimate causes." Madison removed
27 office holders; Monroe gave the axe to 27 more;
and John Quincy Adams removed only 12. Adams' stringent
removal policy proved to be an important political liability and probably contributed significantly to his
failure to win the Presidency for a second term. Adams'
moral integrity prevented him from removing unreliable
office holders even though retaining many clearly jeo-
pardized his political career.[41]

Removals under Jefferson for party reasons set a bad
precedent. However, considering the enormous political
pressure brought to bear on the Republicans, they did an
excellent job of satisfying their most ardent political
followers and at the same time maintaining a civil service of high caliber. Many highly competent and successful Federalists quietly carried out their official duties
without fear of losing their jobs throughout the entire
Jeffersonian era.[42] In essence, the high standards set by
Washington and John Adams continued under the Republicans
except during the first two years. Political scientist
Leonard White attributes this to two major factors: the
high integrity of the Republican leaders, and the decline
of the two-party system as the Federalist party disinte-
grated.[43]

Republican appointment policies never disregarded
party affiliations. All Republican administrations selected
their candidates for public office from party followers.
Within the party circle, however, the appointees came from
the same social group as the Federalists. A candidate had
to possess respectability and high standing in the community, as well as known qualifications for the position.
Nepotism played little influence on the primary political
leaders, but lesser officials made a number of appointments
to family members. Veterans of the War of 1812 pressed
for government jobs, and some acquired good jobs at subordinate levels. Nevertheless, veterans' preference did
not significantly influence selections.[44]

---

[41] Carl Russell Fish, Removal of Officials by the Presidents
of the United States (Washington, D.C.: American Historical
Association, 1899), pp. 65-86.

[42] 1801 to 1829.

[43] Leonard D. White, The Jeffersonians: A Study in Administrative History, 1801-1829 (New York: Macmillan Co., 1951), p. 348.

[44] Ibid., pp. 343-364.

Selection by Examination

The American military introduced examinations as a means of selecting candidates for professional positions. In 1814, the Army Medical Corps developed the first test system to examine Army surgeons. The Navy medical service followed and set up examination boards in 1824 to test doctors for Navy surgeon positions and promote medical officers. They reported a "marked improvement" in the talent acquired through these examinations. In 1818 and 1819 military academy candidates began to sit for examinations. To acquire the status of an officer, academy candidates often sat for an examination on several occasions. The examination system for military academy candidates improved the level of officers attending such institutions. No one seems to have thought of applying an examination system for selecting candidates to civilian positions.

Office Seekers' Deportment

The generally high standards attributable to the four Republican Presidents from 1801 to 1829 with respect to personnel management practices could not overshadow some developments which pointed to a breakdown in these standards. Office seekers grew bolder and bolder, and on more than one occasion embarrassed a President with the intensity of their activities. The reserve and reluctance of office seekers to pursue aggressively their objective, characteristic of the Federalist period, faded rapidly under the Republicans. Applicants "showed no moderation, self-management, or control" in their pursuits.[45]

Tenure of Office Act, 1820

Custom and practice prevented civil servants from establishing property rights to their positions, but longevity in office on the basis of good behavior became the rule. William H. Crawford, Secretary of the Treasury under President James Monroe, conceived a plan to limit the tenure of office of many subordinate positions to four years. Secretary Crawford drafted a bill and sent it to Congress where the Republican-dominated legislature enacted the Tenure of Office Act of 1820. Jefferson, Madison, and John Quincy Adams strongly opposed the law, and Monroe himself later expressed reservations. However, he "unwarily signed the bill without adverting to its real character."[46] The

---

[45]The Jeffersonians, pp. 362-368.

[46]Ibid., p. 388.

Act established a four-year term of office for civil servants dealing with financial transactions. District attorneys, collectors of customs, naval officers, surveyors of customs, money agents, registers of land offices, paymasters in the Army, and the commissary-general of purchases faced removal every four years.[47]

Crawford's motives were not clear and neither were those of President Monroe who signed the bill. Nevertheless, the impact of this provision did not escape the notice of most astute politicians. Jefferson wrote to Madison on November 29, 1820, explaining that the law

> saps the constitutional and salutary functions of the President, and introduces a principle of intrigue and corruption, which will soon leaven the mass, not only of Senators, but of citizens. . . . It will keep in constant excitement all the hungry cormorants for office, render them, as well as those in place, sycophants to their Senators, engage these in eternal intrigue to turn out one and put in another, in cabals to swap work; and make of them what all executive directories become, mere sinks of corruption and faction.[48]

Madison agreed with Jefferson and added complaints about the increased power of the Senate and doubts as the law's constitutionality. John Quincy Adams wrote that "Monroe regretted that he had signed the bill," and resolved to renominate the incumbent in every instance in which there was no misconduct.[49]

Hoping that he and Monroe could establish a precedent, Adams declared: "I determined to renominate every person against whom there was no complaint which would have warranted his removal; and renominated every person nominated by Mr. Monroe, and upon whose nomination the Senate had declined action."[50] Even when reappointment held detri-

---

[47] Tenure of Office Act, 3 Stat. 582 (1920).

[48] Thomas Jefferson, The Works of Thomas Jefferson, 12 vols., ed. Paul Leicester Ford, Federal ed., (New York: G.P. Putnam's Sons, 1904-5), 12:174-175.

[49] Fish, p. 67.

[50] Charles Francis Adams (ed.), The Memoirs of John Quincy Adams, Comprising Portions of his Diary from 1795 to 1848, 12 vols. (Philadelphia: J.B. Lippincott & Co., 1874-77), 6:521.

mental political consequences for him, Adams refused to change his policy.

Increased Congressional Interest

Congressional interest in civil appointments was always present. Washington often consulted legislative representatives when considering a candidate for office. The practice of appointing former congressmen to federal positions increased over the years. In 1811, Nathaniel Macon introduced an amendment to the Constitution to prevent this practice. He wanted to prevent the destruction of the separation of powers principle. His amendment failed to pass. Congressmen continued to seek appointments in great numbers. "In 1821 John Quincy Adams said that one-half of the members of Congress were seeking office, and that the other half wanted something for their relatives."[51] Macon reintroduced his bill in 1826, but because of poor health, relinquished its leadership to Thomas H. Benton. Benton, chairman of a committee to consider Macon's amendment, took the opportunity to attack the executive appointing power (primarily in support of Jackson against Adams), and wrote a scathing attack on the power of patronage vested in the hands of the executive. He described this power of patronage as a potential influence on elections. The author listed many jobs and showed their financial value and to whom they belonged. To remedy the abuses, he recommended transferring the power of appointment from the executive to the legislature. Benton charged that the power of patronage had unsettled the balance between legislature and executive as well as Federal and State governments, and proposed a series of six bills to effect the transfer of patronage to Congress. His stated objective was to reduce the influence of patronage on the elections. Actually, patronage played very little influence on any election up to that time.[52]

> It is of some significance to note that no President before 1829 undertook to buy leadership or legislation with patronage. Congressmen were increasingly eager for influence in appointments and made some inroads on the executive domain, but the practice of using patronage to get votes in either House

[51]Fish, p. 59.

[52]U.S. Congress, Senate, Senate Documents No. 88, 19th Cong., 1st Sess., pp. 1-12.

was rare and would have been thought corrupt.
No President, naturally, was unaware of the
political implications of his appointments
and probably none failed on occasion to smooth
the path of legislative accommodation by a
suitable appointment. The institution of bar-
tering patronage for legislation, however, did
not exist.[53]

State and Local Governments

Perhaps the most ominous sign of future decline
emerged in state and local governments where politicians
were failing to sustain the high standards of the Federal
Government. Carl Russell Fish traced, in some detail, the
practice of rotation in office in state governments. He
attributed the practice to fear of creating an oppressive
elite official class, concern over control of financial
trust, and a desire to educate as many people in government service as possible. Many states enacted into law
numerous tenure restrictions on public positions long before the practice of spoils emerged. Eventually, Fish
contends, the reasons for rotation became obscure and the
rotation per se became the goal.[54]

Rotation in state governments did not necessarily
bring about abuses in political patronage. South Carolina's
constitution limited the term of office on practically all
civil jobs, and no abuse of political patronage developed.
Virginia maintained the high standards of Jefferson, Monroe, and Washington. Large plantation owners controlled
the political life of the state with a strong tradition of
high quality public service. Massachusetts maintained a
high degree of performance with respect to patronage during
most of the Federalist and Republican era, except for one
temporary experiment in political patronage. Governor
Elbridge Gerry, Republican governor in 1810, removed a
number of office holders so that he could replace them
with party followers. The public registered such energetic
protests that Republicans failed to win the next election.
Federalist Governor Strong wisely removed all of Gerry's
appointees and replaced them with the former office holders.
Massachusetts suffered no further excursions into political

---

[53]White, _Jeffersonians_, p. 43.

[54]Fish, pp. 79-85.

patronage during the Republican era.[55]

Political realities in Pennsylvania and New York pre-
cipitated a decline in appointment standards. Pennsylvania suffered intense political struggles from the beginning. Radical thinkers won the original battles in creating the state constitution. They favored a weak executive
and strong legislature. Acquiring power in 1790, the
conservatives reversed the decision and strengthened
the executive, including exclusive appointing power for
subordinate officials. Conservative Thomas Mifflin selected his candidates strictly from Federalist political
supporters. Thomas McKean, Republican Governor in 1799,
determined to reverse the work of his predecessor. Consequently, he threw out Federalist office holders and replaced them with Republicans. McKean justified his actions
as being in harmony with the "common order of nature."
Subsequent Pennsylvania governors continued to practice
party patronage as the accepted norm in public office.[56]

New York began with high standards paralleling those
in George Washington's government. George Clinton, Federalist governor until 1795, emulated Washington's policies.
John Jay, his successor, continued the policy of maintaining
public servants on good behavior but incorporated the restriction of appointing only Federalists. DeWitt Clinton,
nephew of George Clinton, came to dominate New York politics. He initiated party control of patronage after 1801,
using the Council of Appointment to carry out his policy
of "equal participation." Republican administrative activities in New York deteriorated until they included such
questionable practices as allocation of appointments to
party factions, removals of rival political appointees, and
even the sale of public office to the highest bidder.[57]

Before 1829, the employment practices of the Federal
Government constituted a generally consistent pattern.
Federalists and Republicans alike favored partisan selec-
tions for office. They chose individuals from the same

---

[55]James Trecothick Austin, Life of Elbridge Gerry With
Contemporary Letters, 2 vols. (Boston: Wells & Lilly, 1828-
29), 2:322 and Appendix B.

[56]Fish, pp. 92-94; White, Jeffersonians, p. 396.

[57]Howard Lee McBain, DeWitt Clinton and The Origin of the Spoils
System in New York (New York: Columbia University Press, 1907);
Robert V. Remini, Martin Van Buren and the Making of the Demo-
cratic Party (New York: Columbia University Press, 1959), pp. 5-7.

social class who were mostly well educated, men of integrity, and well known in the local community. Both political parties discouraged appointments to friends and relatives, recognized the benefits of a "balanced ticket," and adhered to the principle of appointing local residents to local jobs. Republicans and Federalists held similar views on office holding, and their standards of appointment from 1789 to 1829 conformed to a single pattern.[58]

Changes Ensue

The Tenure of Office Act, the theory of rotation, and party control of appointments developed into three cornerstones of the spoils system. Republicans never used the Tenure of Office Act, passed in 1820, as a political tool. President Andrew Jackson used the law with the theory of rotation and party control of appointments. President Jackson eloquently described the new theory of rotation in his first annual message in December 1829.

> There are, perhaps, few men who can for any great length of time enjoy office and power without being more or less under the influence of feeling unfavorable to the faithful discharge of their public duties. This integrity may be proof against improper considerations immediately addressed to themselves, but they are apt to acquire a habit of looking with indifference upon the public interests and of tolerating conduct from which an unpracticed man would revolt. Office is considered as a species of property, and government rather as a means of promoting individual interests than as an instrument created solely for the service of the people. Corruption in some and in others a perversion of correct feelings and principles divert government from its legitimate ends and make it an engine for the support of the few at the expense of the many. The duties of all public officers are, or at least admit of being made, so plain and simple that men of intelligence may readily qualify themselves for their performance; . . . .

---

[58]White, Jeffersonians, p. 368.

In a country where offices are created solely
for the benefit of the people no one man has
any more intrinsic right to official station
than another. Offices were not established to
give support to particular men at the public
expense. No individual wrong is, therefore,
done by removal, since neither appointment to
nor continuance in office is matter of right.
. . . The proposed limitation would destroy
the idea of property now so generally connected
with official station, and although individual
distress may be sometimes produced, it would,
by promoting that rotation which constitutes
a leading principle in the republican creed, [59]
give healthful action to the system.

This dramatic change in policy did not take place in
a vacuum. Jackson created it in an atmosphere conducive
to such a policy. The concepts which motivated the old
political leaders gave way to new concepts created to cope
with changing political and economic conditions. A dramatic change took place in the business and economic world.
Almost simultaneously with Jackson's inauguration, a general decline in business morality set in. At the same time,
the industrial revolution increased the number of wealthy
businessmen and the amount of fortunes at their disposal.
These industrialists demanded rewards from politicians [60]
for their financial support.

Expansion of the electorate and increased interest in
the political process swelled the number of voters participating in elections. Many men voted in an election for the
first time. A large segment of the new voters identified
with Andrew Jackson who managed to convince many of them
that he represented all of their interests. The electorate
communicated to its leaders a desire to participate in
government. Andrew Jackson provided effective leadership
to this sense of participation and became the first successful political leader to make the majority an important

[59]James Daniel Richardson, ed., A Compilation of the
Messages & Papers of the Presidents, 8 vols. (Washington,
D.C.: Government Printing Office, 1896-99), 2:448-449.

[60]Taylor, pp. 16-17; Leonard D. White, Jacksonians: A
Study in Administrative History: 1829-1861 (New York:
The Macmillan Co., 1954), p. 5.

element in national affairs.[61]

Manifestations of Change

"Hordes" of people inundated Washington, demanding
a share in government. In the home districts, these demands resulted in the direct election of local officials,
but in the national administration this was impossible.
Another solution had to be found. Citizens who supported
General Jackson exerted such strong pressure that it is
unlikely anyone could have resisted successfully.

Along with this great demand for a share in government came a change in the American attitude toward office
holding. Under the old society, the upper class considered
acceptance of public office a duty. They practiced little
manifest seeking of office, and the Chief Executive generally
felt free to seek out likely office holders without undue
pressure from outside. The attitude changed and Americans
developed a passion for office holding. Office seeking became an overt act by candidates to secure a government
position. Following each election a large group of men
sought employment and competed among themselves with great
fortitude and persistence for the relatively few jobs
available: "in short the voice of the people was loud,
brazen, and insistent, and the words of its 'betters'
were only a happy echo."[62]

Expansion of the franchise accompanied the development
of a national party based on the control of delegates to
national and state conventions. A presidential candidate
desirous of being elected or reelected must learn to deal
with national parties. Party workers demanded a reward
for their activities, necessitating a search for ways to
provide it.[63]

---

[61]Goldsmith, 1:168-174; Robert V. Remini, The Age of Jack-
son (Columbia, S.C.: University of South Carolina Press,
1972), pp. xiii-xvii; Harold C. Syrett, Andrew Jackson:
His Contribution to the American Tradition (Westport, Conn.:
Greenwood Press, Publishers, 1971, reprint ed., The Bobbs-
Merrill Company, Inc., 1953), pp. 21-30.

[62]White, Jacksonians, p. 306; Goldsmith, 1:175; Remini,
Age of Jackson, p. x.

[63]McCormick, pp. 13-16; Goldsmith, 1:170.

The general public came into contact with the government employees as Congress expanded executive responsibilities. The government served the public primarily through the legal duties performed by district attorneys, the collection of customs, and post office activities. All three of these government functions became highly politicized during the spoils period.

The use of appointing powers and removal powers for political purposes elevated the authority of the Presidency in its historic struggle with Congress. The President increased his ability to demand party loyalty, reward supporters, and punish opponents.

The general decline in business morality, demands of the people for a share in government, expansion of democratic concepts, development of nationwide parties, change in the American attitude toward office seeking, and the opportunity to expand the powers of the President combined to create the fertile atmosphere in which the "Spoils System" would flourish.

President Jackson may be criticized for overlooking or ignoring the potential consequences of the rotation system, but he acted on laudatory motives. He wanted to prevent public office from becoming the property of the incumbent. He wanted to reduce or eliminate the office holding class, and he sincerely wanted to give every voter an opportunity to acquire public office and participate in self-government. The system of rotation also offered him an opportunity to retire old civil servants who remained in office long after they could contribute to its operations.[64]

Many of Jackson's contemporaries understood the dangers of the system of rotation and made their views known.

Application of the System of Rotation

Confusion reigned in Washington after the inauguration of General Jackson. Incumbents worried about their possible removal, while office seekers clamored for their jobs. This confusion made it impossible to remove or select replacements on a systematic basis according to the principles articulated by the Jacksonians. Some Jackson men fought to save valued employees of their respective

---

[64]Remini, Age of Jackson, pp. xvi-xvii, 43-51; Syrett, p. 28; White, Jacksonians, p. 5.

agencies. Secretary of State Martin Van Buren could not bring himself to remove "old Mr. Maury" because he was a respected George Washington appointee. John A. Hamilton, advisor to Van Buren, prided himself on his ability to save many valued employees. Jackson retained some prominent Adams men. He overruled his close associate Van Buren in reappointing General Solomon Van Rensselaer as Postmaster at Albany after Van Rensselaer came to Washington to protest Van Buren's desire to remove him. Once a Jackson man received an appointment only to find himself removed for another Jackson man before he served one day in office.[65]

The Jacksonians applied a different set of principles to appointments and removals than Republicans. President Jackson gave weight to merit, defined as "honesty, probity, and capability." He wanted well qualified men. He did not confine his appointments to men of "education" as Federalists and Republicans, but gave considerable weight to "moral qualifications" of the candidates. "Merit" for Jacksonians consisted of men with intelligence, honesty, "integrity, loyalty, and patriotism." Jackson rejected the assumption that all government jobs required equal talent. He felt that government jobs fell into many levels of difficulty, and sought men who met the level required of the position. He rejected the principle of seniority as a basis for appointment or retention in office. The Chief Executive declared that qualified personal friends should not be rejected for appointment simply because of their relationship to him. Like his precedessors, President Jackson made party loyalty a requirement for office.[66]

---

[65]Goldsmith, 1:175; Remini, Van Buren, pp. 18-23; John Wien Foiney, Anecdotes of Public Men (New York: Harper & Brother, 1873), pp. 281-282; Benjamin Perley Poore, Perley's Reminiscences of Sixty Years in the National Metropolis, 2 vols. (Philadelphia: Hubbard Bros., 1886), 1:110, 173; James Alexander Hamilton, Reminiscences of James A. Hamilton; Men and Events, At Home and Abroad, During Three Quarters of a Century (New York: C. Scribner & Co., 1869), p. 282.

[66]Aronson, pp. 14-21.

Senator William L. Marcy of New York contributed a powerful slogan to supporters of the spoils system when he coined the phrase "To the Victor Belong the Spoils." Senator Marcy defended the system of rotation during a debate with Henry Clay in January 1832. The two Senators exchanged views during consideration of the confirmation of Martin Van Buren as minister to England. He declared:

> It may be, sir, that the politicians of the United States are not so fastidious as some gentlemen are, as to disclosing the principles on which they act. They boldly preach what they practice. When they are contending for victory, they avow their intention of enjoying the fruits of it. If they are defeated, they expect to retire from office. If they are successful, they claim, as a matter of right, the advantages of success. They see nothing wrong in the rule, that to the victor belong the spoils of the enemy.[67]

From a practical standpoint, Jackson and his successors found it impractical and unwise to discharge every civil servant to satisfy political desires. Political considerations had to give way to some administrative considerations. Experience could not be ignored in the day-to-day conduct of government business. Consequently, a political public service found it necessary to co-exist with a career civil service consisting of those individuals who performed essential government business requiring past experience and acquired skills. Although establishing the principle of rotation, President Jackson initiated no more removals, in proportion, than those undertaken by Thomas Jefferson between 1801 and 1803.[68] These removals were concentrated in the north and west; few office holders lost their jobs in the south.

---

[67]White, Jacksonians, pp. 347-362.

[68]Erik McKinley Eriksson, "The Federal Civil Service Under President Jackson," The Mississippi Valley Historical Review 13 (June 1926 to March 1927): 528-529; Prince, p. 565; Arthur Vernon Wolfe, "The United States Civil Service Employment System--To 1933" (Ph.D. dissertation, University of Chicago, 1966), p. 68.

Selective Factors

Political considerations became the most important factor in selecting appointees. The largest number of appointments went to Jackson men. Political parties demanded and received a great influence in selecting office holders. In the past, applicants usually demonstrated previous or present political activities. Under the new concepts, the party also demanded future commitments before giving its support to a candidate's bid for appointment. Simultaneously, a new practice came into existence with President Jackson. The practice of political assessments from party office holders started slowly at first but gradually grew until it became common practice. In time, this method of financing political parties became so important that it was probably the most important single factor in delaying the introduction of civil service reform. Political parties failed to exert maximum influence on appointments because they seldom agreed on a unanimous recommendation. Factionalism spawned party squabbles and allowed even the weakest of Presidents to act as the final arbiter between them.[69]

Nationwide political parties needed favorable and widespread publicity for their programs. Editors and prominent literary figures thus acquired a high priority in competing for coveted government jobs. In this way party leaders hoped to attract favorable press support for their programs.[70]

Congressional Action

Jackson's introduction of the system of rotation, elevating the powers of the Presidency, sparked a struggle with Congress, especially in the Senate. The Whigs, in control of the Senate, raised the old issue over who should control appointments. Webster, Clay, and other prominent politicians argued that the decision of 1789, giving the executive exclusive power to remove appointees, was in error. Such powers, according to the Whigs, must be shared by the Congress. Attempts to repeal portions of the Tenure of Office Act of 1820 incorporating these views failed because of Jackson's political support in the House of Representatives.

---

[69]Fish, p. 115.

[70]Eriksson, p. 532.

William J. Duane, Secretary of the Treasury, decided to interpret an Act of Congress in such a way as to
allow him to act independently of the President. After
refusing to carry out Jackson's orders, Duane was promptly
removed. Congress supported Duane's interpretation and
condemned the President, but Jackson successfully defended
Presidential removal powers. Jackson established
firmly the "absolute right" of the President to require
his Cabinet members to conform to his policies. Andrew
Jackson's triumph in the Duane incident, a chapter in the
"Bank War," marked a significant victory of the executive
over the legislative branch.[71]

The Senate used another tactic in an attempt to increase its influence over the appointing decision. The
Senate chose to battle the President by refusing to con-
firm many of Jackson's most important nominations. President Jackson fought back by reappointing rejectees or
nominating them for other jobs. Eventually, the futility
of the Senate's effort became evident as Jackson succeeded
in having most of his men confirmed in one position or
another.[72]

In 1831, the Senate passed a resolution demanding
that the executive consult Congress before appointing
citizens to civil service vacancies. In 1832, Senator
Thomas Ewing introduced a resolution which demanded that
the President refrain from removing office holders without the advice and consent of the Senate. In 1835, a
Senate committee recommended that the President submit
to the Senate the reason for each removal. President
Jackson frustrated each of these efforts by simply declaring them unconstitutional and refusing to comply.[73]

The Congress already had powers strong enough to restrict the actions of the executive. The legislative
control of finances permitted it to exercise considerable
influence over the nature of the executive administration.
Throughout this period, Congress refused to appropriate
enough money to hire sufficient staff to conduct the increasing government business. At times, this refusal resulted in a complete breakdown of government services
when the flood of business became too large for the staff

---

[71]Goldsmith, 1:198-234; Remini, The Age of Jackson, pp. 106-110.

[72]Eriksson, pp. 525-535; Fish, pp. 119-120.

[73]Eriksson, p. 534; Richardson, 2:636, 3:132-134.

to handle. Coupled with reluctance to permit the expansion of employees sufficient to carry out government
assignments, Congress refused to appropriate sufficient
funds to pay government employees an adequate salary.

The stingy attitude of Congress toward the government service impeded efficient administrative functions.
Adding insult to injury, Congress advocated retrenchment
after retrenchment, constantly denouncing the government
for excessive employment of clerks.

Congress most effectively exercised influence on
removals and appointments by subtle and indirect means.
Informal consultations increased between officials in
the executive departments and Congressional members.
Congressmen actively contacted department officials on
behalf of their constituents and party followers. They
used petitions, letters from influential men, and testimonials in an attempt to acquire a position for their
constituents. Gradually, Congressmen gained a commanding influence on appointments and even removals in their
respective districts. This tendency to grant Congressmen control over appointments in their districts was
strengthened when the government adopted an apportionment rule in 1853 which allocated clerical appointments
in the Washington offices by state. The apportionment
rule has plagued government recruitment ever since.[74]

Corruption - Customhouses

From the beginning, the spoils system generated
charges that it encouraged corruption. Very little evidence has been found that corruption existed in the civil
service before the introduction of the system of rotation.
Jackson tried to find corruption in the service under
President Adams but instead found the government service
essentially honest.[75] Corruption in Jackson's Administration flourished in many cases. Administration of the customhouses in the major cities offers the most conspicuous
example of corruption. It demonstrates clearly a major
defect of the spoils system. Boston, Philadelphia, Baltimore and New York customhouses followed similar practices.

---

[74]White, Jacksonians, pp. 118, 156.

[75]Syrett, pp. 93-94; Fish, p. 128.

Organizationally, the customhouses operated under the direction of the Secretary of Treasury. Until 1829, collectorships of the customhouses went to experienced civil servants. After that date, they became coveted prizes in the spoils system. President Jackson appointed Samuel Swartwout Collector of the Port of New York. His seven year tenure and that of his successor, Jesse Hoyt, resulted in some of the most corrupt practices ever detected. Swartwout, a prominent politician in New York, worked hard for Jackson's election. Jackson rewarded his efforts, against the advice of Martin Van Buren, with the New York appointment. Swartwout repaid Jackson's confidence by embezzling a million and a quarter dollars from the customhouse. Many of his subordinates collaborated with him. Lax administrative procedures, negligence, connivance, and outright corruption made this one of the best examples of the decline in government administration under the system of rotation.[76]

Van Buren, now President, appointed Jesse Hoyt to clean up the New York Customhouse. Hoyt rewarded his benefactor by embezzling another two hundred thousand dollars. He practiced various forms of corruption during his tenure. He was insubordinate to the Secretary of Treasury, cooperated with fraudulent importers trying to eliminate foreign competition, and accepted private payments from importers. Hoyt collected illegal fees and made illegal seizures to increase his take. He employed graft, extravagance, and bias in making financial transactions. Civil servants found it necessary to pay political assessments and those who complained were removed. Appointees came from party supporters and were frequently absent from duty or required to perform little work. Hoyt benefited from inadequate or inoperative accounting procedures.[77]

The collector of customhouses became one the major patronage prizes. Bitter political battles centered around the appointment of collectors throughout this period. Every time a collectorship changed, great numbers of employees lost their jobs to new, inexperienced party workers. These frequent personnel rotations produced disastrous results with respect to carrying out the duties of the customhouses.

---

[76]U.S. Congress, House, House Document 13, 25th Cong., 3rd Sess., 1838, pp. 19, 29, 47, and 97; U.S. Congress, House, House Report 313, 25th Cong., 3rd Sess., February 27, 1839.

[77]White, Jacksonians, pp. 427-428.

131

Growth of the Spoils System

Martin Van Buren, Andrew Jackson's choice, entered
the White House with a friendly civil service. Jackson
supporters stood firmly behind Van Buren, and many civil
servants worked hard for his election. Consequently,
President Van Buren made relatively few removals. Perhaps the worst abuses of the spoils system could have been
avoided if the Democratic Party proved strong enough to
acquire a long tenure in office. The President improved
working conditions for all government employees when he
issued an executive order restricting the working hours
to ten hours per day without a reduction in compensation.
Van Buren's ambition to secure a second term motivated him
to introduce a new element into the spoils system. Party
loyalty did not suffice; he now demanded personal fidelity
from office holders.[78]

Unfortunately, Van Buren failed to win the election
of 1840, and the Whigs swept into power. The Whigs found
themselves in a very difficult position. Their party
followers demanded removal of the obnoxious Democrats
from Federal positions. In Congress during the Jackson
and Van Buren Administrations, the Whigs championed the
old stable method and opposed the system of rotation.
President Harrison's Administration included Cabinet members Daniel Webster, Thomas Ewing, and Vice President John
Tyler, strong opponents of the system of rotation when out
of power. The temptation proved too much; the system too
strong to reverse; and the actors too weak to resist the
demands of their party followers as the Whigs adopted the
spoils system. Many civil servants fell to the axe as the
Whigs turned out civil servants appointed by Jackson and
Van Buren Democrats according to the principles of the
spoils system. John Tyler accepted the new policy when
he succeeded William Henry Harrison as President even
though he promised to "remove no incumbent from office
who has faithfully and honestly acquitted himself of the
duties of his office. . . ."[79] The behavior of the Whigs
guaranteed the continuation of the patronage system. John
Tyler eventually found that Presidential power over patronage became one of his most valuable assets when his Senate
enemies, Clay Whigs and Van Buren Democrats, thwarted his
executive leadership. Tyler employed the patronage to

---

[78]Arthur H. Schlesinger, Jr., The Age of Jackson (New York:
The New American Library, 1945), p. 111; Fish, pp. 134-135;
White, Jacksonians, p. 309.

[79]Richardson, 4:38.

further his Texas annexation ambitions and create a third
party to support his policies and candidacy for a second
term. As a lame-duck President, Tyler unsuccessfully
applied the spoils tool to protect the influence of his
supporters in the new Polk Administration. Tyler's narrow political base caused him to use nepotism in his
late appointments.[80]

In 1845, the Whigs relinquished the Presidency, and
the Democrats marched back into power under President Polk.
Polk attracted the inevitable horde of office seekers.
President Polk authorized a clean sweep, including Tyler-
ites, without hesitation. His Secretary of War, William
L. Marcy, author of the slogan "to the victor belong the
spoils," labeled himself "altogether the most moderate man
in the whole concern."[81] Office holders submissively ten-
dered their resignations in droves, reducing the necessity
to remove the incumbents. The country took the rotations
in stride, accepting them as common practice. Members of
Congress increased their interest in petty offices, advocating the right to control all appointments in their own
states. Polk resisted this proposition, but his successors
did not. The struggle to control appointments in their
own state did not reduce the constant pressure on the
executive from Congressmen who demanded appointments for
their relatives, friends, and constituents. Factional
struggles complicated the problem. Polk dispensed patronage to further passage of his programs in Congress and thus
freely consulted Congressmen about appointments. The
President's greatest problem with Congress came from the
desire of members to acquire appointments to prestigious
executive positions. Contrary to the traditional concepts
of independence of the legislative and executive branches,
Congressmen greedily pursued Polk for their own appointments.[82]

---

[80]Oliver Perry Chitwood, John Tyler: Champion of the Old
South (Washington: American Historical Association, 1939;
reprinted, New York: Russell & Russell, Inc., 1964), pp. 367-
385; Robert Seager II, And Tyler Too: A Biography of John &
Julia Gardiner Tyler (New York: McGraw-Hill Book Co., Inc.,
1963), pp. 83-84; 224-229; 266-288; 312-313.

[81]William L. Marcy to General Prosper M. Wetmore, July 23, 1845,
William L. Marcy papers, Library of Congress, Washington, D.C.

[82]Norman A. Graebner, "James K. Polk: A Study in Federal Patronage," The Mississippi Valley Historical Review 38 (June 1951-
March 1962): 630-632; Charles Sellers, James K. Polk: Continentalist: 1843-1846 (Princeton: Princeton University Press,

The Chief Executive recognized the defects of the
spoils system. Polk tired of the many visitors who took
his time "seeking office for themselves or their friends."
He observed that the spoils available to a President resulted in six disappointed constituents for every job he
filled and predicted that it "will destroy the popularity
of any President." The President "cannot tell upon what
recommendations to rely " because many submit them for any
individual who. asks. "I now predict that no President of
the United States of any party will ever again be reelected."[83]

Zachary Taylor led the Whigs back into the White House
in 1849. They had a second chance to mute the Democratic
initiated system of rotation. Taylor's Cabinet convinced
him to perpetuate the system as a means of rebuilding the
faction-split party with patronage. The Taylor Administration devoted a great amount of time to patronage matters.
Appointments went to all major party elements, with nepotism a prominent ingredient in the decision. In the one
year of his presidency Taylor replaced thirty-five per cent
of the total civil service.[84] Vice President Millard Fillmore succeeded President Taylor and introduced another
element into the spoils story. Fillmore initiated the
policy of removing President Taylor's appointments as
though an opposing party had come into power.[85]

1966), pp. 267-273, 298-303, 447-448; Spencer, pp. 140-141;
White, Jacksonians, p. 122; Milo Milton Quaife, ed., The
Diary of James K. Polk During His Presidency, 1845 to 1849,
4 vols. (Chicago: A.C. McClurg & Co., 1910), 1:483, 388-
389, 427, 466-67, 497-98; 2:382-383.

[83]Allan Nevins, ed., Polk, The Diary of a President: 1845-
1849: Covering the Mexican War, the Acquisition of Oregon and
the Conquest of California and the Southwest (London: Longmans, Green & Co., 1929), pp. 183-185.

[84]Holman Hamilton, Zachary Taylor: Soldier in the White House
(Indianapolis: Bobbs-Merrill Co., 1951; reprinted, Hamden,
Connecticut: Archon Books, 1966), pp. 203-218.

[85]Robert J. Royback, Millard Fillmore: Biography of a Presi-
dent (Buffalo: Buffalo Historical Society, Henry Stewart,
Inc., 1959), pp. 102-103, 201-203, 255-257, 264-265, 334-377;
Fish, pp. 163-165; Taylor, p. 26.

When the Whigs joined the "patronage bandwagon"
in 1841 and 1849, the last opportunity to modify the
spoils system disappeared until after the Civil War.
The operation of the patronage system expanded rapidly
in the absence of effective resistance.[86]

During the election of 1852, Franklin Pierce managed
to unite the factions of the Democratic Party sufficiently
to defeat the Whigs. By this time, conflicts over dispensing spoils took place between factions in the same
party, for Americans accepted that the defeated party
would lose its jobs. Pierce tried to balance his
patronage among the various party factions and at the
same time apportion his spoils equitably among the states.
His policies satisfied very few. So intense was the competition that it became the custom to devote the first[87]
month of a new term primarily to dispensing patronage.

James Buchanan carried the Democratic Party back
into the White House for a second consecutive term. His
handling of the spoils earned him the reputation as "the
most extreme advocate of rotation."[88] Even though Pierce's
supporters worked hard to help elect Buchanan, he announced that all office holders appointed by the former
President would be removed from office and replaced with
original Buchanan men. Marcy observed that "Pierce men
are hunted down like wild beasts."[89] Buchanan defended
his action by arguing that civil service positions "were
but prizes and should not be enjoyed for more than four
years by any good Democrat."[90] The new policy meant that
party politicians who originally supported a losing candidate for nomination to the Presidency became subject to
removal along with members of the opposing party.

---

[86]Goldsmith, II: 981-982.

[87]Roy Franklin Nichols, Franklin Pierce: Young Hickory of
the Granite Hills, 2d ed. (Philadelphia: University of
Pennsylvania Press, 1958), pp. 247-258; Spencer, pp. 226-229.

[88]Taylor, p. 30.

[89]William L. Marcy, "Diary and Memoranda of William L. Marcy,
1857," American Historical Review 24 (1918-1919): 647.

[90]George Tickner Curtis, Life of James Buchanan, Fifteenth
President of the United States, 2 vols. (New York: Harper
Bros., 1883), 2:185-186.

Many writers designate the Buchanan Administration as the "high tide" for the spoils system.[91] Actually, the honor belongs to Abraham Lincoln. Like many Presidents before him, Lincoln lamented the duty demanded of him to dispense patronage. He saw its dangers and defects and wishfully expressed hope that it would some day be reformed. Vice President Colfax reported that Lincoln once remarked: "I seem like a man so busy letting rooms at one end of his house that he has no time left to put out the fire that is blazing and destroying at the other end."[92] Looking at a multitude of office seekers, Lincoln told a friend: "There you see something which in the course of time will become a greater danger to the Republic than the rebellion itself."[93] In a similar vein, he told Carl Schurz: "I am afraid this thing is going to ruin republican government."[94] Sick in bed with smallpox, Lincoln revealed his humor when he said: "Tell all the office seekers to come at once, for now I have something I can give to all of them."[95]

These and other frequently quoted comments by Lincoln tend to obscure his extensive use of the spoils system. Lincoln's apologists argue that he had good reason to employ the spoils system. The Republican Party consisted of many diverse factions united only in their opposition to the Democratic Party and James Buchanan. Being a realist, Lincoln employed the spoils system to mold the Republican Party into a cohesive political organ.[96] The

---

[91] Philip Shriver Klein, President James Buchanan: A Biography (University Park, Pa.: The Pennsylvania State University Press, 1962), pp. 278-284; Curtis, p. 507; White, Jacksonians, p. 313; Philip Gerald Auchampaugh, James Buchanan and his Cabinet on the Eve of Secession, reprinted, (Boston: J.S. Canner & Co., Inc., 1926: Boston: J.S. Canner & Co., Inc., 1965), pp. 8-9.

[92] Henry J. Carman & Reinhard H. Luthin, Lincoln and the Patronage (New York: Columbia University Press, 1943), p. 6; Ward Hill Lamon, Recollections of Abraham Lincoln, 1847-1865 (Washington: Dorothy Lamon Teillard, 1911), p. 212.

[93] U.S. Civil Service Commission, The Story of the United States Civil Service, unpublished and undated (around 1960), p. I-2-15, CSC Library.

[94] Taylor, p. 32.

[95] U.S. Civil Service Commission, The Story of the United States Civil Service, p. I-2-15.

[96] Carman & Luthin, pp. 6-10; Fish, pp. 169-170.

Republican President made some adjustments in the composition of the government service to eliminate southern
secessionists and reward northern sympathizers.

President Lincoln had many more civil and military
positions at his disposal than any of the previous fifteen Presidents. He and his Cabinet engineered a massive
sweep of the civilian positions, replacing some eighty-
nine per cent. The permanent civil servants who had kept
the government in business during the previous thirty years
survived in only a small percentage of positions.[97] Lincoln further expanded the patronage at his disposal by
politicizing the military. His action brought inefficiency
and incompetency when the pressures of war demanded efficiency. No doubt they contributed to the length of the
war. President Lincoln rarely made only one appointment
per position. Most jobs changed hands many times during
his Administration.[98] Lincoln's use of patronage marks
the pinnacle of the spoils system. He used the system
deftly and with far more skill than any of his precedessors.

Personnel Management

Disposition of most major positions attracted the
attention of the President. Minor positions, on the other
hand, rested with Department Secretaries. Like the President, heads of departments devoted considerable amounts of
their time staffing vacancies. These executives performed
their duties with certain restrictions. Congress wanted a
hand in the selection of inferior positions as well as
presidential level appointments. Over the years, that influence gradually increased, especially in postal and customs positions located in their districts. The executive
never quite satisfied legislators with informal arrangements
to regulate this influence. In 1836, Congress enacted an
apportionment act for appointment of postmasters. The apportionment act assigned quotas to appointments by state.
That idea attracted attention again in 1852 when Samuel
Benton proposed a rule of apportionment by states for departmental clerks in Washington, D.C. Secretary of Interior
Robert McClelland announced in 1853 that he would appoint
departmental clerks according to their representation in
Congress. McClelland's action spread throughout the government until enacted into law in 1883.[99]

---

[97]Fish, p. 170.

[98]Taylor, p. 33; Fish, p. 172.

[99]5 Stat. 80 (1836); Richardson, Messages, 2:636; U.S.
Congressional Globe, 32nd Cong., 1st Sess., 11 August 1852, p. 2189.

137

Appointing relatives of elected officials became increasingly common. President Jackson resisted the pressure but Presidents Tyler, Polk, Taylor, and Fillmore sponsored relatives for government positions. Many lesser political figures did the same, including Daniel Webster and Henry Clay.[100]

Congressmen and politicians by no means agreed on their devotion to the spoils system. Thomas W. Gilmer, Chairman of the House Select Committee on Retrenchment, conducted an extensive investigation into the operations of the Federal government. The Gilmer Committee concluded in 1842:

> In other branches of the Service, the advantages of preliminary examinations, as to the qualifications of those entrusted with duties sometimes less important than the duties of clerks, have been manifested. Cadets, midshipmen, and applicants for appointments as surgeons in the Army and Navy have for years been subject to this test. The Committee have no doubt that the application of the same principles in the original appointment of clerks would be attended with beneficial results.[101]

These recommendations fell on deaf ears, but nine years later the subject surfaced again. Senator Robert M.T. Hunter, also from the State of Virginia, introduced a resolution requesting that Cabinet officers formulate

> some plan of classifying the clerks in the several departments; for apportioning their salaries according to their services and for equalizing the salaries of the clerks of the same grade in each of the departments; also, some plan to provide for a fair and impartial examination of the qualifications of clerks and for promoting

---

[100]Oliver Perry Chitwood, John Tyler, Champion of the Old South (New York: D. Appleton-Century Co., Inc., 1939), p. 391; Quaife, 1:371; Hamilton, 2:140-141, 207-208; Frama H. Severance, ed., Millard Fillmore Papers (Buffalo: The Buffalo Historical Society, 1907), 2:286-287; Claude Moore Fuess, Daniel Webster (Boston: Little, Brown & Co., Inc., 1930), 2:195-196.

[101]U.S. Congress, House, House Reports, IV, Report No. 741, 27th Cong., 2nd Sess., 1842, p. 24.

them from one grade to another, upon due regard to qualifications and service.[102]

On May 1, 1852, five of Fillmore's six Cabinet officers (Webster refused to accept their plan) submitted a plan in compliance with the Hunter resolution.

They recommended departmental boards to examine candidates nominated by the head of the department as to their health and physical energy, education, skill, and other qualifications. No person was to be eligible for appointment without a certificate from the board of examiners, nor to be eligible for promotion without examination and a certificate that he was "fully qualified."[103]

Attracting little attention, Senator Hunter directed the Act of 1853 through Congress. Based on recommendations of Cabinet officers the act stipulated that:

No clerk shall be appointed . . . until he has been examined and found qualified by a Board, to consist of three examiners, one of them to be the Chief of the Bureau or Office into which he is to be appointed, and the two others to be selected by the head of the Department to which the said clerk will be assigned.[104]

This "pass examination" system preceded a similar British system by two years.[105]

Besides establishing examination boards for civilian positions, the Act of 1853 tackled the classification and pay problems of the Federal service. It divided Federal

---

[102]U.S. Congress, Senate, Senate Journal, 31st Cong., 2nd Sess., 7 March 1851, p. 288.

[103]U.S. Congress, Senate, Senate Executive Document 69, 32nd Cong., 1st Sess., 1 May 1852, pp. 1-2.

[104]10 Stat. 189 (1853).

[105]For an excellent comparison of the American "pass examination" system with the "pass examination" system in Great Britain see Arthur Vernon Wolfe, "The United States Civil Service Employment System--To 1933" (Ph.D. dissertation, University of Chicago, 1966), pp. 78-82.

employees into four basic classes with prescribed salaries
attached to each class.

```
Class 1 .............................. $1,200
Class 2 ..............................  1,400
Class 3 ..............................  1,600
Class 4 ..............................  1,800
Chief Clerk of a Bureau ..............  2,000
Chief Clerk of a Department ..........  2,200[106]
```

The Act of 1853 failed to retard the spoils system.
The Pierce, Buchanan, and Lincoln Administrations that
followed increased the decline of the administrative structure with their use of the spoils system. Spoilsmen easily
circumvented the requirement that all government clerks sit
for an examination before acquiring a job. Administration
officials invariably chose political appointees to sit for
the examinations. Examinations varied in complexity according to the individual examiners, but they often consisted of such superficial questions as: "What did you have
for breakfast this morning?"[107]

The classification provision fared a little better.
It brought uniformity to grades and pay for government workers and recognized the principle that employees doing the
same work ought to receive the same pay, and that "there was
work of varying difficulty and importance."[108] The act
failed to insure that those doing the higher level work acquired the higher level grade and pay. It was silent on the
relationship of pay to productivity, efficiency, promotions,
and level of appointment. Pay provisions of the act served
to hold down costs as Congress refused to increase salaries
of government employees for another seventy years.

The real contribution of the Act of 1853 was the fact
that it should have taken place at all. Even though it was
weak, the law represents an unexpected reform passed at a
time when the spoils system flourished.

---

[106] Taylor, p. 27.

[107] Ibid., p. 28.

[108] White, Jacksonians, pp. 391-392.

CHAPTER V

INTRODUCTION OF CIVIL SERVICE REFORM
1864-1868

The man who used the spoils system with more skill
than any of his predecessors contributed to its demise
in two important ways. Abraham Lincoln had enough of
office seekers in his first four years. He turned
against the rising expectations of many politicians and
announced he intended no mass removal of office holders
during his second term. This was a tremendous blow to
the inevitable horde of office seekers.[1] "From that time
the popularity of rotation declined. The tide had turned."[2]

More important, Lincoln inspired men like Carl Schurz,
George William Curtis, and Thomas A. Jenckes with his high
moral tone. These future leaders of the civil service reform movement committed themselves to Lincoln's democratic
moral principles.

Problems caused by staffing government positions with
spoils candidates during Lincoln's administration stimulated three important politicians to consider administrative
alternatives. Independent of each other, William H. Seward, Secretary of State; Charles Sumner, Chairman of the
Senate Foreign Relations Committee; and Thomas A. Jenckes,
House member of the Joint Committee on Retrenchment, ap-
proached the patronage problem from a different direction
than their predecessors. Older reformers thought in terms
of controlling the discharge of government employees,
thereby reducing the number of positions available for
patronage disposition. Seward, Sumner, and Jenckes
turned their attention to the front of the system. They
thought in terms of restricting entrance to the government
service. All three considered, for the first time, the use
of a uniform examination system as a selection device for
the civilian service. In addition, they looked to foreign
governments for inspiration.

Seward and Sumner Ponder

William Seward's and Charles Sumner's official positions gave them a unique opportunity to develop new approaches

---

[1]Carman and Luthin, pp. 301-302.

[2]Fish, p. 172.

to patronage reform. The official position of both gentlemen subjected them to enormous pressure from office
seekers. The scramble for jobs kept the Secretary of
State under constant pressure and absorbed enormous
amounts of his time. He wrote President Lincoln:

> We are at the end of a month's administration,
> and yet without a policy, either domestic or
> foreign. . . . The presence of the Senate,
> <u>with the need to meet applications for patron-</u>
> <u>age</u>, have [sic] prevented attention to other
> and more grave matters. . . . But further de-
> lay to adopt and prosecute our policies, for
> both domestic and foreign affairs, would not
> only bring scandal on the Administration, but
> danger upon the country. To do this we must
> dismiss the applicants for office.[3]

The powerful Republican Senator from Massachusetts lamented the duty, demanded of him from his constituents,
to acquire executive positions for them. Both men knew
first-hand the price paid for the spoils system.

The two most important positions in foreign affairs
were those of Secretary of State and Chairman of the Senate Foreign Relations Committee. These positions gave
their incumbents an excellent opportunity to survey administrative practices in foreign countries.

William H. Seward instructed the American Consul-
General in Paris, John Bigelow, to study the French Revenue
Service in 1862. In August 1863, Bigelow replied that he
found much in the French system which would benefit the
United States. He extolled the French use of examinations
in recruitment and promotion, their ability to create experienced and skilled employees, and their support of the
government in power.[4] In 1864, Seward supported a bill
which passed Congress stipulating that appointment of
"consular pupils" be selected on the basis of an examination.[5]

---

[3] U.S. Civil Service Commission, <u>Fifteenth Report of the United</u>
<u>States Civil Service Commission, July 1, 1897 to June 30, 1898</u>,
p. 471.

[4] See Chapter I.

[5] Taylor, p. 35.

Charles Sumner gave the subject more than superficial
treatment.[6] Never a supporter of the spoils system, he
frequently wrote of his dislike of office seekers, the system of rotation, and the patronage system. No doubt, demands made upon his time by Massachusetts constituents
seeking government jobs irritated him.[7] During the Civil
War Sumner became the spokesman for British political
thought in the Lincoln government. His voluminous correspondence with John Bright, Richard Cobden, William Gladstone,
and the Duke of Argyll kept him well informed of English
events. He most certainly knew of the civil service reform
movement and the Order-in-Council of 1855.

In 1864 Senator Sumner wrote and introduced a bill,
patterned after the English system, for reform of the civil
service. "The object of the bill is to provide a competitive
system of examination in the civil service of the United
States."[8]

> I matured it alone, without consultation, and
> flung it on the table of the Senate as a way
> of drawing attention to the subject. . . . I
> do not doubt that the scale of business now and
> the immense interests involved will require
> some such system. We cannot transact our great
> concerns without serious loss unless we have
> trained men. "Rotation in office" is proper

---

[6]Senator Sumner entered Congress in 1851 and soon became a
strong opponent of slavery. In 1856 his powerful speech
against the Kansas-Nebraska bill ended in his severe injury
when Congressman Preston Brooks of South Carolina physically
assaulted him. Sumner was an uncompromising champion of the
Negro cause and vigorous advocate of emancipation. His career of influence began to decline when he conducted a spirited
attack on President Grant's Santo Domingo policy. His opposition to the Santo Domingo annexation caused him to lose the
chairmanship of the Committee on Foreign Relations in 1871.
Charles Sumner died in 1874 from heart trouble at the age of
63. David Donald, Charles Sumner and the Coming of the Civil
War (New York: Alfred A. Knopf, 1960); David Donald, Charles
Sumner and the Rights of Man (New York: Alfred A. Knopf, 1970).

[7]Charles Sumner to George Sumner, 17 July 1849, Edward L.
Pierce, Memoir and Letters of Charles Sumner, 4 vols. (Boston: Roberts Brothers, 1877-1893), 3:44, 149.

[8]Congressional Globe, 38th Cong., 1st Sess., p. 1985.

enough in the political posts where political direction is determined, but absurd in the machinery of administration. . . . This is a moment for change. Our whole system is like molten wax, ready to receive an impression.[9]

The bill established a Civil Service Commission existing of three commissioners to act as a board of examiners. All candidates would have to obtain a certificate from the board and take a general competitive examination. The bill empowered the board to develop examination rules after consultation with the President and heads of departments. The Commission would establish a register of candidates between 18 and 25 years of age, according to merit and fitness. The candidates became eligible for vacancies according to their grade. The bill authorized removals for good cause only and stipulated that twenty per cent of the promotions be made on the basis of merit and eighty per cent on seniority.[10]

Much to his surprise, Sumner's bill attracted considerable attention from the public. "I am astonished at the echo of my little bill on civil service,"[11] he wrote. Many important newspapers mentioned the bill, including the Washington National Intelligencer, the New York Times, Evening Post, and the Nation. The prominent Union League Club of New York offered to help, while several individuals wrote to tell Senator Sumner of their support and urge him to pursue the bill in earnest.[12]

Next to the destruction of the rebel army in importance to this government is the sweep of your bill for the reform in the appointment and entrance in office of the civil officers in this nation. If you succeed every man in

---

[9] Charles Sumner to Francis Lieber, 15 May 1864, Pierce, 4:192.

[10] Charles Sumner, The Works of Charles Sumner, 15 vols. (Boston: Lee and Shepard, 1874), 8:452-454.

[11] Charles Sumner to Francis Lieber, 15 May 1864, Pierce, 4:192.

[12] E.M. Ward to Charles Sumner, Detroit, 27 May 1864; William E. Dodge, New York, 13 May 1864; Sudovic Bennet to Charles Sumner, New York, 27 May 1864; Conrad Wegard to Charles Sumner, Virginia City, Nevada Territory, 13 June 1864, Charles Sumner Papers, Harvard University.

this country for all time to come, will
have the most potent reasons for gratitude
and thankful remembrance to the statesman
who inaugurated and pressed so valuable
and necessary a law.[13]

Unfortunately, Sumner did not press for passage of
his bill. Most observers attribute Sumner's inaction to
the pressure of other work. One historian suggests that
Sumner introduced the bill for political purposes, and
when the political reasons evaporated, he lost interest.
Whatever reason, Sumner failed to act and the momentum
switched to the House of Representatives.[14]

Thomas A. Jenckes

The real father of the civil service reform movement
in the United States is Thomas A. Jenckes, Congressman
from the State of Rhode Island. Historians find little
evidence that Thomas A. Jenckes, Seward, or Sumner influenced each other. They acted independently, suggesting that
the spoils system began to reach intolerable levels during
the Civil War. Jenckes was born in 1818 of a respected old
New England family, graduated from Brown University with
distinction in 1838, and became an accomplished lawyer
specializing in patent law. Jenckes' political career began
at the age of twenty-two with his election to reading clerk of
the Rhode Island House of Representatives. He served as clerk
of the Landholders' Constitutional Conventions in 1841 and 1842
which drafted a new constitution for the state. From 1843 to
1863, Jenckes held various political positions, including seats
in both houses of the state legislature. He had a number
of business interests, including the Rubber Sole Shoe Company and the American Wood Paper Company (which came to
monopolize the paper pulp manufacturing business). Elected
to the House of Representatives from the First District of
Rhode Island, Jenckes served from 1863 to 1871. In Congress he sat on the Patents Committee, Judiciary Committee,

---

[13]E.M. Ward to Charles Sumner, Detroit, 27 May 1864, Sumner
Papers.

[14]William Harrison Clarke, The Civil Service Law, 3rd ed.
(New York: M.T. Richardson Co., 1897), p. 1; Van Riper,
p. 64; Ari Arthur Hoogenboom, Outlawing the Spoils: A
History of the Civil Service Reform Movement: 1865-1883
(Urbana: University of Illinois Press, 1961), p. 12.

145

and Joint Committee for Retrenchment. Like Trevelyan in
Great Britain, Jenckes had one asset which benefited him
in pursuing his potentially unpopular civil service reform activities. Mr. Jenckes was independently wealthy.
He never had to consider his own welfare or that of his
family in deciding on his political activities.[15] In 1871
Jenckes' National Bankruptcy Bill became law. He assisted
in the prosecution of the Credit Mobilier case from 1872
to 1873.[16]

Thomas Jenckes had good reasons for dissatisfaction
with the employees in the Federal civil service. He found
them greatly inferior to the military and naval administrative staffs.[17] His business interests brought him into
contact with the customhouses where incompetence and corruption were common. The service he received from the Post
Office left much to be desired. His friend Hugh Burgess,
a scientist from the American Wood Paper Company at its
Royersford, Pennsylvania plant, wrote: "It is a bad disgrace to the Post Office that nearly every foreign newspaper is stolen -- I duly receive my scientific periodicals
but never the papers of general interest -- when mailed from
London by my agent."[18]

Congressman Jenckes experienced the usual demands of
office seekers upon entering the legislature. H s papers
contain many letters from anxious solicitors requesting
Jenckes' endorsement. Generally, they demanded support
because of their acquaintance with or support from some
other prominent person or for some humanitarian reason.
The new Congressman received three typical letters from
Elisher Smith shortly after his election:

Providence, December 3, 1863

I am desirous of securing a messenger's appointment in the House of Representatives
and I request your influence in enabling me
to secure said situation. I am much in want
of the office. The recent death of my son-in-

---

[15] In 1871 Jenckes earned $16,000 beyond his Congressional
salary.

[16] Dictionary of American Biography, 1928-36, s.v. "Thomas
Allen Jenckes," by William B. Nunro; Thomas A. Jenckes
Papers, Library of Congress.

[17] U.S. Congressional Globe, 39th Cong., 1st Sess., 1865, p. 98.

[18] Hugh Burgess to Thomas A. Jenckes, Royers Ford, September
30, 1864, Jenckes Papers.

law has thrown on my hands his wife and two
little children to care for besides my own
family. If you will secure for me the place
you will confer on the needy a great favour.

Providence, December 16, 1863

I wrote to you a few days before the meeting
of Congress asking you to use your influence
to secure for me the Office of a messenger
in the House of Representatives. Not having
heard from you since I wrote again I ask you
not to forget me as I am greatly in need of
the situation. Hoping to hear from you soon
I remain, . . .

Providence, December 30, 1863

I would state that Mr. Smith is a gentleman
of good address and one whom [sic] I think
would fill the position for which he applies
with credit for himself and the satisfaction
of all.

                    Very respectfully,
                    James Smith
                    Governor of Rhode Island[19]

These requests for endorsement, typical of the patronage system, probably irritated Jenckes more than most of his
colleagues. He failed to answer most of them and acted
only on those considered politically impossible to avoid.[20]
Jenckes' personality did not lend itself to patronage demands. "Although witty in select company, Jenckes was
frequently described as cold, unsocial, lacking enthusiasm,
and ignoring public opinion."[21]

---

[19]Elisher Smith to Jenckes, Providence, December 3, 1863;
Elisher Smith to Jenckes, Providence, December 16, 1863;
James Smith to Jenckes, Providence, December 30, 1863, Jenckes
Papers.

[20]George Manchester to Jenckes, South Portsmouth, R.I., 21 Feb-
ruary 1865; 10 March 1865; 3 June 1865; D. Kimball to
Jenckes, Providence, 16 December 1865; G.T. Hammond to Jenckes,
Newport, 1 February 1866, Jenckes Papers.

[21]Hoogenboom, p. 13.

The practice of selecting nominees recommended by Members of Congress as appointees to the United States military academies gave Jenckes an opportunity to test an idea he developed in 1863. He revealed plans to "throw open [appointments] to competition" in a letter to H.H. Tilley. Tilley, a clerk in the Navy Department, wanted the Congressman to sponsor his fifteen-year-old brother, B.F. Tilley, as a student of the Naval Academy. Jenckes refused to give his endorsement because it violated his "convictions of duty," for he disagreed with the "manner of making appointments to the public service."[22] He appointed an unofficial examining board, announced that he intended to select his candidate by open competitive examination, and referred all applicants to his board of examiners. The first exam, held on May 6, 1864, tested twenty-two boys for appointment. The board unanimously selected Richard E. Thompson to receive Jenckes' nomination.[23] Jenckes continued to select his appointees at the military academies by competitive examination throughout his tenure in the House.[24] The Mayor of Newport exerted

---

[22]H.H. Tilley to Jenckes, Providence, 18 May 1863; Thomas Jenckes to H.H. Tilley, Washington, 1 June 1863; 4 June 1863, Jenckes Papers.

[23]G.W. Stanley to Jenckes, Lutherville, 16 February 1864; Charles W. Chafee, Newport, 28 March 1864; Stanton Bolden, Providence, 29 March 1864; Charles Briggs, Providence, 12 April 1864; A. Woodbury, Providence, 7 May 1864, Jenckes Papers.

[24]The practice of selecting appointees to the military academies by open competitive examinations began in 1859 with Daniel E. Sickles, a New York Democrat, and was followed by other congressmen such as James A. Garfield and Henry B. Anthony. The practice for Members of Congress using "designation" examinations for Service Academy appointments has continued to the present. The United States Civil Service Commission has conducted such examinations as a courtesy for Members who ask for such service. The results are advisory. There is no fixed pass/fail standard. Some Members follow the written test rankings strictly. Others take into account examination elements of their own, such as oral interviews. John F. Scott, interview at Civil Service Commission, June 1974.

political pressure on Jenckes, forcing him to adjust his
merit principles. The Mayor and one of his examiners protested that pure merit discriminated against Newport citizens. They predicted that Jenckes' two appointments would
go to Providence citizens because of their "superior advantages, education . . . and the sure advantage of being
at home among familiar faces. . . ."[25] The First District
Congressman altered his examination system to give Newport
at least one nomination without regard to the examination
results.[26]

Political considerations probably influenced the Representative from Rhode Island in developing his civil service reform position. As a prominent Radical Republican,
Jenckes opposed President Johnson and worked actively for
his impeachment in the House. Many observers conclude that
Jenckes introduced his civil service bill to weaken the
powers of the Presidency. Certainly his timing suggests
that conclusion.[27]

Jenckes worked on his civil service bill in 1864 and
Hugh Burgess implied that it was ready by September. He
did not introduce it until December 1865. Meanwhile, Andrew Johnson succeeded Abraham Lincoln in the White House
and many feared he planned to use the removal and appointment powers to carry out his reconstruction policies.
Designed to restrict executive and legislative patronage,
Jenckes patterned his proposal after the British administrative system. Notable for its brevity, simplicity, and
clarity, Jenckes' bill created a Civil Service Commission
to examine all applicants for Federal jobs except those
"nominated by the President and confirmed by the Senate,
. . . prescribe qualifications for an appointment. . .,
establish rules . . . [and] report . . . all rules and
regulations. . . to Congress. . . ." The bill granted those
passing the open competitive examination "preference in appointment. . . in order of rank. . . in examinations. . . ."

---

[25] Coggeshill to Jenckes, Newport, 26 June 1866, Jenckes Papers.

[26] Henry M. Fay, Newport, 26 June 1866; Thomas Coggeshill to
Jenckes, Newport, 26 June 1866; Augustus Woodbury, Henry M.
Fay, Dr. Mannan, George Engs, and William A. Marcy, Providence,
R.I., 6 July 1866.

[27] Ari Hoogenboom, "Thomas A. Jenckes and Civil Service Reform," Mississippi Valley Historical Review 47 (March 1961):
637.

Promotions must be made by seniority or open competition
according to Civil Service Commission rules. The bill
conferred tenure on employees appointed by open competition
"during good behavior" with prescribed rules governing misconduct augmented by rights of appeal. Jenckes stipulated
that all citizens "shall be eligible to examination and appointment." He wrote the first equal employment opportunity
provision by specifically granting females equal appointment
and promotion rights "in order of their merit and seniority
and without distinction from those of male applicants or
officers." The Jenckes bill delegated to heads of departments responsibility over employee mobility.

        Jenckes' civil service bill provided that the civil
service examination board consist of at least three commissioners "appointed by the President, by and with the
advice and consent of the Senate." Board members were responsible for examinations, appeals, and setting penalties
for avoiding rules. The bill prescribed the salary of the
Commissioners and authorized the board to hire a clerk
and messenger.

        Jenckes included two options in his original bill.
He delegated heads of departments the right to examine
current employees and authorized the President to require
candidates needing Senatorial confirmation to sit for an
examination.[28]

        The Representative from Rhode Island's bill generated
little notice in the press or from private citizens.
The New York Times noted the bill on January 18, 1866, but
concluded it was "too good and too much in advance of our
civilization to pass as yet."[29] The Nation endorsed the
bill in March. Jenckes got a few letters from interested
citizens.[30] One of these, Isaac Pitman of Providence,
recommended he add a prohibition against sinecure positions

_____

[28]U.S. Congress, House, A Bill to Regulate the Civil Service
of the United States, H.R. 60, 39th Cong., 1st Sess., 1865.
Jenckes introduced the bill on December 20, 1865, at which
time it was referred to the Committee on Judiciary.

[29]"The Public Service--Competitive Examinations," New York
Times, 18 January 1866, p. 4.

[30]David A. Wells to Thomas Jenckes, Washington, 19 January
1866; George W. Searle to Jenckes, 12 January 1866; William Hichborn to Jenckes, Boston, 14 February 1866; William
Allen to Jenckes, New York, 14 March 1866, Jenckes Papers.

and a requirement for the election of postmasters "by the
constituency with whom he resides. . . ."[31]

Apparently unaware of Jenckes' bill, the New York
Times published an article in its Sunday, January 7, 1866,
edition lamenting the inefficiency in government caused by
patronage and drawing the reader's attention to the English
system. In conclusion, the Times wrote: "All of us see
the evils of our present system. When shall we begin to
initiate remedies?"[32]

David A. Wells, Chairman of President Johnson's Revenue
Commission, issued a Revenue Commission Report at the end of
January. Wells' report gave further weight to the discontent expressed by the Times with the quality of government
service. Once again the New York Customhouse provided the
basis of his investigation. The report described continued
corruption, waste, and inefficiency, costing the taxpayer
up to a quarter of a million dollars each year. Wells
turned to Great Britain for a solution. He recommended removing the customhouse from the spoils arena and creating
an independent board of custom commissioners to examine and
appoint employees. Perhaps the Revenue Commission arrived
at this solution after reviewing Jenckes' bill since Wells
wrote to Jenckes on January 19, 1866, about it. The press
gave considerable attention to the Revenue Commission Report but generally ignored its recommendations.[33]

Congress took rudimentary steps in response to this
agitation. In March 1866, the House of Representatives
created a Select Committee on the Civil Service, and in June
Senator B. Gratz Brown of Missouri headed a Senate committee
to inquire into the expediency of reforming the civil service.[34]

---

[31]Isaac Pitman to Thomas Jenckes, Providence, 24 March
1866, Jenckes Papers.

[32]"Want of Efficiency in the American Civil Service," New
York Times, 7 January 1866.

[33]David A. Wells to Jenckes, Washington, 19 January 1866,
Jenckes Papers.

[34]U.S. Congressional Globe, 39th Cong., 1st Sess., 1865,
pp. 1342, 1365, 1341, 1350-51, 3825.

The Legislative War on the Executive Branch

One of the reasons Jenckes' bill attracted so little attention was the titanic power struggle between President Andrew Johnson and Congress. Radical Republican leaders, opposed to President Johnson's reconstruction policies, chose to attack him through executive patronage powers. Tension grew in the Senate throughout the Civil War over the immense expansion of presidential powers. On several minor occasions, the Congress restricted presidential removal powers by requiring the President to submit reasons for removals. Some sort of conflict over the expanded presidential powers seemed inevitable after the Civil War. Through the year 1866 apprehension over the President's reconstruction policies grew, and President Johnson began to strengthen his position as the struggle for supremacy became inevitable. He used three Cabinet resignations to appoint men favorable to his policies. He selected A.W. Randall, the Postmaster-General, to plan strategy for the expected battle. The President decided to employ his patronage power as a major weapon in the struggle. During 1866 he began to remove opponents and replace them with supporters. In this way he replaced some fifteen per cent of all Executive Branch government employees.

Radicals decided to challenge the Presidential appointment powers, originally fought over in 1789. In that year Congress agreed to grant the executive exclusive removal power. The Whig Party raised the issue again in 1830 during their unsuccessful challenge with President Andrew Johnson. In late 1866 the issue surfaced again. This time the debate led to passage of the Tenure of Office Act of 1867. The bill, reported out of the Joint Select Committee on Retrenchment, proposed to grant the Senate a share in the removal powers. It contained four sections: granting presidential office holders the right to remain in office until the President appointed and the Senate confirmed a successor; granting the President suspension powers subject to Senate approval; restricting presidential powers to fill vacancies caused by removal, death, or resignation; and forbidding any action to change terms of office already limited by law. The bill passed Congress and became law over President Johnson's veto in March 1867.[35]

---

[35]U.S. Congressional Globe, 39th Cong., 2nd Sess., pp. 17-18, 382-90, 404-410, 438-41, 460-61, 470, 524-43, 547, 938, 969, 1514, 1964, 1977; Fish, 192-198; Edmund G. Ross, History of the Impeachment of Andrew Johnson: President of the United States by the House of Representatives and his Trial by the Senate for High Crimes and Misdemeanors in Office: 1868 (New York: Burt Franklin, 1896), pp. 57-65.

Secretary of War Edwin M. Stanton worked energetically
to thwart President Johnson's reconstruction policies.
Radical Republicans designed the Tenure of Office Act of
1867 to protect Congressional friends such as Stanton from
removal by the President. Johnson confronted Congress and
the law by asking Edwin Stanton to resign on May 5, 1867.
The Chief Executive's strategy called for the appointment
of General U. S. Grant to replace Stanton. After the anticipated Senate rejection of Stanton's removal, Johnson expected Grant to remain in office, forcing Stanton to take
his case to the courts and test the constitutionality of
the Tenure of Office Act. General Grant, appointed secretary ad interim, withdrew from office when the Senate refused to concur in the suspension on January 13, 1868, and
Secretary Stanton returned. Johnson then announced, in
direct violation of the Tenure of Office Act, the removal
of Stanton and his replacement by General Lorenzo Thomas.
Stanton refused to leave; accused Thomas of violating the
Tenure of Office Act; and ordered military protection
from General Grant.

The House of Representatives moved immediately to im-
peach the President. The Senate held a trial which acquitted Mr. Johnson on May 26, 1868. Stanton resigned and
General Schofield replaced him as Secretary of War, which
the Senate confirmed on May 28.[36]

Most observers believed that Congress would repeal
the Tenure of Office Act when the new President took office,
since it was aimed at a specific President and a specific
policy advocated by that President. The House agreed but
the Senate refused to relinquish everything it had gained
on the executive. In December 1869 the Congress amended
the act to remove any restrictions on the President with
respect to suspensions and placed cabinet officers under
the same restrictions as other officials. The Congress
directed the President to nominate replacements for vacancies within thirty days after the beginning of each session. All other provisions remained unchanged.[37]

---

[36]Michael Les Benedict, The Impeachment and Trial of Andrew John-
son (New York: W.W. Norton & Co., Inc., 1973), pp. 95-180;
Lately Thomas, The First President Johnson: The Three Lives of
the Seventeenth President of the United States of America (New
York: William Morrow & Company, Inc., 1968), pp. 402-607;
David Miller DeWitt, The Impeachment and Trial of Andrew Johnson:
Seventeenth President of the United States: A History (New York:
The Macmillan Co., 1903), pp. 180-596; Fletcher Pratt, Stanton:
Lincoln's Secretary of War (New York: W.W. Norton, 1953), reprint
ed., Westport, Ct.: Greenwood Press, 1970), pp. 447-452;
Ross, pp. 63-173.

[37]Richardson, 7:38; 16 Stat. 6-7 (1868).

Civil Service Reform Attracts Attention

The civil service bills, sponsored by Thomas A. Jenckes, became entangled in the legislative-executive struggle in the minds of their sponsor, the public, and politicians. On January 13, 1866, Jenckes introduced his second civil service bill with changes designed to appeal to opponents of President Johnson. H.R. 673 narrowed the coverage of the previous bill by exempting "postmasters whose compensation is less than 1000 dollars per annum." The Board of Commissioners would consist of three commissioners serving for five years. Striking at Johnson, Jenckes stipulated that the President could appoint or remove the board only "with the assent of the Senate." He provided provisions for holding examinations in designated district locations. The author expanded the rules to permit promotions on the basis of merit, seniority, and "advancement for meritorious service and special fitness for a particular branch of service." In all other provisions the 1866 bill, reported favorably to the House by the Select Committee on Civil Service, emulated the earlier version.[38] Jenckes persuaded his colleague Henry B. Anthony, Senator from Rhode Island, to introduce an identical civil service bill in the Senate, even though Anthony showed no sympathy for the measure.[39]

Representative Jenckes' second attempt fared even worse than the first. The press ignored the bill, and he failed to receive any letters or comments from interested individuals. It appears that the attention of the country centered on the activities of President Andrew Johnson and Radical Republicans.

The next month Congress created a new forum for Mr. Jenckes' civil service reform campaign by creating the Joint Select Committee on Retrenchment. Senators George F. Edmunds of Vermont, George H. Williams of Oregon, and Charles R. Buckalew of Pennsylvania joined Representatives Samuel J. Randall of Pennsylvania, Robert S. Hale of New York, Robert C. Schenck of Ohio, John L. Thomas of Maryland, and Thomas A. Jenckes on the committee.[40]

---

[38]U.S. Congress, House, A Bill to Regulate the Civil Service of the United States, and Promote the Efficiency Thereof, H.R. 673, 39th Cong., 1st Sess., 1866.

[39]U.S. Congressional Globe, 39th Cong., 1st Sess., 1866, pp. 1342, 1365, 3141, 3450-51, 3825; Hoogenboom, p. 19.

[40]U.S. Civil Service Commission, Fifteenth Annual Report of the Civil Service Commission, July 1, 1896, to June 30, 1897, p. 477

On December 13, 1866, Representative Jenckes introduced a third bill for consideration by the Joint Select
Committee on Retrenchment. H.R. 889 was substantially the
same as its predecessors. This time all postmasters fell
outside the coverage of the bill. The other major change
reflected Jenckes' anti-Johnson sentiments. He granted
the Senate and the President equal powers to administer an
examination to presidential appointees.[41]

The bill attracted immediate and widespread attention.
Jenckes received a number of letters from interested observers. John Wightman, a government employee from Washington,
suggested that he add a provision giving preference to
veterans.[42] Former colleague John Law wrote: ". . . it
is surprising to me that since the foundation of the Government, a similar bill has not been brought before Congress."[43]
Allen Goodridge predicted that the bill was in for a difficult time. "I fear you cannot enact the Bill. You will be
assailed on all sides by the incompetent, and vicious who
will employ all the ingenuity of the Lobby to defeat the
measure. . . . God grant it may become a law."[44] Jenckes'
friend and business associate Hugh Burgess encouraged
Joseph George Rosengarten to offer his services to the
Rhode Island Congressman. Rosengarten, a Philadelphia lawyer and businessman, became interested in administrative
reform while studying in France and Germany. He returned
to the United States with a collection of European books
on the subject just in time to read about Jenckes' bill.
Rosengarten wrote: "Excuse my asking you if the bill is
in such a shape as to be helped by anything I can do or
write and my offer to do either according to your suggestion or direction."[45]

---

[41]U.S. Congress, House, A Bill to Regulate the Civil Service of
the United States, and Promote the Efficiency Thereof, H.R.
889, 39th Cong., 2nd Sess., 1866.

[42]John Wightman to Jenckes, Washington, 15 December 1866,
Jenckes Papers.

[43]John Law to Jenckes, Evansville, 4 January 1867, Jenckes
Papers; John Law was a former Member of Congress and friend
of Jenckes. They served together on the 37th and 38th Congresses.

[44]Allen Goodridge to Jenckes, Washington, 14 December 1866,
Jenckes Papers.

[45]Joseph George Rosengarten to Jenckes, Philadelphia, 16
December 1866, Jenckes Papers.

Presumedly encouraged by Jenckes, Rosengarten took
the first steps in what proved to be a sixteen-year struggle
for the enactment of a Civil Service Reform bill. He sent
the Congressman a handwritten extract from a paper on government service by French writer Edouard Laboulave in hopes
that Jenckes could use it as an introduction to his bill.
He proceeded to write an article in support of the civil
service bill and offered it to the Nation, which published
it on January 10, 1867.[46] Rosengarten's January article
described the political and financial weaknesses of the
spoils system. He supported Jenckes' bill as a solution
and called for the united effort of all those who suffer
from the inefficient system of government.[47]

Two weeks later Congressman Jenckes delivered a major
speech in support of his civil service bill. The January
29, 1867 speech set the stage for civil service reform.
The bill, according to Jenckes, came about without regard
to party politics or the existing conflict between the
executive and legislative branches, but in response to
conditions in the government service. He indicated that
the system proposed may not have been necessary in the
early years when government was small, but its great growth
required reform in the system of recruiting and promotions.
He described the effects of the spoils system from the political, administrative, and financial standpoint. The
American people have a right to expect good government.
We must eliminate incompetence and admit men of honesty.
This can best be accomplished by introducing a new system
of examinations, open to all, which is monitored by a
board of examiners. Such a system, according to Jenckes,
has American and European prototypes which have led to
eliminating "patronage" and inefficiencies that accompany it.

> . . . this proposed system will stimulate edu-
> cation and bring the best attainable talent
> into the public service, it will place that
> service above all considerations of locality,
> favoritism, patronage, or party, and will give
> it permanence and the character of nationality
> as distinct from its present qualities of in-
> security and of centralized power. A career
> will be opened to all who wish to serve the

---

[46]Rosengarten to Jenckes, Philadelphia, 21 December 1866;
12 January 1867, Jenckes Papers.

[47]"The Civil Service Bill," The Nation (New York), 10
January 1867.

Republic; . . . The nation will be better
served; the Government will be more stable
and better administered; property will be
more secure; personal rights more sacred;
and the Republic more respected and powerful.
The great experiment of self-government which
our fathers initiated will have another of its
alien elements of discord removed from it, and
in its administration, in peace as well as war,
will have become a grand success.[48]

Jenckes may have denied that he designed the bill to
reduce the powers of President Johnson, but he encouraged
the impression that it would accomplish this objective.
He described "the direct interference of the Chief Executive in the appointment of officers" as an evil "which
may become of greater magnitude and threaten greater danger to the Republic than any other. . . ." The Joint Select Committee on Retrenchment wanted to eliminate the
"interference of the Chief Executive" as well as party
officials from appointment control.[49]

These points were not lost on the press, which gave
Jenckes' speech a favorable response. Rosengarten enthusiastically reported: "The newspapers have given such
a thorough report of your Bill and speech that the public
have the 'Civil Service' well before them."[50] The New
York Times supported the bill saying that it would eliminate the "spoils system" and reduce the "overgrown power"
of the President.[51]

At first Jenckes' supporters were exuberant. Hugh
Burgess expressed considerable optimism. George O. Chase
of Providence wrote: "I hope there are enough of virtue
and good sense in Congress to insure its adoption." H.W.
Fuller of Boston wrote: "I hope you will persevere -- and
if you do, you will, at least, have the satisfaction of re-
ceiving the hearty thanks of all true men." Rosengarten
predicted success as did S.W. Macy of the Customhouse in

---

[48]U.S. Congressional Globe, 39th Cong., 2nd Sess., 1867,
pp. 837-841.

[49]Ibid., p. 838.

[50]J.G. Rosengarten to Jenckes, Philadelphia, 31 January
1867, Jenckes Papers.

[51]New York Times, 30 January 1867, p. 1.

Newport, Rhode Island, who wrote that Congress will
"pass it . . . without doubt."[52]

Enthusiasm gave way to sober reflection on the difficulties ahead. "You are right: but your course is hopeless -- for want of virtue and courage enough in the majority and in the people to adopt the meritorious candidates
instead of the availables." Rosengarten lamented: "I wish
I could stir up people here. . . . It is surprising that
at a time when the country suffers so noticeably from the
mischiefs for which you propose a remedy, the journals of
a great town like this, should be indifferent and silent."
Four days later he reported: "Everyone to whom I speak,
say that the politicians there will never give it a
chance. . . ."[53]

He was right. On February 6, 1867, Frederick E. Woodbridge, a Republican from Vermont, led the attack against
the Jenckes bill. Woodbridge, claiming credit for scuttling
Jenckes' original bill, opposed civil service reform on
three major points. (1) Theoretically perfect, the bill
was too moralistic and not practical. (2) It was too expensive, and the fee system too burdensome for the poor and
needy. (3) The bill was designed for aristocratic countries and therefore "anti-Democratic." It would provide
employment for the powerful ruling class only.

Jenckes answered, ". . . in my judgment a more vicious
system does not exist in any civilized nation on the face
of the earth. Every other civilized nation has reformed
its system except ours." Experience in the American military as well as countries in Europe demonstrated that the
proposed system would work. The "small fee . . . will
pay all the expenses, and perhaps even more than that."
Finally, he refuted Woodbridge's argument that the system
was aristocratic.

Thaddeus Stevens, Radical Republican leader from Pennsylvania, "moved that the bill be laid on the table." He
carried the day by a vote of 72 to 66.[54]

---

[52]Hugh Burgess to Jenckes, Royers Ford, 2 February 1867; George
O. Chase to Jenckes, Providence, 31 January 1867; H.W. Fuller
to Jenckes, Boston, 31 January 1867; J.G. Rosengarten to
Jenckes, Philadelphia, 31 January 1867 and 4 February 1867;
S.W. Macy, Newport, 5 February 1867, Jenckes Papers.

[53]H.W. Fuller to Jenckes, Boston, 31 January 1867; J.G.
Rosengarten to Jenckes, 31 January 1867 and 4 February
1867, Jenckes Papers.

[54]U.S. Congressional Globe, 39th Cong., 2nd Sess., 1867, pp. 1034

In the minds of many political analysts, the Jenckes
bill constituted an alternative to the Tenure of Office
bill. The New York Times, the Nation, and New York World
connected the two bills as reform measures.[55] Perhaps
this accounts for the Jenckes bill's attracting forty-eight
per cent of the votes cast on February 6, 1867. Not discouraged by the setback in Congress, reformers flocked to
the cause and laid plans to carry the battle to the public.
Henry E. Wallace, Commissioner of the Court of Common Pleas
in Philadelphia, wrote: "I see your bill did not pass. . . .
If you shall succeed. . . I am of the opinion you will
have established your name and fame as a jurist and Statesman of the first order, and secure the grateful admiration
of coming ages of this Great Nation." Another correspondent
declared: "We fear that party spirit will not permit so beneficial a change without a considerable struggle and long
delay. . . ."[56]

Campaign for Reform

The attention of the country, the press, the Congress,
and Thomas Jenckes focused on the impeachment of Andrew
Johnson during the remainder of 1867. Nevertheless, the
seeds planted by Jenckes' Civil Service Reform bill continued to grow until it became the focal point for most
political reformers. Julius Bing, an obscure clerk of the
Joint Select Committee on Retrenchment who probably acquired
his job with the help of Charles Sumner, became an ardent
devotee of civil service reform. Bing drew up plans for
an extensive reform campaign. By performing administrative
duties in the Committee, writing and publishing articles,
encouraging Jenckes to maintain the "agitation," lobbying
in the Senate, and soliciting support from government employees, Bing played an indispensable role in the new civil
service reform campaign. Between the last quarter of 1867
and second quarter of 1868, Bing wrote some twenty articles
in support of Jenckes' Civil Service bill. His articles
appeared in the Chicago Tribune, New York Round Table, and
North American Review. He distributed pamphlets, fielded
questions, and lobbied for the support of Senators Charles
Sumner and William D. Kelley. "JB," as Bing referred to
himself in letters to Jenckes, worked six months preparing
for the famous report issued May 25, 1868. The basis of

---

[55]Nation, 7 February 1867, p. 101; New York Times, 4 March 1867,
p. 4; "Tenure of Office Bill," World (New York), 22 January
1867, p. 4.

[56]Henry E. Wallace to Jenckes, 6 February 1867; B. White Car-
ter to Jenckes, The Phoenix National Bank of Providence, 23
February 1867, Jenckes Papers.

the report consisted of answers compiled from three
questionnaires written by Bing inquiring "into the present condition of the administrative departments of the
government." Eighty-one per cent of the 446 replies endorsed the Jenckes bill while three per cent were opposed.
The other sixteen per cent failed to provide a decisive
reply. This inquiry and many letters from government employees indicate that Jenckes held strong support from
the government service.[57]

This famous report, which became the "Bible" for
civil service reformers, compiled most of the literature
on civil service reform in one easy-to-use reference book.
Bing published the thirty-seven questions contained in the
circular letter along with excerpts from some 155 replies,
all but one favorable. The report contained a short history of civil service reform and extracts from the writing
of former Presidents and prominent politicians "upon the
principles which should govern appointments to office."
It described conditions in the government service under
the spoils system. The report published selected articles
in the press and portions of the report applied to Jenckes'
1867 bill (H.R. 889). The largest section continued discussions of the civil service system in China, Prussia,
France, and Great Britain.[58]

Convinced that the 40th Congress offered better hope
for success than waiting for the 41st Congress, Bing set
about to create as much attention as possible. He distributed the report to every opinion maker he could find. JB
collected articles written on civil service reform and
sent them to Jenckes. He suggested that Jenckes make an
attempt to get civil service reform included in the Republican platform and that all "Stump Speakers" be provided
a copy of the report for their use. He followed developments in Europe, especially in England, and advised Jenckes

---

[57]Bing to Jenckes, Washington, 27 November 1867; 6 May 1868;
22 May 1868;   26 November 1868;   31 December 1868;   JB to
Jenckes, Tuesday;   two no date letters;   Note from JB to
Jenckes;   Julius Bing, "Civil Service of the United States,"
North American Review 45 (October 1867):   478-495;   Julius
Bing to Jenckes, Washington, 4 December 1867;   23 January
1868;   19 June 1868;   U.S. Congress, Joint Select Committee
on Retrenchment, Civil Service of the United States, H.
Rept. 47 to accompany H.R. 948, 40th Cong., 2nd Sess., 1868,
Jenckes Papers.

[58]Report No. 47, Civil Service of the United States.

on the campaign strategy, contributed articles to the
Round Table and Putnam's Magazine, sent copies to newly
elected Congressmen and Senators, made appointments for
Jenckes to talk to reform supporters, and talked to a
number of newspaper editors, including Godkin of the
Nation. Bing was enthusiastic about Nathaniel Gale's
suggestion to create a "Civil Service" gazette. "It is
an idea, worth while pushing among your acquaintances.
There may be somebody ready to furnish the means; I will
undertake to furnish the brains."[59]

        Jenckes wrote to a number of editors in 1868 to
solicit support for his bill, including George William
Curtis, political editor of Harper's Weekly.[60] In Boston he contacted Nathaniel Gale who turned out to be an
enthusiastic campaigner for reform. Gale was a full-time
government clerk in the Boston Customhouse. He had a
broad circle of friends among prominent businessmen and
former government employees. Quickly responding to Jenckes'
request for help, Gale submitted the names of a number of
his acquaintances he felt would work to secure the passage
of Jenckes' bill. He continued to submit names and encourage supporters of the movement to write directly to
the Representative from Rhode Island throughout the year
1868. "I have no doubt you will soon get from some, if
not all the gentlemen whose names you received from me
many facts and much valuable matter for your purpose."[61]
Gale distributed copies of Jenckes' report and speeches to
businessmen, newspaper editors, current and former government employees, a "Commercial Convention" at Worcester, the
Board of Trade in Boston, and the Social Science Association.
He encouraged supporters to write and contribute articles
on civil service reform and on Jenckes' bill to newspapers,
and personally urged numerous editors to publish pertinent
articles. "I have arranged for a series of short articles
for the 'Bulletin.'"[62] Gale organized a group of government

---

[59]Julius Bing to Jenckes, Boston, 6 August 1868; 12 August
1868; 27 August 1868; Washington, 27 October 1868; 31
October 1868; 26 November 1868; 4 December 1868; 5 December 1868; 8 April 1869; 21 May 1870; New York, 5 December
1870; no place, 12 December 1868, Jenckes Papers.

[60]George William Curtis to Jenckes, New York, 5 June 1868,
Jenckes Papers.

[61]Nathaniel Gale to Jenckes, Boston, 11 January 1868,
Jenckes Papers.

[62]Ibid., 16 January 1868, Jenckes Papers.

employees to write and work for reform, including soliciting the support of the Boston Collector of Customs,
highest ranking government employee in Boston. "I think
of starting a petition in favor of your measure and it
will be a monster one if it is started, as everybody is
ripe for it here."[63]

Gale's vitality must have been encouraging to Thomas
Jenckes. Gale took it upon himself to keep Jenckes posted
on reform activities in Boston. He collected articles,
sent Jenckes a correspondent from the London _Times_ in
hopes he would report favorably on the bill, and kept informed on arguments against the bill. Gale was a strong
opponent of the spoils system and continually urged
Jenckes to push for reform. "Now is the time to press
the matter -- this Congress, I mean."[64] "I hope and pray
you will press this matter to the 'bitter' end -- _I know
you will_."[65] He reported on the prospects for passage
as he could determine in Boston. "I am not really sanguine that your bill will be passed by this Congress.
But that it will pass eventually I cannot in the least
doubt nor does anyone here interested in the subject have
doubts on that point."[66]

> General Banks, I understand, when here a few
> days since expressed an opinion that there
> was not the slightest chance for the passage
> of your bill. On the contrary, it gives me
> great pleasure to read a letter. . . from
> Mrses [sic] Loughridge and Price, M.C. from
> Iowa, expressing not only decided opinions
> as to the great need of the measure, but
> little or no doubt of its passage in this
> session. I earnestly hope the result will
> prove that the latter gentlemen are right
> in their belief; but if it turns out other-
> wise, you will find, sir a band a persons in
> this city who have enlisted for the war in
> this cause, and increasing their forces they
> will write and work together until the right-
> eous reform is accomplished.[67]

---

[63] Nathaniel Gale to Jenckes, 16 January 1868, Jenckes Papers.

[64] Ibid.

[65] Ibid., Boston, 27 January 1868, Jenckes Papers.

[66] Ibid., Boston, 8 May 1868, Jenckes Papers.

[67] Ibid., Boston, 22 June 1868, Jenckes Papers.

Jenckes received two suggestions from his supporters
in Boston that, when combined at a later date, played an
important role in civil service reform. Gale and his
friend "Mr. Jas. A. Dupee of our Board of Trade. . . an
able and zealous laborer in the good work," proposed establishing "a new independent Journal to be devoted to
Civil Service reform." Gale drew up elaborate plans for
the project, suggesting potential subscribers and con-
tributors. General Henry Villard, Recording Secretary of
the American Social Science Association in Boston and supporter of Gale's "independent Journal" proposal, notified
Representative Jenckes that a "civil service reform league
is now in process of formation and will formally appear
before the public in a few days."[68] Apparently, independent
of Villard's efforts, Dr. W.L. Richardson proposed the same
idea in 1870. "A number of young men, formerly friends at
Harvard, are talking in a quiet sort of way about forming
a club here, which should have for its main object the
advancement, in the next few years, of the great question
of reform in our Civil Service, so far as our influence
may count in Boston."[69] These two suggestions, an independent journal and civil service reform league, never
made a major contribution to the reform campaign led by
Thomas Jenckes, but became important in the late 1870's
and early 1880's.[70]

Early supporter Joseph George Rosengarten threw himself into the 1868 campaign with his usual energy. "It is
so long since I have written regularly for publication, that
I have got quite out of the habit, and only do so now because I think your Bill ought to get all the help it can.
. . ."[71] He began a vigorous writing campaign by submitting

---

[68]Henry Villard to Jenckes, Boston, 29 March 1869, Jenckes Papers.

[69]Dr. W.L. Richardson to Jenckes, Boston, 29 November 1870,
Jenckes Papers.

[70]Nathaniel Gale to Jenckes, Boston, 3 January 1868; 11 January 1868; 16 January 1868 (2); 22 January 1868; 27 January
1868; 4 February 1868; 9 May 1868; 25 May 1868; 22 June 1868;
25 November 1868; 28 March 1870; Jas. A. Dupee to Jenckes,
Boston, 9 March 1868; 29 March 1868; 7 April 1868; 4 June
1868; 10 November 1868; 23 November 1868; Dr. W.L. Richardson,
Boston, 29 November 1870; 7 December 1870, Jenckes Papers.

[71]J.G. Rosengarten to Jenckes, Philadelphia, 19 May 1868,
Jenckes Papers.

an article to the Nation which printed it as a leader on
May 28, 1868. He followed with a succession of articles
in Lippicott Monthly Magazine, Morning Post, Evening Bulletin, Princeton Review, and North American Review. Rosengarten urged fellow supporters to contribute articles
and campaigned among Philadelphia editors to keep up the
agitation. He collected articles from every possible
location, including London, and sent them to Jenckes. He
even collected articles from those periodicals which opposed reform for he felt that keeping the subject before
the public, even though the articles may be unfavorable,
benefited the cause.

        J.G. Rosengarten distributed copies of Jenckes' speech
and report to those he thought would support the bill. He
urged the National Board of Trade and the Union League to
endorse the bill in hopes that they could lead a nationwide campaign for civil service reform. Joseph Rosengarten
came to Washington to get guidance from Jenckes on further
efforts. He reported on campaign results and prospects
for passage and prepared a paper for the Social Science
Association meeting in Philadelphia. He proposed to organize a series of public meetings and offered to undertake the job. He followed through with the suggestion by
scheduling a series of public meetings on reform sponsored
by the Philadelphia Social Science Association and invited Congressman Jenckes to deliver the keynote speech
on civil service reform. Finally, Rosengarten kept informed of developments in England and sent Jenckes copies
of many articles concerning the English experience and
the new Order-in-Council.[72]

        With support from Bing in Washington, Rosengarten in
Philadelphia, Gale in Boston, and a favorable New York
press, Jenckes directed the campaign from Congress.

                    Congressional Campaign

        In July 1867, Thomas Jenckes reintroduced his bill
but no further action resulted.[73] Political developments

---

[72]J.G. Rosengarten to Jenckes, Philadelphia, 19 May 1868;   29
May 1868; 9 June 1868; 18 December 1868; 9 January 1869;
13 January 1869; 14 January 1869; 12 March 1869; 24 January 1870; 6 May 1870; 15 May 1870; 4 July 1870; 15 December 1870; and 20 January 1871, Jenckes Papers.

[73]U.S. Congress, House, A Bill to Regulate the Civil Service of the United States and Promote the Efficiency Thereof,
H.R. 113, 40th Cong., 1st Sess., 1867.

in the executive-legislative struggle motivated him to
alter his bill to reflect the current events. He introduced H.R. 948 on March 23, 1868, which would replace
the former Civil Service Commission with a "Department
of Civil Service; that the head. . . shall be the Vice-
President of the United States . . . who shall be a member
and president of the board of commissioners. . . ."
This time the board would consist of four commissioners
instead of three as in the former bills. Jenckes dropped
the requirement that commissioners could only be removed
with the advice and consent of the Senate. He gave the
Vice-President, as Head of the Department, power to make
temporary appointments to the Commission pending Senate
confirmation "of the commissioners authorized to be appointed by this act." All other provisions remained
the same.[74]

Representative Thomas A. Jenckes took the floor of
the House on May 14 to urge its members to embrace civil
service reform. He reiterated most of his now famous
arguments against the spoils system: ". . . for the money
it pays there is no Government in the world more poorly
served than ours." The Federal government under the spoils
system employs the incompetent, uneducated, inexperienced,
and those largely incapable of learning the duties of their
offices. As a result, the government received poor service from its employees and endured periodically great
frauds from "bold operators." Besides the evils perpetuated on the American government the system had a degrading
effect on the "many good and faithful servants who do the
work of these unfaithful politicians."

It was necessary, Jenckes argued, to make the civil
service respectable by obtaining "better recruits. . . for
the service." Jenckes designed The Bill to Regulate the
Civil Service of the United States and Promote the Efficiency
Thereof to effect these changes. The reform succeeded in
other countries,and it would destroy the evils of patronage
here. Again he stressed that "it is not urged as a measure
of temporary expediency, or to promote any partisan interest;
its purpose is to place the administrative departments of
this Government in the hands of skillful and honest men, and
thus to renew the health and life of the Republic."

---

[74]U.S. Congress, House, A Bill to Regulate the Civil Service
of the United States and Promote the Efficiency Thereof,
H.R. 948, 40th Cong., 2nd Sess., 1868.

The Representative from Rhode Island argued that
creating a new government department headed by the Vice-
President would enhance the prestige of both the new
civil service board and the office of Vice-President.
The people can expect "a higher grade of talent and character" from candidates for Vice-President "than many that
they have been compelled to vote for or against heretofore."
This was a slap at President Johnson.

Jenckes used the Bing Report to demonstrate that the
great majority of responsible government employees favored
his reform. "The preponderance of evidence in favor of
the proposed reform is so great that there can hardly be
said to be a minority."[75]

Congressman Jenckes tried to acquire the widest possible coverage of his civil service speech. He wrote to
Gale in Boston and Rosengarten in Philadelphia and requested
their help in getting broad press coverage for his speech.
He wrote to the important New York editors for the same
purpose.[76] The result disappointed Jenckes and his supporters as civil service reform proved unable to compete
with the Johnson impeachment trial and Republican National
Convention for headlines. Gale commented: "I felt somewhat disappointed and mortified in not being able to induce
any of our Boston editors to publish your last noble speech
in full."[77] Perhaps Jenckes' timing was not perfect but
his campaign managed to grow, nevertheless. Many newspapers in Boston, Philadelphia, New York and Washington
carried excerpts of his speech. Interest began to expand
to other parts of the country. He received comments from
Detroit; Buffalo; Charlottesville, Virginia; Cumberland,
Maryland; Oberlin, Ohio; Castine, Maine; Brighton, Vermont; Terre Haute, Indiana; De Soto, Missouri; Jacksonville, Illinois; Mobile, Alabama; Rochester, New York;
Minneapolis, Minnesota; and San Francisco, California.[78]

---

[75]U.S. Congressional Globe, 40th Cong., 2nd Sess., 1868, pp.
2466-2470.

[76]Nathaniel Gale to Jenckes, Boston, 9 May 1868; J.G. Rosengarten to Jenckes, Philadelphia, 15 May 1868; George William
Curtis to Jenckes, New York, 5 June 1868; Financial Editor
of Evening Post to Jenckes, New York, 19 May 1868, Jenckes Papers

[77]Nathaniel Gale to Jenckes, Boston, 22 June 1868, Jenckes Papers

[78]E.B. Ward to Jenckes, Detroit, 6 April 1868; Frederick Far-
thingham, Buffalo, 20 May 1868; Michelle DeVere, University of
Virginia, 16 May 1868; Geo. W. Harrison, Cumberland, Maryland,
20 May 1868; J.E. Hitchcock, Oberlin, Ohio, 21 May 1868;

Jenckes tried again to bring his bill to a vote.
In July 1868 he moved to suspend the rules in order to
consider the Civil Service Bill.[79] He failed to get the
necessary two-thirds majority.

Expectations of General Grant

Reformers flocked to the banner of Ulysses S. Grant.
In him they saw a champion strong enough to control the
"politicians" and noble enough to support reform and
thwart corruption. Influenced by a forged letter stating
that Grant pledged not to reward supporters with office,
reformers interpreted the Republican platform, which
attacked corruption and promised economy in government,[80]
as including support for the Jenckes bill. H.J. Mead
told Jenckes: "With this bill, and the Nation with General Grant, in the Executive Chair, I am persuaded our
future will be bright."[81] "General Grant being favorable
to the reform I build strong hopes upon his influence on
the matter."[82] "I think Gen. Grant just the man to
grapple with this evil."[83]

Reformers found much to be thankful for in the election of 1868. They thought they could count on support
in the executive branch from President Grant. They reelected Jenckes to continue the battle in the House and
gained a new champion of reform in the Senate with the
election of Carl Schurz from Missouri. James G. Blaine

S.K. Devereaux, Castin, 22 May 1868; James B. Anger,
Brighton, Vermont, 11 June 1868; H.J. Keeler, Terre
Haute, Indiana, 29 June 1868; John H. Fix, De Soto, Missouri, 10 July 1868; J. Edward Wright, Jacksonville,
Illinois, 13 July 1868; Theo F.H. Gomezto, Mobile, Alabama, 3 August 1868; Henry George, San Francisco, 16 May
1868, Jenckes Papers.

[79]U.S. Congressional Globe, 40th Cong., 2nd Sess., 1868, p. 4003.

[80]Nation (New York), 19 December 1867, p. 493; J. Bing to
Jenckes, Washington, 26 May 1868, Jenckes Papers.

[81]H.J. Mead to Jenckes, Custom House, District of Natchez,
28 August 1868, Jenckes Papers.

[82]Bing to Jenckes, Washington, 27 October 1868, Jenckes Papers.

[83]A.G. Blissing to Jenckes, Washington, 20 February 1869,
Jenckes Papers.

of Maine, a strong opponent of the Civil Service Bill,
paid tribute to reform by sending a congratulatory letter
to Jenckes in which he wrote: "Your return to Congress
is hailed with pleasure all over the country on account
especially of yr [sic] authorship of the measure to purify,
improve & elevate the civil service of the country -- Pray
advise me of the present attitude of yr [sic] Bill. I
mean its parliamentary status -- Is it in such a position
as will insure its being readied & acted on at the ap-
proaching session?"[84]

Grant Alienates Reformers

Grant's cabinet appointments signaled the first signs
of disappointment among reformers. He did not seek the
advice of professional politicians or reformers. Grant
"treated the task of Cabinet-making as if he were hiring
servants for his home."[85] The appointments of Elihu Washburne as Secretary of State and A.T. Stewart as Secretary
of Treasury came in for the most criticism. Nevertheless,
reformers had some joy in the appointment of Jacob D. Cox
as Secretary of the Interior, and Ebenezer Rockwood Hoar
as Attorney General. Curtis discussed Grant's cabinet
selections in a letter to his friend Charles Eliot Norton
on March 13, 1869. He expressed disappointment and predicted little reform progress.[86]

Grant's refusal to consult "respectable and cultured
men" about administrative policy or appoint them to influential policy jobs in his Administration became an underlying
cause for ferment among the reformers. Henry Adams came to

---

[84]James G. Blaine to Thomas A. Jenckes, Augusta, Maine, 7
November 1868, Jenckes Papers. The letter was probably motivated by Blaine's desire to become Speaker of the House.

[85]Hoogenboom, p. 52.

[86]George W. Curtis to Charles Eliot Norton, Staten Island,
13 March 1869, George William Curtis Papers, Harvard University. Charles Eliot Norton (1847-1908) was Professor of History of Fine Arts at Harvard University from 1874 to 1898 with
a special interest in the study and translation of Dante.
From 1863 to 1868 he was joint editor with his friend James
Russell Lowell of the North American Review.

Washington to seek a job but found the door locked.[87]
Carl Schurz found tnat Grant ignored his right to influence
the appointments in St. Louis.[88] Grant appointed none of
Horace White's recommendations to his administration and
removed David A. Wells, Jacob D. Cox, and Ebenezer R. Hoar
because of their relations with reformers.[89] These re-
buffs heightened the reformers' interest in Jenckes' Civil
Service Bill and account for the rapid growth of the civil
service reform campaign. If Grant had opened the door to
reformers and satisfied some of their desires, it is doubt-
ful if they would have continued to advocate civil service
reform with so much intensity. "Reform was their weapon --
the battering ram that would splinter the shut door."[90]

The foundations on which civil service reform rested
were introduced between 1864 and 1868. They grew out of
inefficiency and corruption displayed in the federal
bureaucracy during the Civil War. Far-sighted reformers
adopted the basic principles of their system from Great
Britain. These principles survived the long struggle
for reform.

---

[87]Henry Adams, The Education of Henry Adams: An Autobiography
(New York: Houghton, 1931), p. 262.

[88]Carl Schurz to William H. Grosvenor, Washington, 29 March
1869, Schurz Papers.

[89]Joseph Logsdon, Hoarace White, Nineteenth Century Liberal
(Westport, Connecticut: Greenwood Publishing Corporation,
1971), pp. 170-171; Richard E. Welch, Jr., George Frisbie
Hoar and the Half-Breed Republicans (Cambridge: Harvard
University Press, 1971), pp. 38-39; John G. Sproat, "The
Best Men": Liberal Reformers in the Gilded Age (New York:
Oxford University Press, 1968), pp. 74-75.

[90]Hoogenboom, p. 70.

CHAPTER VI

RELUCTANT REFORM
1869-1871

Climax of Reform Campaign

The outlook for the Jenckes bill improved considerably
with the opening of the special session of Congress in 1868.
C.A. Trowbridge, a friend of General Grant, predicated:
"It should be passed early in December -- I don't think
Johnson will veto it -- as his time is so near out."[1]
Thinking that the bill was "so nearly accomplished,"
James A. Dupee supported risking the "time and money"
to "start a weekly periodical" on civil service reform.[2]
Nathaniel Gale, encouraged by Senator James W. Patterson's
prediction that the bill would pass, wrote: "Others here
who had little hope a few months ago are quite sanguine
now of an early favorable result."[3] Julius Bing agreed:
"Public opinion seems to be fully alive to the Civil Service Bill."[4] "Your Civil Service Bill is now all the talk,"
wrote another correspondent.[5] Joseph Rosengarten added:
"I congratulate you on the strong public opinion that has
grown up in support of your Bill."[6]

The campaign gained considerable prestige and power
when it acquired the support of organized pressure groups.
The outgoing Secretary of the Treasury, Hugh McCulloch,

---

[1] C.A. Trowbridge to Jenckes, New York, 20 October 1868,
Jenckes Papers.

[2] James A. Dupee to Jenckes, Boston, 23 November 1868,
Jenckes Papers.

[3] Nathaniel Gale to Jenckes, Boston, 25 November 1868, Jenckes
Papers; James W. Patterson was a senator from New Hampshire.

[4] Julius Bing to Jenckes, Washington, 5 December 1868,
Jenckes Papers.

[5] I.M. Dalzell, Ohio, 19 December 1868, Jenckes Papers.

[6] Joseph Rosengarten to Jenckes, Philadelphia, 18 December
1868, Jenckes Papers.

equated the Jenckes bill with revenue reform and called for its passage.[7] The Union League Club of New York endorsed competitive examinations in government service.[8] The National Manufacturers' Association passed a resolution in support of the Jenckes bill in their Cleveland meeting and sponsored its support at the New England Manufacturers Convention and Washington meeting.[9]

The American Social Science Association, founded in 1865 to advance education and promote sound principles of economy, trade, and finance, adopted civil service reform as an issue in December 1868. Henry Villard, Recording Secretary, invited Thomas A. Jenckes "to explain his Civil Service Bill to the Boston membership."[10] The Representative from Rhode Island rose to the occasion and delivered an inspired speech before a distinguished audience on the practical aspects of his bill. He walked away with a signed petition from all those attending.[11] The Boston experience motivated Villard to sponsor a similar meeting in New York City. He issued an invitation to a select list of New York citizens for another Jenckes speech for January 16, 1869. This time Jenckes stressed the historical aspects of the civil service.[12]

Moving from the Jenckes speeches to a membership campaign designed to expand its influence in other parts of the country, Villard went to Washington to consult with members of the new Administration and sign up prominent government officials. President-elect Grant, Vice President-elect Schuyler Colfax, and Chief Justice Salmon P.

---

[7]Nation (New York), 10 December 1868, p. 469.

[8]John Jay to Jenckes, New York, 21 January 1869, Jenckes Papers.

[9]G.B. Stebbins to Jenckes, Detroit, 15 November 1868, Jenckes Papers.

[10]Henry Villard to Jenckes, Boston, 17 December 1868, Jenckes Papers.

[11]Alexander H. Rice to Jenckes, Boston, 27 December 1868, Jenckes Papers; New York Times, 3 January 1869, p. 1.

[12]Henry Villard to Jenckes, New York, 14 January 1869, Jenckes Papers; New York Times, 23 January 1869, p. 4.

Chase headed the list of new members. Pleased with the
rapid expansion Villard wrote Jenckes: "Our Association
is now rapidly extending its organization throughout the
country and we propose, with the aid of our branches, to
carry on a regular campaign for reform in the civil service between now and the next winter in the Eastern as
well as the Western States."[13]

Spoilsmen Counterattack

Early in January 1869 Congressman John Alexander Logan
opened the Stalwart attack on Jenckes' civil service bill.
The choice of Logan was particularly significant because
he switched sides. He was considered before his speech a
supporter of civil service reform and author of a narrow
civil service reform bill introduced a year earlier.[14]
Logan declared the Jenckes bill unconstitutional and undemocratic in the same sarcastic tone as most speeches opposing civil service reform. He charged that Congress
could not legislate economy and integrity. He speculated
that the Jenckes bill would obliterate "all that is republican in our Government." Logan asked the Members of Congress to imagine the situation if, during the Civil War,
office holders had tenure for life. Mr. Lincoln could not
have evicted known spies. Logan argued that another war
would happen sometime, and the country should not strap
its hands before the event.

Logan predicted that Jenckes' bill would give the
Vice President more power than the President because of
his control over appointments. He devoted most of his
attack to the charge that the Jenckes bill was aristocratic and monarchical and thus un-American. Jenckes'
bill would create a caste system, unresponsive to the people
and monopolize government jobs through education and nepotism. "This bill is the opening wedge to an aristocracy
in this country." "This is a new danger to the country,
and it comes not with the bold front of revolution but
with pleasing show of reform. . . . The disguise is thin,
and he who looks beneath may see the true lineaments of a
monster which will destroy us all."[15] George W. Woodward,

---

[13]Henry Villard to Jenckes, Boston, 5 February 1869,
Jenckes Papers.

[14]U.S. Congressional Globe, 40th Cong., 2nd Sess., 1868, pp.
366 and 806.

[15]Ibid., 3rd Sess., 1868, pp. 262-265.

a Democrat from Pennsylvania, carried the attack further.
Woodward applauded Logan's speech and echoed his charge
that the Jenckes bill was unconstitutional. He objected
to the expense of the bill and ridiculed the competitive
examination provision by asking: "Who has examined the
examiners, and tested their fitness for the work in hand?"
He questioned whether President Grant could pass the examination. The bill was designed for foreign governments
"founded on privileged classes and aristocratic ranks"
and was therefore anti-republican and anti-American. The
Jenckes bill, he charged, was biased toward college educated New Englanders and would "tax the many for the benefit of the few." Actually, according to Woodward, the
United States government needed no change: "We can afford
to leave well enough alone." We need, if we want to make
changes, to increase public morality by eliminating excise taxes, revenue tariffs and government subsidies.
Real savings can be initiated by paying increased salaries
to the remaining staff.[16]

Other than protest Woodward's innuendo that he spent
Congressional funds to purchase copies of an article in
the North American Review, Jenckes made no public comment
on Woodward's speech. He responded to Logan's unexpected
attack by denying his bill was "contrary to the spirit of
the Constitution and the wishes of the people." Life tenure does not grant a government employee immunity from removal, he declared, since he may be removed for cause.
The Commissioners can "prescribe by general rules what
'misconduct and inefficiency' shall be." Jenckes denied
that life tenure was anti-republican or anti-democratic.
"I say that the present mode of appointment is one which
we have derived from monarchies and foreign nations." The
Civil Service bill, contrary to Mr. Logan's statement,
had economical implications for it would reduce corruption.
We would no longer allow "money of the people to be squan-
dered upon incompetent or inefficient officers, or upon
favorites of this or that President or Heads of the Departments." "Under this bill the Vice President of the United
States has no patronage or appointment power whatever."
The Vice President would merely assist the other Commissioners
in prescribing the rules and regulations. There is nothing
impractical in the operation of the civil service system.
"The competent are selected, the incompetent and unqualified
are rejected. Is this impractical?" Representative Jenckes

---

[16]U.S. Congressional Globe, 40th Cong., 3rd Sess., 1869,
pp. 747-751.

ended with a rousing call to action. "The foundations
of our institutions are to be sapped and weakened, the
structure is to be made to crumble and fall, being the
insidious effects of those who take away from the Government its life-blood, the money, the taxes by which it is
supported and carried on. Let us have this measure."[17]

Friends of reform responded to the Logan and Woodward attacks with their usual energy. Rosengarten wrote
an article in the Philadelphia Morning Post on Logan's
speech appropriately titled, "Save Me From My Friends."[18]
Henry Medley, editor of the Round Table wrote an article
attacking Logan's speech.[19] It was not enough. Within
a few days of Woodward's speech, reformers in New York,
Boston, and Providence advised Jenckes to give up the
battle for the special session and concentrate on the next
Congress. One wrote: "I hope you will meet with success
but see by the papers that there is to be a good deal of
opposition."[20] Villard reflected the reformer's plight
when he wrote: "It is my firm consideration, that it
will be wiser not to push the bill to an issue during the
present session of Congress, but to deter the final decision upon it until the next one. . . . The best course
for you appears to me to be to make as strong an argument
as possible for it before the adjournment and then let
the measure rest until it can be revised in the next Congress."[21] The special session closed without further
action on civil service reform.

---

[17]U.S. Congressional Globe, 40th Cong., 3rd Sess., 1869,
pp. 266-269.

[18]J.G. Rosengarten to Jenckes, Philadelphia, 13 January 1869,
Jenckes Papers.

[19]Henry Medley to Jenckes, New York, 13 January 1869,
Jenckes Papers.

[20]Charles Adams to Jenckes, Providence, 10 February 1869,
Jenckes Papers.

[21]Henry Villard to Jenckes, Boston, 2 February 1869,
Jenckes Papers.

In the meantime, against the opposition of many prominent reformers, Congress amended the Tenure of Office Act of 1867. The House desired to grant the President complete relief from the restrictions in the 1867 version, but the Senate refused to relinquish all it had gained. A compromise relieved the President from restrictions on suspensions from office, but required that he nominate a new candidate within thirty days for Senate advice and consent.[22]

Jenckes' Bill Changes Again

Now that President Johnson vacated the White House, Jenckes revised his bill accordingly. He withdrew the provisions calling for the creation of a department level commission headed by the Vice President and reverted back to the original concept of a presidential commission. This eliminated a number of constitutional objections which the other proposal generated. He specifically granted the commission power to administer oaths and hold hearings under conditions it prescribed. Jenckes granted the President power to remove civil servants from office but gave employees legal recourse to this action. He cleared up one administrative problem by declaring that a department which eliminates an office may also discharge its incumbent. Departments retained the right to assign employees to any place in the United States as long as the Treasury paid their travel expenses. Jenckes introduced a period of probation for new employees and eliminated the provision allowing for temporary commissioners pending confirmation by the Senate.

Early in the new session of Congress, Jenckes spoke to the House in defense of his revised bill. Thomas Jenckes encouraged others to propose a better measure. He stressed, as he had in his earlier version, that the appointing power was an executive function, and that the legislators should refrain from interfering.

> . . . it was an unfortunate hour for the Republic when the representatives of the people abdicated their high functions and consented to become the recipients and dispensers of what is called "executive patronage." . . . It has paralyzed the executive in the administration of the Government and destroyed its independence.

---

[22] 16 Stat. 6 (April 5, 1869).

His bill "would restore the executive to its original independence, and remit the Legislative to its appropriate sphere."

In the rest of the speech, Jenckes defended his bill against the charges of Woodward and Logan. His bill would help reduce the national debt by giving the government honest officials and thereby saving the money siphoned off by corruption. He reminded Woodward that he conveniently ignored the fee provision which would offset the cost of salaries and expenses of the Commission. This bill, Jenckes assured his listeners, would not create an aristocracy. That charge is "a mirage of an over-heated intellect." The aristocratic element in our system is the patronage which bestows its gifts upon favorites."[23]

Jenckes' speech captured favorable press report.[24] Julius Bing thought it contained convincing arguments and triumphant refutation of the speeches of Woodward and Logan. He suggested a revision of the 1868 report to include current excerpts from the press.[25] Henry Villard went to Philadelphia to assess the chances of support for his fall campaign on civil service reform and found reformers in that city actively campaigning for civil service reform. He reported success in getting George William Curtis to deliver a public paper on civil service reform and tried to get Jenckes to set the date for his Philadelphia speech.[26]

New Leaders Join the Campaign

1869 saw the commitment of two major political leaders to the principles of civil service reform. George William Curtis and Carl Schurz joined the battle and soon assumed a leadership role in the civil service reform campaign.

George William Curtis

George William Curtis was born in 1824 at Providence, Rhode Island, of an English Puritan family. Largely self-educated, Curtis lived two years at Brook Farm before be-

---

[23] U.S. Congressional Globe, 41st Cong., 1st Sess., 1869, pp. 517-523.

[24] Harper's Weekly (New York), 8 May 1869, p. 291.

[25] Julius Bing to Jenckes, Washington, 8 April 1869, Jenckes Papers.

[26] Henry Villard to Jenckes, Boston, 19 July 1869, Jenckes Papers.

coming a disciple of Ralph Waldo Emerson which took him to
New York and Concord, Massachusetts, for two years. He
traveled to Europe, Egypt, and Palestine until 1850 when
he returned to New York to become a journalist on the
staff of the New York Tribune. He became a popular author,
literary scholar and political editor, joining Harper's
Weekly in 1863. Curtis took an avid interest in politics,
worked actively in Republican party affairs, giving Lincoln
his valuable support in the Convention of 1860. He cru-
saded for an end to slavery, opposed the Tweed Ring in
New York City, and advocated women's suffrage.[27]

Curtis devoted the summer of 1869 to preparing his
fall speech. He studied documents supplied by Villard,
which included Jenckes' speeches, reports, and bills. He
added to these documents with his own sources and became
thoroughly versed on the subject.[28] In October 1869 Curtis delivered a well attended speech to the New York meeting of the Social Science Association. The editor began
by defining the civil service as "all of the public service that is not military." He attacked the spoils system as "the most wasteful, the most awkward, the most de-
structive, possible. It fosters personal and official
corruption, it paralyzes legislative honor and vigilance,
it poisons the spring of moral action, and so, vitiating
the very character of the people, it endangers the permanence of the nation." Curtis put more emphasis on the
relationship between Civil Service reform and business
than Jenckes. He argued that civil service reform is
nothing more than good business practices: ". . . there
is no reason. . . that the United States should not manage
its affairs with the same economic ability, and honesty
that the best private business managed." The principles
of the Jenckes bill, Curtis argued, had been thoroughly
tested in other countries. He acknowledged that examinations tested only knowledge and not ability or morality.
The probation provision, he noted, provided an opportunity
to test ability. The existing system failed to test either
knowledge, ability, or morality. Curtis ridiculed the argument that civil service reform creates an aristocracy,
and contended that we should borrow ideas from any country
which will improve the United States government.[29]

---

[27]Charles Eliot Norton, ed., Orations and Addresses by George
William Curtis (New York: Harper & Br., 1894); Gordon Milne,
George William Curtis & The Genteel Tradition (Bloomington,
Ind.: Indiana University Press, 1956).

[28]Henry Villard to Jenckes, Boston, 19 July and 21 July
1869, Jenckes Papers.

[29]Norton, 2:1-30.

Henry Adams

Henry Adams added his voice to the growing supporters
of civil service reform in an article published in the
October 1869 edition of the North American Review. Adams
charged that the Grant Administration employed the rotation
system to extremes. The President disappointed many supporters because reformers neglected to defend him from
office seekers. According to Adams, Congress should stay
out of the appointment business and by this he included
Jenckes. The Jenckes bill imposed Congressional dictation
on the executive. He advocated that the executive initiate
civil service reform through an executive order, as accomplished in Great Britain. Congress should encourage this
by passing a resolution recommending the President initiate
competitive examinations in the entire government.[30]

Carl Schurz

Carl Schurz, Senator from Missouri, publicly embraced
civil service reform. Born in Cologne Germany, in 1829,
Schurz entered politics as a revolutionary in the Prussian
Revolution in 1848. He was wounded and narrowly escaped
only to return from exile to engineer the escape of his
friend Gottfried Kinkel from prison. Moving from France
to England he came to the United States and settled in
Wisconsin, where he became a prominent representative of
the German-American citizen. He embraced the anti-slavery
causes which carried him to influence in the Republican
party.

Even in the beginning, Schurz's career was characterized by his eloquent speeches. One observer described his
introduction to a convention as initially "painful." "I
think nearly every delegate in that convention felt as I
did that we had made a terrible blunder in nominating him.
. . ."

. . . our suspense was happily relieved by
one of the finest impromptu addresses I ever
heard, which convinced all of us that we had
made no mistake, but that the ablest man in
the hall was Carl Schurz.[31]

---

[30]Henry Brooks Adams, "Civil Service Reform," North American
Review 109 (October 1869); 443-470.

[31]"Glimpses of Early-Day Politics," Milwaukee Sentinel,
1 April 1900, Schurz Papers, Library of Congress.

Schurz carried out a spirited campaign for Abraham Lincoln in 1860 who rewarded him with the post of Minister to Spain and later appointed him brigadier general in the field. He served in the Union Army at Manassas, Chancellorsville, and Gettysburg. After the war Schurz toured the South for President Johnson and recommended Negro suffrage in his report as a condition for reconstruction. He settled in St. Louis, Missouri, in 1867 as editor of the St. Louis Westliche Post until his election to the Senate in 1869.[32]

Two motives seem to have converged to bring Carl Schurz into the civil service reform camp. First, he wanted to be a "brilliant" Senator and spent some time searching for a cause to "make his mark." He wrote his wife after one week on the job: "I bring too much reputation to the Senate to allow myself to remain at the customary level. I must be a brilliant Senator or people will say I disgraced myself."[33] Like most Members of Congress, Senator Schurz devoted much of his time in the new session trying to secure spoils appointments for his political supporters. By the end of April, however, he was discouraged with Grant, frustrated by his lack of influence, and seriously questioning the spoils system as a means of selecting competent government officials. Schurz visited President Grant about the St. Louis Post Office appointment only to have the President reproach him with: "Why, Mr. Schurz, I know Missouri a great deal better than you do."[34] He told a friend: "The utter absurdity of our system of appointment to office has this time so glaringly demonstrated itself that even the dullest patriots begin to open their eyes to the necessity of a reform."[35]

[32] Claude Moore Fuess, Carl Schurz, Reformer (1829-1906) (New York: Dodd, Mead & Co., 1932); Carman & Luthin, pp. 82-84; Carl Schurz, The Autobiography of Carl Schurz (New York: Charles Scribner's Sons, 1961); Chester Verne Easum, The Americanization of Carl Schurz (Chicago: University of Chicago, 1929).

[33] Carl Schurz to Margaretha Schurz, New York, 24 February 1869. Translated by the author, Arthur B. Hogue, "Civil Service Reform, 1869," The American-German Review (June 1952), p. 6.

[34] Carl Schurz to Margaretha Schurz, Washington, 20 March 1869, Joseph Schafer, ed., Intimate Letters of Carl Schurz, 1841-1869 (Madison: State Historical Society of Wisconsin, 1928), pp. 475-476.

[35] Carl Schurz to James Taussig, Washington, 18 April 1869, Frederic Bancroft, ed., Speeches, Correspondence, and Papers of Carl Schurz, 6 vols. (New York: G.P. Putnam, 1913), I:482-483.

On March 29, 1869, Schurz won a seat on the Committee
on Retrenchment and became a member of the Sub-Committee
on Civil Service with Jenckes and Senator Patterson. Julius
Bing sent him a copy of Jenckes' April 5 speech and reported
"that he proposed to make the Civil Service Reform the
special object of his legislative attention and requests me
to make him suggestions." He had already assessed the
chances for Jenckes' bill in 1869 and proposed a means of
helping it. "It is certain. . . that civil service reform
measures have little if any chance of success in Congress,
unless we manage to produce a pressure." He predicted that
there was a good chance for a successful campaign in the
winter.

In April, Schurz reported to his wife that he had de-
cided to make civil service reform his big task as a Senator.
He saw himself uniquely qualified to lead the civil service
reform campaign in the Senate. "This is a great field and
I am determined to be the leader of the reform in the Senate.
This problem required the kind of talent which I have. . . .
I have about 8 months left to prepare myself. . ." He
blamed the prevailing system for the worst mistakes of the
Grant Administration. By the end of May Schurz completed
plans for drafting a civil service reform bill and the
outline of a speech in support of it.[36]

Senator Schurz introduced his bill to the Senate on
December 20, 1869. Twice as long as Jenckes' proposal,
Schurz incorporated a number of paragraphs directly from
the House bill. He created a board of examiners, provided
for appointment by examination, and gave the board judicial
powers and responsibility for making rules applicable to
the entire government service, similar to those granted in
the Jenckes bills. Schurz excluded fewer civil servants
than Jenckes, exempting only foreign service, Cabinet, and
certain court positions. His board of examiners included
nine Commissioners to serve for twelve years.

Carl Schurz's bill, however, was much weaker than
Thomas Jenckes'. He accepted the system of rotation by em-
powering the executive to request another examination when

------

[37]Julius Bing to Jenckes, Washington, 8 April 1869, Jenckes
Papers; Carl Schurz to Preetorius, Washington, 29 March
1869; Carl Schurz to Margaretha Meyer Schurz, 12 April,
18 April and 30 May 1869, Washington and St. Louis, Hogue,
pp. 5-7 and 39-40.

it was dissatisfied with the eligible candidates listed on the original examination register. He authorized un-limited removals in the first year and permitted depart-ments to make appointments of individuals who did not take an examination, subject to an investigation "concerning the candidates', 'character, antecedents, social standing, and general ability.'" He established classification of employees by their tenure of office, ranging from four to twelve years duration.

The New York Times published a favorable article on the Schurz bill, and George William Curtis supported it. The Senate, however, twice refused to debate the bill even though it accepted a modified version of the rotation system. Schurz never got an opportunity to deliver his speech in support of the bill.[38]

Jenckes' Last Speech

On the last day of February 1870, Mr. Jenckes re-introduced his civil service bill. The Committee made some minor changes in the 1869 version before reporting it out in May. The new Commission consisted of three commissioners appointed for a term of five years. It included a new section authorizing the Commission to inspect and reexamine all government employees.[39]

A major debate of Jenckes' Civil Service Bill began on May 3, 1870. The speeches generated few new ideas on either side of the aisle but contained a compendium of arguments on civil service reform. Opponents attacked the basic assumptions underlying civil service reform, arguing that the present system functioned well and reformers over-rated its defects. After all, the present system uncovered frauds in the New York Customhouse. The existing system allowed supervisors to select the best man and permitted managers to release incompetent people after they proved a

---

[38]New York Times, 14 January 1870, p. 4; U.S. Congressional Globe, 41st Cong., 2nd Sess., pp. 2953 and 4309; George William Curtis to C.E. Norton, Staten Island, 3 May 1870, Curtis Papers, Harvard University; D.F. Murphy to Jenckes, no date and place, Jenckes Papers.

[39]U.S. Congressional Globe, 41st Cong., 2nd Sess., 1870, pp. 3182-84.

failure. Defects described by advocates of the Jenckes
bill resulted from human behavior, and no system could
alter human behavior.

Stalwarts unleashed a torrent of abuse against the
bill's Board of Commissioners. They charged that the bill
was unconstitutional because it gave appointment power to
the Board. Civil Service Reform was undemocratic for it
took power from the people and gave it to the Commissioners.
It gave the Commission control of patronage by taking the
power from the Heads of Departments to run their department.
The Jenckes bill did nothing more than move the spoils
from elected politicians to appointed Commissioners. Opponents asked: "Who will examine the Commission?" Mr.
Jenckes replied that the Commissioners had no appointment
power and no control of departments. His bill did not
affect the rights of Department Heads but only restricted
hiring of incompetents. The Army and Navy, according to
Jenckes, already used the examination system without restricting the power of the War Department. Civil Service
Reform would produce a more democratic system than the
existing spoils system because it would open appointments
to all citizens.

Opponents charged that the machinery was impractical.
One Congressman estimated that government employees and
candidates for civil service jobs would require twelve or
thirteen years to examine. Besides, the Jenckes bill would
not solve all the problems associated with government service. Congress could not cure all evils. Other means
would be found to get the right men in and the wrong men
out. Jenckes called the time estimate ridiculous since the
commission would examine only those who applied. He
challenged his colleagues to "try it."

Spoilsmen further charged that restriction on unlimited
removals would diminish the power of supervisors. It would
prevent the President from removing undesirable employees.
Imagine what problems this law would have imposed on Lincoln
if he had been unable to relieve subversives from office
in 1861. Jenckes' bill would insure placing Democrats and
Rebels in office, and the Administration needed to have
friendly people at all levels to do its business. Congressman Jenckes pointed out that the turnover rate was so great
that an employee did not have time to learn his job. Rebels
could not take the oath of office. Since the bill did not
cover high offices, there would be no Democrats in policy
positions. The President, Jenckes contended, had sufficient
power to remove incompetent civil servants.

The bill was expensive, according to Jenckes' antagon-
ists, for it increased the number of government employees and
therefore added to the amount of salary required. Not so,
refuted Jenckes, since the Commission would replace nearly
thirty government employees than working in department personnel offices. It also would not add operating expenses
because the bill contained a provision to collect a fee for
the cost of examining. Besides, Jenckes argued, the revenue
flowing into the Treasury would increase by almost $50 million
when collecting taxes siphoned off by fraud and incompetence.

Appealing to anti-intellectual sentiments, adversaries
charged that the civil service system would fill the departments with incompetent intellectuals and reject those
skilled in practical business life. Examinations measured
a man's intellect but not his morals or loyalty. The problem was not lack of skills anyway but lack of honesty.
The Representative from Rhode Island refuted these arguments
by reminding his opponents that his bill included tests for
integrity and loyalty through probation and personnel investigations. Dishonesty and negligence did not constitute
the biggest problem, Jenckes declared. That honor went to
incompetent employees and their lack of loyalty to the
government. The spoils system attracted incompetents;
the civil service reform program eliminated them.

Spoilsmen charged that the Jenckes bill discriminated
against veterans. They predicted that the bill would result in firing disabled veterans and widows. Jenckes declared that every American could compete for government
jobs under the bill, and it discriminated against no one.

Jenckes told the House that his bill brought "good
business practice" to the federal government. His opponents responded that businessmen did not hire people by
examinations. They further charged that the system humili-
ated government employees, but Mr. Jenckes pointed out
that he had strong support from civil service employees.

Jenckes charged patronage advocates with attacking
the details and not the principles of his bill. He said
that they offered no alternative proposals even though
several Congressmen advocated Henry Adams' suggestion that
Congressional referrals be declared illegal. Jenckes
ignored this alternative.

The debate, begun by Jenckes with high hopes, soon
turned against him. Congressman Horace Maynard of Tennessee
skillfully directed the opposition, virtually isolating the
Congressman from Rhode Island as the sole supporter of his

184

bill. Adversaries flooded the Chair with amendments designed to weaken the bill and negate its impact. Congressmen proposed amendments to apportion government jobs
among the states, eliminate the fee provision, legalize
sex discrimination, and promote unlimited removals. To
keep it from total destruction, Jenckes decided to recommit his bill to committee.[40]

Political Events of 1870

President Grant came more and more under the influence
of conservative spoilsmen like Roscoe Conkling of New York
and Benjamin Butler of Massachusetts. He narrowed the party
base of the Administration by disposing of its more liberal
elements. Judge Ebenezer Rockwood Hoar, Grant's Attorney
General, attracted the wrath of Ben Butler and Roscoe Conkling who engineered a Senate rejection of his appointment
to the Supreme Court. Hoar's opposition to the annexation
of Santo Domingo and Southern demands for a Cabinet post
prompted Grant to ask for his resignation. Charles Sumner,
Chairman of the Senate Foreign Relations Committee, came
out against the Santo Domingo project. Grant began an
attack on Sumner, which eventually resulted in his being
ousted as chairman, by dismissing his friend John Lothrop
Motley as Minister to England. David A. Wells, a leading
advocate of revenue reform, left the Administration when
Grant refused to reappoint him to the Revenue Commission.[41]

---

[40]U.S. Congressional Globe, 41st Cong., 2nd Sess., 1870,
pp. 3182-4, 3222-25, and 3258-61.

[41]Donald, Charles Sumner and the Rights of Man, pp. 516-17;
Sproat, p. 75; Logsdon, pp. 180-186; Welch, pp. 38-43; Milne,
p. 146; John M. Dobson, Politics in the Gilded Age: A New
Perspective on Reform (New York: Praeger, 1972), p. 40; David
M. Jordan, Roscoe Conkling of New York: Voice in the Senate
(Ithaca: Cornell University Press, 1971), pp. 67-68; E.L.
Godkin to Charles Eliot Norton, 15 April 1869, William M. Arm-
strong, ed., The Gilded Age Letters of E.L. Godkin (Albany:
State University of New York Press, 1974), pp. 135-136; E.L.
Godkin to Carl Schurz, New York, 5 April 1871, Schurz Papers;
David J. Rothman, Politics and Power: The United States Sen-
ate; 1869-1901 (Cambridge: Harvard University Press, 1966),
pp. 21-24; Rothman concludes that Sumner's ouster was not the
result of his opposition to the annexation of Santo Domingo
but was caused by his refusal to communicate with the President and Secretary of State about the issue.

Secretary of the Interior General Jacob Dobson Cox,
supported by reformers, fell out of favor with the President. Cox's actions attracted the wrath of the spoilsmen.
He initiated tough civil service examinations for the
Patent Office, Census Bureau, and Indian Bureau. Under
Cox's pass-fail system, fifty per cent of the candidates[42]
referred to him by politicians failed the examination.
Cox alienated Grant and his spoils advocates most by his
action over the issue of political assessments and his
opposition to the Santo Domingo venture. Assessments
obtained from civil servants provided political parties
with one of the most secure sources of funds. Secretary
Cox published a letter attacking the practice and issued
a departmental order forbidding employees from taking a
"paid vacation" to go home to work for and vote in the
November election. That was too much for the spoilsmen.
Senator Zachariah Chandler of Michigan went to the Interior Department and announced to employees that President Grant planned to remove Secretary Cox. At the White
House President Grant prepared to issue an executive
order to reverse Cox's policy and thus to force the[43]
Interior Secretary to submit his resignation.

Cox's attack on political assessments, a practice
heretofore ignored, attracted the attention of the civil
service reform advocates such as Schurz, Godkin, and Curtis. Hereafter, opposition to political assessments became an integral part of the civil service reform program.

Reformers, frozen out of the Administration by President Grant and his Stalwart advisors, prepared to form a
separate Liberal group. Carl Schurz began the movement in
Missouri when he led a revolt at the State Republican Convention. Liberal Republicans bolted the party and nominated Benjamin Gratz Brown for governor. He captured the
state house in the election.

---

[42]U.S. Department of Interior, 1870 Report of the Secretary
of Interior, p. xiv; Jacob D. Cox, "The Civil Service Reform,"
North American Review 62 (1871): 101-4.

[43]Logsdon, p. 182; Geoffrey Blodgett, "Reform Thought and the
Genteel Tradition," Wayne Morgan, ed., The Gilded Age, 2nd ed.
(Syracuse: Syracuse University Press, 1970), 64-68; E.L.
Godkin to George P. Marsh, New York, 6 October 1870; E.L.
Godkin to his wife, New York, 1 December 1870; E.L. Godkin
to Jacob Dawson Cox, New York, 3 December 1870, Armstrong,
pp. 157-8, 160-66, 167; Hoogenboom, pp. 78-80.

Liberal Republicans, in conjunction with the Free Trade League, organized a convention in New York in the fall of 1870. The Liberals favored a platform embracing civil service reform, revenue reform, and civilian control over the military. They failed to create a new party, primarily due to the efforts of James G. Blaine, Republican Speaker of the House. Blaine counseled caution on the part of the liberals and promised reformers certain important Congressional seats and other political positions. Blaine's efforts helped prevent a party break.[44]

The election of 1870 resulted in a stinging defeat for the Administration. Republicans lost their two-thirds majority in the Congress, and polled less votes in the key states of New York and Indiana than the Democrats.

Although generally pleased by the election results, reformers suffered a major setback in Rhode Island. Discontent with the way Jenckes dispensed his patronage and genuinely frightened by the growing civil service reform movement, Senators Henry B. Anthony and William Sprague joined forces with Governor Stevens to defeat Congressman Thomas A. Jenckes with some highly questionable election tactics.[45]

Grant's Endorsement

It became obvious to most political observers that the Grant Administration was rapidly losing support. The combined controversy over Grant's appointments and dismissals, Cox's resignation, the Missouri revolt, the political assessments controversy, the Liberal convention, and most of all the election defeats necessitated a change in policy.

---

[44]Logsdon, pp. 183-184; Sproat, pp. 78-79; Hoogenboom, p. 84.

[45]Charles Adams to Jenckes, Providence, 21 February 1870; Ezra D. Fogg to Jenckes, Providence, 24 February 1870; A. Payne to Henry B. Anthony, Providence, 25 February 1870; George Manchester to Jenckes, South Portsmouth, 25 April 1870; Ezra D. Fogg to Jenckes, Providence, 19 April 1870; Charles Adams to Jenckes, Providence, 23 May 1870; J.W. Marshall to Jenckes, Washington, 21 June 1870; J.H. Coggeshall to Jenckes, Providence, 30 June 1870; William W. Douglas to Jenckes, Providence, 10 December 1870; Ulysses Mecur to Jenckes, Towanda, Pennsylvania, 26 December 1870, Jenckes Papers.

President Grant changed policy in his second annual message to Congress delivered on December 5, 1870.

> Always favoring practical reforms, I re-
> spectfully call your attention to one abuse
> of long standing, which I would like to see
> remedied by this Congress. It is a reform
> in the civil service of the country. I would
> have to go beyond the mere fixing of the ten-
> ure of office of clerks and employees who do
> not require "the advice and consent of the
> Senate" to make their appointments complete.
> I would have it govern, not the tenure, but
> the manner of making all appointments. There
> is no duty which so much embarrasses the Ex-
> ecutive and heads of Departments, nor is there
> any such arduous and thankless labor imposed
> upon Senators and Representatives, as that of
> finding places for constituents. The present
> system does not secure the best men, and often
> not even fit men, for public place. The ele-
> vation and purification of the Government civil
> service will be hailed with approval by the
> whole people of the United States.[46]

Lame-duck Congressman Thomas A. Jenckes introduced the last version of his civil service bill in January 1871. He broadened its scope to include all civil servants ex- cept legislative and judicial officials, Cabinet members, and Ministers abroad. A commissioner and two assistant commissioners composed his Civil Service Commission. Jenckes introduced a shortened bill, consisting of only nine sections. He eliminated references to promotion regu- lations and removals as well as those paragraphs pertaining to the judicial responsibility of the Commission. Emulating the Order-in-Council of 1870 in England, Jenckes added a section authorizing the Commission to write rules governing the hiring of professional applicants without requiring an examination.[47]

---

[46]Richardson, 7:109.

[47]U.S. Congress, House, A Bill to Regulate the Manner of Making Appointments in the Civil Service of the United States, H.R. 2633, 41st Cong., 3rd Sess., 1871.

188

President Grant endorsed the Jenckes bill, but none of his Congressional colleagues gave it support, and the Congress ignored it. Schurz's bill received the same treatment, as did the civil service bill of Senator Henry Wilson of Massachusetts. Wilson's bill eliminated the Civil Service Commission by placing examination responsibility with the department heads. Overall, Wilson drafted an excellent bill which was particularly noteworthy as the first bill to forbid political activity by civil servants and prohibit political assessments on government employees.[48]

The Senate turned its attention to the civil service bill of Senator Lyman Trumbull, Republican from Illinois. Originally introduced in December 1869, Senator Trumbull's bill made it illegal for Congressmen to advise the President on appointments. Trumbull's original version permitted Congressional recommendations in writing, but the committee eliminated this provision. Trumbull's intent was "that it is improper for the persons charged with the legislative department of the Government to be mixed up with this matter of appointments."[49] Senator John Sherman of Ohio supported Trumbull while Oliver P. Morton of Indiana strongly opposed the bill. The Senate failed to pass Trumbull's bill.[50]

It became obvious that a lack of consensus on the form of civil service reform hampered reformers in the Congress. In the closing days of the special session they managed to get White House approval of a statement authorizing the President to appoint a board to create rules for appointing candidates. The resolution, authored by Representative William H. Armstrong of Pennsylvania, stated:

> That the President of the United States be, and he is hereby authorized to prescribe such rules and regulations for the admission of persons into the civil service of the United States as will best promote the efficiency thereof, and ascertain the fitness of each candidate in respect to age, health, character,

---

[48] U.S. Congress, Senate, S. 1228, 41st Cong., 3rd Sess., 1871; New York Times, "Civil Service Reform," 23 January 1871, p. 4.

[49] U.S. Congressional Globe, 41st Cong., 2nd Sess., 1870, p. 1078.

[50] U.S. Congressional Globe, 41st Cong., 3rd Sess., 1871, pp. 292-294.

knowledge, and ability for the branch of
service into which he seeks to enter; and
for this purpose the President is authorized
to employ suitable persons to conduct such
inquiries, to prescribe their duties, and
to establish regulations for the conduct of
persons who may receive appointment in the
civil service.[51]

On January 30, 1871, William Armstrong introduced the
joint resolution in the House. Senator Trumbull introduced
the same resolution in the Senate as a rider to the civil
appropriation bill stating: "I hope there will be no objection to it." But there was! By a one vote margin (25
to 26) a motion to table the amendment lost. The Senate
then attached the amendment to the civil appropriations
bill by a vote of 32 to 24. It was the last bill of the
special session which passed the Senate on the night of
March 3, 1871.[52]

In the House, which had been waiting for the bill before adjourning, Massachusetts Congressman Henry L. Dawes,
floor leader for the bill, endorsed the entire Senate version to avoid creation of a conference committee. James
A. Garfield of Ohio and Representative Armstrong strongly
supported the rider while John A. "Black Jack" Logan,
long time opponent of the Jenckes bills, attacked it
furiously as a deceptive parliamentary ruse. The appropriations bill with the civil service amendment passed the House
by a vote of 90 to 20, thus putting Congress on record as
supporting civil service reform.[53]

---

[51]U.S. Congressional Globe, 41st Cong., 3rd Sess., 1871, p. 1997.

[52]Ibid., pp. 1935-97.

[53]Ibid., pp. 1935-6; Mark M. Krug, Lyman Trumbull: Conservative
Radical (New York: A.S. Barnes, 1965), pp. 292-294; Carl Schurz's
maiden speech on civil service reform came on January 27, 1871.
He reintroduced the bill as a substitute for Trumbull's proposal
making legislative referrals illegal. Schurz delivered a long
speech attacking the spoils system with graphic examples from his
own experience and from testimony taken by the Joint Committee on
Retrenchment. He dismissed the argument that civil service reform
will create an aristocracy as "ludicrous." The anti-Republican
charge, according to Schurz, has no validity since Republican
government does not depend on spoils. "I predict," Schurz warned
the Senate, "the time is not far [off] when a political party
can disregard it with impunity."

CHAPTER ·VII

BRITISH INFLUENCE
DURING THE JENCKES ERA
1864 to 1871

To understand the extent of the British influence on
the civil service reform movement it is necessary to re-
vert back to 1864. This separate treatment will make both
the course of events and special aspects of the subject
clear.

Charles Sumner independently developed his civil service bill, introduced in the Senate on April 30, 1864. As
far as we know, he consulted with no one about its content.[1]
His position as Chairman of the Senate Foreign Relations
Committee and provisions of the bill suggest that he closely
followed the examples of the civil service system in Great
Britain. He followed the British system in recommending
establishment of a Civil Service Commission consisting of
three commissioners to act as a board of examiners. He included the British requirement that all candidates must obtain a certificate from the board and take a general competitive examination. Sumner followed the British example
in stipulating that the board develop examination rules in
conjunction with the Chief Executive and department heads.
He followed the British precedent in requiring the Commission
to establish a register of candidates according to merit and
fitness. Reflecting the American political conditions, he
departed from the British example in his final two provisions
pertaining to removals and promotions.[2]

The English system influenced David A. Wells, Chairman
of President Johnson's Revenue Commission. Wells' Revenue
Commission report, published in January 1866, recommended a
reorganization of the entire revenue system on the British
model. The report proposed establishing an independent
Board of Custom Commissioners with responsibility for testing candidates and making appointments.[3] The Nation picked

---

[1] Pierce, 4:190-191.

[2] See Chapter V.

[3] U.S. Revenue Commission, Revenue System of the United States,
House Executive Documents, 30th Cong., 1st Sess., 1866,
VII, No. 34, pp. 44-51.

up this recommendation and enthusiastically urged its
adoption, but the rest of the press failed to mention it.[4]

On Sunday, January 17, 1866, the New York Times published a provocative article on the U.S. civil service.
Apparently unaware of Jenckes' recently introduced bill,
the author compared the American system to the British system. The article, entitled "Want of Efficiency in the American Civil Service," asked its readers to "compare the pre-
cision, accuracy, and promptness of a foreign Custom-house,
for instance, with the slowness, slovenliness, and confusion
of an American." It used the "perfect machinery of the
British system" to show that the Americans "are at least
a generation behind England." We are so far behind because
"we do not train men for offices, and do not leave them
in when they are trained."

In England politics is "not considered in the appointments. . . . Each official is educated for his place and
rises alone by merit." The paper described the English system and contrasted it to the American, using examples in
the customhouses, post offices, and foreign office. The
author contended that the British attracted able men and
"the public reap the benefit." Every American "suffers
from the friction and slowness of our civil machinery."

The article concluded with the question: "All of us
see the evils of our present system. When shall we begin
to initiate remedies?"[5]

Jenckes and the British Precedent

Thomas Allan Jenckes, Representative from Rhode Island,
proposed an answer. The Jenckes Papers contain a copy of
the New York Times article, but he had already come to a
similar conclusion and introduced a civil service reform
bill. Jenckes undoubtedly knew a considerable amount about
civil service reform developments in Great Britain because
he received British newspapers regularly from his friend
Hugh Burgess.[6] Jenckes stated in 1867 that he turned to
England after his early experience with the spoils system
in Congress.

---

[4]Nation (New York), "The Way the Government is Served,"
15 February 1866, p. 198.

[5]New York Times, 7 January 1866, pp. 6-7.

[6]Hugh Burgess to Jenckes, Royers Ford, 30 September 1864,
Jenckes Papers.

When I first entered the public service of
this Government during the war, I could not
but be struck at once at the great difference between the military and naval administrations and that of the civil departments.
It led me to inquire into the course of this
great difference, and to see whether such
difference existed in the systems of other
nations. I found that in England, during
the Crimean War, what indeed I had in part
known previously, great complaint existed
against the civil service from its almost
total inefficiency, arising and admitted and
proclaimed, from the vicious mode of appointments to office in that service.

I learned that the evil in England had almost been entirely cured, and I looked into
her history to find the reason of the change.
I found it, sir, in the adoption of a wise
and practical system regulating the appointments in the different departments of the
civil service.[7]

We know that Jenckes entered into correspondence with
prominent English officials, but that correspondence is no
longer available. Perhaps he began his correspondence
through the efforts of the London agent of The American
Wood Paper Company, where Jenckes had a major business
interest. At any rate, his bill showed he possessed a
thorough knowledge of the British system, as he adopted
many of its most important features.[8]

Admission to the civil service through examinations,
open to all citizens, administered by a three man Civil
Service Commission with power to establish rules and regulations followed British precedent. Open competitive examinations, advocated by Macaulay, but not yet part of
the British system, indicated that Thomas Jenckes may have
been in touch with advanced British thought on administrative theory.[9]

---

[7]U.S. Congressional Globe, 39th Cong., 2nd Sess., 1867, p. 1034.

[8]Hugh Burgess to Jenckes, Royers Ford, 30 September 1864, Jenckes
Papers; Burgess worked as a scientist for the Royersford Pennsylvania plant of the American Wood Paper Company. Hoogenboom, pp. 16-17.

[9]U.S. Congress, House, H.R. 60.

On January 29, 1867, Representative Jenckes gave his
first important speech in support of civil service reform.
In this speech, summarized in some detail in Chapter V,
the Congressman supported many points with numerous references to Great Britain. He pointed out that in England
the "evils resulting" from the spoils system were prevented
by "regulating the appointments" in such a way as to give
an appointment to the person proving himself "better qualified on a test examination."

An appointment system consisting of a central board of
examiners empowered to issue examination certificates to
successful candidates "has worked with great success" in
Prussia, France, and England. "In England the system. . .
has given new life to the home service, and its full application to the colonial service is the vital element in its
administration." English job seekers, Jenckes told the
House, do not view the examination requirement as a "hard-
ship, but the opportunity has been accepted as a favor by
the aspirants for the service. In the colonial department
the door is swung open to all."

"What is practicable in and for Great Britain and
its vast colonial possessions is practicable for the United
States." Jenckes argued that his bill contained improvements on the one operating in Great Britain in that English
applicants had to travel to London to sit for an examination
while his bill authorized commissioners to "go to Maine
or Oregon."

Jenckes adopted Jowett's argument that the examination
system would prove a great benefit to education. It would
"raise the standard of excellence in all the schools and
colleges in the country."

> The certificate of the commissioners will
> have the same advantage over the diploma
> of a college as the bill of a national bank
> has over that of a State institution; it
> will have currency throughout the country
> by virtue of the national indorsement. Edu-
> cation is thus stimulated and nationalized;
> the result will be felt in every family in
> the nation, and the benefit will inure to
> the whole people and not alone to the edu-
> cated individuals.

He quoted from John Stuart Mill's letter to Sir Charles
E. Trevelyan written on May 22, 1854.

The proposal to select candidates for the
civil service of Government by a competitive examination appears to me to be one of
those great public improvements the adoption of which would form an era in history.
The effects which it is calculated to produce in raising the character both of the
public administration and of the people
can hardly be overestimated.[10]

Jenckes followed up this speech with a report from
the Joint Committee on Retrenchment in support of his bill.
The sixty-three page report contained: (A) Testimony from
two employees in the New York Customhouse who asserted that
a system like the one Jenckes proposed would "unquestionably" improve the quality of employees and increase "the efficiency of the entire revenue service." (B) A letter from
the Commissioner of Customs to the Secretary of Treasury
maintaining that the spoils system paralyzed the public
service and destroyed its efficiency. Appendix B also included a large segment of David A. Wells' Revenue Commission
Report of 1866. (C) Rosengarten's abstract of Edouard Labou-
laye's article on the administrative system in Germany. (D)
Bigelow's letter to Secretary of State Seward. (E) Translation of M. Delandre's work on the French system. (F) Statistical information on the civil service system in Britain.
(G) Guide to the British Civil Service including a history
of the Civil Service Commission. (H) Examples of British
competitive examinations. The report collected most of the
literature on the subject into one volume.

Thomas Jenckes issued the report to show that his system was practical and workable, as demonstrated by similar
systems in other countries. Segments of the report on Great
Britain were particularly comprehensive, and Jenckes stated
that his bill was substantially the same as that existing
in England.[11]

Frederick E. Woodbridge of Vermont took the floor on
February 6, 1867 to attack the Jenckes bill.[12] Among other
arguments, Woodbridge appealed to Anglophobic sentiments in
the United States. He charged that the Jenckes bill "is

---

[10]U.S. Congressional Globe, 39th Cong., 2nd Sess., 1867,
pp. 837-841.

[11]U.S. Congress, Joint Select Committee on Retrenchment, Civil
Service of the United States, House Reports, No. 8, 39th
Cong., 2nd Sess., I, 1967.

[12]See summary in Chapter V.

195

anti-democratic" because it proposes adopting an aristocratic "system of appointing officers to the civil service."

> But where is the analogy between England and
> this country? That, sir, is a country of aristo-
> cracy, a country of classes, where as a rule a
> man cannot rise unless he is born to position.
> In England the coal-heaver of to-day is a coal-
> heaver on the day of his death. . . . How dif-
> ferent here! . . . The rail-splitter of to-day
> becomes to-morrow the President of the United
> States.

To climax his argument Woodbridge declared: "Here the
avenues to position, to power, to wealth, are open to
all . . . and I think it would be dangerous for us to close
these avenues to the many and provide a royal road for a
fortunate or favored few."[13]

Congressman Jenckes rebutted Woodbridge's argument:

> The effect on the system in England and Prussia
> has been, not to bring the scions of the aristo-
> cracy into the service as heretofore, but to
> exclude them. Those who have gone to work "with
> peasant's heart and arm" have crowded out the
> sons of the aristocracy. . . .

Robert Cumming Schenck, Civil War General and Speaker
of the House during the debate, amplified Jenckes' comments
by rejecting the "anti-democratic" charge against the bill.
The "anti-democratic" charge, according to Schenck, applied
more accurately to the "present system of making official
appointments" which "depend upon the personal and political
influence which the applicant may be able to bring to bear,
without regard to his want of qualifications for the position sought." He outlined its democratic provisions and
concluded that the bill "throws open these places in the
different Departments of the Government, to be occupied
without distinction by all men, rich and poor, and by persons of both sexes, according to their merits."[14]

---

[13]U.S. Congressional Globe, 39th Cong., 2nd Sess., 1867,
p. 1034.

[14]Ibid., pp. 1035-1036.

The foreign precedent impressed some reformers favorably. H.W. Fuller of Boston wrote to congratulate Jenckes on his speech. "You are right -- : but your course is hopeless -- for want of virtue and courage enough in the majority and in the people to adopt the meritorious candidates instead of the availables." He went on to say: "What you propose, or its equivalent, seems our only remedy. I was not aware that you could cite the examples of England and France with so much propriety."[15]

J.G. Rosengarten of Philadelphia wrote to the Congressman to give him more information on the civil service in Europe. Commenting on the prospects he wrote: "Everybody to whom I speak, says that the politicians there will never give it a chance -- but I think better of men than that. . . . Still it must have been harder to make the change in France and Germany, and yet it has been done."[16] Markinfield Addey of New York proposed to write an article for the Tribune on the results of examinations in Great Britain.[17]

Report Number 47

Thomas Jenckes, with the help of Julius Bing, added to the material on foreign countries contained in the original 1867 report with an in-depth analysis of the civil service systems in China, Prussia, England and France. Report No. 47, issued on May 25, 1868, gave broad coverage to the British system, incorporating a number of tables selected from various official government reports designed to show that "the service has not only become more efficient under the system of qualified employees by competitive examination, but also more economical."[18]

Appendix F consisted of several newspaper articles which utilized the foreign example to support Jenckes' proposals. The Chicago Tribune wrote: "of all civilized nations, the United States alone has not adopted such a system [competitive examinations]. . . . England, later

---

[15]H.W. Fuller to Jenckes, Boston, 31 January 1867, Jenckes Papers.

[16]J.G. Rosengarten to Jenckes, Philadelphia, 4 February 1867, Jenckes Papers.

[17]Joint Select Committee on Retrenchment, Report No. 47, p. 138.

[18]Ibid., p. 90.

to adopt this system, accomplishes its work with few officials and no fraud."[19]   The author observed: "The fear of an American bureaucracy as a result of a competitive system is absurd. . . . The humblest clerk would be as much a candidate for the presidency then as now, and, in the majority of cases, with vastly superior qualifications."[20]

The North American Review wrote:

In the foreign service of England much improvement has taken place in the subordinate branches, the secretaries of legation being subjected to a severe examination. But the heads of the legations themselves, having been secretaries at a period when such stringent tests had not yet been introduced, are in many instances comparatively inferior men, often of elegant manners and social accomplishments, but not proficient in the higher branches of statesmanship and cosmopolitan culture, and thus incapable of grappling with the manifold relations of foreign countries, and unable to give to their own government comprehensive views of the respective countries to which they are accredited.[21]

In an article on "How to Prevent Official Corruption" the New York Tobacco Leaf recommended adopting a civil service system "resembling that of Great Britain" and quoted from Alexander Pope:

Vice is a monster of such hideous mein
That to be hated needs but to be seen;
But, seen too oft, familiar with its face,
We first endure, then pity, then embrace.

"We have embraced too long already; now let us have a look at virtue's beautiful and benign countenance."[22]

---

[19] Joint Select Committee on Retrenchment, Report No. 47, p. 91.

[20] Ibid., p. 92.

[21] Ibid.

[22] Ibid., p. 95.

The *Boston Advertiser* lamented that civil service reform "is a work in which the United States ought to have been the pioneer, but unwittingly it has been delayed till even the conservative governments of Europe are far in advance of us."[23]

The New York *Evening Post* wrote that the Jenckes bill "retains the essential features of the system which has produced such satisfactory results in Great Britain and yet is far more simple, leaving all the details to grow up as circumstances require."[24]

The bill's sponsor devoted a few moments to the British experience in his May 14, 1868 House speech. Jenckes quoted Ben Johnson's admiring observation of the King of Prussia's ability to "choose a man to an office merely because he is the fittest for it." He noted that the result had been achieved in England and the success "is so great and so beneficial as to encourage the attempt to obtain the same end in our own."[25] He indirectly used the British experience to refute the argument that his system "is in its tendency bureaucratic, exclusive, aristocratic, and that the system was formed under monarchic institutions."

> It is our present system that is borrowed from that of monarchies and gives us the will and choice of the person having the appointing power, and not merit, as the passport to office, as under monarchies the king is the fountain of honor and the giver of employment. No measure could be more republican than that which we now present. The gates of the avenues to the public service are thrown open to all. Merit can only enter, and merit only can keep its place.[26]

The Jenckes Papers contain a number of letters which show that he kept close contact with events in England. The State Department provided him with a package of documents on

---

[23] Joint Select Committee on Retrenchment, *Report No. 47*, p. 97.

[24] *Ibid.*, p. 107.

[25] *Ibid.*, p. 5.

[26] *Ibid.*, p. 11.

the reorganization of the British Civil Service including
the 1855 <u>Northcote-Trevelyan Report</u> and the <u>Thirteenth
Annual Report of the Civil Service Commission</u>.[27] Julius
Bing reviewed the English press and drew Jenckes' attention to pertinent articles including one by Sir Charles
Trevelyan "advocating the adoption of the competitive
system. . . to higher military appointments."[28] Alive to
the benefits of gaining favorable foreign support, reformers
worked to inform the British press and officials about the
American campaign. Nathaniel Gale introduced Jenckes to a
London correspondent. Bing sent copies of the civil service
bill and report to American diplomats in foreign countries.
"You know how much foreign opinion tells upon the public
mind, tho I do not know why it should. But it is a fact
nevertheless." Henry Howard of New York asked John Bright
of Gladstone's cabinet to say a word "for the purpose of
helping you [Jenckes] and your great work."[29]

Foreign Influence Attacked

John A. Logan concentrated his attack on the charge
that the Civil Service Bill "is taken openly, boldly and
without disguise from monarchical Governments." Logan predicted that "life tenure" will produce an elevated class
which is insensitive to the needs of the people.

> A person who although he may have been ori-
> ginally of the people and from the people,
> yet soon will become by the immunity which
> he enjoys, by the security of his place, by
> the hardening of long continued position,
> removed from the people, with but few feel-
> ing in common with them, and at last to have
> an utter disregard and contempt for them.[30]

---

[27]Theodore W. Dixon to Jenckes, Department of State, 30 May
1868; W.J. Custer to Jenckes, Department of State, 16 December 1868, Jenckes Papers.

[28]Julius Bing to Jenckes, Boston, 27 August 1868; Julius Bing
to Jenckes, Washington, 27 November 1868, Jenckes Papers.

[29]Nathaniel Gale to Jenckes, Boston, 27 January 1868; Julius
Bing to Jenckes, 12 December 1868; Henry Howard to Jenckes,
New York, 7 January 1869, Jenckes Papers.

[30]U.S. <u>Congressional Globe</u>, 40th Cong., 3rd Sess., 1869, p. 264.

"The bill," according to Logan, "is the opening wedge
to an aristocracy in this country." His objection "is that
the system begets a caste in this country. . . . There is
the aristocratic tendency which inevitably comes to class."
In England and France the "king or queen is not to be
reached by any voter, nor can the existing Government be
ever changed no matter how oppressive, unless by violence
and arms."[31]

The system may be suited for England but the "same
reasons which make this system a good one there make it a
bad one here."

Representative Jenckes refuted these statements, arguing
that the spoils system and not the civil service reform bill,
came from monarchies. Life tenure, Jenckes continued, did
not grant government employees immunity from removal and
would not result in creating an unresponsive class in the
United States.[32]

George W. Woodward continued the emotional attack on
the "foreign influence" of the Jenckes bill. Woodward applauded Logan's speech, in his January 30 speech, and charged
that we should never permit ideas "drawn from despotic and
monarchical government . . . to become a rule for our free
Republic." He declared that competitive examinations allow
the "landed aristocracy . . . to leave the Church, the
Army, and the civil service open to younger sons."

> But all such systems of government are founded
> on privileged classes and aristocratic ranks.
> There is no sympathy with the common masses
> in them. The Church, the Army, and the civil
> service become as aristocratic as the landed
> nobility, while with us government is founded
> on a basis that is truly popular.

Woodward concluded that "one of the great vices of this bill"
is that it is based on the Old World and "not built upon
the American ideas of government."

Woodward took "pot-shots" at Jenckes' contention that
the spoils system is inefficient and expensive. The 1868
report indicated that the English paid less wages for the

---

[31]U.S. Congressional Globe, 40th Cong., 3rd Sess., 1869, p. 265.

[32]See Chapter VI for a complete analysis of Logan's speech
and Jenckes' rebuttal.

same amount of work. Woodward gloated that "the payments
to the civil service are not niggardly. They are larger
than those paid . . . in England."[33]

Direct Contact With Reformers in England

Thomas Jenckes exchanged extensive correspondence with
English reformers throughout his efforts to reform the civil
service in the United States. He gave those letters to
George William Curtis, first Civil Service Commission President, in 1871 for his use in the work of the Grant Civil Service Commission (1871-1875), but they cannot be located now.
Charles Loring Brace of New York, famous for his child welfare interest, supported Jenckes' civil service reform campaign. Brace, independently wealthy and extensive traveler,
wrote his friend John Stuart Mill for information on civil
service reform which might be helpful to Jenckes. Mill referred the request to Sir Charles E. Trevelyan, the father
of civil service reform in Great Britain. Trevelyan responded
with a six-page letter to Brace and Jenckes discussing the
history, experience, and philosophy of civil service reform
in England. He accompanied the letter with copies of the
Northcote-Trevelyan Report, Lord Macaulay's Report to the
Indian Civil Service, and the Thirteenth Report of the British Civil Service Commission.

Trevelyan began his letter by outlining the history of
civil service reform in England. He followed with a discussion of open competition as practiced in the Indian Civil
Service and the Artillery and Engineer service. Sir Charles
quoted from the 1860 Northcote Commission Report stating
that, "the best method of procuring competent persons to
fill the junior clerkships in the Civil Service would be
through a system of competitive examinations, open to all
subjects of the Queen." "The intellectual test of the competitive examination," Trevelyan continued, "is almost [as]
efficacious as a guarantee of moral character" as the
character check performed by the Civil Service Commission.

Trevelyan supported Jenckes on two major arguments
advanced by his opponents. He stated that civil service
reform was both economical and democratic. "The mode of
appointment by open competitive examination also creates a
strong tendency towards the economy of the public money.
. . . The political tendency of the system is to favor
democracy in it's [sic] highest and best sense."

---

[33]U.S. Congressional Globe, 40th Cong., 3rd Sess., 1869, pp.
749-750; see Chapter VI for a complete analysis of Woodward's
speech.

Education will open the door to government employment.

> Without solicitation, without the slightest
> sacrifice of personal independence, everybody
> in every part of the country, however remote
> from the center of political power, can merely
> by giving his son a good education reasonably
> hope to obtain from him an honorable place in
> the service of the State.

Sir Charles stressed another point seldom used by
Representative Jenckes up to this time. "The influence
of the system upon national education is of the best possible kind."

> . . . the whole of the schools and colleges of
> the country have, for every practical purpose,
> been converted by this system into a single
> university; the rewards of which are provided
> by the State, not only without additional cost,
> but with a striking improvement both in economy
> and efficiency of the public service.

Admitting that the struggle for open competition "is
still in progress here," Trevelyan argued that the new system has a great effect on reducing corruption. "Open
competition cuts up this growth of corruption by the roots.
Public appointments can no longer be used as bribes or
retaining fees. . . ."

He concluded with the statement: "This is our experience. It is for you and those who are acting with
you, to judge how far it is applicable to the circumstances
of the United States."[34]

Jenckes continued to receive information from Great
Britain. J.G. Rosengarten sent Jenckes a copy of the Pall
Mall Gazette of February 6, 1869, which published a leading
article on "The American Civil Service."[35] Walter E. Lawton

---

[34]Sir Charles E. Trevelyan to C. Brace, Esq. of New York,
London, 8 February 1869, Library of the U.S. Civil Service
Commission.

[35]J.G. Rosengarten to Jenckes, Philadelphia, 12 March 1869,
Jenckes Papers.

of New York introduced Jenckes to Peter Rylands, Member
of Parliament from Warrington, England, and the two
legislators agreed to exchange information on their respective civil services.[36]   In November, Benjamin Morgan,
Secretary of the U.S. Legation in London, sent the Congressman the "14th Report of Her Majesty's Civil Service
Commission."[37]

Response to Logan and Woodward

Brace forwarded the Trevelyan letter to Jenckes on
March 10, 1869, just in time for its use in preparing the
Congressman's next speech in the House of Representatives.[38]
The speech delivered on April 5, 1869 contained most of the
points outlined by Trevelyan. He paraphrased Trevelyan's
contention that open competition is the best means of obtaining competent government employees. "It simply provides means for obtaining for the service of the Government
in its subordinate offices the best quality of servants to
be obtained for the price paid for their services." He
argued, as Trevelyan had, that competitive examinations
would guarantee high moral character. "Fidelity in the
minor offices will secure integrity in the higher." "The
great element of success in the proposed system is the encouragement and development in the civil service of the
sentiment of honor."

Jenckes echoed Trevelyan's argument that civil service
reform was democratic.

> Every one is to have a fair chance. Every young
> man in the country is to have the opportunity, if
> he chooses, of competing for the privilege of
> entering the public service, and to be entitled to
> the right to enter it if he proves that he has
> prepared himself for it better than his competit-
> ors. Its principle is that the people have a
> right to the service of the best men, and that
> the best men have the best right to serve the
> people. If this be not the true idea of the
> Republic my studies have been in vain.

---

[36]Walter E. Lawton to Jenckes, New York, 13 October 1868;
Lawton to Jenckes, New York, 19 October 1869, Jenckes Papers.

[37]Benjamin Morgan, Secretary of the U.S. Legation in London to
Jenckes, London, 20 November 1869, Jenckes Papers.

[38]C.L. Brace to Jenckes, New York, 10 March 1869, Jenckes
Papers.

Like Trevelyan, Jenckes had no doubts that civil service reform was economical. "It is presented as a practical measure to enable the Administration to get its business done most effectually and economically." "In its economical aspect I also ask for this measure the approval of the House and of the country." Jenckes made direct reference to England in a strong refutation of Mr. Woodward's contention that "one of the great vices of the bill" was that it drew from other Government examples.

> . . . the idea that we should not take a hint
> from the improvements in the machinery of ad-
> ministration made in other countries because
> their Governments are "despotic and monarchical"
> is as ridiculous as it is preposterous. The
> same rule would require us to reject the steam-
> engine, the railway, and the locomotive because
> they came from Great Britain.

He argued that "our present system of appointments to office is of monarchical origin and is copied from that of the parent nation." He reminded the Congressmen that "we are constantly borrowing ideas in jurisprudence and in legislation from other countries." "All our jurisprudence is based upon that of the country from which our first colonists emigrated, England, monarchical England. Our Government itself, with an executive chief, our representative legislature and independent judiciary, are all copies from the same model." England, Jenckes stated, gave us our inheritance of common law which underlies "all our constitutions, and all our legislation, colonial, State and national."

Congressman Jenckes devoted a good portion of his speech to refuting Logan's charge that his bill would create an aristocracy. "That merit shall have the places it deserves is the true republican doctrine, and the measure which is devised to bring forward and advance merit and merit alone in the public service, is the keen edge of the axe to the root of these alien, corrupt aristocratical practices."[39]

British Example -- Curtis and Adams

George W. Curtis referred frequently to the British in his speech delivered before the American Social Science Association in October 1869. Curtis declared that the principles of the Jenckes bill have been thoroughly tested in other

---

[39]U.S. Congressional Globe, 41st Cong., 1st Sess., 1869, pp. 517-523; see Chapter VI for summary of the entire speech.

countries and especially in Russia and England." He explained that the Order-in-Council of 1855 established civil service reform in England on the basis of examinations "of those only who have been previously nominated." Curtis declared, the principle of open competition had been recognized by the Northcote Committee of 1860, and a Parliamentary bill introduced by Mr. Fawcett in 1865.

> This principle has not yet been fully adopted; but it will be a happy day for England when no lord of the bedchamber can nominate a favorite to be clerk in the Treasury, as it will be a day of thanksgiving in America when the mere party politician in Congress shall no longer quarter his bittle-holders and runners upon the purses of the American people.

Curtis dismissed the charge that civil service reform would lead to an aristocracy. ". . . of course, it is not seriously urged that such a system leads to an aristocracy, for to the idea of an aristocracy some kind of privilege or special political power is essential." The present system fulfills those criteria, but the reform will have the opposite effect for it "throws open these offices to every citizen with proved qualifications."

The editor addressed the charge that the new system was not suited to American institutions because it "is taken from monarchical governments." "The truth is that a nation not yet a hundred years old would find itself seriously perplexed if it scornfully rejected whatever is approved by foreign experience." He concluded that "the genius of our institutions is reason and common-sense, and therefore we will have anything from anywhere that may be of service."[40]

Henry Brooks Adams' intimate familiarity with British administrative practices obtained from years of residence in England resulted in the advocacy of a different approach than that of Thomas A. Jenckes. Convinced that "Congress has seized and now claims as its right the most important executive powers," Adams advocated strict separation of powers between the Executive, Legislative, and Judicial branches of government. "So far as the legislature is concerned, there is but one rule to follow. Let Congress keep its hands off executive powers. Let it not undertake to interfere by mandatory legislation in matters which

---

[40]Norton, ed., pp. 20-25; see Chapter VI for summary of the speech.

are beyond its sphere." Thus, the Jenckes bills, "however excellent in purpose, must be held wrong both in principle and in detail."

Americans should emulate British precedent and carry out civil service reform with existing executive powers, Adams wrote. "Let it imitate the example of the British Parliament, which, omnipotent as it is, respects the principles of government so far that it wisely contents itself with advising or approving competition in the civil service, but has never ventured to legislate upon it."

Adams concluded with two recommendations which paralleled English developments, ". . . one, recommending the President to extend the principle of competitive examinations to all branches of the service in which it might in his opinion be usefully applied; the other, declaring the opinion of Congress that, in respect to removals from office, the executive should return to the early practice of the government."[41]

Familiar Arguments Persist

During the three-day debate on civil service reform in the House in May 1870, Horace Maynard of Tennessee revived the anti-foreign arguments of the spoilsmen. "I beg to call attention of gentlemen to the fact that the European system and our system are very different. The object of government in Europe is to get as far as possible away from the people. . . . The object of this country is to keep the Government near to the people."

John A. Bingham of Ohio renewed the charge "that this is a bill to create an aristocracy, a privileged class in this country, in the very face of that wise provision in our Constitution that neither the United States or any State of this Union shall confer titles of nobility." Mr. Covody of Pennsylvania repeated the argument. "I am disposed to vote against this bill" because "I look upon it as an attempt to establish an aristocracy of officeholders, and to follow in the lead of the Governments of Europe, disregarding the voice of the people who are instrumental in putting the men in power who control the public offices."

Thomas Jenckes addressed these statements when he urged the Congress to give the proposal a fair test. "If it were a new invention or discovery of mine, I should hesitate to

---

[41]Adams, pp. 443-475.

ask consideration for it at all. But it has been tried and found valuable in the experience of all civilized nations, and I have the hope that it may be tried with advantage here." Americans have not "invented or discovered all that is useful either in government or in administration," Jenckes argued. Other nations have many innovations we may learn from and adopt "with benefit to our own."

Jenckes ridiculed the argument his bill would create an aristocracy. Light-house keepers, inspectors, and Department clerks making less than $1,200 are not likely to form a powerful aristocracy. "What a fearful, nay terrible aristocracy to plant among the institutions of a representative republic!" He dismissed the subject by calling it "ludicrous" and inviting his opponents "to make free use of this 'aristocracy' argument."[42]

British Developments Reported

Many eyes looked to England for inspiration in civil service reform. Interested observers reported to the Representative from Rhode Island English developments as activities increased in connection with the forthcoming Order-in-Council of 1870. Professor G.W. Shurtleff from Oberlin College requested information on the British Commission and directed Jenckes' attention to the "testimony of the Duke of Buckingham, found on page 144 of the 14th Report of English Commissioners."[43] Jenckes sent Joseph Rosengarten "notes in reference to the English Civil Service Reform." Rosengarten responded by referring Jenckes to an article in the Spectator on the effect of the new Order-in-Council, and discussed the legal implications of the Order. He told Jenckes of finding "a couple of articles on Civil Service Reform in 1860, -- one by Horace Mann," and wondered if he could use them to advantage by contrasting "ten years experience in England, with our slothful indifference." Later Rosengarten wrote for more documents on civil service reform to send to a friend in England who "is likely to be of service to our reform, by advocating it in England."[44]

---

[42] U.S. Congressional Globe, 41st Cong., 2nd Sess., 1870, pp. 3182-4, 3222-5, 3258-61.

[43] G.W. Shurtleff to Jenckes, Oberlin, Ohio, 28 January 1870; 28 February 1870; and 15 March 1870, Jenckes Papers.

[44] J.G. Rosengarten to Jenckes, Philadelphia, 4 July 1870; 15 December 1870, Jenckes Papers.

Congressman Jenckes received a mysterious undated
letter from the "Observer" written on paper with a Congressional watermark. "Permit me very respectfully," the
writer began, "to call your attention to the fact that in
your 'Civil Service Bill' modelled as it is in some of
its features after the English system, you have omitted
one of their predominant ones. . . ." The bill needed a
pension plan. "It seems to me," he wrote, "that such an
amendment to your bill, would give it strength. . . ."[45]
Located near this letter in the Jenckes Papers is an undated handwritten section incorporating the Observer's
suggestion.

> Sec. And be it further enacted, That when any
> individual has served as a clerk in either of
> the Executive Departments, or Bureaus attached
> thereto, at the seat of Government in a period
> of thirty-five years, and shall have arrived at
> the age of seventy-five years, he may retire
> from the active duties of his position, and re-
> ceive, during the remainder of his life,
> of the salary paid him at the time of his so
> retiring; the same to be paid at the same time,
> and in the same manner as theretofore.[46]

Jenckes used the information he obtained from England
on the new Order-in-Council of 1870 to write another section in his last bill, introduced on January 9, 1871. The
new section authorized the Civil Service Commission to prescribe rules which would permit the Administration to hire
professional applicants without subjecting them to a competitive examination.[47]

Use of British Influence in Reform Campaign

Supporters and opponents of civil service reform found
the use of British example in particular and European example in general somewhat enigmatic. Reformers needed the
British to demonstrate that civil service reform was practical and would solve the problems created by the spoils

---

[45]Undated letter from the "Observer" to Jenckes, Jenckes
Papers.

[46]Undated paper located in Container Number 47, Jenckes
Papers.

[47]U.S. Congress, House, A Bill to Regulate the Manner of
Making Appointments in the Civil Service of the United
States, H.R. 2633, 41st Cong., 3rd Sess., 1871.

system. The Jenckes bill, closely modeled after the British system, offered a total package designed to meet most defects of the patronage system. It left very little room for a partial program or compromise, thus confronting opponents with a choice between total rejection or total acceptance.

Opponents responded by trying with emotional, illogical arguments and scare and fright tactics to divert attention from the practical and logical system proposed by reformers to a wholly hypothetical monster of their own creation. Relying on ignorance and prejudice in place of arguments, they appealed, again and again, to isolationist sentiments of the American public with charges that civil service reformers proposed a foreign, monarchist system that would create an oppressive aristocracy.

Representative Jenckes reduced his use of the English example by calling attention to other countries which applied examinations to recruiting government employees. After 1868 he contributed few new arguments to the debate on the foreign origins of civil service reform. Perhaps he felt that continued emphasis injured the movement because of strong isolationist and Anglophobic sentiments in the United States. Opponents may have decreased their appeal to isolationism and Anglophobia at the same time, for fear that it might backfire and attract attention to the reformers' argument supporting the practical success of the system in England. Consequently, in future debates concerning civil service reform, both sides appear to under-emphasize the reliance placed on European experience.

Spoilsmen and reformers frequently exaggerated conditions in Britain during the civil service reform debates. Congressman Woodbridge, for example, labeled the British government as "despotic" and Jenckes characterized the British system as "republican." This kind of exaggeration was typical throughout the debates.

The choice of words reflects an attempt by politicians and journalists to appeal to the broader masses of voters. They selected emotional terms in an attempt to generate predictable responses from their listeners or readers. The propaganda techniques contained many exaggerations with a frequent dose of sarcasm. Neither side concerned itself with correcting the misconceptions their public statements represented, even though the speakers were usually well informed about conditions in Great Britain. The battle over civil service reform reflected the public relations skills of the participants. The strength of public appeal for both sides depended on the propaganda methods employed.

CHAPTER VIII

ABORTIVE EFFORT
1871 to 1880

Returning to the major chronicle of events, inter-
rupted at the end of Chapter VI to examine details of
British influence on them, the center of attention moved
from the Congress to the White House as reformers looked
to see how the President would implement the 1871 rider.
President Grant appointed an eminently qualified civil
service advisory board. He assigned the board responsibility to recommend "rules and regulations for the admission of persons into the civil service. . . ."
Chaired by civil service reformer George William Curtis,
the seven-member board consisted of three from inside the
civil service and four from outside. Journalist Joseph
Medill, owner of the Chicago Tribune and political friend
of Presidents Lincoln and Grant, was a most influential
member. Grant appointed recently defeated Senator Alexander G. Cattell of New Jersey as the third member from
outside the government. Cattell, a friend of President
Grant, was a banker and corrupt politician who espoused
the "stalwart" view of civil service reform. Judge Dawson
A. Walker of Georgia completed the outside members of the
board. E.B. Elliott of Connecticut, elected Secretary of
the Board, had practical administrative experience with
competitive examinations. Secretary of the Treasury
George S. Boutwell had appointed Elliott to the board of
examiners in the Treasury Department. He developed stringent written examinations and supervised the first competitive examination in the United States civil service in
1870. David C. Cox, Interior Department Clerk, and J.H.
Blackfan, Superintendent of Foreign Mails in the Post Office Department, completed the government members of the board.[1]

Curtis wrote immediately to Jenckes and Schurz asking
for "any suggestion . . . in regard to the details of the
system to be recommended. . ." "What we want now," he

---

[1]Lionel V. Murphy, "The First Federal Civil Service Commission: 1871-1875," Public Personnel Review (January, July,
October, 1942), p. 33; Alexander G. Cattell was "involved
in several financial scandals" and removed as Treasury agent
in London because of "dishonesty"; Interior Department Clerk
is the equivalent of an Under Secretary for Administration.

wrote to Jenckes, "is a simple practicable method which will be likely to be adopted and the lessons of your experience and thought upon the subject would be very valuable."[2] By the time the Commission began its meetings on June 28, 1871, Curtis had prepared his objectives and strategy.[3] His preparation and dynamic personality allowed him to exercise the most decisive influence on the deliberations.

The Board agreed that his powers "were limited to the preparation of rules and regulations for the approval of the President."[4] Curtis focused the discussion directly on the central issue of competitive examinations with a resolution to "recommend to the President that all admissions to the civil service of the United States . . . shall be determined by a competitive examination open to all. . ."[5] Medill and Cattell led the opposition while Elliott, Blackfan and Cox supported the resolution. In the end, the major argument, initially brought up by Medill, that open competitive examinations would destroy "the Constitutional power of appointment vested in the heads of departments," caused the Board to "refer informally to the Attorney General for his opinion on the question whether Congress can under the Constitution delegate to the President authority to prescribe rules for admission to the civil service which would practically defeat the power of appointment vested by law in the heads of department."[6] The Board adjourned from July 10 to October 17, 1871, to await the Attorney General's decision.

---

[2]G.W. Curtis to Jenckes, West New Brighton, Staten Island, 5 June 1871, Jenckes Papers; G.W. Curtis to Schurz, West New Brighton, 5 June 1871, Schurz Papers.

[3]G.W. Curtis to Jenckes, New York, 24 June 1871, Jenckes Papers.

[4]U.S. Civil Service Commission, Minutes of the Civil Service Commission, 28 June 1871, 1:6, Library of the U.S. Civil Service Commission.

[5]Minutes, June 30, 1871, p. 9.

[6]Minutes, July 6, 1871, p. 18.

From the beginning George William Curtis wrote comprehensive letters to Thomas A. Jenckes on the issues which
surfaced in the Commission deliberations. Jenckes served
the cause of civil service reform one last time. He wrote
to Attorney General Amos Tappan Akerman on July 15 about
the requested opinion. Akerman proposed "a loose notion . . .
that an examination for admission into the class of candidates may lawfully be present; but that, under the Constitution, the selection of the individual who shall have the
office must be the act of the appointing power -- President,
Head of Department or Court." At Akerman's request, Jenckes
prepared an exhaustive list of citations dating back to the
beginning of the republic to prove that competitive examinations were constitutional. Akerman delivered his opinion
along the lines he originally outlined to Jenckes on August
31. He held that the board could not designate "a single
person for appointment," but the President may "regulate
the exercise of the appointing power now vested in the
heads of departments. . . ."

Although not getting all that he wanted, Curtis accepted Akerman's decision and looked toward the next steps.
"This brings it just where I told the President it lay,
upon his shoulders. . . . If he will make the reform it
can be made. If not, not." "The difficulty," according to
Curtis, "is to arrange it without expense so as not to depend on Congress which is radically hostile."[8]

The ten meetings held by the Board between October 17
and October 30 concentrated on drafting the first seven
rules. They restricted appointments to citizens who passed
an adequate examination. Admissions "shall be filled. . ."
from those "who shall have passed a further competitive
examination." Those passing the competitive examination
would be placed on a register in order of their score and

[7]G.W. Curtis to Jenckes, West New Brighton, New York, 5 June
1871; Curtis to Jenckes, New York, 24 June 1871; Curtis to
Jenckes, New York, 24 June 1871 [2nd letter]; Curtis to
Jenckes, Washington, 2 July 1871; Curtis to Jenckes, Ash-
field, Massachusetts, 6 August 1871; A.T. Akerman to Jenckes,
Washington, 18 July 1871; Akerman to Jenckes, Washington, 5
August 1871, Jenckes Papers; Minutes, 10 July 1871, p. 21;
13 op. Atty. Gen. 516 (August 31, 1871.

[8]G.W. Curtis to Charles Eliot Norton, Ashfield, 10 September
1871, Norton Papers, Harvard University.

certified to heads of departments in groups of three for each vacancy existing. The rules called for competitive examinations for promotions and a six-month probation period. To reduce expenses and therefore dependence on Congress, the Commission authorized the heads of each department to appoint a board to carry out the rules and regulations developed by the Commission and adopted by the President.[9]

Chairman Curtis took the new rules to President Grant on October 31 who "approved generally of the rules" and obtained the favorable consent of the Cabinet. Privately, Grant and his Cabinet considered the rules impracticable but wanted to give them an adequate trial. In November the Board made several amendments to the original rules. They now included provisions to classify all positions into groups and allow employees no longer able to work in their upper-level jobs because of injury or illness to obtain positions in lower grades. Finally, the rules contained a prohibition against political assessments. The Commission formally submitted the recommendations in December 1871 and Grant promulgated them on January 1, 1872. The President transmitted the rules to Congress in a report, mostly prepared by George Curtis, modeled after Jenckes' 1868 report.[10]

President Grant assigned the Commission responsibility for implementing the new rules and regulations. Unfortunately for those hoping for success, the date was premature and the rules had to be suspended ten days later. Classification problems for the government service outside Washington proved to be the stumbling block. Application of the rules to the great majority of government employees posed an enormous amount of problems for the board. The Advisory Board of the Civil Service, which they chose to call themselves during this period, met several times each week to work out the problems they faced. The composition and function of the departmental boards attracted a lot of attention. Curtis delineated between the functions of the Advisory Board and Departmental Boards. He described the new role of the Advisory Board as "a formal and ceremonial kind, while the determination of subjects for examinations and so forth would fall under the examining boards."[11] The Advisory Board

---

[9] Minutes, October 19, 1871, p. 25; October 26, pp. 31-32; October 27, p. 34; October 31, p. 37.

[10] See Murphy for an in-depth analysis.

[11] Minutes, April 16, 1872, p. 142.

214

devoted another large block of its time to considering
the systemic and political problems associated with the
Post Office Department and the Department of State.[12] They
discussed the composition of the excepted service,[12] and
how it would relate with the regular service staffed on
the basis of merit alone. The Board also considered promotions, classifications, and grading. On March 20, 1872
George Curtis discussed the Board's progress with the
President and obtained clearance by the Cabinet in time
for it to issue a new report on April 11, 1872. The rules
and regulations became effective May 16, 1872, allowing
the Treasury Department to hold the first competitive examination on June 5, 1872.

Political Atmosphere Surrounding
the Commission's Deliberations

The Conkling-Fenton feud continued to affect civil
service reform in Congress.[13] The Tweed ring, dominant
element in the Democratic Party in New York, lost power
in New York City. In November 1871, Grant replaced Thomas
Murphy with Conklingite Chester A. Arthur as Collector of
the New York Customhouse, where Murphy's close connection
to the Tweed ring created sufficient pressure to force a
change. Conkling forces defeated efforts of Lyman Trumbull
to reconstitute the Joint Committee on Retrenchment in
Congress. The Senate, however, created a Committee of Investigation and Retrenchment, which concentrated its efforts
on investigating the New York Customhouse. The investigation uncovered extensive corruption, especially on the part
of George Leet and Wilbur T. Stocking. These findings pro-

---

[12]The excepted service was to be a small number of high ranking
or confidential positions, recognized as necessary and appropriately filled on a political patronage basis, to give the party
in power control of administration, consistent with its mandate
of election by the voters.

[13]President Grant supported Roscoe Conkling in a complex party
struggle in New York. The New York factional battle between supporters of Reuben Fenton and Conkling took place over the control
of patronage at the New York Customhouse. Grant's first appointment went to businessman Moses H. Grinnell, a member of neither
faction. Unhappy with the benefits Grinnell dispensed, both sides
demanded a change. Grant supported Conkling, demoted Grinnell to
Naval Officer and removed pro-Fentonite, Edwin A. Merritt. In
his place Grant appointed Thomas Murphy Collector. Fenton and
Conkling fought it out in the Senate over Murphy's confirmation.
Both sides used unethical tactics, but with Grant's help Conkling
won and Murphy received his confirmation. Jordan, pp. 132-138.

vided civil service reformers additional data for their
Anti-Grant campaign.[14]

Senator Matthew Carpenter of Wisconsin introduced an
anti-Civil Service reform resolution on January 10, 1872,
and supported it with an excellent speech in the Senate.
Carpenter advanced the same arguments used against the
Jenckes bills. He concluded that the civil service rules
and regulations were unconstitutional and anti-republican.
They benefited the rich who could afford an expensive
education for their sons and discriminated against disabled veterans. Other Senators attacked the new rules and
regulations with charges they were impractical, an attempt
to destroy the Republican party and incapable of detecting
immoral candidates.[15] Carpenter's speech upset the Advisory Board, but Grant came to their defense with a letter
to Commissioner Joseph Medill. "It is my intention that
Civil Service shall have a fair trial," he assured Medill.[16]

Many Congressmen opposed the new civil service rules
and regulations. John B. Hay, William T. Clark, George Mc-
Crary, Thomas J. Speer, as well as Elizur H. Prindle, Henry
Snapp, Simon Cameron, Zachariah Chandler and John A. Logan
worked to derail the new civil service rules. The most
important conflict took place over the appropriations for
the Commission. Supporters hoped to get an appropriation
of $100,000 but finally settled for $25,000 after a monumental effort on the part of James A. Garfield of Ohio,
Chairman of the House Appropriations Committee.[17] Some of
the most conspicuous opponents of civil service reform in

---

[14]Rothman, p. 27; Hoogenboom, pp. 75-76; Krug, 294-296; Milne
pp. 142-144; Ari Hoogenboom, "Civil Service Reform and Public
Morality." The Gilded Age, H. Wayne Morgan, ed. (Syracuse:
Syracuse University Press, 1970), 2nd ed., pp. 90-91; Jordan,
pp. 172-173.

[15]U.S. Congressional Globe, 42nd Cong., 2nd Sess., pp. 333, 441-
445, 453-458, 463-464, 810-812; Louis A. Dimitz to Carl Schurz,
Louisville, 20 January 1872, Schurz Papers.

[16]Minutes, 20 January 1872, 1:104; Ulysses S. Grant to Joseph
Medill, Washington, 1 February 1872, William Best Hesseltine,
Ulysses S. Grant (New York: Dodd Co., 1935), p. 264.

[17]U.S. Congressional Globe, 42nd Cong., 2nd Sess., pp. 1354, 1502
1507, 2398, 3020-3021, 3053-3055; James A. Garfield to Joseph
Medill, Washington, 13 April 1872; Garfield to David A. Wells,
Washington, 22 April 1872, Garfield Papers.

these debates were generally strong and loyal supporters of the Grant Administration. This did not help create an atmosphere conducive to reform.

A political movement, begun by Schurz in Missouri in 1870, developed by 1872 into a major split in the Republican Party. Missouri Liberal Republicans proposed convening a national convention in Cincinnati to select a candidate to run against General Grant in November. Politicians of many divergent political persuasions attended the Convention. They were united primarily in their opposition to President Grant. Horace Greeley and John W. Forney received the nomination of the delegates to run for President and Vice President. Liberal Republicans who had hoped to nominate Charles Francis Adams for President fell into disarray over Horace Greeley's candidacy. Some followed Edwin L. Godkin and returned to the Republican Party; some followed Carl Schurz and threw their support to Horace Greeley; and some, like George William Curtis, remained in President Grant's corner from the beginning. The Cincinnati movement, resulting as it did in a colossal defeat for Horace Greeley, severely weakened the reform movement and thus exposed civil service reform to attack by stalwarts.[18]

Grant did not exploit his victory immediately. He continued to give verbal support to the Advisory Board in Civil Service and at one point showed his interest by holding a long meeting between the Commission and the Cabinet.[19] In time, however, powerful stalwarts gained in influence over President Grant, and his appointments soon reflected adversely on the civil service reform movement. Representative Henry Snapp of Illinois delivered a devastating attack on civil service reform in December 1871.[20] Grant appointed Simon

_____

[18]Sproat, pp. 51, 65-66, 72, 76-88; Earle Dudley Ross, The Liberal Republican Movement (New York: AMS Press, 1971; reprint ed., New York: 1919), pp. 86-191; Richard Allan Gerber, "The Liberal Republicans of 1872 in Historiographical Perspective," The Journal of American History 62 (June 1975): pp. 40-73; Krug, pp. 303-338; Logsdon, pp. 192-253.

[19]The Diary of Hamilton Fish, January 28, 1873, 3:353, Library of Congress; "Memorandum of a Meeting of the Advisory Board, January 27, 1873 in Civil Service Reform 1853-1883," 1:115A-116, E.B. Elliot Papers, Library of the U.S. Civil Service Commission.

[20]U.S. Congressional Globe, 42nd Cong., 3rd Sess., pp. 194-199.

Cameron's supporter as Postmaster of Philadelphia and
John Logan's candidate as Postmaster of Chicago. George
Bliss, an associate of Thomas Murphy, became U.S. District
Attorney in New York City. These appointments of spoilsmen
disturbed reformers but did not violate the Civil Service
rules. The true test of Grant's intentions came over the
appointment of the New York Surveyor. Alonzo Cornell resigned his position and Grant, after consulting with Curtis, nominated Deputy Surveyor James I. Benedict, in compliance with the Civil Service rules. Before Congress
took up the nomination Grant acceded to the demands of
Senator Conkling and other stalwarts and withdrew the nomination. He appointed a three-member committee consisting
of Curtis, Collector Chester A. Arthur, and Jackson S.
Schultz to select a surveyor, in accordance with the Civil
Service rules. Unfortunately, the severe illness of George
Curtis delayed action of the committee. Grant violated
the Civil Service rules by appointing George H. Sharpe,
political supporter of Senator Conkling. Curtis felt
himself "publicly snubbed" and submitted his resignation
on March 18, 1873.[21]

Dorman Bridgeman Eaton

President Grant appointed Dorman B. Eaton of New York
City to replace George William Curtis. The fifty year old
Eaton was graduated from the University of Vermont and Harvard Law School. He practiced law from 1850 to 1870. He
helped edit a new edition of Judge James Kent's famous four
volume book Commentaries on American Law. Eaton contributed legal skills to the New York Citizens Association after
1864 and helped to create the fire department, police judiciary, and departments of health and docks. Probably his
most significant client was the Erie Railroad. His energetic
participation in the legal controversies of the railroad and
his reform work led to a severe physical attack by unknown
assailants. The "unknown assailants" may have worked for the
Tweed Ring. These injuries prompted him to give up his law
practice and travel to England for a "rest cure."

Eaton's interest in civil service reform possibly came
from his work with the Erie Railroad and the New York City
government. He followed the efforts of Thomas A. Jenckes
and attended his 1869 lecture in New York, sponsored by

---

[21]Nation (New York), 20 February 1873, pp. 126-127; Nation,
20 March 1873, p. 189; Jordan, pp. 268-269; Milne, pp. 150-
151; Sproat, pp. 160-161; Hoogenboom, p. 122; Murphy,
pp. 305-306.

Henry Villard. Eaton occupied his time in Europe studying the administrative systems of several European countries. He found friends in England with "deep and friendly interest in the prospects of civil service reform in the U.S." and wrote to Representative Jenckes on Christmas Day, 1871 for copies of his bills, speeches, and "other writings on civil reform."[22] Eaton wrote again from London a month later to thank Jenckes for his material. He urged the Congressman to continue his efforts outside of Congress, for he felt that the election of 1872 would decide the issue. "No question of so great a moment -- save that which was decided by the Election of Mr. Lincoln -- has, in my opinion, ever been decided by a presidential election." Eaton had no illusions that the struggle would be easy. He cautioned: "I have some fear that the opposition of partisans will be more desperate and powerful than has been anticipated."[23]

The Washington Post, obviously pleased with Grant, wrote that Eaton's "appointment is just tribute to one who is worthy of all confidence."[24] Eaton, who felt Curtis' resignation hasty, applied considerable energy and enthusiasm to his new job. The Commission, now composed of Eaton, Cattell, Walker, Elliott, Blackfan, Cox, and Samuel Schellabarger who replaced Joseph Medill, met with Grant and the Cabinet on May 24, 1873. They agreed to several adjustments in the civil service rules; examinations should recognize fitness for special duties, and jobs should be more evenly distributed among the states. Working rapidly under Eaton's chairmanship, the Commission issued a Report of June 4, 1873, which surveyed existing conditions and recommended ten new rules which the President implemented on August 5.

The new rules authorized government officials to accept recommendations for jobs in written form only. Removals could not be made solely for the purpose of creating a vacancy for another employee. Rule 6 permitted examinations "in anticipation of vacancies," and Rules 7 and 8 authorized appointments to certain fiscal positions "without examination of persons." The most significant addition to the rules established five Civil Service Districts of equal population size. The Commission hoped that the district concept would

---

[22] Dorman B. Eaton to Jenckes, London, 25 December 1871, Jenckes Papers.

[23] Dorman B. Eaton to Jenckes, London, 4 February 1872, Jenckes Papers; Gerald W. McFarland, "Partisan of Nonpartisanship: Dorman B. Eaton and the Genteel Reform Tradition," The Journal of American History 54 (December 1967): pp. 806-811.

[24] The Washington Post, 16 April 1873.

increase the opportunity for candidates from distant
states to compete for government jobs.[25]

These new rules satisfied no one. Stalwarts continued to attack the Commission in Congress and at state and
national conventions. Reformers continued to attack Grant's
intentions and his nominations. Eaton tried to protect
President Grant against impatient reformers and find a means
of improving relations with Congress through rule changes
and other approaches. Commissioner Eaton decided that the
rules which led to Curtis' resignation should be withdrawn
and persuaded the Commission to eliminate them. These rules
required the executive to fill Customhouse collector and
surveyor vacancies from subordinates in the organizations
concerned. Eaton felt them impractical and ineffective because competitive examinations were inoperative for appoint-
ive positions. He incorporated these changes into a comprehensive report issued April 18, 1874.

The Commission tried to defend civil service reform in
the 1874 report. The report discussed in considerable detail
the problems, both political and administrative, encountered
by the Commission. It contained segments on the history of
civil service reform and major arguments against reform, including the constitutional question. The report recognized
that the struggle for reform centered on whether the executive or legislative branches would control the federal administration. The Commission explained the evils which
Congress intended the civil service act to remedy. It discussed problems pertaining to political parties, public relations, and creation of the essential condition of reform.
The Commission restated the rules and their results with comments on the future prospects of civil service reform. The
report incorporated several sections dealing with the activities of the Chief Examiner, tables showing the home state of
federal employees, examples of examination questions for admission and promotion, investigation results of charges
against the board of examiners, excerpts of executive statements on civil service, and opinions of the heads of departments and offices affected by the rules.[26]

---

[25]U.S. Civil Service Commission, Report of Civil Service
Commission, June 4, 1873.

[26]U.S. Civil Service Commission, The Civil Service of the
United States: The Theory, Methods, and Results of the Reform
Introduced by the President Pursuant to the Act of March 3,
1871, Stated by the Civil Service Commission in a Report to
the President, April 15, 1874.

The Civil Service Commission never enjoyed much support from Congress, but the message of the President transmitting the 1874 report showed declining support from the White House.

> I advise for the present only such appropriation
> as may be adequate to continue the work in its
> present form, and would leave to the future to
> determine whether the direct sanction of Congress
> should be given to rules that may, perhaps, be
> devised for regulating the method of selection
> of appointees, or a portion of them, who need to
> be confirmed by the Senate.[27]

Dorman Eaton thought the appropriations struggle in 1874 untimely. He feared Grant's veto of a monetary inflation plan may have irritated Congress. Ben Butler, supporter of the inflation scheme, thought the timing good to cripple civil service reform. In the House, Butler and John A. Kasson defeated an attempt to appropriate $25,000 for the Commission and passed an amendment abolishing the Civil Service Commission. A conference committee failed to reach an agreement. This resulted in dropping the money appropriated by the House and abandoning the legislation intended to repeal the law creating the Commission. Thus, the Commission remained legal but penniless.[28]

The unwillingness of Congress to appropriate funds to the Civil Service Commission and unrelenting attacks on civil service reform by spoils politicians resulted in weakening the resolution of department heads to apply the rules. E.O. Graves, Chief Clerk of the Treasury Department in Washington, and Silas W. Burt, Deputy Naval Officer in New York Customhouse, did all in their power to promote civil service reform and scrupulously apply the Commission rules. However, they encountered increasingly less support from the politicians above them. Burt, for instance, as chairman of the local supervisory board, administered one of the first competitive examinations in the United States civil service. Burt published a report in the New York Times praising the accomplishments of the Customhouse experiment with examinations. When his close friend Chester A.

---

[27] The Civil Service of the United States, op. cit.

[28] Dorman B. Eaton to John Bright, Washington, 21 May 1874, John Bright Papers, British Museum; U.S. Congressional Record, 43rd Cong., 1st Sess., 1874, pp. 4888-4889, 4919, 4974-4976, 4997.

221

Arthur assumed the Collector's post, he relieved Burt of his examination duties and proceeded to limit applicants to political associates.[29]

In face of this constant public and private hostility, the members of the Civil Service Commission continued to deliberate on new rules and regulations. The Commission developed and promulgated new rules for lighthouse keepers, and President Grant extended the jurisdiction of the Commission to all federal offices in the city of Boston. These two steps mark the last advances of the Civil Service Commission.

The election of November 1874 resulted in a severe defeat to Republicans in the Congress. Democrats captured control of the House and reduced the Republican strength in the Senate to a slim majority. In December 1874 President Grant decided to press for a decision on the Civil Service Commission. He sent a message to the lame-duck Forty-third Congress that he supported civil service reform but declared it necessary to secure Congressional support. "If Congress adjourns without positive legislation on the subject of 'civil service' reform, I will regard such action as a disapproval of the system and will abandon it. . . ."[30]

President Grant's tactic failed to stimulate the Congress into action, and he had no other choice but to suspend the Commission and abandon its rules. On May 9, 1875, the first experiment with civil service reform came to an inglorious conclusion.

Grant's motives for terminating the activities of the Commission are not clear. He supported the system consistently for five years and had sufficient funds available for more than one additional year of operation. Perhaps he simply tired of the constant struggle. Maybe he wanted to reward his stalwart supporters in Congress or changed his mind about the benefits of civil service reform. Many historians think that Grant's political philosophy decided the

---

[29] "Civil Service Reform: Its Working in the Custom-House-- Report From an Official Engaged in Applying the Rules," New York Times, 24 March 1873, p. 8; Silas W. Burt, "Writings: Civil Service Reform 1886-1900," written about 1905, Burt Writings, New York Public Library.

[30] Richardson, 3:301.

issue. He believed that Congress should determine policy and the President should execute it.[31]

Two months after the experiment ended Eaton, assigned blame to Congress and party managers. According to Eaton, Grant lacked the necessary "zeal" and "self-denial" to carry out a reform. Nevertheless, "he was the first President who had the moral courage and the disinterestedness to attempt the overthrow of the spoils system, and he was the last of the great forces of his party to leave the field."[32]

The Grant Civil Service Commission established a number of administrative and legal precedents with long range implications. Most of the rules and regulations created by the Grant Commission became part of the Pendleton Act of 1883 or Civil Service Commission rules and regulations.[33]

Hayes Arrests Decline

Corruption in the Grant Administration, particularly the Whiskey Ring exposed by Treasury Secretary Benjamin H. Bristow, and the election of 1876, helped to revise the fortunes of civil service reformers. Henry and Charles Francis Adams, Jr. managed to form a united front among reformers with a meeting held on April 27, 1875. They convinced Schurz and other reformers to support Rutherford B. Hayes for Governor of Ohio. Hayes' victory and eventual nomination as President by the Republican Party over James G. Blaine, Roscoe Conkling, Oliver P. Morton and Benjamin Bristow managed to revise the enthusiasm and optimism of the reform elements in the country. The Democratic candidate Samuel James Tilden attracted a number of reformers, giving a considerable amount of promise that

---

[31]White, The Republican Era, p. 286; Murphy, p. 318; Hoogenboom, pp. 133-134.

[32]Dorman B. Eaton, The Experiment of Civil Service Reform in the United States: Paper. . .Read Before the American Social Science Association of Detroit, May 1875, pp. 1-37.

[33]Murphy, p. 332: The basic enactment of 1871 giving the President power to regulate the civil service was never repealed. Grant simply stopped using his existing authority. To this day the 1871 law is cited as one authority in Executive Orders for directives administering the civil service system.

either candidate would advance the cause of civil service reform.[34]

Hayes consulted with Curtis and Schurz who urged him to "devote the whole energy" of his Administration to civil service reform. Hayes assured them that "I think as you do -- probably precisely as you do, on the Civil Service reform" question and promised to "make that the issue of the canvass."[35] He followed through by making a strong endorsement of the principles of civil service reform in his July 8 letter of acceptance. Reformers felt it "hit the nail on the head."[36]

Rutherford B. Hayes failed to meet reformers' expectations on many occasions. Even though Schurz campaigned vigorously for him, the Republican presidential candidate relegated the question of civil service reform to a relatively minor place in the campaign. He employed archspoilsman Zachariah Chandler as Republican National Committee Chairman and allowed him to collect political assessments from government employees over the strong objection of Schurz. Hayes won the election in United States history's most disputed presidential election. Democratic candidate Samuel J. Tilden received 250,000 more votes than Republican Hayes. The votes of four states -- South Carolina, Florida, Louisiana, and Oregon -- came under dispute, and Republican Party officials employed considerable political manipulations to capture the electoral votes of each one, resulting in a one-

---

[34]David Saville Muzzey, James G. Blaine: A Political Idol of Other Days (New York: Dodd, Mead & Company, 1934), pp. 77-116; Kenneth E. Davison, The Presidency of Rutherford B. Hayes (Westport, Connecticut: Greenwood Press, Inc., 1972), pp. 19-37; Keith Ian Polankoff, The Politics of Inertia: The Election of 1876 and the End of Reconstruction (Baton Rouge, Louisiana: Louisiana State University Press, 1973), pp. 16-93; H.J. Eckenrode, Rutherford B. Hayes: Statesman of Reunion (Port Washington, N.Y.: Kennikat Press, 1930), pp. 100-138; Jordan, pp. 229-242; Webb, pp. 216-262; Logsdon, pp. 305-307; Welch, pp. 54-58; Milne, pp. 150-151.

[35]Carl Schurz to Hayes, Fort Washington, Pennsylvania, 21 June 1876, Bancroft, 3:250-251; Hayes to Schurz, Columbus, Ohio, 27 June 1876, Schurz Papers; George W. Curtis to Hayes, West New Brighton, 22 June 1876, Hayes Papers, The Rutherford B. Hayes Library.

[36]George W. Curtis to Hayes, Ashfield, Massachusetts, 13 July 1877, Hayes Papers.

vote victory for Hayes. A Congressional Electoral Commission confirmed the victory.[37]

Once elected, the President gave reformers sufficient
encouragement to sustain their support. He incorporated
a strong civil service endorsement in his inaugural speech
along the lines of the letter of acceptance. Cabinet selections received a favorable response, especially Carl
Schurz for Secretary of Interior and William M. Evarts
as Secretary of State.[38]

Carl Schurz, with encouragement from Hayes, moved
early to establish a competitive system for appointments
and promotions in the Interior Department. He created a
competitive examination system which followed closely the
bill he submitted to Congress in 1871. He established a
board of inquiry to investigate and recommend to the
Secretary of Interior nominations for appointment, promotions, and removals. The Interior system restricted candidates for examinations to those approved by the Secretary, and made all nominations subject to his approval.
This effectively limited the candidates eligible to sit
for examinations to those whose political affiliation
corresponded to the Secretary of Interior. Schurz's
examination procedures improved the caliber of candidates
entering the Department. Coupled with a policy decision
to make "no dismissals without cause," Schurz's examination

---

[37]John C. Hopper to Schurz, New York, 14 March 1877; William
Endicott, Jr., to Schurz, Boston, 22 March 1877; William
Welsh to Schurz, Philadelphia, 24 March 1877, Schurz Papers;
Carl Schurz to Hayes, Fort Washington, 14 July 1876; Schurz
to Hayes, Fort Washington, 14 August 1876; Schurz to Hayes,
Fort Washington, 3 September 1876, Hayes Papers; C. Van
Woodward, Reunion and Reaction: The Compromise of 1877 and
the End of Reconstruction (New York: Doubleday & Co., 1956),
p. 20; Mary Karl George, Zachariah Chandler: A Political
Biography (East Lansing, Michigan: Michigan State University
Press, 1969), pp. 249-260; Davison, pp. 40-46; Polakoff,
pp. 94-314; Eckenrode, pp. 139-234.

[38]Richardson, 7:444-445; Nation (New York), 15 March 1877,
p. 153; "The President and the Civil Service," Harper's
Weekly (New York), 24 March 1877, p. 223.

system strengthened the civil service reform posture of the Hayes Administration.[39]

President Hayes turned his attention from the Southern Question to civil service reform in April 1877 when he wrote in his diary: "Now for civil service reform. . . . We must stop interference of federal officers with elections."[40] On June 22, 1877, he issued an Executive Order prohibiting government employees from taking "part in the management of political organizations, caucuses, conventions, or election campaign," and interdicted political assessments. Reformers and reform journals applauded the order. Harper's Weekly, for instance, wrote: "The purpose is one which ought to be heartily commended by every good citizen, for it is nothing less than the emancipation of politics from official control, and their restoration to the great body of the citizens."[41]

New York Stalwarts -- Attempts to Weaken

The Executive Order gave Hayes a weapon to help him attack the political power of anti-Hayes Republicans in New York State. President Grant had transferred control of patronage in the New York Customhouse to Roscoe Conkling, boss of New York State Republicans. Rutherford Hayes refused to accept this decision and decided to reassert his

---

[39]"The Civil Service," New York Times, 6 April 1877, p. 1; Nation (New York), 12 April 1877, pp. 4-5; U.S. Department of Interior, U.S. Patent Office, Special Order, 10 April 1877; S.L. Bayliss to Schurz, Keakuk, Iowa, 17 March 1877; W.M. Ampt to Schurz, Washington, D.C., 20 March 1877; Horace H. Higgens to Schurz, St. Louis, 24 March 1877; Dr. C.A. De-Marsan Spencer, Ellicott City, Maryland to Schurz; John F. Wait to Schurz, Norwalk, Connecticut, 9 April 1877; Commissioner Patent Office to Schurz, Washington, D.C. "Civil Service Reform as Applied to the Interior Department," 23 April 1877, Schurz Papers.

[40]Charles Richard Williams, ed., Diary and Letters of Rutherford Birchard Hayes, 5 vols. (Columbus, Ohio: The Ohio State Archaeological and Historical Society, 1922-1926), 3:430.

[41]"The President's Order," Harper's Weekly (New York), 21 July 1877, p. 55; Nation (New York), 28 June 1877, p. 373; "The Hopes of the Office-Holders," Nation, 28 June 1877, pp. 376-377; Richardson, 7:450-451.

226

authority. He began cautiously by appointing John Jay, a
reform advocate, to investigate the Customhouse in New York.
The Jay Commission found the Customhouse managed for political purposes and recommended a twenty per cent reduction
in staff and an increase in working hours. Inefficiency,
incompetence, and corruption pervaded the work force, which
devoted much of its time to political activities. The Commission observed that party leaders with the help of Customhouse officials systematically pressed employees to pay
political assessments. ". . . the existing system . . .
with little or no examination into the fitness of the appointee. . .[is] unsound in principle, dangerous in practice,
[and] demoralizing in its influence. . . ." The Commission
declared that no improvements are possible "until the service is freed from the control of party. . . ." President
Hayes endorsed the report and issued instructions to his
Secretary of Treasury, John Sherman:

> It is my wish that the collection of the reve-
> nues should be free from partisan control, and
> organized on a strictly business basis, with
> the same guarantees for efficiency and fidelity
> in the selection of the chief and subordinate
> officers that would be required by a prudent
> merchant. Party leaders should have no more
> influence in appointments than other equally
> respectable citizens. No assessments for poli-
> tical purposes on officers or subordinates
> should be allowed; no useless officer or em-
> ployee should be retained; no officer should
> be required or permitted to take part in the
> management of political organizations, caucuses,
> conventions, or election campaigns. Their
> right to vote and to express their views on
> public questions, either orally or through the
> press, is not denied, provided it does not
> interfere with the discharge of their of-
> ficial duties.[42]

Sherman, who disapproved of Hayes' approach, sent a
considerably weaker letter to Collector Chester A. Arthur,
ordering him to reduce the staff but playing down or eliminating the political elements of Hayes' instructions.

---

[42]U.S. Congress, House, Commissions to Examine Certain Custom-
houses of the United States, House Executive Documents, 45th
Cong., 1st Sess., I, No. 8, 1877, pp. 14-16; "Reform in the
Custom-House," Harper's Weekly (New York), 16 June 1877, p. 458.

Reformers, demanding the removal of Collector Arthur,
Surveyor Sharpe and Naval Officer Alonzo Cornell, found
the Sherman letter disappointing. Harper's Weekly satir-
ized the Sherman letter: "Mr. Collector, the President
wishes the Custom-house to be taken out of politics. You
will please do it in your own way, only -- you will, of
course, leave politics in."[43]

Naval Officer Alonzo Cornell offered Hayes another
opportunity to resume the battle against Senator Conkling.
Probably on Conkling's advice Cornell flaunted Hayes' order instructing government employees to desist from participation in political party activities. He openly attended party meetings and helped organize the New York
State Convention. Reformers demanded his resignation or
removal. Hayes announced that he continued to believe
in the soundness of the June 22 order and notified Secretary of Treasury, John Sherman, to relieve all three
Customhouse officials. Sherman announced on September 6
the President's decision. "After full consideration it
has been determined by the President that the public interests would be better served by the appointment of new
officers for the three leading positions in the New-York
Custom-house."[44]

Conkling lost no time in attacking Hayes and the reformers who supported him. He delivered a stinging speech
against President Hayes at the New York State Republican
Convention in Rochester with "Mephistophelean leer and
spite" reserved for George William Curtis. He followed
that with a demonstration of his strength in Congress by
leading the Senate rejection of Hayes' nominees, Theodore
Roosevelt, Sr., L. Bradford Prince, and Edwin A. Merritt
for Collector, Naval Officer and Surveyor respectively.
Hayes resubmitted the trio several months later. The Senate debate on the renomination of Hayes' appointees elevated the struggle from that of a Republican party factional
struggle to one between the President and Senate over control

---

[43] "The Prospects of Reform," Harper's Weekly (New York), 7
July 1877, p. 518; "Reform in the Custom-House," Harper's
Weekly, 16 June 1877, pp. 458-459; Thomas C. Reeves, Gentleman Boss, The Life of Chester Alan Arthur (New York: Knopf,
1975), pp. 119-120.

[44] John Sherman, Recollections of Forty Years in the House,
Senate and Cabinet: An Autobiography (Chicago: The Werner
Co., 1895), 2 vols., 2:679-681; "New York Custom-House,"
New York Times, 7 September 1877; Nation (New York), 6 Sep-
tember 1877, p. 143; Nation, 13 September 1877, p. 159; "Re-
movals from Office," Harper's Weekly, p. 878.

of spoils. Again Hayes lost by a vote of 31 to 25.[45]

Senator Conkling's three lieutenants continued in office under the provisions of the Tenure of Office Act. Hayes waited until after the election of 1878 and the adjournment of Congress when the Tenure of Office Act no longer applied to Arthur and Cornell. He removed both men and appointed Edwin A. Merritt Collector, Silas W. Burt Naval Officer, and George K. Graham Surveyor. These nominations passed the Senate on February 3, 1879, and represent a major victory of President Hayes over Senator Conkling.[46]

The Hayes-Conkling controversy catapulted Alonzo Cornell into the Governorship of New York State and Chester A. Arthur into the Vice Presidency and eventually Presidency of the United States. Nevertheless, it produced the first crack in Conkling's armor which came crumbling apart under President Garfield. The newspapers characterized Conkling as the "villainous" spoilsman and Hayes as the "white knight" reformer. Neither is accurate or fair and represents a simplistic view of the conflict. The Hayes-Conkling controversy not only involved control over the spoils in New York Customhouse but New York State political issues, Republican Party politics, and personality conflicts. It was a key chapter in the struggle between the legislative and executive branches of government.

Hayes Fails

The Hayes Administration failed to fulfill its reform promise. It contributed very little to the advancement of civil service reform even though publicly committed to it. Even the discredited Grant Administration could claim more credit for advancing the cause of civil service reform than the Hayes Administration. The Grant Commission rules and

---

[45]Alfred Ronald Conkling, The Life and Letters of Roscoe Conkling, Orator, Statesman, Advocate (New York: C.L. Webster & Co., 1899), pp. 538-549; Jordan, pp. 275-287; G.W. Curtis to Norton, Ashfield, 30 September 1877, Norton Papers; Carl Schurz to Henry Cabot Lodge, Washington, 1 December 1877, Schurz Papers; Nation (New York), 13 December 1877, p. 357; Nation, 20 December 1877, p. 373.

[46]Venila Lovina Shores, The Hayes-Conkling Controversy, 1877-1879 (New York: Northampton, Mass., Department of History of Smith College, 1919), pp. 254, 262-266; Jordan, pp. 293-301; Milne, pp. 154-159; Eckenrode, pp. 273-279; Davison, pp. 164-165; H. Wayne Morgan, From Hayes to McKinley: National

and regulations established a solid foundation for future advances in reform. The Hayes Administration included three strong advocates of civil service reform -- Hayes himself, Secretary of State William Evarts, and Carl Schurz, a giant among civil service reformers. Ironically, the most thorough reform occurred in the New York Customhouse after the departure of Chester Arthur under the control of Secretary of Treasury John Sherman, one of the least enthusiastic supporters of reform in the Cabinet. In his letter of acceptance Hayes promised a "thorough radical and complete" reform of the civil service. His diary of April 22, 1877, began with: "Now for civil service reform." He wrote the same words on December 8, 1878. Reformers who supported Hayes constantly complained about his lack of progress. William Grosvenor told Schurz on March 26, 1877: "I am afraid the President is making haste too slowly." On July 10 C. Tenney wrote from Kansas: ". . . at present he [President Hayes] seems to have a painful hesitation. . . compromising between the professions of civil service reform. . . and the professed politician. . . ."[47]

Even its most conspicuous successes in civil service reform had major defects. Schurz's competitive examinations in the Department of Interior opened the door only to candidates approved by the Secretary. Hayes' June 22, 1877 order, prohibiting political assessments and participation in political activities by government employees, accomplished little except in the Hayes-Conkling controversy. The order was openly and flagrantly disregarded during the election campaigns of 1878 and 1880. The Hayes victory over Conkling in the New York Customhouse benefited civil service reform because the appointment of Deputy Naval Officer Silas W. Burt to Naval Officer placed an ardent civil service reformer in a key position to influence the development of new customhouse rules and regulations. Hayes himself recognized his lack of progress. On April 11, 1880, he wrote in his diary: "I have not done as much to improve the System and methods of the Civil Service as I hoped and tried to do."

Party Politics, 1877-1896 (Syracuse: Syracuse University Press, 1969), pp. 67-69; Rothman, pp. 30-31.

[47]Williams, 22 April 1877 and 8 December 1877; W.M. Grosvenor to Schurz, New York, 26 March 1877; C. Tenney to Schurz, Lawrence, Kansas, 10 July 1877; William M. Grosvenor was editor of the St. Louis Democrat and later contributed articles to the New York Tribune. He was an Independent Republican and supporter of Carl Schurz. Charles Daniel Tenney was a supporter of civil service reform. He later went to China as an American missionary and became the first president of Imperial Chinese University, Tiensin.

President Hayes' inability to effect civil service reform during his Administration most likely resulted from his concept of the power of the Presidency. Like Ulysses S. Grant, Rutherford Hayes looked to Congress to establish civil service reform. He never seriously considered taking the matter in his own hands. He made three major public appeals to Congress for action. Congress failed to act on his appeals in his letter of acceptance and inauguration speech. It failed to respond to his third annual message on December 1, 1879, in which he asked for an appropriation to renew the Civil Service Commission. Finally, the Congress took no action on his final message in 1880 which renewed the request for an appropriation to revive the Civil Service Commission and abolish political assessments. Hayes attributed his failures to public opinion and an unresponsive Congress. He wrote in his diary on July 11, 1880: "I would like to make it clear. . . that public opinion and Congress must be right on the question before we can have a thorough and complete Reform. The President has neither time, nor authority, neither means nor men, to gather the information required to make appointments and removals."[48]

---

[48]Williams, p. 283; Richardson, 7:562 and 603.

CHAPTER IX

REFORMERS GO TO ENGLAND

During the decade of the 1870's reformers continued
to draw inspiration from Great Britain. The decade began
with the work of the Grant Civil Service Commission and
concluded when Dorman Eaton published his comprehensive
book on the Civil Service in Great Britain. The Grant
Commissioners designed a system modeled after the one in
Britain. The Commissioners maintained close contact with
British officials between 1871 and 1875. Eaton's trip
to England and subsequent book is one of the most important
contributions to reform. It provided reformers with an intimate understanding of civil service reform in Great Britain, and contributed significantly to British influence on
the American civil service system.

The Grant Commission Looks to
Britain for Inspiration

The Grant Civil Service Commission met for the first
time on June 28, 1871.[1] The Washington Evening Star speculated that the first order of business would be to organize and adopt "some plan by which statistics of the civil
service in the different countries of Europe may be obtained." Chairman George William Curtis secured this information before the meeting, allowing the board to move
directly into a discussion of the Commission's authority.
The second day Curtis read "a letter to himself from Mr.
Jenckes on this subject, followed by a discussion of various ideas on reform of the civil service."[2] George Curtis
led the committee into a discussion of substantive issues
by offering a resolution to regulate admissions to the
civil service through open competitive examination. The
Chairman supported his resolution by drawing attention to
the British. He told them that "competitive examinations
. . . had revolutionized the whole civil service of Great
Britain." Competitive examinations "would, he thought, insure a moral stability, as it had done in England, which
would endear itself to the people and they would in time
require it to be incorporated into the law of the land."[3]

---

[1]Minutes, June 28, 1871, p. 5.

[2]Ibid., June 29, 1871, p. 7.

[3]Ibid., June 30, 1871, p. 9.

233

Joseph Medill opposed the resolution. "A general objection is that this is the Chinese system, adapted to
a paternal Government, but unsuitable in a republic
where parties do and must exist."[4]

Throughout the first session Chairman Curtis submitted various documents relating to foreign experiences.
On July 5, Commissioner Blackfan delivered "certain documents . . . from the English Civil Service" which Curtis
introduced. On July 7, the Chairman

> submitted a letter received from Geo E.
> Brown, Esq., offering the loan of certain
> documents in references to the British
> Civil Service.
>
> He also submitted a copy of the Report of
> the Select Committee appointed to inquire
> into the Constitution of the English Dip-
> lomatic and Consular Service, dated May
> 18, 1871.[5]

On the same day he received a letter from John Hitz, Consul
General of the Swiss Confederation, "on the subject of civil
service of Switzerland."[6]

Between the first and second sessions Curtis received
from Thomas Jenckes his correspondence and documents with
British officials, and entered into discussions with British
officials directly. The Secretary of the English Civil Service Commission sent him "several documents . . . comprising
the latest orders and directions of the Commission and showing the working of the British System."[7] This helped the
Chairman to reinforce his demand for open competitive examinations. Curtis added to the material received from Jenckes
by entering into correspondence with Sir Charles Trevelyan

---

[4] Minutes, July 1, 1871, p. 10.

[5] Ibid., July 7, 1871, p. 19.

[6] Ibid.

[7] Ibid., October 17, 1871, p. 23.

and Sir Stafford Northcote. He became familiar with the
views of John Stuart Mill, Benjamin Jowett, and members of
the British Civil Service Commission. Curtis incorporated
into the minutes of the Commission the important 1869 letter [9]
from Sir Charles Trevelyan to Charles Brace of New York City.
On November 3, 1871, Chairman Curtis read another letter
from Benjamin Jowett, the Secretary of the British Civil Service Commission. Later he quoted Gladstone and made reference "to the progress of British Civil Service Reform."[10]

The Commission turned again to Great Britain in developing its examinations. At the request of Chairman Curtis,
the Commission invited Reverend Doctor James McCosh to speak.
He was a Scotch philosopher, educator, and writer who was
professor of logic and metaphysics at Queen's College, Bel-
fast, before coming to the United States to serve as President of Princeton College. The Reverend Doctor "offered
some suggestions in regard to the scope of examinations,
based upon his experience in connection with the civil service system of Great Britain."[11] The Commission, through
Chairman Curtis, maintained such close contact with British
officials that it sent them a copy of Attorney General
Akerman's decision on competitive examinations and asked
them for comments.[12]

George W. Curtis prepared the first report to the
President and Congress of an American civil service commission. The report attributed the adoption of open competitive
examinations to the example of Great Britain. It explained
the rule requiring selection from a list of three as more
advanced than the rule in England. "It appears probable
that this method, which is precisely the one we have adopted,
will also be approved in England."[13]

The report quoted Prime Minister Gladstone reviewing
the results of his administration. Gladstone said:

---

[8]Murphy, p. 219.

[9]Minutes, November 1, 1871, p. 38. See Chapter VIII.

[10]Ibid., November 13, 1871, p. 45.

[11]Ibid., February 2, 1871, p. 112.

[12]Report of the Civil Service Commission, December 1871, p. 16.

[13]Ibid.

It has been our happy lot, in almost every
department of the State . . . to give up
that which has always been considered the
special patronage and the highly prized patronage of a government, namely, the appointment of clerks to the civil offices of the
country. We have abandoned that power; we
have thrown every one of them open to public
competition. The transition is now nearly
complete, and, with regard to the future, I
can say that, as to the clerkships in my own
office -- the office of the treasury --
every one of you have just as much power over
their dismissal as I have.

The Prime Minister went on to state, "every man belonging
to the people of England, if he so pleases to fit his
children for the position of competing for places in the
public service, may do it entirely irrespective of the
question, what is his condition in life, or the amount of
means with which he may happen to be or not to be blessed."[14]
The Civil Service Commission proposed to do the same thing,
according to the report. "We propose also that in this
country the places in the public service shall be restored
to those who are found to be fitted for them."[15]

The rules and regulations recommended by the Commission
closely followed the system operating in Great Britain. Dorman Eaton acknowledged the debt to Great Britain in his book
on the Civil Service in Great Britain. "It is a matter of
general information, that under President Grant a trial, beginning January 1st, 1872, was made of the merit system in
a limited way; the regulations, competitions and examinations being closely analogous to those so long in practice
in Great Britain."[16]

---

[14]Report of the Civil Service Commission, December 1871, p. 22;
the quote is from a speech delivered at Greenwich, England,
on 28 October 1871.

[15]Ibid., pp. 22-23.

[16]Dorman B. Eaton, Civil Service in Great Britain: A History
of Abuses and Reforms and Their Bearing Upon American Politics
(New York: Harper & Brothers, 1880), p. 445.

British Influence Under the New Chairman

In March 1873, Chairman George William Curtis resigned. President Grant appointed staunch civil service reformer Dorman B. Eaton to succeed Curtis and ex-Congressman Samuel Shellabarger to replace Chicago Mayor Joseph Medill. Eaton possessed a thorough knowledge of English administrative practices obtained from his sojourn to Great Britain between 1870 and 1873. During his stay he studied British practices first hand as well as administrative systems of other European countries.

The new Chairman of the Civil Service Commission wrote immediately to John Bright, member of Gladstone's cabinet, upon hearing of his appointment. Bright responded with an unequivocal endorsement of the civil service reform system in England. He declared that "it would be impossible to go back to the old system." The British civil service reform system then in use was "more just" and "calculated to supply more capable men" than the previous patronage system. He indirectly criticized the "spoils system" in the United States by promoting permanent tenure. "No changes in persons employed in government offices . . . take place on a change of government, and thus we avoid a vast source of disturbance and corruption. . . ." Bright wrote that expanded government service "in these days" makes it "absolutely necessary to take precautions against the selection of incompetent men, and against the corruption which under the purest administration is always a menacing evil."

John Bright endorsed Eaton's reform efforts and declared: "All the friends of your country in other nations will congratulate you in your success . . . [if] the good sense of your people will enable you to complete it." He closed by sending Eaton "some of our Parliamentary publications, that you may know the latest facts connected with what is doing here in the matter of our civil service."[17]

The new Commission rapidly developed modifications to the rules and regulations and published them in the Report of

---

[17]John Bright to D.B. Eaton, London, 29 April 1874, Dorman B. Eaton, Civil Service in Great Britain: A History of Abuses and Reforms and Their Bearing Upon American Politics (New York: Harper & Brothers, 1880), pp. 433-434; D.B. Eaton to John Bright, Washington, 21 May 1874, Bright Papers, British Museum.

June 4, 1873. The report contained ten new rules; the
most important one pertaining to conducting examinations
in various outlying geographic locations came directly
from Britain. The report acknowledged this fact when it
defended the new rule by saying: "we think . . . it would
be the case here, as it now is in England, that such examinations would be sought by worthy young men, . . ."[18]

On April 15, 1874, the Commission under Eaton made
its last major attempt to defend civil service reform and
get support in Congress and among the people. It issued
a comprehensive report covering the entire range of rules
and regulations and discussed the major political arguments for and against reform. The report referred to the
English system frequently. The Commission incorporated a
rather extended section on: "The Experience of Other
Countries" in the 1874 report. The report mentioned China,
but it moved rapidly to Great Britain. "Besides considering the administrative methods of several continental nations, we looked especially into the political history of
England. . . to see what we might learn from the experience
of a country. . ." from which we have obtained many of
our institutions. The "demand for civil service . . . was
a republican, a democratic protest against the privileges
of royalty, aristocracy, and the state church. . . . "We
think," the report stated, "it may be fairly doubted whether
any single public measure in England has ever inaugurated
a movement more republican, more democratic in tendency,
more threatening to any of those institutions, than civil
service reform."[19] The report returned often to the theme
that civil service reform was suited to republican institutions and eliminated many aristocratic procedures. "We
could see nothing which a monarchy ought alone to desire,
or which a republic would have occasion to fear, but rather a spirit and an influence in harmony with our system
of general institution, and with our theory of equal rights
and opportunities to all, which the aristocracy of England
still oppose."[20] Civil Service reform had reduced corruption,

---

[18] U.S. Civil Service Commission [Grant Commission], Report of
Civil Service Commission, June 4, 1873, p. 7.

[19] U.S. Civil Service Commission [Grant Commission], The Civil
Service of the United States: The Theory, Methods, and Results of the Reform Introduced by the President Pursuant to
the Act of March 3, 1871, Stated by the Civil Service Commission in a Report to the President, April 15, 1874, p. 25.

[20] Ibid., p. 26.

advanced "the cause of general education," and "increased
the equality of . . . administration."

These observations were not conjecture but expressions
of the true contribution of civil service reform. They "have
been confirmed by the observations of a member of this Commission,"[21] and prominent English citizens including Prime
Minister Gladstone, Cabinet members Mr. Foster, John Bright,
Professor Fawcett, Secretary of the Queen's Privy Council,
Arthur Helps, M.P. Neate and John Stuart Mill.[22]

The 1874 report devoted a large amount of space to a
discussion of the most important arguments against civil
service reform. It refuted the contention that reform would
"establish a bureaucracy of officeholders." "So far from
creating an aristocracy, we have shown that the adoption of
civil service rules in England has been a great victory in
the spirit of republicanism, won by the common people, under
the lead of the liberal party, over the lords, the bishops,
and the landed aristocracy."[23] Opponents charged that "the
rules are intended to destroy parties." The Commissioners
emphasized again that "it is the party most republican in
England which promotes civil service reform, and that this
reform has gained strength there just in proportion as the
privileges of royalty and class have given place to republican principles." Rather than being hostile to parties
"the rules seem to us to carry out the spirit, and substantially the letter, of the resolutions of all the parties"
in the United States.[24] Eaton, writing for the Commission,
pointed out that several British civil service rules were
not adopted in the United States. He denied the argument
that civil service reform favored college graduates to the
exclusion of the less educated.

> In England, when the aristocratic classes were
> unable longer to keep what they call the com-
> mon people from the public service, they
> naturally tried to raise the standard of lit-
> erary attainments so high as to secure a mono-
> poly to that higher education in which such
> classes might excel. They also tried to es-
> tablish a permanent tenure of office and pro-
> motions by seniority rather than by competition.

---

[21] Dorman B. Eaton.

[22] 1874 Report, pp. 26-27.

[23] Ibid., pp. 71-72.

[24] Ibid., p. 73.

Those features of the English system, we have
regarded as hostile to the theory of our institutions; and the rules adopted have, therefore, most regard for practical, business
qualities, exacting only so much general information as seems most desirable.[25]

The increased quality of candidates recruited under
the English open examination concept sometimes resulted
in a decrease in the number of employees needed to accomplish a task.[26] Thus, civil service reform had the potential of reducing the cost of government.

Some opponents stated that pass examinations "have
been as effective as competitive examinations." Administrative experience in the United States with the Act of 1853
proved that they were inadequate. The English civil service
began in 1855 with pass examinations which after a "trial
for fifteen years, were found as inadequate as in our service."[27] The report quoted John Stuart Mill writing in
1867: "A mere pass examination never, in the long run,
does more than exclude absolute dunces."[28] Other opponents
wrote that "competitive examinations are no test of the special capacity required in the public service."[29] Experience
with competitive examinations in England did not verify this
conclusion. Bearing in mind that no absolute test was possible, the English report of 1872 gave extensive evidence of
a dramatic increase in the quality of employees entering
the public service through competitive examinations.[30]

The Report of April 15, 1874 met with an unresponsive
Congress and declining interest in the White House. Within
the next year America terminated its first experience with
civil service reform.

---

[25]1874 Report, p. 77.

[26]Ibid., p. 78.

[27]Ibid.

[28]Ibid., p. 79; quote taken from John Stuart Mill, Considerations on Representative Government (New York: Harper, 1862),
p. 108.

[29]1874 Report, p. 80.

[30]Ibid., pp. 80-84.

Congressional Debate

Spoilsmen dominated Congress during the 1870's and successfully thwarted the efforts of Presidents Grant and Hayes to bring reform to the government establishment. Before 1875 the attack centered on efforts to derail the Grant Commission; after 1875 it centered on efforts to prevent its reconvening. During the debates many members of Congress tried to undermine the British and their reform success. On December 18, 1871, during the debate over the election of members to the Committee on Retrenchment, Senator Oliver P. Morton refuted the entire assumption underlying the reform movement. "I believe," he declared, "our civil service . . . [is] the best in the world. . . ." Examination "will show that greater abuses exist in the civil service" of England, France, Germany or Russia, "than exist in ours." He argued "that there is as much integrity in ours as in any other; that there is more ability; and that there is from one third to one half more labor performed by our civil service than by any other."[31]

Later Henry Snapp, Representative from Illinois, sponsored a resolution against the Civil Service Commission. He declared that the Civil Service Commission was a "Star Chamber" with power to "fill the offices in these United States." The Commission, according to Snapp, "promise that somebody else than the people shall fill these offices. And not only do they make such proposition, but they further insult this same people by proposing to make the tenure of these offices perpetual." This "Star Chamber," this "commission," he charged "gravely propose to gag the people." Snapp declared himself the "watch-tower of liberty" and charged that a "proposition not one half as infamous as this [set of Civil Service rules] made by the Parliament of Great Britain, drove our fathers through a seven years' war."[32]

Thomas J. Speer, a Republican Congressman from Georgia, delivered a long attack against the rules and regulations of the Civil Service Commission on March 2, 1872. He openly touted the benefits of the spoils system and declared: "I am not willing, under the guise of reforming the civil ser-

---

[31]U.S. _Congressional Globe_, 42nd Cong., 2nd Sess., 1871, p. 165; Morton returned to that same argument in a speech delivered one month later, p. 464.

[32]_Ibid._, pp. 444-445.

241

vice, to saddle upon the country the expensive, impractical, anti-republican, and un-American scheme which
the civil service commission has proposed."[33]

> We are told that in England such a system is
> in full operation. Possibly so; but did the
> commissioners remember that the area of the
> United States is nearly sixty times that of
> England? So what can be done in England and
> what can be done in this country are wholly
> different questions both as to practicability
> and expense.[34]

If we promulgate these civil service rules, Speer argued,
"we take a great stride toward the overthrow of republican
government and the establishment of a monarchy." The Commissioners would lead us "to ruin" if we adopted their plan.
"They recommend in a great measure the plan of civil service
which has obtained in England. If it goes that far now,
does not that indicate the tendency to go still farther,
and imitate the entire Government of England?"[35]

In the House of Representatives Henry Snapp of Illinois
returned to the attack of the Civil Service Commission on
December 14, 1872. He charged that the Commission was
"composed mainly of editors" and the report a "production
of those editors." He then attacked the reform press for
its conceit: "It being my conviction that the civil service rules were a humbug." The Commission intended "to
strip the Government offices of all political power and influence." It is nothing more than a "self-styled and arro-
gant" body intent on stripping the Members of Congress of
their power. Snapp said that the Commissioners "refer to
the British plan of competitive examination as though it
were a success."[36] It is not a success and to prove it you
need only read the London Quarterly Review of July 1872.
The author of the London article declared competitive examinations to be absurd. We must, according to the author,

---

[33] Congressional Globe, Appendix, p. 130.

[34] Ibid.

[35] Ibid.

[36] Ibid., p. 197.

242

end competitive examinations "which otherwise may linger
long and do an infinity of mischief before any political
party has the courage boldly to denounce them as unsound
and pestilent." "The idea of one 'board' selecting qualified persons for every appointment in the civil service
is preposterous." Snapp charged that civil service reform
would eliminate good men simply because they have "deficiencies in spelling and history [which] will not in the
least interfere with the efficient discharge of the duties
of the office." Henry Snapp concluded his speech with a
call to act. "Let the members of this Congress rise up
in the might of their power and crush this insidious monster. Let this Congress boldly proclaim to the world the
humbug of 'civil service reform' and it will receive the
blessing and the plaudits of this generation, and of pos-
terity in all coming time."[37]

Democratic Senator John B. Gordon of Georgia, upset
by the corruption in the revenue service revealed in the
"whisky ring," delivered a strong speech in support of the
"English system." Senator Gordon's objective in delivering the speech was "if possible, . . . to ascertain the
defects which make such frauds under our revenue system
possible and apply the remedy." Gordon pointed out that
the American revenue system came "largely from Great Britain" but we "have proceeded to knock the very breath out
of it by refusing to incorporate her methods for securing
honest men to administer it." The English collected ten
times more revenue than the United States because: "England
appoints her officers solely to collect her taxes, while
here they are appointed to collect the taxes and to aid the
party which happens for the time to have the appointing power." He went on to explain that the English revenue officials were forbidden to belong to a political party while
American officials had to belong to a party to secure a job.
The English system produced "competent" employees while the
American system produced "a political partisan, without any
experience, without any training, without any examination,
often, alas, without any qualifications." "England's method"
secured "honest and competent agents." America's method secured dishonest agents, impure politics and revenue frauds.
Under England's

system of selecting honest men, non-partisans,
this revenue system is a success, the pride of

---

[37] Congressional Globe, p. 199.

> her people, and the glory of that island.
> Under our system of selecting partisans to
> administer it, it is famous only from fail-
> ure and conspicuous only from crime. It is
> the shame of the people and the disgrace of
> the country that so many of its officers
> have become embezzlers of the revenue.[38]

The trouble with the American system was "refusing to
adopt the English policy of selecting non-partisans for
collectors of revenue."

> Sir, we must remove these collectors of
> money from party temptation and party in-
> fluence. . . . These revenue officers
> should hold their positions . . . during
> life if need be, or during good behavior,
> placed upon moderate salaries, and remov-
> able by the head of the Treasury only for
> incapacity and disreputable conduct.

Senator Oliver P. Morton dismissed Gordon's proposal
with a slur against his patriotism. "The Senator has eulo-
gized the government of England. It would appear from his
remarks that he admires it very much more than he does a
republican form of government."[39]

Reformers Make Infrequent
Use of British Example

Carl Schurz delivered his first major speech on civil
service reform in the Senate on January 27, 1871. In that
speech Schurz made no mention of the British system and
devoted only three sentences to discussing the charge that
civil service reform would create an "aristocratic class
among our population." "In fact," Schurz argued, "the idea
of a class of aristocrats, consisting of departmental clerks
of Washington and of customhouse and post-office clerks at
New York and other cities, seems to me somewhat ludicrous."[40]

---

[38] Congressional Globe, p. 1580.

[39] Ibid., p. 1581.

[40] U.S. Congressional Globe, 41st Cong., 3rd Sess., 27 January 1871, p. 161.

244

Schurz did not return to the subject until 1881 when he delivered a speech titled "Business, Public and Private." Civil Service reform was nothing more than good business and not an "outlandish philosophy, borrowed from the effete monarchies of the old world," he said. "The idea is that we should apply to the public business the same common sense principles upon which every sensible man or woman conducts his or her private business."[41]

George William Curtis frequently used the British example in his writing and speeches. Curtis attributed corruption in the New York Customhouse to political influence on appointments. "The only practical method yet suggested" for eliminating political influence on appointments "is competitive inquiry; and . . . this method works so well in England. . ." "The English are quite as practical as we," he wrote, "and understand politics and parties quite as well; and their successful practice constantly, from month to month and from day to day, disproved the theory of the American spoils system."[42] Curtis used the English example again in September 1877. He argued that "the reform of the service does not concern elective offices" and will not "destroy political activity." The English example showed that "a tenure of proved fitness and good behavior" would "take away one of the chief illicit sources of the power of 'the machine,'" and would not establish "a worse machine" in its place.[43] Three months later George Curtis ridiculed the arguments of spoilsmen against the necessity of reform.

> The scarecrows of an "English system," of a "permanent class," of an "aristocracy of office-holders," and even the latest and most ingenious device of "the anomaly of an elective officer appointing other officers during good behavior" -- a very familiar fact in the case of judges -- all gradually cease to scare.

He continued: "Thus the reform is taking root in the public conviction." Curtis concluded by predicting: "Happily the events of every day are enlightening the public mind, and confirming the public desire of a methodical correction of the notorious evils of the civil service."[44]

---

[41]"Business, Public and Private," 1881, Schurz Papers.

[42]"Official Responsibility," Harper's Weekly (New York), 25 August 1877, p. 658.

[43]"Reasonable Reform," Harper's Weekly, 1 September 1877, p. 678.

[44]"The People and Reform," Harper's Weekly, 1 December 1877, p. 746.

On September 20, 1878, Curtis delivered an address before the Unitarian Conference at Saratoga, New York. He referred to the British system on several occasions during the speech. He reminded his listeners that the "cost of collections" in the custom-houses is "nearly five times as great as in Great Britain" because of patronage. He went on to quote Gladstone who declared that the English civil service system limited its removals and appointments "to a few scores of persons" after each party election. English ministers, Gladstone declared, "seem to us not infrequently to be more sharply served from one another in principle and tendency than are the successive presidents of the great Union."[45]

The next day Harper's editor attacked Congressional "dictation of appointments" and suggested that "a method free of personal influence must be introduced. That this is practicable the experience of England shows."[46] One month after Curtis' Saratoga speech, "Treasury officers" denied the allegation that it cost five times more to collect customs in the United States than in England. Curtis used the denial to deliver a stinging attack on the cost of patronage. He directed the attention of the "Treasury officers" to the Jay Commission inquiry into the Custom-house, second report, dated July 4, 1877, which "did state in a detailed statistical appendix that the cost of our collection on 'the total importations' was nearly five times as large as in Great Britain." He went on to quote various statistics from the years 1874-5 and 1876 which were unchallenged and concluded "that the cost of collection on our total importations is nearly five times as large as in Great Britain."[47]

Edwin L. Godkin, editor of the influential New York weekly, The Nation, addressed the charge against the "European system" twice in the 1870's. He used speeches by Senator Oliver P. Morton and Massachusetts Governor Rice to dismiss the argument with a heavy dose of sarcasm. During the debate to revise the Retrenchment Committee in the Senate, Morton declared

---

[45] Norton (ed.), pp. 129-137.

[46] "Young Republicans," Harper's Weekly (New York), 21 September 1878, p. 746.

[47] "Corrections that do not Correct," Harper's Weekly, 26 October 1878, p. 846.

that our civil service is "better than that
of any European country, more free from abuses,
equal in integrity, and more efficient than
any other," and, in short, "the best in the
world." This reminds one of the minister in
Berlin who maintains that the world is flat
and the sun goes around it, and says the
"philosophers may laugh as they please, but
he is happy as a child." Statements like
this are not the articulate utterances of a
legislator but the snortings of a war-horse.[48]

The Nation accorded remarks by Governor Rice no more
respect than those of Senator Morton. Governor Rice declared "that it has sometimes appeared to those who have
given thought to the matter that it [civil service reform]
would engraft on our republican government the characteristics of the civil service of monarchies. . . . Many of
the complaints made against the American civil service are
complaints against the republican form of government itself."
Godkin ridiculed the Governor's remarks:

Now we suggest to the Govenor that he shall
lay his hand on his kindly heart and ask
himself these questions, as a means of getting to the bottom of this troublesome question. As a matter of fact, was the present
"spoils system," as it is called, introduced,
like the election of members of Congress,
for instance, into this Government deliber-
ately, as part and parcel of republican institutions, and with the view of promoting
republicanism? If not, how, by whom, and
for what reasons was it introduced? In what
way does the American people profit by it,
and how would the American people be injured
by the proposed changes? . . . We are greatly
afraid that "those" whom the Governor quotes
are not persons who "have given thought to
the matter."[49]

---

[48] Nation (New York), 21 December 1871, p. 393.

[49] Nation (New York), 10 January 1878, p. 18.

Dorman Eaton to England

Newly elected President Rutherford B. Hayes continued
to recognize Dorman B. Eaton as Chairman of the Civil Service Commission, even though the Commission held no meetings. The President instructed Secretary of State William
M. Evarts to write Eaton and request that he "investigate
and make a report to him concerning the action of the
English Government in relation to its Civil Service, and
effects of such action since 1850."[50]   No one could possibly
have been better qualified for the assignment than Dorman
Eaton. He possessed a thorough foundation in the British
system acquired from independent study in England during
the early 1870's. He continued to receive information on
English developments while serving as Chairman of the Grant
Civil Service Commission.

Commissioner Eaton accepted the President's invitation
and booked passage on a ship for England leaving July 18,
1877, at his own expense. He wrote to Schurz and other
reformers requesting "a note of introduction to any one
who would be willing to aid my investigations."[51]   Eaton
returned from England on the 11th of September "well satisfied" with his trip. He "gathered documents and information
of various kinds" and entered into conversations with many
prominent British officials, including Sir Charles Trevelyan,
father of the reform in Great Britain, and Horace Mann,
Secretary of the British Civil Service Commission.[52]   Three
days before Eaton arrived in New York, George William
Curtis notified the readers of Harper's Weekly that
"Eaton is in England, and . . . will make a careful investigation of the English methods, upon which he will
report, that the inquiry in this country may be conducted
with full and accurate knowledge."[53]

---

[50]W.M. Evarts to Dorman Eaton, Washington, 25 June 1877,
Eaton, Civil Service in Great Britain.

[51]Dorman B. Eaton to Carl Schurz, New York, 8 July 1877,
Schurz Papers.

[52]Dorman Eaton to Schurz, New York, 14 September 1877, Schurz
Papers; a number of scholars report that Eaton spent "more
than a year" studying in England in preparation for the book.
This is accurate only if one considers his travels in the
early 1870's. He actually devoted from July 18 to September
11 in travel status, a period of fifty-five days from which
actual travel time consumed about half of the time.

[53]"Secretary Sherman and the Civil Service," Harper's Weekly
(New York), 8 September 1877, p. 698.

Trevelyan Writes Eaton

Sir Charles Trevelyan's letter to Dorman Eaton parallels a similar letter he wrote to C. Brace and Thomas Jenckes in 1869. He thought that open competition was well suited to the American political system, and felt its adoption would correct "some of the worst results of the United States political system." At first, Sir Charles admitted civil service reform was unpopular, "and if the matter had been put to the vote, . . . the new system would have been rejected by an overwhelming majority." The reform grew in popularity because "large as the number of persons who profited by the former system of patronage were, those who were left out in the cold were still larger." Members of Parliament grew to support the system because "they had been relieved from a degrading yoke." Before patronage held them bondage to "attendance on the Patronage Secretary of the Treasury" and "having to carry on a large and annoying correspondence with their constituents." The reform "has purified the constituencies and increased the independence and public feeling of members of Parliament."

Trevelyan asserted that "the change upon the efficiency of the administrative service" was spectacular. "As the persons appointed have no party connections, and are generally unknown to the political chiefs, there is now nothing to prevent their being promoted according to qualification and merit, which is the key to administrative efficiency." Besides leading "to a great improvement in the efficiency of the administrative service" the change "has given a marvellous stimulus to education." "All this . . . is proved by the general acceptance of the new national institution, so that no sane person has any idea of abrogating it and reviving the former state of things."[54]

Eaton Reports

Upon his return, Eaton wrote immediately to Schurz trying to find out the Administration's policy on the subject. He reported that "the English have done a wonderful work since 1850, and the taking of their administration out of politics and favoritism is their greatest advancement in later times. . . . The subject is more complicated than I

---

[54]Sir Charles Trevelyan to Dorman B. Eaton, Braemore, England, 20 August 1877, Civil Service in Great Britain, pp. 430-433.

had suspected and the reform has been greater in England."[55]
Schurz recommended that Eaton come to Washington and hold a
series of conferences with the President and Cabinet officials.
Eaton informed Schurz he was willing to come to Washington
after October 13. "The English system is far more varied,
matured and diverse than I had suspected -- immensely more
so than our Civil Service friends who have not specially
studied it have any idea of." Eaton suggested that the
President announce in the annual message in December that
he would "convey the results of the investigation" to Congress shortly after the regular session began in March 1878.[56]

     The two reformers could not agree on a date for Eaton's
visit during the last two weeks of October, and Eaton suggested November 6. "When I come," he wrote, "I shall regard
it as fortunate if I can have a full and free exchange of
views, first with you and then with the President; and I
desire also to learn from Mr. Evarts his policy on the
Civil Service question." The Chairman of the Civil Service
Commission informed Schurz that he had some definite ideas
on the reform as a result of his study. "The considerable
attention I have given to the subject, both here and in England, has unfortunately, perhaps you may think, resulted
in fully distinct convictions, both as to what is best and
what is practicable and what is unsuitable, in the present
state of our affairs -- always open to change however."[57]

     The intended meeting apparently never took place because
Eaton finally wrote directly to President Hayes informing him
of his return and repeating some of the findings he conveyed
to Schurz earlier. On January 10, 1878, he wrote: "I am
astonished at the immense length the English have distanced
us, in the great cause of honest & efficient administration;
and I assure you our partisan & venal ways -- our frauds our
intrigues & our inefficiency -- will show a sad contrast with
their regular & upright methods."[58] The President responded
on March 16, 1878, urging Eaton to "push forward the good
work" and "send in his report."[59]

---

[55] Dorman Eaton to Schurz, New York, 14 September 1877,
Schurz Papers.

[56] Dorman Eaton to Schurz, Brattleboro, Vermont, 6 October
1877, Schurz Papers.

[57] Dorman Eaton to Schurz, New York, 27 October 1877, Schurz
Papers.

[58] Dorman Eaton to Rutherford B. Hayes, New York, 10 January
1878, Hayes Papers.

[59] Thomas Harry Williams, ed., Rutherford Birchard Hayes, The
Diary of a President, 1875-1881; Covering the Disputed Election,

Eaton's return gave President Hayes an opportunity to think ahead about his plans on civil service reform. He planned

1. To separate office holding from . . . political management. . . .
2. To . . . restore . . . the legitimate and constitutional exercise of the appointing power to the Executive. . . .
3. To provide by legislation appropriate means to secure information as to the fitness of applicants for appointment. . . .
4. Let the Cabinet officers have seats in the House of Representatives and in the Senate with the right to speak on questions pertaining to their respective departments. . . .
5. Congress should provide for a revival of the Civil Service Commission. . . .
6. In the absence of legislation by Congress to promote the desired reforms, it will not be practicable to give a fair trial to the great political parties of the Country prior to the last National elections. . . . [60]

The writing of the report proved more time-consuming than expected. Nine months later President Hayes reviewed his plans for a special message declaring:

The first step in any adequate and permanent reform is the divorce of the Legislative from the nominating power. With this, reform can and will successfully proceed. Without it reform is impossible. . . . The people must be educated to expect and require their M.C.'s [Members of Congress] to abstain from appointments. They must not expect them to obtain places. Congressmen must not claim to have a share of the appointments, either principal or minor places. [61]

In July Eaton felt compelled to write Secretary Schurz with an apology for the delay. He did not complete the report until December 1879 [62] two years and three months after his return from England.

---

the End of Reconstruction, and the Beginning of Civil Service (New York: David McKay Co., 1964), p. 129.

[60] Williams, ed., 30 March 1878, pp. 134-135.

[61] Ibid., 8 December 1878, 175-176.

[62] Dorman Eaton to Schurz, 2 July 1879, New York; Dorman Eaton to Carl Schurz, New York, 19 December 1879, Schurz Papers.

Contents of the Report

The report traced English administrative developments from the Magna Carta to the Playfair Commission of 1875. Eaton wrote the report in such a way as to convey the impression that the English moved steadily forward in the art of administration until reaching the inevitable and logical decisions to implement a merit system. Throughout the historical discussions Eaton drew analogies between English and American developments. His first and last chapters dealt almost exclusively with the American scene. Eaton opened with a direct attack against spoilsmen's anti-foreign, anti-republican, and anti-democratic charges. "The authors of our constitution accepted good material whenever they found it; but from no quarter did they gather so much as from the experience of England." Eaton noted that "all the leading nations, except the United States, have recently, and as a matter of policy, made searching investigations not only into their own administrative methods but into the methods of other governments." "British experience," the author contended, "is present as richer, riper, and more varied, as well as vastly more extensive, than that of the United States." "It will appear," Eaton argued, "that either in the home government or in India, substantially all the abuses we have endured, and all the specious arguments by which their continuance has been excused, were familiar to English statesmen long before we began to talk about political corruption."[63]

Eaton continued the same arguments in the conclusion. "The reform, therefore was as democratic and republican in its operation, as it was moral and educational in its origin and influence." The reform accomplished all the objectives envisioned by reformers. Corruption had been eliminated, administration improved, education advanced and merit applied. "In the beginning, a man was in the public service because a corrupt and arbitrary king wished him there; at the end, he was in that service because a fair test of his worth gave him the place, as the best man to fill it."[64]

The final chapter, added to the second edition of the report, dealt with "The Bearing of British Experience Upon Civil Service Reform In The United States." The author

---

[63]Eaton, _Civil Service in Great Britain,_ pp. 2, 6, 11a and 11c.

[64]_Ibid._, pp. 355 and 357.

reminded the reader that "the people of Great Britain have so much more than any other people in common with ourselves." He listed fourteen "principles and conclusions which have become accepted in the . . . experience of Great Britain." They included: (1) the public's right to have the "worthiest citizens" service as civil servants; (2) the "highest claim upon an office" is determined by the "personal merits of the candidate"; (3) open competition is "the most just and practicable means" of selecting "fit persons for appointment"; and (4) the merit system "invigorated national patriotism, [and] raised the standard of statesmanship." These principles and conclusions, according to Eaton, "have obtained almost universal acceptance in British administration."[65]

Dorman Eaton returned repeatedly to the theme that the merit system, as applied in England, was conspicuously suited to the United States. "It would be little less than an insult to the intelligence of the reader to gravely argue that a policy, which would bring into places of public trust the moral character and the intelligence needed for the proper discharge of their duties, is at least as appropriate and needful in a republic as in a monarchy."[66] He argued that the merit system did not interfere or restrict the party system in any way.

Let is be borne in mind that the merit system does not interfere with the freedom of choice on party ground in any popular election; that it leaves unimpaired the power of the party majority to control the enactment of all laws; that the officers its majorities have elected will have the right of instruction and control. . . . The system thus gives to parties the broadest field of discretion and responsibility.[67]

Dorman Eaton outlined the steps which reformers needed to take to insure administrative reform. He declared that the real question was whether America has the moral strength

---

[65]Civil Service in Great Britain, pp. 362, 365-366.

[66]Ibid., p. 378.

[67]Ibid., p. 384.

to implement the needed reform. "This generation, which
has made the greatest sacrifices for liberty and justice
recorded in human annals, must surely have the moral ele-
vation needed for the removal of any abuses that can be
developed in administering the government whose righteous-
ness and honor it has greatly exalted."[68]

Impact of the Report

Eaton's report played an important role in the civil
service reform movement. It documented a successful application of the merit system. Reformers, editors, and authors
quoted or referred to it on numerous occasions when advocating aspects of the reform proposals. The publication
came at a convenient time for President Hayes. Reformers
were upset with Hayes after the elections of 1879, and Hayes
needed to lift their spirits to maintain their support.
The Eaton report did just that.[69]

The press responded to the report favorably. The New
York Times called it "the most important contribution that
has yet been made to the reform of the civil service in this
country."[70] Favorable press reaction pleased the author.
"The book," he wrote to Curtis, "has attracted more attention
than I anticipated and strange enough, I have not, as I have
seen, been abused." He noted favorable comments in the
Democratic Utica Herald and in papers in Texas.

> But no notice pleased me so much as that in
> the Tribune of January 16th by Mr. [George]
> Ripley -- not because he speaks so favorably
> of the book, but because it shows such a
> change in the attitude of the paper toward
> the subject. . . . That the Tribune should
> so feel its mistake & the tendency of public
> opinion as to substitute Ripley for Gail
> [Hamilton] & soberness for ridicule, is cer-
> tainly significant.[71]

---

[68] Civil Service in Great Britain, pp. 427-428.

[69] "The Fallibility of Rumor," Harper's Weekly (New York),
8 December 1877, p. 958.

[70] "New Publications," New York Times, 29 December 1879, p. 2.

[71] Dorman Eaton to George William Curtis, New York, Monday, 1880,
Curtis Papers; Gail Hamilton (Mary Abigail Dodge) was a relative of James G. Blaine and caustic opponent of civil service
reform.

254

The Chairman of the Civil Service Commission followed
up his success by arranging for publication of his report
in a hard back cover edition. He changed the introduction
and added a final chapter to the report. Eaton hoped the
book "may be a sort of text book for reformers." He requested that George William Curtis write an introduction
to the work but added: "do not write so much better than
I have as to make my pages unbearable."[72] In October 1880
he wrote again to Curtis to urge him to complete the introduction rapidly so that he would "have the publication made
before November 1st." He planned to travel to Washington
"and have a long talk, before October 25" with Administration officials. He thought "that an early publication, may
help the President in making a strong presentation of the
subject in his next message."[73] For this purpose he wanted
Curtis to "say some encouraging words of President Hayes'
contribution to reform." Eaton added that I "shall be much
gratified if you can so say it as to imply that I wished it
said, without saying so."[74]

Curtis' Introduction and
Hayes' Last Message

The introduction arrived in time for Harper & Brothers
to publish the book before the end of 1880. Curtis began
with a short summation of the book and its purpose. He then
devoted a large portion to the history of civil service reform movement in the United States. Curtis wrote that the
"law of 1871 . . . was the last public service of Mr. Jenckes."
He made short reference to the Grant Commission in saying
that "the rules . . . were never effectively carried into
practice at any point of the service. The reasons for this
failure were many . . . ." The largest segment of the
introduction he reserved for President Hayes, at Eaton's
request. Curtis discussed Hayes' letter of acceptance,
quoted from Hayes' inaugural address, and pointed to the
selection of Carl Schurz as Secretary of the Interior as
evidence of the reform sympathies of the Administration.
Noting that President Hayes' actions have "been inexplicably
inconsistent," he declared that nevertheless "very much more
reform has been accomplished than under any previous administration." He noted the advancements at the New York Custom-

---

[72]Dorman Eaton to George William Curtis, New York 7 September 1880, Curtis Papers.

[73]Dorman Eaton to Curtis, Brattleboro, Vermont, October
1880, Curtis Papers.

[74]Dorman Eaton to Curtis, Vermont, 11 October 1880, Curtis Papers.

house and Post Office. "These are results which are due wholly to the sincere conviction and purpose of the President, and, however imperfect and incomplete, they are of great importance and significance." George Curtis returned to the contents of the book, quoted from Prime Minister Gladstone, and concluded that "the readers of this book will decide whether the abuses of the worst days of English party politics -- abuses which the good sense of England has entirely removed -- are necessary either for the maintenance of party government or for the promotion of political morality in the United States."[75]

President Hayes made good use of the Eaton report by announcing its pending publication in his Third Annual Message delivered on December 1, 1879.

> In view of the facts that during a considerable period the Government of Great Britain has been dealing with administrative problems and abuses in various particulars analogous to those presented in this country, and that in recent years the measures adopted were understood to have been effective and in every respect highly satisfactory, I thought it desirable to have fuller information upon the subject, and accordingly requested the chairman of the Civil Service Commission to make a thorough investigation for this purpose.[76]

He justified looking to Great Britain for inspiration: "While the reform measures of another government are of no authority for us, they are entitled to influence to the extent to which their intrinsic wisdom and their adaptation to our institutions and social life may commend them to our consideration."[77]

The Eaton book was destined to make a major contribution to the final reform campaign leading to passage of the Pendleton Act. It fulfilled Eaton's expectations expressed to Curtis when he wrote: "I hope the Book . . . may be a sort of text book for reformers."[78]

---

[75] Eaton, _Civil Service in Great Britain_, pp. x and xii.

[76] Richardson, 7:561.

[77] _Ibid._

[78] Dorman Eaton to George William Curtis, New York, 7 September 1880, Curtis Papers.

256

CHAPTER X

VOTERS DEMAND REFORM

1881 to 1883

After President Hayes relieved Chester A. Arthur and Alonzo Cornell from the New York Customhouse and appointed Edwin A. Merritt and Silas W. Burt, he instructed them to make the Customhouse a conspicuous model of reform. "My desire is that your office shall be conducted on strictly business principles, and according to the rules which were adopted on the recommendations of the civil service commission by the administration of General Grant." Make all[1] appointments and removals "independent of mere influence."[1] Collector Merritt, unenthusiastic about reform and convinced of its ultimate failure, turned over implementation of the President's instructions to Naval Officer Silas W. Burt. Burt, an active civil service reformer, took Hayes' letter seriously and convinced himself that "behind the purge [of the Customhouse] lay a sincere concern on the part of Hayes for civil service reform."[2] Burt pleased his fellow reformers by publishing a comprehensive set of rules applicable to all but a few of the highest positions. The rules included competitive examinations for the lowest grade entries and promotions, selection from the highest three candidates, and three boards of examiners to administer the examinations. Silas Burt added his own twist with a provision inviting "well-known citizens" to observe the examinations. This proved to be a highly successful public relations technique. Most contemporary observers agreed with E.O. Graves that the experiment in the New York Customhouse with open competitive examinations produced "excellent" results.[3]

---

[1]Rutherford B. Hayes to Edwin A. Merritt, Washington, 4 February 1879, Hayes Papers.

[2]Thomas C. Reeves, "Silas Burt and Chester Arthur: A Reformer's View of the Twenty-first President," The New York Historical Society Quarterly 54 (October 1970): 330.

[3]E.O. Graves to Hon. H.F. Fruela (?), Assistant Secretary of the Treasury, 16 June 1881, in Silas Wright Burt, A Brief History of the Civil Service Reform Movement in the United States (unpublished work written about 1905 and located in the Burt Writings, New York Public Library), pp. K-L; G.W. Curtis to Hayes, Staten Island, 28 June 1879, Hayes Papers; "The

Civil Service Reform League

Proposals to create an organization devoted to promoting civil service reform go back to the beginning of the movement. For one reason or another such an organization never attracted sufficient support to make a major contribution. The most recent effort took place in May 1877 when several supporters of civil service reform organized the New York Civil Service Reform Association. Members of the association appointed Henry W. Bellows, founder and president of the United States Sanitary Commission and well known Unitarian minister in New York City, first president. The constitution of the association, developed with strong support from Dorman B. Eaton, pledged its members to "contribute to the development of a sound public opinion concerning the Civil Service."[4] The first public meeting met with good attendance and wide press coverage. Unfortunately, the association was unable to sustain itself as membership declined and attendance at meetings fell sharply. By May 1878 it adjourned indefinitely. Renewed interest in the New York gubernatorial race motivated its leaders to resume meetings in 1879.

The Presidential election campaign of 1880 and determination by reformers to avoid the disastrous split in their ranks (which occurred in 1872) created the necessary atmosphere to successfully germinate a permanent association of civil service reformers. Reformers unanimously favored a second term for President Hayes, but he refused to serve more than one term. Because of this, they divided their support among Senator George F. Edmunds, Elihu B. Washburne, Congressman James A. Garfield and Treasury Secretary John Sherman. While they could not agree on which candidate to support, they united against the candidacy of former President Grant and James G. Blaine, the front-runner. This opposition to Grant and Blaine stimulated "Independent Republicans" to hold several anti-Grant/Blaine meetings in New York, Philadelphia, and St. Louis. The weakness of the Independents became evident when the Republican Convention in Chicago refused to endorse a strong civil service plank. When the deadlock over Grant and Blaine occurred on June 7, Independents united with other anti-Grant forces to nominate James A. Garfield.

Civil Service Reform in the Custom-House," New York Times, 9 July 1879, p. 4; Dorman B. Eaton, Civil Service Reform in the New York City Post-Office and Custom-House, House Executive Documents, 46th Cong., 3rd Sess., 28 No. 94, pp. 35-37.

[4] Minutes of the Executive Committee of the New York Civil Service Reform Association, National Civil Service League Collection, U.S. Civil Service Commission Library.

The weakness of reformers surfaced again when they proved powerless to prevent the nomination of Chester A. Arthur as Vice Presidential candidate. "Why in the name of sense," G.M. Lockwood asked, "when the 'machine' was broken in Garfield it should have been recognized in Arthur I cannot understand."[5] Editor Grosvner tried to rationalize the Arthur nomination as "a necessity" to keep Conkling and Company from bolting the party. "Many pleasanter things, but not many wiser, have been done," he told Schurz.[6]

Reformers found themselves generally ineffective in influencing the course of the election campaign when they acted as individual politicians. Attempts failed to persuade Garfield to incorporate a strong civil service reform statement in his acceptance letter. "I consider it a duty," Schurz wrote the Republican candidate, "to say to you that your letter of acceptance has been a great disappointment. . . ." Garfield responded by suggesting that "the pressure of public opinion should be brought to bear on Congress rather than the President. . . ." He attacked Hayes' order against political assessments. "I have never doubted that portion of his Order No. 1 was a mistake -- and was an invasion of proper rights of those who held Federal office."[8] Reformers found much to complain about in Garfield's visit to New York, which resulted in securing Conkling's campaign support. Garfield paid less and less attention to civil service reform as the campaign progressed but reformers congratulated themselves on his election.[9]

---

[5]G.M. Lockwood to Schurz, New York, 8 June 1880, Schurz Papers.

[6]W.M. Grosvner, editor of The Public, to Schurz, New York, 9 June 1880, Schurz Papers.

[7]Carl Schurz to Garfield, Indianapolis, 20 July 1880, Schurz Papers.

[8]James A. Garfield to Schurz, Mentor, Ohio, 22 July 1880, Schurz Papers.

[9]Jordan, pp. 330-359; Herbert J. Clancy, The Presidential Election of 1880 (Chicago: Loyola University Press, 1958), pp. 22-252; Morgan, From Hayes to McKinley, pp. 57-121; Welch, pp. 95-98; Sproat, pp. 103-108; Chester L. Barrows, William M. Evarts: Lawyer, Diplomat, Statesman (Chapel Hill: University of North Carolina Press, 1941), pp. 405-407; Milne, pp. 163-4; Logsdon, pp. 311-314; Muzzey, 161-177; Hoogenboom, pp. 179-186.

Reformers wrote immediately to the President-elect trying to exercise some measure of influence on the administration. Schurz warned Garfield that the Republicans were in danger of losing the leadership of civil service reform to the Democrats. "You will want at least one man in your official family who believed in it and understands it," he advised. Eaton asked Garfield for an interview to discuss the "administration at the Customs-House and Post Office" in New York. Curtis urged the new President to preserve the reform of the New York Customhouse and Post Office. "The approval and continuation of these reforms would be full of good augury for the new administration. Abandonment of them would be exceedingly discouraging."[10]

The sense of frustration over the lack of influence during the convention and campaign of 1880 motivated reformers to organize themselves. The spark which fired the zeal to organize came from a letter to the editor of the Nation, signed by F.G.S. of Hartford, Connecticut, in the July 30, 1880 issue. F.G.S. declared that civil service reform could not be won unless supporters agitated. "We must begin with the agitation, and the charge I make against the Independents and civil-service reformers is that they have rejected this agitation."[11] Two issues later the Nation published another letter from F.W.H.[12] of Mt. Vernon, New York. F.W.H. suggested that Independent Republicans form a society to sponsor civil service reform. He proposed that the society promote reform with "education and enlightenment" by using political, social, and religious agitation. He urged the society to concentrate its arguments exclusively on the moral issue. F.W.H. proposed publishing a periodical and called on Independent Republicans to act immediately by scheduling a meeting. He asked interested readers to send in letters.[13]

The response to F.W.H.'s call was excellent, and the Nation promised action. Curtis suggested to Burt that reformers revise the New York Civil Service Reform Association

---

[10]Carl Schurz to Garfield, Washington, 15 January 1881; Dorman Eaton to Garfield, New York, 16 April 1881, Garfield Papers; "Political Prospects," Harper's Weekly (New York), 4 December 1880, p. 770.

[11]Nation (New York), 5 August 1880, p. 93.

[12]F.W.H. probably stands for Frederick William Holls, a lawyer who practiced in New York City.

[13]Nation (New York), 19 August 1880, pp. 134-135.

and make it "the nucleus of an efficient organization."[14]
One week later members of the association met and appointed
a committee to revise the organization. The association
adopted committee recommendations to "open" membership "in
every part of the country." It extended membership to those
individuals who wrote letters to the Nation in response to
F.W.H.'s call. The committee revised the association's
constitution and distributed it to important opinion makers.
George William Curtis promised that the organization "will
enter at once upon an active campaign of publication and
diffusion of information. . . ."

> The new constitution just adopted expresses
> the objects of the Association and of the
> reform in the plainest and most comprehen-
> sive manner. It will be adopted, we hope,
> by similar associations which may be formed
> elsewhere, with which the Association here
> will most gladly correspond and co-operate.[15]

The Civil Service Reform Association grew rapidly for
the next three years. The executive committee established
control, and George William Curtis replaced Henry Bellows as
President. Two major committees, legislation and publication, headed by long-time reformers Dorman Eaton and Edwin
Godkin, assumed a major role in the activities of the association. Membership in the reform associations during these
critical years tended to attract men of similar background
and interest. From 1877 to 1881 ecclesiastics, attracted
by the moral aspects of the reform movement, directed the
association before giving it up to journalists and public
relations specialists after the reorganization of 1880.
The typical member was just under fifty years of age in
1880, usually Protestant, with family ties in the northeastern states, well educated, had attended a prestigious
New England college, had prominent social recognition, and
supported other reform movements. He generally was a member
of the Independent wing of the Republican party. As a whole
the group was made up of conservative politicians with a desire to return to the good old days before President Jackson.[16]

---

[14]G.W. Curtis to Silas W. Burt, Ashfield, 10 September 1880,
Burt Collection, New York Historical Association.

[15]"The Prospects of Reform," Harper's Weekly (New York), 11
December 1880, p. 786.

[16]Hoogenboom, pp. 186-197.

Under new leadership, the association concentrated
its efforts in three areas. Curtis directed efforts to
expand by organizing association groups in other parts
of the United States. Auxiliary associations sprang up
in Boston, Cincinnati, Milwaukee, Philadelphia, San Francisco, Buffalo, St. Louis, and Baltimore in rapid succession.
Edwin L. Godkin's publication committee issued five publications and directed their wide distribution within the
first five months of its operation. Boston and Cambridge
associations began to issue the first civil service reform
publication, Civil Service Reform, which later merged with
a similar periodical from Baltimore to form Good Government,
which is still printed. Eaton's legislative committee set
about to study the political situation in Congress and began to draft an ideal civil service reform bill.[17]

Garfield Administration

President-elect Garfield faced a Republican party
deeply split among three powerful factions. Senator Conkling led the Stalwart or Grant faction. Although assured
of a prominent position in the Administration through Vice-
President Chester Arthur, Conkling demanded that Garfield
appoint his lieutenant Levi P. Morton as Secretary of Treasury and acknowledge his control of all New York patronage
positions. Half-Breeds, as the supporters of James G. Blaine
were called, demanded the post of Secretary of State for their
leader and help in weakening the Conkling machine in New York.
Independent Republicans, generally synonymous with civil service reformers, demanded a prominent cabinet post and retention of the advances made by President Hayes in the Interior
Department, New York Post Office, and New York Customhouse.[18]

President Garfield devised his Cabinet after months of
negotiations. He appointed Blaine Secretary of State to
satisfy the Half-Breeds, Wayne MacVeagh Attorney General as
the Independent representative, and settled for Postmaster
General on Thomas L. James, generally considered a Conkling
man but highly favored by reformers because of his strong

---

[17]G.W. Curtis to Charles Norton, West New Brighton, 21
December 1880, Curtis Papers.

[18]Goldsmith, 2;1003-4; Morgan, From Hayes to McKinley, pp.
121-125; Clancy, 252-253; Logsdon, pp. 313-315; Welch, pp.
96-98; 102-213; Jordan, pp. 362-363; Muzzey, pp. 177-183;
C.E. Henry to Garfield, New York, 26 July 1880 (2); C.E.
Henry to Garfield, New York, 27 July 1880 (2), Norris &
Shaffer, pp. 283-286.

administration in the New York Post Office. Senator
William Windom of Minnesota received the coveted Secretary
of Treasury post, while Iowa Senator Samuel J. Kirkwood
succeeded Schurz as Secretary of the Interior. Garfield
completed his Cabinet with military posts going to William
H. Hunt of Louisiana as Secretary of the Navy and Robert
Todd Lincoln, son of the Sixteenth President, Secretary of
War. The appointments drew praise from many corners. Garfield wrote in his diary: "The result is better than I expected."[19] Hayes agreed and wrote the new President; "Your
cabinet is simply perfect. It could not be better."[20] Cabinet selections elevated Half-Breed influence over Stalwarts
in the administration. When the President turned to second
level appointments, the Blaine and Conkling feud broke into
the open.

President Garfield refused to consult with Senator
Conkling in making appointments in New York. He promoted
Assistant Postmaster Henry G. Pearson to succeed James and
removed Edwin A. Merritt as collector of the Port of New
York for anti-Conklingite William H. Robertson. The Soli-
citor General appointment went to Half-Breed William E.
Chandler. The appointments satisfied few. Reformers ap-
plauded the appointment of Pearson but lamented the loss of
Merritt and appointment of Chandler. Conkling "raged and
roared like a bull of Bashan for three mortal hours."[21]

The Robertson appointment represented a direct attack
against the political authority of Senator Conkling in New
York. As a member of the Republican State Committee, William Robertson was a powerful Garfield ally. Many correctly
saw the hand of Secretary Blaine in the nominations. Conkling collected his political allies, including Postmaster

---

[19]Theodore Clarke Smith, Life and Letters of James Abram Garfield, 2 vols. (New Haven: Yale University Press, 1925), 2:1098.

[20]Rutherford B. Hayes to Garfield, Altoona, Pennsylvania, 6
March 1881, Garfield Papers.

[21]Henry L. Dawes to Electa Sanderson Dawes, Washington, 30
April 1881, Dawes Papers, Library of Congress; "Postmaster
Pearson," Harper's Weekly, 2 April 1881, p. 210; "The New
York Nominations," Harper's Weekly, 9 April 1881, p. 227; "The
President's New York Appointments," Nation, 31 March 1881, pp.
216-217; "The Robertson Nomination," Nation, 21 April 1881,
pp. 272-3.

James and Vice-President Arthur, to work out his plan of attack. He sent a parade of supporters to the White House to protest the appointments and to suggest a withdrawal of Robertson's name. Postmaster Thomas James, Senator Platt, John Logan, and Vice-President Arthur all returned empty-handed. Conkling then turned to his Republican colleagues in the Congress and threatened to destroy the party unless the Garfield Administration dropped Robertson. Frightened by the prospects of an internecine war, the party caucus sent Henry Dawes of Massachusetts to talk with the President. When this failed, Conkling obtained the permission of the committee to consider the nominations in two parts -- un-contested and contested nominations. In this way he could delay consideration of Robertson's nomination indefinitely. Garfield retaliated by withdrawing five major New York Stalwart nominations, leaving Conkling with no appointments to his credit. Conkling and Arthur decided to use the press. They caused the New York Herald to publish an attack against Garfield, charging that he had failed to keep his word because he wanted to destroy the New York party. The Herald concluded that the real enemy was Blaine. The crucial meeting in the drama between President Garfield and Senator Conkling came on May 9, 1881, when the Republican caucus decided to abandon Conkling and support the President in fear of destroying the party. Five days later Senator Thomas C. Platt persuaded Conkling to join him in resigning from the Senate. He reasoned that a joint resignation would allow both men to return triumphantly after reelection by the state legislature.

Universally condemned by the press and fellow senators, Conkling and Platt found themselves too weak to win reelection from the New York State Legislature. Vice-President Arthur rushed to Albany to help his old boss, but nothing could save the situation, since Conkling no longer controlled the all-important patronage which was the foundation of his strength.[22]

Garfield and Civil Service Reform

President Garfield upset Independent Republicans al-most as much as he upset Stalwarts. His selection of Wayne MacVeagh to represent their interest in the Cabinet pleased

[22]Reeves, Gentleman Boss, pp. 220-237; Rothman, pp. 32-35; Clancy, pp. 254-260; Morgan, From Hayes to McKinley, pp. 129-137; Jordan, pp. 379-407.

most, but they worried when Garfield neglected to consult MacVeagh before removing Edwin Merritt. The Robertson appointment appeared to be the first step in destroying the merit system in the New York Customhouse. This suspicion did not subside until Collector Robertson assumed his duties in August and promised to continue the civil service rules.[23]

The President's inaugural address caused reformers great concern. Garfield ignored reformers' demands for a major change in the appointment system brought about by civil service reform. Instead he reverted to an earlier proposal by advocating limited tenure as the solution to civil service reform. ". . . I shall, at the proper time, ask Congress to fix the tenure of the minor offices of the several Executive Departments and prescribe ground upon which removals shall be made during the term for which incumbents have been appointed."[24] Reformers charged Garfield with "back sliding" and feared it was "an adroit measure to defeat the whole scheme without openly opposing it."[25]

The new Secretary of Interior Samuel J. Kirkwood, former Governor and U.S. Senator from Iowa, made short work of the Carl Schurz civil service system. He not only terminated the Schurz system but removed Schurz's Commissioner of Pensions, J.A. Bentley, to make way for his own patronage candidate.[26]

Postmaster General Thomas L. James threw another scare into reformers when he tried to enhance his position with Congress by advocating Congressional control of patronage. Candidates sponsored by Congressmen would then be required to pass a competitive examination. The James plan attracted a chorus of complaints from Schurz, Burt, and Senator Dawes without picking up supporters. The idea never surfaced again.[27]

---

[23]"The Progress of Reform," New York Times, 14 September 1881, p. 4; "Collector Robertson," Harper's Weekly, 13 August 1881, p. 547.

[24]Robertson, 8:11-12.

[25]I.J. Wister to Burt, Philadelphia, March 12, 1881, Burt Collection; Nation, 17 March 1881, pp. 180-181.

[26]E.P. Hanna to Schurz, 13 June 1881, Schurz Papers; J.A. Bentley to Schurz, Washington, 17 June 1881, Schurz Papers.

[27]Silas W. Burt to Schurz, New York, 20 July 1881; Burt to Schurz, New York, 22 July 1881, Schurz Papers; New York Times, 30 July 1881, p. 4; "Defining Reform," New York Times, 22 July 1881, p. 4.

Star Route Frauds

Another example of corruption under the spoils system surfaced shortly after President Garfield took office. The Star Route Frauds, exposed by Postmaster General James and Attorney General MacVeagh, involved a scheme to defraud the government by padding the cost of operating some ninety-three remote postal routes in the west. The frauds involved former Senator and current secretary of the Republican National Committee, Stephen W. Dorsey. Between 1878 and 1880 Second Assistant Postmaster General Thomas J. Brady authorized expansion of the ninety-three star routes and awarded the contracts to Dorsey and his relatives. They pocketed the money for personal and political purposes, including financing the Garfield political campaign in Indiana. The corruption exposed by this fraud gave weight to reformers' arguments that the spoils system spawned corruption.[28]

Congress and Civil Service Reform Activities

Up to 1880 civil service reform advocates came largely from the Republican party. It was the most consistent part of the program of the Independent Republican faction. The Democratic party, out of power since 1861, continued to support the spoils system even though the Republicans exploited its most valuable rewards, political assessments. By 1880 the Democratic party included a small but important segment in favor of reform. This embraced such men as Thomas F. Bayard, Senator from Delaware, Everett P. Wheeler of New York, a member of the National Civil Service Reform League, and Senator George Hunt Pendleton of Ohio.

Senator Pendleton came from a prominent American family. He entered the House of Representatives in 1857, ten years after passing the bar, and served through the Civil War. In 1864 the Democratic party nominated him to run with General George B. McClellan as Vice-Presidential candidate. Pendleton returned to the Congress after election to the Senate in 1878. In between his Congressional duties, George Pendleton contributed his skills to the railroad industry as president of the Kentucky Central Railroad. He gained a reputation as an advocate of the "Ohio Idea" which promoted the use of inflated greenbacks to pay the national debt.[29]

---

[28]Nation (New York), 28 April 1881, p. 287; Reeves, The Gentleman Boss, pp. 297-305; Morgan, From Hayes to McKinley, pp. 156-157; Norris and Shaffer, p. 295.

[29]Hoogenboom, p. 200.

Sometime during his business career Senator Pendleton
was attracted to civil service reform. He entered the
civil service reform battle on December 10, 1880, when he
acted to submit President Hayes' comments on the civil service system, delivered in his last annual message, "to the
Select Committee to Examine the Several Branches of the
Civil Service, with instructions to report at an early day,
by bill or otherwise."[30] Five days later Pendleton introduced two bills in the Senate, one to regulate the civil
service and promote its efficiency with competitive examinations, and the other to forbid political assessments.[31]
Pendleton modeled the bill he introduced to regulate the
civil service on those written by Representative Jenckes.
The bill proposed creating a Civil-Service Examination Board
to administer examinations and issue regulations. He empowered the five-man board to regulate removals. The bill
provided equal opportunities to both men and women and established a network of five districts to administer examinations. It contained a provision which required agencies to
appoint candidates at the top of a register.

George Pendleton's timing was perfect. Reformers, recently organized in the New York Civil Service Reform Association, responded immediately to Pendleton's initiative.
Suspicious at first that the bill constituted a Democratic
party "scheme" to "discredit the cause," reformers soon
concluded that the Senator from Ohio planned to conduct a
genuine and sincere reform effort.[32] Pendleton invited
Silas W. Burt to criticize its provisions. "I may say that
it was framed after much consideration," he declared,
". . . and whilst I am not wedded to it, as it stands, I
desire extremely to see the idea embodied in it, carried out."[33]
E.L. Godkin wrote in the Nation that the bill was fundamen-
tally sound and deserved serious consideration.[34] George W.
Curtis, after talking to Eaton, gave the Pendleton bill a

[30]U.S. Congressional Record, 46th Cong., 3rd Sess., 1880,
p. 49.

[31]Ibid., p. 44.

[32]George W. Curtis to Charles Eliot Norton, West Brighton,
21 December 1880, Curtis Papers.

[33]George H. Pendleton to Silas W. Burt, Washington, 22 December 1880, Burt Collection, New York Public Library.

[34]Nation (New York), 23 December 1880, p. 433.

strong endorsement. "The Pendleton bill, although defective in details, has been prepared with a clear conception
of the indispensable conditions of reform."[35] Dorman Eaton
felt Pendleton needed to amend certain provisions he considered unconstitutional and impractical but told former
President Hayes: "For a man who has not technical familiarity, he has done well -- exceedingly well."[36]

The Pendleton bill spurred Eaton, already working on
a draft civil service reform bill with his legislative
committee, to complete his version of a bill in time to
submit it to the executive committee of the New York Civil
Service Reform League on December 30, 1880. The committee
approved the bill in time for Eaton to take it to Washington and persuade Senator Pendleton to substitute it for the
original bill, which he did on January 10, 1881. The Committee To Examine The Several Branches Of The Civil Service,
consisting of Senator West (Chairman), Senator Pendleton,
Senator Brown, and Senator Dawes, opened hearings on January 13, 1881. It heard Dorman B. Eaton and Everett P.
Wheeler defend the bill, with Eaton assuming most of the
responsibility for the testimony.

The committee reported out the new Pendleton bill
with a recommendation for its passage on February 16, 1881.[37]
The new version of the Pendleton bill did not differ radically from the original version. It corrected the errors,
which reformers considered made the original version unconstitutional, by incorporating a provision allowing the
selection officer to choose one of the top three candidates
to fill a vacancy. It eliminated restrictions on the power
of the executive to remove employees and "goes into operation at first only in the Treasury and Post Office Department
in offices having 50 or more employees, and that afterwards
the extension depends on the request of the President. . . .
You will see," Edward Carry wrote, ". . . that the bill requires a period of probation; that it admits promotion on
the basis of 'merit and competition,' and provides for special appointments where competition is not practicable."[38]

---

[35]Harper's Weekly (New York), 8 January 1881, p. 18.

[36]Dorman B. Eaton to Hayes, New York, Wednesday, Hayes Papers.

[37]U.S. Congress, Senate, The Regulation and Improvement of the
Civil Service, Senate Report No. 872, 46th Cong., 3rd Sess, 1881.

[38]Edward Carry to Carl Schurz, New York, 22 January 1881,
Schurz Papers.

Generally, the Pendleton bill incorporated most of the rules and regulations promulgated by the Grant Civil Service Commission between 1871 and 1875.

Reformers applied considerable pressure on Congress to schedule the bill for a debate and vote, and on the new President to urge its passage. The Nation reported on the bill's progress, and Harper's Weekly urged President Garfield to support the bill. "The best bill ever matured is that which Senator Pendleton introduced. . . . It contains the principles that have been approved and tested by experience, and made applicable in the most reasonable manner."[39] Schurz told Garfield that the reform movement in the Democratic party is "a serious thing. Pendleton believes in it and will honestly push it." Schurz wrote: "The Republican party cannot afford to let this movement pass to the credit of the Democrats. If the Republicans in Congress are wise they will take it out of the hands of their opponents and carry it on themselves."[40] Supporters of the National Civil Service Reform Association sent petitions to Congress urging them to act on the Pendleton bill.[41] Unfortunately, Congress, still under the control of spoils leaders, took no action on the Pendleton bill or on the Civil Service Reform Association's other effort to prevent political assessments contained in a bill introduced by Congress Albert S. Willis of Kentucky.[42]

Senator Henry L. Dawes of Massachusetts, considered a civil service reform supporter, and member of the Senate committee which reported favorably on the Pendleton bill, surprised reformers by introducing a new civil service reform bill. The Dawes plan contained many of the same features of the Pendleton bill but eliminated a civil service commission. Dawes delegated responsibility for selecting appointees to the lowest level of authority. Reformers attacked the plan immediately. Silas Burt charged that "the remedies proposed by

---

[39] Nation (New York), 24 February 1881, p. 122; Harper's Weekly (New York), 5 February 1881, p. 82.

[40] Carl Schurz to Garfield, Washington, 16 January 1881, Schurz Papers.

[41] U.S. Congressional Record, 46th Cong., 3rd Sess., 1881, pp. 899, 1089, 1279-80, 1332, and 1539.

[42] Ibid., p. 491.

Mr. Dawes are impractical. . . . The proposition," he
told Schurz, "that the constituents shall pledge themselves not to importune 'their members' is refreshingly
child-like."[43]   Henry Hitchcock of Rhode Island accused
Dawes of "conceding the principle" but trying to destroy
reform "under color of suggesting remedies which amount
to nothing."[44]   The Nation claimed that the Dawes system
would "not abolish pressure, but only transfer most of it
to the point where it would meet with the least resistance."
The newspaper went on to suggest that "Senator Dawes will
do well to push Mr. Pendleton's bill."[45]

Assassination of President Garfield

       While reformers worked to publicize civil service re-
form and lobby for a strong reform bill in Congress, the
new Administration struggled with the horde of office seekers who flocked to Washington to secure jobs as payment for
their political support.   One of those job seekers was a
forty-eight year old man from Illinois named Charles Guiteau.
The product of mentally disturbed parents, Guiteau had tried
employment as an attorney, theologian, swindler, preacher,
and politician with the same result -- failure.   Considered
by many observers to be insane, Guiteau attached himself to
the drive to re-elect Ulysses Grant to a third term as President.   When Grant failed to get the nomination, Guiteau
chose to switch his loyalty to the Garfield-Arthur ticket.
During the campaign he hung around the Fifth Avenue Hotel
in New York trying to persuade politicians to permit him to
deliver a speech he had written.   After the election he immediately pressed the President-elect for a diplomatic position.   At first he sought the ministry in Vienna and later
the consul-generalship in Paris.   He came to Washington and
spent much time pestering the President and Cabinet officials,
especially at the State Department.   Eventually Garfield and
Blaine both refused to see him.   Unemployed, hungry, and
desperate for attention, Guiteau convinced himself that the
President should be eliminated to save the country.   He purchased a pistol with borrowed money and followed Garfield
around the city until the morning of July 2, 1881.   About
9:30 a.m. that Saturday, on their way to catch a train to

---

[43]Silas W. Burt to Schurz, Port of New York, 22 July 1881,
Schurz Papers.

[44]Henry Hitchcock to Schurz, Naragasset Pier, R.I., 30 July
1881, Schurz Papers.

[45]"The Dawes Plan," Nation (New York), 4 August 1881, p. 86.

New England where they planned to attend commencement exercises at Williams College, President Garfield and Secretary Blaine walked into the near-empty Baltimore and Poto-
mac Railroad Station in Washington. At this moment a small
bearded man came up behind him, drew his revolver, and shot
Garfield in the back. He ran closer and fired again before
turning toward the exit. Officer Patrick Kearney of the
Washington police force seized the gunman before he escaped.
Charles Guiteau calmly declared "I did it and will go to
jail for it. I am a Stalwart, and Arthur will be President."[46]

Impact of Assassination

Guiteau's endorsement of the Stalwarts and Vice President Arthur while Arthur campaigned in New York for the reappointment of Conkling to the Senate, in direct opposition
to President Garfield's policies, combined to generate a
nationwide press attack against Arthur and Conkling. Many
editorials linked Conkling and Arthur to Guiteau. This was
fostered by papers and letters found among Guiteau's possessions. The anti-Arthur and anti-Stalwart mood soon turned
attention to the policy most associated with them, the spoils
system. To friend and foe alike Chester A. Arthur represented
the arch proponent of the spoils system. His entire political
career depended on his skill in manipulating the spoils system to his advantage. The assassination attempt stunned the
Nation, which expressed great dissatisfaction at the prospects
of having Arthur succeed to the Presidency. The newspaper
feared that Conkling would run the government.[47] The New
York Times lamented: "Gen. Arthur is about the last man who
would be considered eligible to that position, did the
choice depend on the voice either of the majority of his own
party or of a majority of the people of the United States."[48]
Former President Hayes expressed similar reservations. He
wrote: "Arthur for President: Conkling the power behind the
throne, superior to the throne!"[49]

---

[46]Charles E. Rosenberg, The Trial of the Assassin Guiteau:
Psychiatry and Law in the Gilded Age (Chicago: University of
Chicago Press, 1968), pp. 2-3; The United States vs. Charles
J. Guiteau (Washington: 1882; reprint ed., New York: Arno
Press), 1973, 2 vols.

[47]Nation (New York), 7 July 1881, p. 836.

[48]"To Whom It May Concern," New York Times, 3 July 1881, p. 1.

[49]Williams, 4:23.

271

Soon after the assassination attempt many Americans placed the blame on the spoils· system. The <u>National Republican</u> wrote:

> This desperate deed . . . was mainly, if not entirely, the promptings of a disappointed office-seeker. There is but little doubt that if Guiteau had not come here for the purpose of getting an office and had failed to do so he would not have attempted to shoot the President.[50]

The <u>New York Mail</u> predicted that "Guiteau's bullet did not do fatal injury to President Garfield, as there is daily increasing reason to hope, but it inflicted a wound upon the spoils system which is likely to prove fatal to that conspicuous curse of the country."[51] Mr. Scoville, the prosecutor at Guiteau's trial, came to the same conclusion. In his opening statement he declared: "Who is to blame for this great crime? . . . The blame must rest somewhere."

> . . . I think it is due to the American people, and I think the people ought to consider it: that this continuous strife after office, this element of politics that has entered in during the last few years when there has been no principle at the bottom of political contents, when the political parties of the country have not been divided by a hair's breadth on any great question of public interest or public policy, this question has entered into the contest and has been the question of the day in politics.[52]

The <u>Nation</u> paid tribute to this conclusion in urging its readers to support the Pendleton bill in Congress. "We do not think we have taken up a newspaper during the last ten days which has not in some manner made the crime the product of 'the spoils system.'"[53]

---

[50]"The Civil Service," <u>The National Republican</u> (Washington), 18 July 1881.

[51]"The Tide of Reform," <u>The Evening Mail</u> (New York), 1 August 188

[52]<u>U.S. vs. Guiteau</u>, 1:340.

[53]"The Moral of It," <u>Nation</u>, 14 July 1881, p. 26.

Exploiting Garfield's Illness

Reformers immediately grasped the importance of the situation. Henry Hitchcock, President of the recently created Missouri Civil Service Reform Association, expressed these views when he told Schurz: "Never before have the signs been so favorable for this movement. . . ."[54] They uniformly proposed exploiting the situation with a massive public relations campaign. Burt declared: "It is obvious that the first stage of the reform movement is passed. Everyone now concedes the necessity. . . ." "The important point now," he urged, "is to show that the method of open competitive examination is the only feasible remedy that is satisfactory." If the Publication Committee of the Reform League was ready, "the country press would gladly sow this seed for us and perhaps in time to have an effect upon Congressional legislation during the coming session."[55] One reformer outlined a three point "practical programme" which closely resembled the one eventually adopted by the Reform Association: (1) try "in every way to arouse and stimulate public opinion. . ."; (2) "individually and collectively" urge action in Congress; and (3) carry out "the widest possible discussion of the proposed methods. -- competitive examination [,] etc., -- so as to inform intelligent men generally of what is actually proposed, and how it has actually succeeded, and how absurd and for the most part dishonest are the objections made to it."[56]

While President Garfield clung tenaciously to life, the New York Civil Service Reform Association organized its first nationwide conference. Twenty-seven days after the assassination attempt, the executive committee invited other associations to meet in Newport, Rhode Island, for the purpose of (1) exchanging views "as to measures and methods" to promote the movement; (2) promoting passage of the Pendleton bill; (3) reaching agreement "on the question of tenure"; and (4) considering organizational questions. Besides the benefits in bringing together fifty-eight delegates from thirteen states interested in promoting reform, the conference agreed on several resolutions. Eaton sponsored a resolution which recognized a centralized civil service com-

---

[54] Henry Hitchcock to Schurz, Naragasset Pier, Rhode Island, 21 July 1881, Schurz Papers.

[55] Silas Burt to Schurz, New York, 12 July 1881, Schurz Papers.

[56] Henry Hitchcock to Schurz, Naragasset Pier, Rhode Island, 30 July 1881, Schurz Papers.

273

mission as essential to reform. Delegates agreed to push for passage of the Pendleton and Willis bills through a massive promotional program and local lobbying efforts in every Congressional district. The question of tenure, as expected, generated most attention. The conferees failed to back a resolution supporting "tenure during good behavior" and substituted a compromise opposing interference from Congress and arbitrary removals. The delegates created the National Civil Service Reform League to coordinate the activities of the various associations. The New York Association's executive committee was appointed to serve temporarily as the central committee for the national league.[57]

By August 1881, many reformers concluded that President Garfield would not resume his Presidential duties. They began to transfer the public image of Garfield from an ineffectual executive under the domination of Half-Breed politicians to a martyr who sacrificed his life for the cause of civil service reform. They collected and published early articles and speeches by Congressman Garfield in support of reform and the Grant Civil Service Commission. Orlando B. Potter, a member of the New York Association and sewing machine manufacturer, donated $2,000 to publish "the late President's opinions and utterances upon the importance and necessity of reform in the civil service of the country. . . ." The Reform League used the money to publish pamphlets, posters, and articles with Garfield's words quoted prominently.[58]

Chester Alan Arthur

Late at night on the 19th of September, James A. Garfield lost his battle with the assassin's bullet and died in a cottage on the New Jersey coast at Elberon. His successor, Chester Alan Arthur, generated considerable apprehension in all areas of the political spectrum. Stalwart

---

[57]William Potts to Schurz, Chesterfield, Massachusetts, 3 August 1881, Schurz Papers; "The National Civil Service Reform League," Harper's Weekly, 27 August 1881, p. 278; Hoogenboom, p. 211.

[58]"President Garfield and Reform," Harper's Weekly, 15 October 1881, p. 691; National Civil Service Reform League, The Assassination of President Garfield in Washington, July 2, 1881, pamphlet, National Civil Service Reform League Collection, Library of the U.S. Civil Service Commission; O.B. Potter to Curtis and Wheeler, New York, 29 September 1881, National Civil Service Reform League Collection; Buffalo Express Poster, National Civil Service Reform League Collection; Burt, A Brief History, pp. N-O.

friends of Arthur observed that "he assumed a totally different manner to his friends and former advisors" during
the long months of Garfield's illness. Reformers warned
their followers not to expect much from the new President.
"Mr. Arthur's political associations and proclivities are
well known, and we must expect no miracles."[59] Half-Breeds
lamented the loss of political influence and prepared to
relinquish their Cabinet posts.

In the last days of August, Vice-President Arthur
received a letter from a woman who signed it Julia Sand.
This was the first of a long series of penetrating, blunt,
and heart-warming letters which she sent to Arthur. She
began: "The hours of Garfield's life are numbered -- before this meets your eye, you may be President. The people are bowed in grief; but -- do you realize it? -- not
so much because he is dying, as because you are his successor." She chided Arthur: "If there is a spark of true
nobility in you, now is the occasion to let it shine."
I "write to you -- but not to beg you to resign. Do what
is more difficult & more brave. Reform!" She continued
by urging him to support civil service reform and appoint
worthy men to office. "It is for you to choose whether
your record shall be written in black or in gold. For the
sake of your country, for your own sake & for the sake of
all who have ever loved you, let it be pure & bright."[60]

Arthur on Civil Service Reform

Chester Arthur was already on record with a position
on civil service reform. In July 1880, he released a letter
accepting the nomination for Vice-President. In that letter
he took his first public notice of the civil service reform
movement. He disapproved of restrictions against political
assessments and doubted the wisdom of introducing competitive examinations "because they have seemed to exalt more
educational and abstract tests above general business capacity, and even special fitness for the particular work in
hand." Arthur expressed belief in the need for honest and
efficient public servants. Public business should be conducted on the same principles as "successful private business."

---

[59]"The Vice-President," Harper's Weekly, 24 September 1881,
p. 642; Julia M. Crowley, Echoes From Niagara: Historical,
Political, Personal (Buffalo: C.M. Moulton, 1890), p. 228.

[60]Julia Sand to Arthur, New York, August 1881, Arthur Papers,
Library of Congress.

Original appointments should be based upon
ascertained fitness. The tenure of office
should be stable. Positions of responsibility
should, so far as practicable, be filled by
the promotion of worthy and efficient officers.
The investigation of all complaints, and the
punishment of all official misconduct, should
be prompt and thorough.[61]

The new President returned to the subject in his
first message to Congress delivered in December 1881.
He repeated his objection against competitive examinations
but stressed his desire for honest and efficient public
servants with appointments based on fitness. He proposed
creating a central board of examiners to pass on the qualification of applicants "without resort to the competitive
test." However, "if Congress should deem it advisable at
the present session to establish competitive tests for
admission to the service, no doubts such as have been suggested shall deter me from giving the measure my earnest
support." If Congress failed to enact such a measure,
Arthur recommended that they appropriate $25,000 to reac-
tivate the Civil Service Commission.[62]

Congress Changes Tactics

Senator George Pendleton and Congressman Albert S.
Willis, Democrat from Kentucky, reintroduced the bills
written by the Civil Service Reform League in December
1881. One bill outlawed political assessment of government employees and the other provided for a civil service
commission with power to issue rules applicable to all
civil servants. The content of the two bills was eventually unified in a new one drafted by the Senate Committee.
The new bill called for competitive examinations of all
entry level positions and promotions on the basis of merit
and competition. It expressly relieved employees from the
obligation of contributing to political parties. It authorized the Commission to investigate violations of its rules
and required it to submit an annual report to the Congress.
Departments were assigned responsibility for developing a
"more perfect classification of clerks and employees."[63]

---

[61]Richardson, 8:60.

[62]Ibid., 8:60-63.

[63]U.S. Congressional Record, 47th Cong., 1st Sess., 1881,
p. 82.

Pendleton attacked the spoils system in his intro-
ductory speech, declaring that it brings "injustice, bru-
tality, wastefulness, recklessness, fraud, peculation, de-
gradation of persons and of parties." The assassination
of President Garfield illustrated this. "That system is
the real assassin of Garfield. . . . We must supplant this
system" with a "better system [merit system]." The bill,
Pendleton said, "is very limited" and "its provisions are
very simple." It "concerns itself only with the admission
to and promotion in the civil service."

It affects only a small number of "inferior offices"
and does not deal with "tenure of office, or removals from
office," or incumbents, "except in the case of promotion."
The Senator from Ohio pointed out that competitive examinations are necessary because "pass examinations has [sic]
proven an utter failure." Pendleton concluded his speech
with a spirited attack on the bill introduced by Senator
Dawes of Massachusetts. Dawes failed to include a civil
service commission because of "the power given to the
commissioners." Senator Dawes, according to Pendleton, has
"grossly exaggerated" these powers. "The Senator [from
Massachusetts] is entirely mistaken" when he objects to the
Commission on the grounds that managers and supervisors
responsible for "the work to be performed are to have no
voice in the selection of the men who are to perform it."
Pendleton objected to Dawes' contention that legislative
action was not necessary. "I deny that there has been
ample legislation to cope with the evils which we wish to
eradicate." Senator Pendleton concluded his comments with
an appeal to action. "Let us put the Senate, the Congress,
actively on the side of reform."[64]

Senator Dawes responded to Senator Pendleton's attack
mildly and declared himself a supporter of reform. "The
Senator from Ohio will not find me antagonizing his commission, if that is essential to the enactment of any mandatory
law. I only express my doubt about the manner in which it
will work." But Senator Benjamin Hill, Democrat of Georgia,
responded for the spoils supporters. Senator Hill expressed
grave doubts that the "remedy will ever be found in legislation." The solution "must come from the people," but "I
doubt whether the people themselves are capable of applying
the remedy." He reminded his listeners that Garfield was
no sooner buried than citizens began to appeal to President
Arthur "to make appointments" to their advantage. It is

---

[64] Congressional Record, pp. 79-84.

ironical that "civil service reformers at the North . . .
voted for that very man for Vice-President." "I believe,"
Hill concluded, "that the evil grows out of our system.
. . . Democratic or Republican, in office many years, will
be guilty of it. . . . It proves that the people ought not
to allow any party to remain in power too long." The solution to the spoils system is to vote the Republicans out
of office. "It is time they should go out."[65]

Pendleton's speech included many statements that contained Eaton's views. He undoubtedly reviewed a draft before its delivery.[66] The portion pertaining to the Dawes
bill caused internal dissension among National Civil Service
Reform League members which smoldered below the surface until
1886 when it exploded into a nasty personal attack against
Dorman Eaton. Eaton acquired few close personal friends
among reformers. He wrote and received letters written in
more formal tones than those of Curtis, Burt, or Schurz.

Eaton attacked the Dawes plan in a series of articles
published in the Boston Advertiser. He considered the Civil
Service Commission essential to reform and thought that many
elements of the spoils system would continue without it.
Curtis expressed exasperation with Eaton when he told Burt
and Norton that he found Eaton's position too inflexible.
He refused to permit the National Civil Service Reform
League to republish Eaton's articles.[67] He urged Dawes and
other supporters in Congress to avoid a fight for fear the
two plans threatened to split supporters and weaken the reform movement's impact.[68]

---

[65]Congressional Record, pp. 84-85.

[66]George Pendleton to Schurz, Washington, 10 December 1881,
Schurz Papers.

[67]George W. Curtis to Schurz, New York, 26 October 1882,
Schurz Papers.

[68]G.W. Curtis to Norton, West New Brighton, New York, 7 March
1882, Curtis Papers; Curtis to Dawes, West New Brighton, 8
March 1882, Dawes Papers; Civil Service Record (Boston/
Cambridge), February 1882, pp. 22-23; Civil Service Record,
March 1882, pp. 27-32.

The public blamed Garfield's assassination on the spoils system. Congress received hundreds of petitions and appeals from concerned citizens, many sponsored by civil service reform associations. The "best citizens" from almost every major urban center contributed their names and prestige to petitions urging Congress to take action on various reform proposals, especially civil service reform. This outpouring of public sentiment motivated unsympathetic politicians to adopt another tactic to protect their patronage. Senators and Congressmen flooded the bill hoppers with a mass of reform bills covering every conceivable approach to the problem. This insult to public opinion generated proposals to: (1) elect office holders by direct election; (2) create firm tenure of office rules for all employees; (3) prohibit discrimination against veterans; (4) assign designated positions to Members of Congress for disposition to their constituents; and (5) apportion patronage among voting districts. Meanwhile, legislators thwarted efforts to revise the Grant Civil Service Commission by refusing to appropriate $25,000 requested by President Arthur. They ensured that the Pendleton and Dawes bills would not advance rapidly by stacking the Committee on Civil Service with opponents of reform. These stalling tactics ensured that the first session of the Forty-Seventh Congress passed no reform legislation.[69]

Political Assessments

Congressional elections in 1882 sparked a major battle over the fundraising technique of assessing political contributions from government employees. Democratic strategists and Independent Republicans who considered prohibitions against political assessments part of their civil service reform package, combined to make the practice a major election campaign issue. Democrats opposed political assessments because incumbent Republicans profited by the practice. The Republican campaign committees generally demanded office holders contribute two per cent of their annual salary, but many overzealous election committees demanded and received much higher percentages. Republicans denied accusations that political assessments were compulsory and termed them nothing more than "voluntary contributions." Unfortunately

---

[69]U.S. Congressional Record, 47th Cong., 1st Sess., 1882, pp. 85, 94, 96, 100, 471, 930, 1093, 1697, 2099, 2357, 3925, 6013-16, and 5810-12; "Reformers Who Do Not Wish to Reform," Nation (New York), 15 June 1882, p. 496; Nation, 13 July 1882, p. 22; Nation, 20 July 1882, p. 41.

for Republicans, the mood of the public had changed in response to Garfield's assassination, and citizens responded to press reports exposing the practice. Civil servants began to heed prohibitions against political assessments and contributions declined.[70]

The New York Civil Service Reform Association decided to challenge violations of the Executive Order of 1876 prohibiting "inferior" government employees from soliciting and collecting money for political purposes. The Reform Association notified Secretary of the Treasury Charles J. Folger that General Newton M. Curtis, a special agent in the Treasury Department, violated this statute. Folger, hoping to avoid a major conflict, persuaded Curtis to resign and referred the case to the United States District Attorney. The District Attorney, much to the surprise of Folger and the Reform League, decided to prosecute the case. The press charged the Republican Administration with foul play when the court threw out the first indictment on highly technical, but legally important, grounds created when a copy clerk misspelled the defendant's first name. Julia I. Sand, suspecting Arthur, asked the President: "Who is responsible for this mean little trick. . . the trick was a blunder," she assured him, "as everybody sees through it. . . ." The unfavorable public reaction forced the Administration to hold a second trial which resulted in a conviction.[71]

Jay A. Hubbell, Congressman from Michigan and Chairman of the Republican Congressional Campaign Committee, unaware of the change in public opinion, issued the usual assessment letter to civil servants in May 1882. It generated a considerable amount of protest from reformers and Democrats. Senator Pendleton delivered a strong attack against it on the floor of the Senate on June 26, 1882. He attacked the tone of the text, which made it clear that assessments were not voluntary. "Authorized! By whom authorized; for what purpose authorized? . . . Voluntary contribution! Voluntary as the contribution the traveler makes to the pocket of the highwayman when commanded to stop and hold up his hands."[72]

---

[70]"Which Raised Most Money for the Canvass," Nation (New York), 10 November 1881, p. 369.

[71]Julia I. Sand to Arthur, Saratoga, April 1882, Arthur Papers; Silas W. Burt, A Brief History, p. P.

[72]U.S. Congressional Record, 47th Cong., 1st Sess., 1882, pp. 5329-33.

The New York Civil Service Reform Association exploited the unpopular reception of the Hubbell letter.
The organization issued a warning to office holders that
if they make political assessments, they become liable
for prosecution. Hubbell received support from the Attorney General who declared that the statute of 1876 did not
apply to legislators. The antiassessment campaign failed
in eliminating "voluntary assessments" as a major source
of revenue for the Republican party, but the unfavorable
publicity weakened the appeal of spoils candidates.[73]

Second Annual Meeting of the Reform League

The National Civil Service Reform League scheduled
another meeting at Newport, Rhode Island, for August 2, 1882.
President George William Curtis used the occasion to attack
political assessments and the appointment practices of President Arthur. He raised the possibility of creating a new
political party pledged to reform principles. Delegates
agreed to pursue a more active role in the 1882 Congressional
elections. They decided to interview Congressional candidates
on their civil service reform position and publish the responses. If necessary, they proposed to sponsor their own
candidates.[74]

The Reform League campaign came at a time when the public was more receptive to their appeal than ever before.
Most state party conventions incorporated civil service reform statements in their platforms. Several important politicians, sensing the change in public sentiment, began to
change their public positions. James G. Blaine, challenged
by Independent Republicans in Maine, decided to make his own
reform proposals. He advocated a fixed tenure of seven years,
but reformers dismissed it as insincere. Even vitriolic Benjamin F. Butler felt compelled to ring the bells of reform.
Butler ran for the governorship of Massachusetts on a reform

---

[73]Civil Service Record (Boston), July 1882, 11-14; National
Civil Service Reform League, Report on the Expediency of
Asking Candidates For Public Office Their Views of Civil-Ser-
vice Reform, June 22, 1882, National Civil Service Reform
League Collection, U.S. Civil Service Commission Library.

[74]National Civil Service Reform League, Proceedings at the
Annual Meeting of the National Civil-Service Reform League
Held at Newport, Rhode Island, August 2, 1882, with the
Address of the President Hon. George William Curtis (New
York: William S. Gottsberger, 1882), 5-35.

platform. Democrats wisely nominated Grover Cleveland, the reform mayor of Buffalo, to run against Charles J. Folger, Secretary of the Treasury, for governor of New York. The campaign against political assessments contributed to the failure of Jay Hubbell to win renomination to the House of Representatives.[75]

Election of 1882

Voters registered a general discontent with politicians who stood for "more of the same." Blaine and Butler were lucky enough to climb on the bandwagon before the election. Others waited until the voters evicted many prominent Republican politicians who opposed reform. Democrats benefited from the stunning defeat of Republicans. Republicans from northeastern states suffered major setbacks. Voters in the west and south gave less weight to the reform appeal. Analysts interpreted the election results as a repudiation of the "boss system" and a demand for action on a reform system.[76]

President Chester A. Arthur led a chorus of politicians who publicly withdrew their opposition to the Pendleton bill. In his annual message to Congress, Arthur took note of the election results by saying, "the people of this country, apparently without distinction to party, have . . . given expression to their earnest wish for prompt and definite action." He agreed that the burden of dispensing appointments to the civil service "has become greater than he [the Executive] ought to bear" since it "diverts his time and attention from the proper discharge of duties . . . [that] cannot be delegated to other hands." The President also supported the abolition of political assessments. "I have always maintained and still maintain that a public officer should be as absolutely free as any other citizen to give or withhold a contribution for the aid of the political party of his choice." Arthur extended his support to the Pendleton bill and thus abandoned his opposition to competitive examinations.[77]

---

[75]*Nation* (New York), 31 August 1882, p. 168; *Nation*, 14 September 1882, p. 210; "Mr. Blaine as a Reformer," p. 214; *Nation*, 21 September 1882, p. 232; *Nation*, 28 September 1882, pp. 251-2; *Nation*, 12 October 1882, p. 298; "General Butler's Acceptance," p. 300.

[76]*Nation*, 19 October 1882, p. 324; *Nation*, 9 November 1882, p. 389.

[77]Richardson, 8:145-7.

The election convinced many long time opponents of
civil service reform to follow the President's direction
and reverse their position. Jóhn A. Kasson came around
to vote for the Pendleton bill as did Senator John A. Logan
of Illinois. Senators John Sherman and James Z. George
tried to water down the Pendleton bill but supported it in
crucial votes.[78]

The Pendleton Bill

The lame-duck session of the Forty-Seventh Congress
convened in December 1882. Both Republicans and Democrats
recognized that they must deal with the civil service reform question without further delay. Republicans retained
the balance of power because of their victory in 1880, but
knew that Democrats would supersede them in March when the
Forty-Eighth Congress convened. Both parties looked ahead
to the election of 1884 in deciding what action to take on
the reform question. Republican party leaders decided to
support the Pendleton bill in order to protect their appointments should the Democrats acquire power. They also
wanted to claim credit as champions of reform. Democrats
needed to retain support of the Independent voters who demanded civil service reform and hoped to weaken Republican
fund-raising sources by outlawing political assessments.

Several opponents of reform tried to side track the
Pendleton bill by sponsoring alternative bills. House Republicans drafted a bill, introduced by Congressman John
A. Kasson, which established fixed tenure to ensure rotation
and appointment without competitive examinations. Senator
Henry L. Dawes reintroduced his reform bill designed to
eliminate the centralized civil service commission, and
Senator James Z. George proposed a constitutional amendment requiring election of all federal employees. These
proposals failed to generate serious consideration because
they came too late.[79]

Republican leadership called up the Pendleton bill for
debate soon after the new session opened. Committee hearings
took place in the first session. The report on these hearings

---

[78]U.S. Congressional Record, 47th Cong., 2nd Sess., pp. 246-7,
319-21, 660-1, 860-67.

[79]U.S. Congressional Record, 47th Cong., 2nd Sess., pp. 204-8;
246-7, 319-21, 650.

accompanied the bill and contained the only detailed discussion of its provisions. Dorman Eaton assumed responsibility for defending the Pendleton bill, section by section, before commenting on the defects of the Dawes bill. He read a letter from Silas W. Burt, Chief Examiner at the Customhouse in New York, defending the system as practical, and stressing the need of establishing a Commission to train examiners and ensure uniformity in standards. The Committee heard statements by Henry G. Pearson, Postmaster of New York; Edward O. Graves, Chief Examiner under the Grant Civil Service Commission; George William Curtis, first Chairman of the Grant Civil Service Commission; and John L. Thomas, long-time Collector of the Customhouse in Baltimore. These statements constitute a comprehensive analysis of the Pendleton and Dawes bills and discuss the arguments for and against the civil service reform movement. All of the points raised had been discussed in considerable detail in previous debates or hearings.[80]

George Pendleton began the debate on December 12, 1882, with a speech similar to the one he had delivered a year earlier. He stressed the need for competitive examinations to create an efficient government service. His bill extended democracy by opening government employment to all citizens. Experience in the New York Customhouse, Pendleton stated, showed that competitive examinations need not restrict eligible candidates to college students.[81]

The Senate allotted the rest of December 1882 to the debate. Speakers paid little attention to the merits of civil service reform proposals or the defects of the spoils system, which the Pendleton bill hoped to eradicate. Spoils advocates tried to weaken the bill with a barrage of amendments. Leaders in both parties thought that the Democratic party was in a strong position to capture the White House in 1884 and the speeches delivered during the debate concentrated on strengthening the position of the respective parties in preparation for this event.

Democrats sponsored amendments designed to weaken the Republican strength in the government services. James L. Pugh introduced amendments to require all incumbents to sit for competitive examinations. Positions vacated by those

---

[80] U.S. Congress, Senate, Committee on Civil Service and Retrenchment, Report, Senate Bill 133 to Regulate and Improve the Civil Service of the United States, 47th Cong., 1st Sess., 15 May 1882.

[81] U.S. Congressional Record, 47th Cong., 2nd Sess., pp. 204-8.

who failed would be apportioned among the states. In this
way, he hoped to increase the percentage of Democrats
holding office. Joseph E. Brown sponsored an amendment which
required appointing officials to fill vacancies equally between Republicans and Democrats. Zebulon B. Vance tried to
expand coverage of the Pendleton bill to internal revenue
offices employing more than fifty people. Preston Plumb
successfully sponsored amendments to reduce the salary of
the Chief Examiner to $3,000 but later sponsored amendments
to eliminate the job altogether. Democrats supported changes
designed to eliminate "voluntary contributions." Republicans voted down all of these Democratic-sponsored amendments.

The Senate passed three major amendments that weakened
the Pendleton bill. The original bill applied competitive
examinations to entry level jobs. The Democrats backed an
amendment to open all grades to competitive examinations.
In this way they hoped to redress the balance, then in favor
of Republicans, by shortening the time required to equalize
the distribution of jobs. Southern Democrats and Western
Republicans combined to pass an apportionment amendment
which allocated jobs according to population. These regions
of the country wanted to ensure that all government jobs did
not go to the better educated populations in the north.
Republicans sponsored an amendment introduced by the Chairman of the Committee on Civil Service and Retrenchment which
outlawed political assessments but accepted "voluntary contributions." Republicans could not accept a total cessation
of a major financial source.

Senators gave their approval to the Pendleton bill by
a vote of thirty-eight to five. The vote did not indicate
broad support for reform. The assassination of Garfield
and the election results of 1882 required both parties to
support reform. Many notorious spoilsmen voted in the af-
firmative. Those included Pennsylvania's Don Cameron,
Louisiana's William Kellogg, and Illinois' John A. Logan.
Nevertheless, Georgia's Senator Joseph E. Brown refused to
conform and voted against the bill. He expressed his exasperation by suggesting the Senate title the Pendleton bill
"a bill to perpetuate in office the Republicans who now
control the patronage of the Government."[82]

---

[82]U.S. Congressional Record, 47th Cong., 2nd Sess., pp. 660-
661, 204-208, 273-79, 282-84, 316-21, 268-72, 468-70, 505-
528, 555, 559, 561-2, 566-71, 586, 591-95, 600-11, 620-30,
642-45, and 657-58.

New York Congressman Abram S. Hewitt persuaded colleague Samuel Sullivan (Sunset) Cox to move that the House
consider the Pendleton bill without debate. The lower
house agreed to restrict debate to half an hour divided
equally among supporters and opponents. Texas Democrat
John Reagan spoke for the opponents who accused the Republican party of cheating the Democratic party. Kentucky
Democrat Phil Thompson moved to recommit the bill to committee but lost by a vote of 113 to 85. The debate ended
when the House sent the Pendleton bill to the White House
by a final vote of 155 to 47.[83]

President Chester Arthur Signs

The attention of reformers turned to Chester A. Arthur,
arch advocate of the spoils system in its most extreme form,
of political corruption during the decade of the 1870's. At
the beginning of 1882 Julia I. Sand urged the President to
fight for civil service reform.

> The vital question before the country today
> is "Civil Service Reform." The vital ques-
> tion before you is how you will meet it.
> . . . Are you content to sit, like a snake-
> charmer, and let loathesome serpents coil
> about you, priding yourself on it that not
> one of them dares sting you? I would ra-
> ther think of you, like St. George, in
> shining armor, striking death to the heart
> of the dragon.[84]

At the end of the year she chided him again:

> Cannot you make up your mind to put all
> double-dealing out of your life? If you
> think Civil Service Reform trash, and
> don't care a fig if it fails, say so, and
> have done with it. That would be a pity --
> but the country will live. . . . But if,
> with your present opportunities for observ-
> ing, you believe that Civil Service Reform

---

[83]U.S. Congressional Record, 47th Cong., 2nd Sess., pp.
860-867.

[84]Julia I. Sand to Chester Arthur, New York, 7 January 1882,
Arthur Papers.

286

is a real public need, then stand by your
conviction openly and earnestly. . . . Do
not waver. If a thing is worth doing, do
it with your whole soul.[85]

The Pendleton bill became the Pendleton Act when
Conkling's former lieutenant, Chester A. Arthur, fulfilled his promise and signed it on January 16, 1883.

---

[85]Julia I. Sand to Chester Arthur, Saratoga, New York,
29 December 1882, Arthur Papers.

CHAPTER XI

BRITISH INFLUENCE ON THE PENDLETON ACT

1880 to 1883

The pattern established by earlier debates over civil
service reform continued during the final push for adoption.
Reformers supported their recommendations with examples
from the experience of Great Britain. Spoilsmen charged
that civil service reform was a foreign, undemocratic,
and anti-American system. The assassination of President
Garfield and subsequent election defeats for opponents to
civil service reform created an atmosphere conducive to
reform. President Arthur led the way to passage of the
Pendleton Bill when he removed his opposition to the
"English System."

Continued Use of the British Example

George William Curtis, president of the National Civil
Service Reform League, addressed the Independent Republican
conference of May 20, 1880, on the subject of "Machine Politics and the Remedy." He predicted that "the party of the
future is a party of Civil-Service reform."

> It is too late to denounce it as impracti-
> cable, a dream and a folly and the politics
> of the moon. Is England the moon? Is John
> Bull a dreamer? Is an English government
> any less a party government than ours? On
> the contrary, English parties are more
> thoroughly disciplined than ours and party
> spirit burns more fiercely.

Curtis reminded his listeners that the Tory administration
had just been defeated but "not a single office-holder was
assessed to sustain it or removed to strengthen it" except
policy positions like the Governor-general of India or
Viceroy of Ireland. "On the other hand," every government employee in the United States fears removal while others
struggle to replace them as a "result of the election upon
which we are entering."[1]

---

[1] Norton, ed., pp. 166-167.

Curtis pointed out that the patronage system deprives the average citizen of his individual political rights. The system produces "machine" politics which leads to political control by political bosses. Abolish patronage and "such officers and all present 'bosses' will be equal with all other citizens."

> When the power of patronage was at its height in England, official interference at elections was so mischievous that the whole minor office-holding class was disfranchised. When patronage was abolished, the disability was removed, because the evil had disappeared.[2]

In December 1880, George Curtis returned to the same theme he used before the Independent Republican conference.

> In the late general and exciting election in England not a man in the minor Civil Service was prohibited from taking part, or gained or lost his place in consequence of the total change of administration. There is no reason that the United States should be the only great country to hold on to the ridiculous and exploded medieval tradition of patronage.[3]

Eaton's Book Motivates Reformers

The series of letters in the Nation which led to formation of the National Civil Service Reform League frequently referred to the English experience as portrayed by Dorman Eaton. F.G.S. of Hartford wrote that reform would not be accomplished by the President. "Our reform is to be accomplished as the English reform was accomplished -- by agitation and a bill in Congress. We must begin with the agitation. . . ."[4]   F.W.H. of Mt. Vernon, New York, suggested

---

[2] "General Garfield and Reform," Harper's Weekly (New York), 14 August 1880, p. 514.

[3] "The Prospects of Reform," Harper's Weekly, 11 December 1880, p. 787.

[4] "Letter to Editor from FGS, Hartford, July 30," Nation (New York), 5 August 1880, p. 93; actually, FGS was incorrect in his assertions, for the British reform owed very little to agitation and almost nothing to a bill in Parliament.

that those interested in reform read Eaton's recent book
on civil service in Great Britain to learn about "the
evils of the old system and the benefits of the new. . . ."[5]
Mr. I.J. Wister of Philadelphia suggested that Eaton "con-
dense his valuable work on the history of this reform in
England for popular use" and sell it in a paperback version
for wide distribution.[6]

Another correspondent to the Nation wrote that the demand for reform meant emulation of the British system.

> Let it be clearly understood that the "reform"
> demanded is based upon the English system of
> civil service, which has for its essential fea-
> tures competitive examinations in appointments
> to the subordinate offices, with absolute in-
> dependence of political consideration, succes-
> sive promotion to the highest grades of the
> service as in the army and navy, and, for all
> except the heads of departments, assured ten-
> ure of place during good behavior. When the
> last is fully secured the assessment of
> salaries and similar abuses may be safely left
> to regulate themselves.[7]

William F. Kipp of Buffalo agreed with I.J. Wister
that the civil service movement needed a concise article
on the reform in England. Kipp wrote to Schurz that he
planned to write an article giving a "bird's eye view"
of "the establishment of the English civil service . . .
with direct reference to our efforts at civil service reform in America."[8]

---

[5]Nation (New York), 19 August 1880, pp. 134-35.

[6]"Letter to Editor from I.J. Wister, October 20, 1880,"
Nation, 28 October 1880, p. 307; Eaton published a hard-
back version in 1881 which received a wide distribution.

[7]"Letter to Editor from F.H., Pittsburgh, November 9, 1880,"
Nation (New York), 18 November 1880, p. 357.

[8]William F. Kipp to Carl Schurz, Buffalo, New York, 18
March 1881, Schurz Papers.

Eaton's book remained the major textbook of reform. Harper's Weekly referred to it in its article on the Pendleton bill. Introduction of the reform bill by a prominent Democrat proved that "reform is essentially non-partisan." "The Pendleton bill, although defective in details, has been prepared with a clear conception of the indispensable conditions of reform." One of those "indispensable conditions" was the provision establishing a centralized commission with power to make and enforce regulations.

> That such a body may be perfectly impartial
> and thoroughly efficient, the action of the
> English board proves. Party spirit and poli-
> tical corruption are not less rife in England
> than in this country, but from the first there
> has been no question or suspicion of the good
> faith of the Civil Service Board.

Harper's advised that Eaton's book "upon the history of the English civil service is one of the most valuable contributions to the literature of the subject." The writer referred to England to prove that candidates appointed through competitive examinations are high quality employees who seldom "failed in their probation."[9] Curtis used Eaton's book again in an article on "Elections and Reform."[10]

Committee Hearings on the Pendleton Bill

While reformers used Eaton's book to advertise reform, he came to Washington to testify before the Senate Select Committee established to examine the several branches of the Civil Service. Eaton, as Chairman of the Legislative Committee of the New York Civil Service Reform Association, assumed responsibility for most of the testimony at the hearings. He wrote the new bill which Pendleton substituted for the original version. Eaton consistently used the English experience to show that civil service reform proposals worked and that they would accomplish the objectives claimed for them. The English found, according to Eaton, that examinations "brought into the service a body of men so superior

---

[9]"The Pendleton Bill," Harper's Weekly (New York), 8 January 1881, p. 18.

[10]"Elections and Reform," Harper's Weekly (New York), 29 January 1881, pp. 66-67.

292

that for all the higher positions below cabinet officers a
large portion of them would be taken by promotion from the
lower service."[11] The pass-fail examination system authorized under the law of 1853 did not protect examinees from
the abuses of patronage. "That system was long tried in
England, but was found to break down for the reason that
it could be attacked with all the force of the holders of
patronage, and officials in authority in detail, by bringing pressure to bear on each board, and thus to pass men
through, because the clerks would not have courage enough
to stand up against it."[12]

The Chairman of the defunct Grant Civil Service Commission suggested that one of the duties of the civil service commission would be to preserve records of the examination results "so that at any subsequent time the making and
grading of any person examined may be shown to be correct by
reference to the papers that are kept on file. . . . It is
the case to-day that of 185,000 who have been examined com-
petitively for admission to the British service that records
are so preserved that it is possible to test with entire
accuracy the justice of the examination of every single one
of those individuals, precisely as it was when reported after
the examination was made."[13]

Eaton defended limiting the competitive system to large
post office establishments on the basis that postmasters of
small offices have the time to acquire knowledge of their
employees' "personal fitness." The British Government used
a similar system, except that they limited examinations to
"post-offices where the business is such that the income is
125 pounds a year in England and 100 pounds in Ireland."[14]

Dorman Eaton described the experience of the British
and American Governments with pass-fail examinations. By
keeping out "dunces and blockheads" the administration improved but the system was "entirely defective." It "enabled
the entire pressure to be brought to bear upon this individual
board of examiners from the whole army of partisans and of-
fice-mongers."[15]

---

[11]U.S. Congress, Senate, Select Committee to Examine the Several
Branches of the Civil Service, The Regulation and Improvement of
the Civil Service, Report No. 872, 46th Cong., 3rd Sess., 1881,
p. 15.

[12]Ibid.

[13]Ibid., p. 18.

[14]Ibid., p. 20.

[15]Ibid., pp. 21-22.

Eaton used a large segment of his testimony to describe the British experience and its relation to the American political system. "I hold that an English precedent is
no precedent for us, except where it is wholly consistent
with our social life, with our constitution, with our political matters, and with party government." The struggle for
political change in England "has been . . . between the
democratic and republican elements in favor of reform and
the bishops and the nobility opposed to it." The English
carried patronage to extremes far greater than in the
United States. "But against all this prejudice, . . .
they opened the service to open competition . . . so that
. . . there is not a spot into which a member of the British
parliament can force any favorite whatever."[16] "Once the
system got into operation," the witness observed, "public
opinion, the sense of common justice and right rallied to
its support to such an extent that it now stands as strongly
entrenched. . . ." He attributed the near-defeat of Disraeli in 1876 to a violation of the civil service rules.
A study by Lord Salisbury of the effects of open competition
showed that it "had not only given superior men in all the
lower grades, but it had supplied superior administrative
talent for the higher grades." The examinations did not
open government employment to "a sort of highly educated
person, a scholarly and dilettanti sort of man, but men
who have got practical knowledge, who have got the administrative ability which the government needs."[17] The experience of the government of British India proved this
statement. Eaton used the British example in discussing
tenure for good behavior. He briefly explained that England's civil service retirement system actually saved the
government money because it attracted superior employees
who acquired valuable experience with long service.[18] He
defended the proposal to examine candidates in several geographic locations by referring to the British experience,
which proved it was practical. Eaton argued that it would
be easier to discharge a man for "good cause" since "there
is nothing behind the man but his record. He comes un-
recommended." This rule was so strong in Britain that a
recommendation of a member of Parliament would exclude any
man from a government job. Eaton quoted from "a distin-

[16] Report No. 872, p. 26.

[17] Ibid., p. 27.

[18] Ibid., pp. 28-29.

guished member of the British administration" to show that
members of the House of Commons supported civil service
reform because it relieved them of pressure from office
seekers.[19]

The Senate Committee accepted Eaton's arguments and
approved the bill. The report it rendered took note of
Eaton's book on the British Civil Service and pointed to
the experience of Great Britain as "further evidence of
the good effects of tests of merit, through competitive
examinations." The Committee refuted the charge that civil
service reform was aristocratic and anti-democratic. "Patronage destroyed in Great Britain was mainly controlled by
the privileged or aristocratic classes. . . ." "The reform
there has been substantially a triumph of common justice
and republican principle over class and official monopoly."[20]

President Arthur Attacks
the "English System"

President Chester Arthur devoted a large segment of
his First Annual Message to Congress to civil service reform. Arthur repeated his statements, first delivered in
his letter accepting the nomination for the Vice Presidency.
He accepted the principle that "original appointments should
be based upon ascertained fitness" but opposed the proposal
to determine fitness by "competitive examination." The
strongest argument for adopting this system in the United
States, the President said, is "the success which has attended that system in the country of its birth," Great
Britain. "That this system as an entirety has proved very
successful in Great Britain seems to be generally conceded
even by those who once opposed its adoption." However,
three segments of the British system "have not generally
been received with favor in this country, even among the
foremost advocates of civil service reform." The three
segments which most Americans oppose are life tenure, age
limitations, and a retirement system.

The President continued by attacking numerous additional
features of the "English system." He opposed the English
rule limiting admission to the lowest ranks, the use of competitive examinations which cannot test "probity, industry,

---

[19]Report No. 872, pp. 30-31.

[20]Ibid., p. 10.

good sense, good habits, good temper, patience, order, courtesy, tact, self-reliance," and which would probably exclude older applicants. Arthur objected to the proposal of selecting officers by promotion from the lowest grade. "An infusion of new blood from time to time into the middle ranks of the service might be very beneficial in its results." Arthur implied that Americans may be trying to do too much too fast. "The present English system is a growth of years, and was not created by a single stroke of executive or legislative action." "It may be that before we continue ourselves upon this important question within the stringent bounds of statutory enactment we may profitably await the result of further inquiry and experiment."

Arthur told the Legislature that he would support a law "to establish competitive tests for admission to the service," if "Congress should deem it advisable." If not, Arthur urgently recommended that Congress appropriate $25,000 to revise the Grant Commission. "With the aid thus afforded me I shall strive to execute the provisions of that law according to its letter and spirit." He closed his remarks with a vote of confidence in the employees of the Government who "in my judgment," deserve "high commendation."[21]

Senator George Pendleton's Speech
in Defense of the Civil Service Bill

One week after President Arthur delivered his first annual message, Senator Pendleton reintroduced his civil service bill and spoke in defense of it. Pendleton extracted figures from Dorman Eaton's book to show that the cost of collecting customs duties in the United States was much higher than in Great Britain. He summarized the history of England on civil service reform. The Senator characterized the English spoils system as more extensive and complex than the United States. Yet, "after one hundred and fifty years of luxuriant growth, while the nobility and the minority and the members of Parliament were in full enjoyment of the patronage in Church and State, in the face of an adverse Parliament, in May 1855 Lord Palmerston, by an order in council, cut up the system, root and branch, and introduced competitive examination." Parliament at first condemned the system, but in less than one year supported it financially and later recommended its extension. Like President Arthur, Pendleton suggested that life tenure, age

---

[21]Richardson, 8:60-63.

of entrance, and retiring pensions "perhaps cannot and
ought not to be transplanted here." The "British Empire presents to us a splendid example of self-denial
and courage and power in eradicating an acknowledged
abuse." Americans must not be told that they "cannot do
as much in this direction as the Parliament and ministry
of Great Britain."[22]

Committee Hearings on the Pendleton Bill

Reformers, led by Dorman B. Eaton and George William
Curtis, testified extensively on the virtues of the Pendleton bill again in February 1882. Eaton assumed responsibility for defending the provisions of the Pendleton bill
section by section. He testified on each section of the
Dawes bill and compared it with the Pendleton bill. Eaton
recalled that Congress authorized President Grant to establish rules and regulations for admission to the civil service in 1871. The President "and his Cabinet considered
the subject and looking especially to the British experience
and its results became satisfied that competitive examinations
were the most effective, and that a commission was necessary
for their supervision. Such a commission was appointed. . . ."[23]
Unfortunately, American Congressmen refused to "have their
patronage taken away from them, as competitive examinations
would take it from them, as they had taken it from the members of the British Parliament."[24]

Eaton supported the provision in the Pendleton bill
which provided for filling vacancies "by selection from
those graded highest as the result of competitive examinations."
He opposed the article in the Dawes bill which confined that
section to the highest three on the certificate. "The English
Government in 1874 or 1875, having limited it by their rules
to the three highest, modified the rules so that the selection
might be made from a larger number. . . ."[25] Eaton explained
that sections on merit promotions and on reporting selections
to the commission, followed British rules.[26] Section 6 pro-

---

[22]U.S. _Congressional Record_, 47th Cong., 1st Sess., 1881, pp. 80-1.

[23]U.S. Congress, Senate, Committee on Civil Service and Retrenchment, _Report, Senate Bill 133 to Regulate and Improve the Civil
Service of the United States_, 47th Cong., 1st Sess., 1882, p. 12.

[24]_Ibid._, p. 13.

[25]_Ibid._, p. 15.

[26]_Ibid._, pp. 16-17.

vided for the classification of all clerks. By the 1853
law no person could be appointed to any one of the existing
departmental classifications without sitting for a pass
examination. The pass examinations "are defective, and have
not accomplished any more than they did in England." A
"competitive system is now needed here, as I am convinced,
and as the English Government was convinced after a much
longer trial" of pass examinations.[27]

Senator Dawes asked Dorman Eaton to explain how the
system proposed in the Pendleton bill planned to handle
the large volume of candidates who might apply for competitive examinations. Eaton told Dawes that competitive
examinations should be given to candidates with "prima
facie qualifications." The British determined prima facie
qualifications by giving applicants a "preliminary examination to see who shall compete -- to weed out the hopeless
dunces." Eaton testified that he did not think the United
States needed preliminary examinations. He recommended
that rules be developed to specify age requirements,
certification of reading and writing ability, U.S. citizenship, health requirements and character references from "a
proper number of citizens." These qualifications had to be
met before allowing a candidate "to come in and compete."[28]

The speaker opposed Section 12 of the Dawes bill which
exempted all employees with a salary less than $900 from
examination. The "nature of the duties required, and not
the salary, should indicate whether there should be an examination or not." "The experience of Great Britain"
showed that examinations for "boys and women" who received
salaries lower than the general clerkships are appropriate.[29]

Dorman Eaton concluded his testimony with a discussion
of the "British experience." Based on "my experience in it
here and my study of it there would lead me to think . . .
that no other system would be practicable." He explained
the powers of the British Civil Service Commission. In addition to those recommended in the Pendleton bill, the British Commission had power to deny retirement to those who
had not passed a Commission examination. The examinations
selected such high quality candidates that business firms
often required their applicants to pass a civil service
examination.[30] "The standing attained before the commission

[27] Report, Senate Bill 133, p. 20.

[28] Ibid., pp. 26-27.

[29] Ibid., p. 30.

[30] Ibid., p. 34.

298

is of value to young men who wish to go elsewhere, even
if they fail to get in the British service." The British
civil service system had improved the general education
of its population. "The growth of the common school system has been greatly stimulated by these examinations."
Attendance in the common school system increased one hundred per cent since the introduction of competitive examinations. "The general effect has been to stimulate public
education, and such is the accepted view in Great Britain."
"Appointments to the civil service" no longer went exclusively
to the higher classes for the "result of the examinations
has been to fill the service with those educated in the public schools, and to bring in but a small number of those
educated in the colleges." Eaton declared the system "eminently" democratic and described the attempt of Lord Palmerston to exert influence on behalf of one of his followers
without success. The Disraeli administration suffered a
setback in Parliament over allegations that his government
violated the "spirit" of the civil service rules. The
Civil Service Commissioner explained that the English system
had no relation to the question of tenure in office. Neither the British system nor the Pendleton bill applied to
positions with a fixed tenure. Some have argued that the
competitive system was "very good for a permanent tenure,
but not for a short term." This was "entirely a mistaken
view of the subject," according to the witness. "Such
examinations are all the more indispensable and useful in
proportion as the term is short." Employees with a short
term had to be more effective at the beginning because they
would not have time for on-the-job training.

Dorman Eaton discussed the competitive system in British India. According to Lord Salisbury the system "not
only had secured superior officers for detail administration,
but that through promotions it had resulted in securing
ability of the highest order for the general management of
the administration."[31]

Edward O. Graves testified about his experience as a
member of the board of examiners for the Treasury Department
and chief examiner under the Grant Civil Service Commission.
He argued that the establishment of a commission was essential to civil service reform. Graves outlined briefly the
British reform developments and implied that these developments could not have evolved from pass examinations to

---

[31] Report, Senate Bill 133, pp. 36-38.

limited examinations and ultimately to open competitive examinations without the "central supervision" exercised by the British Civil Service Commission.[32]

George William Curtis, editor of the influential New York newspaper Harper's Weekly, former Chairman of the Grant Civil Service Commission, and President of the New York National Civil Service Reform League, contributed his views to the hearing on the Pendleton bill. He reviewed the history of the spoils system and outlined the evils of that system. Curtis explained the debate that took place at the outset of the Grant Commission deliberations over the best approach to civil service reform. Joseph Medill of Chicago wanted to restrict the power to remove employees while he wanted to control the entrance of employees into the government. "I proposed a resolution to the effect that it was desirable that appointments to the minor civil service should be made upon a competitive examination." To support competitive examinations Curtis used Thomas Jenckes' "correspondence with Sir Charles Trevelyan and Sir Stafford Northcote. . . whose inquiries elicited the first English blue-book" on the subject. The Northcote-Trevelyan report gave the Grant Commission "the views of the most eminent men in the British service and out of the service." In addition, the Grant Commission benefited from "very friendly communications" with the "civil service commission in England" whose Secretary "apprised us of everything that was doing on that side, for the benefit of our inquiries and discussions here."[33]

The spoils system, the witness observed, "while not to be defined as aristocratic, is absolutely oligarchic." "The English system, open to competition, is the most absolutely democratic." The "son of the Archbishop of Canterbury, the son of the Duke of Leeds, has no possible advantage over the son of a coal-heaver." Chancellor of the Exchequer Gladstone publicly declared that he had "no more voice in the appointment of clerks in the treasury than any of you who hear me." Member of Parliament Mundella of Liverpool agreed when he told a New York audience that he had no influence to employ "a friend of his" in any government job.

George Curtis went on to discuss the developments during the Hayes Administration, the Dawes bill, the Pendleton bill with its provision for a centralized commission, and the

---

[32]Report, Senate Bill 133, p. 130.

[33]Ibid., p. 155.

300

Reform League and concluded with a discussion of Presidential powers. "The whole thing presupposed a friendly President." If the President chose to disregard the provisions of the Pendleton bill, "he would take no action, and there would be no remedy except in public opinion."[34]

The Senate Committee on Civil Service and Retrenchment[35] reported favorably on the Pendleton bill May 15, 1882. Those hearings held prior to this report turned out to be the last Congressional attempt to evaluate the issues and principles of civil service reform.

Congressional Debate on the Pendleton Bill

President Chester A. Arthur withdrew his opposition to the various "plans which in the main were modeled upon the system which obtains in Great Britain" in his Second Annual Message to Congress of December 4, 1882. "In my judgment such action should no longer be postponed."[36] Many speakers referred to the British precedent during the long debate on the Pendleton bill which occupied most of the last half of December 1882.

Senator Joseph Hawley of Connecticut, chairman of the Senate's Committee on Civil Service and Retrenchment, defended the Pendleton bill (S. 133) and told his colleagues that it did not adopt the British system completely. He did not think it appropriate to illustrate reform with "the example of Great Britain, chiefly because many of the circumstances there are quite different." We have a different history and different form of government. "There are various provisions there for which our public sentiment is not ripe," such as life term and pensions.[37]

---

[34] Report, Senate Bill 133, p. 178.

[35] The Committee consisted of Senators Joseph R. Hawley of Connecticut (Chairman), James D. Walker of Arkansas, John S. Williams of Kentucky, Henry L. Dawes of Massachusetts, Edward H. Rollins of New Hampshire, John I. Mitchell of Pennsylvania, and Matthew C. Butler of South Carolina.

[36] Richardson, 8:145.

[37] U.S. Congressional Record, 47th Cong., 2nd Sess, p. 241.

Senator Joseph E. Brown of Georgia denounced the Pendleton bill with familiar arguments. "I have learned the British system spoken very highly of" but "the forms of the two governments are entirely different." "The system that may work well there in a limited monarchy . . . is not appropriate to a republican form of government like ours." Brown elaborated on the differences and charged that civil service reform "is one step in the direction of the establishment of an aristocracy in this country, the establishment of another privileged class." The civil service reform system "is contrary to the very genius and spirit of our Government."[38]

Senator Warner Miller, who succeeded Thomas C. Platt in New York, favored the Pendleton bill in a major speech. Miller outlined the role of the State of New York in promoting the spoils system before President Jackson introduced it nationwide. "I say New York must hold itself responsible for the introduction of the spoils system into the Federal Government; and New York today . . . stands by the measure which we are now considering, for it knows the evils which it is intended to remedy."[39] The Pendleton bill is the work of "patriotic gentlemen" who "not only studied the civil service of our own country but the civil service of the principal European nations." He denied the statement by Senator Brown of Georgia that it was impractical and would fill the offices with incompetent persons. Experience in "the two chief Federal offices, the customhouse and the post-office" proved that "the service has been vastly improved since competitive examinations went into operation. . . ." Not only has it been tried there," Miller continued, "but also in England." "The reports from there are alike favorable."[40] The Senator from New York charged that the Senator from Georgia (Joseph E. Brown) twisted the facts when he said that because civil service reform comes from England, it is undemocratic and aristocratic, and would create an office-holding class. We took universal suffrage, civil rights, trial by jury, habeas corpus, and common law rules from England. "The fact then, that the system is English should not be any bar to our adopting it." Actually, the existing English system did not exercise the appointing power for the benefit "of the aristocracy or of any privileged class, they are to-day free and

---

[38] *Congressional Record*, p. 277.

[39] Ibid., p. 282.

[40] Ibid., p. 283.

open to competition to every person within the realm."
This was not undemocratic but the spoils system was, and
we had "an aristocracy in office-holding." Senator Miller used the example of the last election in England, when
the Liberal party defeated the Conservative party, to prove
that political parties did not require patronage to finance
elections. Great "change in the policy of the Government of
Great Britain was made without changing more than fifty
offices in the entire civil service of Great Britain."[41]

Republican Senator John Sherman, former Secretary of
the Treasury, objected to comments attributed to E.O. Graves
that the Bureau of Engraving and Printing had "1,700 'sinecures' that are paid out of the Treasury of the United States
without any specific appropriation."[42] He questioned "what
is it that we want by a civil-service bill?" We want to
end the power to make appointments "by favoritism."

> I therefore will vote for any law which will
> enable any man, rich or poor, whatever may
> be his condition, wherever he may live, to
> go at the proper time before proper offices
> and be examined. In other words, the English
> rule, which has been adopted there only within
> a few years, has worked wonderfully well, so
> that any person there can go before the pro-
> per offices and be examined and he may be ap-
> pointed if he proves himself to be more
> meritorious than any one else. I am in favor
> of any law that will accomplish that.[43]

Sherman favored another law "to forbid members of the
legislative department of the Government from even applying
to the Departments for any position or any office."[44]

Debate ceased on December 27, 1882, when the Senate
passed the bill. George William Curtis wrote: "The passage of the Pendleton bill by the Senate is an important
event in our political history. . . . It is a measure

---

[41]Congressional Record, p. 283.

[42]Ibid., p. 362.

[43]Ibid., p. 363.

[44]Ibid., p. 364.

303

should it become law, will overthrow the aristocracy of patronage and spoils, and open the public service to all the people. . . ."[45] It passed the House on January 4, 1883, and received the approval of the President, January 16, 1883. The United States adopted the "English system" as civil service reform became the law.

---

[45]"Passage of the Pendleton Bill," Harper's Weekly (New York), 6 January 1883, p. 2.

CHAPTER XII

BRITISH LEGACY

1883 to 1886

The public debate over civil service reform continued throughout the remainder of the nineteenth century. Spoilsmen and reformers persisted in making the same arguments for and against civil service reform as they did in the years before January 16, 1883. The Pendleton Act applied to less than ten per cent of government employees at the time of its implementation and never to more than eight-three per cent. Both sides referred to the British influence less and less each year. Spoilsmen found the American public unresponsive to anti-British rhetoric, and reformers no longer needed the British example to demonstrate the practicality of civil service reform.

Attention turned to integrating the British civil service reform system into American political and administrative traditions. Politicians and scholars stressed the differences between the American and British systems rather than the similarities. They spoke in proud tones about those features of the civil service system which Americans rejected, leaving the public with the impression that the United States greatly altered the British principles. When Dorman B. Eaton retired from the Commission in 1886, the most important link between the British and American systems terminated. No other important policy maker with knowledge about administrative events in Great Britain took his place until Professor Leonard D. White accepted the chairmanship of the Civil Service Commission in 1933.

Examinations

One of the most important deviations from the British system was the development of "practical" examinations. Americans objected strongly to the British dependence on "literary" examinations because they feared it would lead to a public service completely dominated by college-trained employees. This did not prevent Americans from borrowing ideas from the British on the mechanics of using examinations.[1]

---

[1]Moreover many of the examinations contained elements which carried an implicit educational requirement; that is to say, it was extremely unlikely that one could do well enough in the examination to be within reach of certification for appointment

305

Silas W. Burt adopted the British system of assigning numbers to examination candidates to insure objectivity in
administering examinations and grading papers. Burt applied the system at the New York Customhouse and recommended
it for the Commission to eliminate the possibility of "legal
prosecutions against examiners" from dissatisfied candidates.[2]
The Commission incorporated the technique in its regulations.

Burt turned to the English example again in developing
a weighted system for grading examinations under the New
York Civil Service Commission. In the capacity of Chief
Examiner of the New York Civil Service Commission, he
studied the British technique and developed an improved
method of grading examinations. He recommended his method
to the Chief Examiner of the national Civil Service Commission.[3]

Some reformers suggested that competitive examinations,
the major component of the British Civil Service system, had
potential application beyond the public service. The New
York Times published an article which suggested applying the
examination system to private industry. Examinations, according to the article, "had been found so beneficial in the
public service of Great Britain that they had been copied by
great firms and corporations." The superior skills of those
individuals who passed the civil service examinations en-
hanced the candidate's chances of securing a position in private industry. In time, private employers required their
applicants to sit for civil service examinations. The practice became so common that the English Commission had to
deny examinations "to those who will not declare they do not
seek them [exams] for the purpose of securing private employment!"[4] Eaton incorporated a similar statement into the

---

unless he had completed study at a high-level educational
institution.

[2]U.S. Civil Service Commission, First Annual Report of the
United States Civil Service Commission, p. 53; Nation (New
York), 26 April 1883, p. 35; Nation, 3 May 1883, p. 382.

[3]Silas W. Burt, "A Brief History of the Civil Service Reform
Movement in the United States," Burt Papers, New York Public
Library.

[4]Reprint of New York Times article in the Civil Service
Record, April 1885, Schurz Papers.

<u>Third Annual Report</u>. He noted that English banks, rail-
roads, "and great business houses have resorted to examinations in the selection of their clerks." Some American
businesses planned to adopt the examination method also.[5]

Promotions

President Arthur's Civil Service Commission considered
the subject of promotions in mid-year 1883. It reviewed
the English method and found that most promotions came on
the basis of seniority. The British Civil Service Commission
offered the departments a "merit" alternative by conducting
competitive examinations for those departments which requested it. Relatively few departments accepted the "merit"
alternative available to them. Section 7 of the Pendleton
Act provided for promotion examinations as did Rule VI,
but the Commissioners decided to postpone implementation of
these provisions because of the complexity of the subject.[6]

<u>Harper's Weekly</u> outlined England's problems with the
seniority method and supported the English Commission's
attempt to persuade authorities in the government service
to employ their "merit" alternative. The seniority system,
according to the New York newspaper, unquestionably resulted in promoting "incompetent men." The editor suggested
"three ways to meet promotions: selection at pleasure,
equal competition among employees, and equal competition with
insiders and outside applicants."[7]

The Federal Civil Service Commission may have avoided
the promotion issue, but the New York Civil Service Commission did not. In January 1884 the New York Commission published rules on promotion. The difficulty with promotion
regulations lay

> in the fact that if you leave promotion wholly
> to the discretion of heads of departments or of
> bureaus, you open the door to favoritism and the
> use of political influence. If, on the other hand,

---

[5]U.S. Civil Service Commission, <u>Third Annual Report of the
United States Civil Service Commission</u>, January 16, 1885, to
January 16, 1886, p. 33.

[6]Great Britain, Civil Service Commission, <u>30th Report of Her
Majesty's Civil Service Commissioners</u>, 1886, p. xx.

[7]"Promotion in the Civil Service," <u>Harper's Weekly</u>, 11 August
1883, p. 498; "Promotion in the Civil Service," <u>Harper's
Weekly</u>, 15 September 1883, p. 578.

you make it depend on competitive examination, you diminish the responsibility of
the chief, and enable him to excuse short-
comings in his office by saying that he
could do no better with the employees which
the new system had put into high places.[8]

Rule 31 established provisions for competitive examinations,
and Rule 33 discouraged candidates from securing recommendations from influential people.

The promotion issue did not surface again until the
end of 1886 when the Federal Civil Service Commission decided to promulgate promotion rules and regulations. Silas
W. Burt tried to influence the deliberations by publishing
proposals in the New York Evening Post on how to use exams
for promotions. The Commissioners adopted rules, but difficulties in administering the rules caused the government
to suspend them.[9]

Aristocratic Classes

The charge that the British civil service system would
create a superior aristocratic class continued to plague
reformers in the early years of the Pendleton Act. Spoilsmen, particularly in Congress, stressed the aristocratic
argument. Representative Randall of Maryland, for example,
introduced a rider to an appropriation bill nullifying the
competitive system. Congressman Cox of North Carolina,
Chairman of the Committee on Civil-Service Reform, argued
against Randall's charges that the civil service system
would create an aristocracy. "Talk about it being aristocratic to appoint men on account of merit instead of political influence! Why, sir, it is the very genius and essence of democracy. It brings the offices within the reach
of the people. . . ."[10]

---

[8] Nation (New York), 3 January 1884, p. 3.

[9] "Promotion in the Civil Service," Harper's Weekly (New
York), 25 December 1886.

[10] Nation (New York), 17 June 1886, p. 497.

All of the major reformers felt compelled to respond
to this criticism. George William Curtis told the Civil
Service Reform League:

The objection which is expressed in the cry of
"life tenure" and "a privileged class" is one
of the most ancient and familiar appeals of the
spoils system to ignorance and prejudice . . .
we are told that a life tenure and a privileged
class are odious and un-American, as if anything
were so odious as a system tending to destroy
the self-respect of public offices, or anything
so really un-American as turning out an honest,
efficient, and experienced agent because somebody else wants his place.[11]

"So long as the power of removal remains free," Curtis told
the League in 1885, "and while it is committed to agents appointed by officers whom the people elect, a life tenure in
any un-American or undesirable sense is impossible."[12]

Dorman B. Eaton addressed the question in every one of
the three Civil Service Commission reports he wrote. He told
readers of the first report that it was far more difficult to
introduce civil service reform in Great Britain than in the
United States "for the reason that such examinations are re-
pugnant to the exclusive spirit and class distinctions of an
aristocracy." "That change," Eaton wrote, "was essentially
republican in spirit which compelled the sons of lords,
bishops, and the great landowners to compete side by side
with the sons of the humblest classes for admission to the
administrative service of their country."[13] Eaton expanded
the discussion in the second report and repeated it verbatim
in the third. He wrote that the reform movement "was largely
a contest between those -- who stood for the old aristocratic
patronage - monopoly of appointments . . . and those . . .
who stood for the just claims of character and capacity in

---

[11]Civil Service Reform League, Proceedings, 1884, pp. 11-12,
National Civil Service Reform League Collection, U.S. Civil
Service Commission Library.

[12]Civil Service Reform League, Proceedings, 1885, p. 22,
National Civil Service Reform League Collection, U.S. Civil
Service Commission Library.

[13]U.S. Civil Service Commission, First Annual Report, p. 14.

humbler life." The aristocracy opposed civil service reform because it "would weaken their means of influencing
the Government . . . [and] would give great opportunities
and influence to the sons and daughters of the common people." Commissioner Eaton concluded his remarks: "These
examinations are, therefore, thoroughly democratic and republican in spirit, and nothing so forcibly illustrates
the prejudice and lack of information concerning them in
this country as the fact that the opposite view should
have been accepted by candid or intelligent persons."[14]

Carl Schurz, who found the aristocracy argument absurd and seldom commented on it, devoted a large portion
of his address before the Boston Civil Service Association
in December 1885 to the subject. "The spoils politicians
are fond of pretending that civil service reform is nothing
but an aristocratic notion imported from England. If it is
an English notion at all, it is a notion grown with the
growth of democracy in England." Schurz outlined the spoils
system in England before civil service reform and declared
that "the spoils system lost its foothold as the ascendancy
of the aristocracy declined." Carl Schurz told his audience that civil service reform grew "as the government became more democratic in composition and spirit." "Strange
democrats are those in this republic who, in the name of
democracy, rail at civil service reform as an English notion, the product of democratic England, while they cling
to the patronage and spoils system, one of the worst abuses with
which aristocratic England ever was identified."[15]

Government Stability

George Curtis frequently used government changes in
England to dramatize the ludicrous scramble for jobs which
accompanied a change in administration in the United States.
He liked to quote Gladstone who observed: "We limit to a
few scores of persons the removals and appointments on these
occasions, although our Ministries seem to us not unfrequently
to be more sharply served from one another in principle and
tendency than are the successive Presidents of the United
States." "There is no more reason," Curtis wrote, "for

---

[14]U.S. Civil Service Commission, Second Annual Report of the
United States Civil Service Commission, January 1885, pp. 48-9,
U.S. Civil Service Commission, Third Annual Report of the
United States Civil Service Commission, January 1886, pp. 30-31.

[15]Article in Boston Daily Advertiser, 12 December 1885, on the
Anniversary of the Boston Civil Service Reform Association,
Schurz Papers.

changing a good postmaster or a good collector, . . . because of a party change in the national administration,
than for changing a surrogate or a bell-ringer."[16]

In July 1885 Curtis turned again to England. He pointed
out the benefits of the English system when administrations
change. "The English service experiences no great upheaval
allowing it to give the people continuous high quality service."[17] Six months later he returned to the subject.
He used the British elections to refute arguments by "political wise-acres. . . that without patronage practical
politics must languish, all interest in elections will die
out, political principles and policies will arouse nobody,
and nobody will take the trouble to accept a nomination or
to vote." "The recent elections in England," Curtis stated,
"have been quite as exciting as any elections in the United
States." Yet, "members of Parliament have no patronage,
not even a post-office. . . ."[18]

Ridley Commission

Late in 1886 the recently appointed Conservative Administration of Lord Salisbury established the Ridley Commission
to inquire into the operation of the British government service. The purpose of the commission, according to Lord Ran-
dolph Churchill, was to investigate the cost and details of
organization in the civil service. James G. Blaine, smart-
ing over the defection of the Independent Republicans in 1884
which cost him the election, delivered a speech at Huntington,
Pennsylvania, using the inquiry into the British system to
attack civil service reform. In his speech and subsequent
letter to the editor of the Kennebee Journal he said:
". . . the English Civil Service, which was held up as a
model for our own Government by those who left the Republican party two years ago, is now under investigation and
apparent condemnation by the English themselves." Blaine
agreed with George W. Smailey that the civil service in
England "is worse in all the departments of the Government

---

[16]"Appointments and Removals," Harper's Weekly, 21 March 1885,
p. 178.

[17]"A Lessson for the Day," Harper's Weekly, 4 July 1885.

[18]"Victory Without Spoils," Harper's Weekly, 19 December
1885, p. 835.

than it was forty years ago." The Republican Party leader
went on: "My argument implied and was intended to imply
that . . . the English system with the life-tenure and its
large pension list and all the attendant evils . . . have
at last demanded investigation by a ministerial commission."
He attacked the Cleveland Administration for advocating
civil service rules that "conformed to British policies
just at the very time when the British themselves were
finding a fatal weakness in these policies." "I meant to
convey my belief that the very worst leaders and guides
for a continental republic are those who persist in seeing
the perfection of human government in an insular monarchy,
whose foundations are in all respects radically different
from conditions in our own broad land." Independents,
Blaine concluded, "should learn that American inspiration
ends where imitation of England begins."[19]

E.L. Godkin, editor of the Nation, responded to Blaine's
comments with typical sarcasm. ". . . the attention of the
whole country has been called to the fact that not only Mr.
Blaine did sneer at civil service reform, but that in order
to find a reason for the sneer, he totally misrepresented
the condition of the English civil service."[20]

George William Curtis editorialized in Harper's Weekly
two days later. "But his assertion that the Independent
Republicans . . . have held up the English civil service as
a model for our own is entirely unfounded in fact." "What
civil service reformers in this country have done is to
show that the principle of open competition, so far as it
has been introduced in the English service, has abolished
the abuses of personal favoritism in appointment."[21]

Recently retired Civil Service Commissioner Dorman B.
Eaton supplied the most comprehensive refutation of Blaine's
attack. Eaton agreed to write an article on "Civil-Service
Reform in Great Britain" for the Civil-Service Reformer.
Blaine's attack came in time for him "to undeceive those
fair-minded people who may have been misled by the ignorant
and erroneous statements of Mr. Blaine. . . ." The editor

---

[19]"Mr. Blaine and the Civil Service," New York Tribune, 17
September 1886, p. 1.

[20]Nation (New York), 25 November 1886, p. 425.

[21]"Mr. Blaine's Letter," Harper's Weekly (New York), 27
November 1886, p. 759.

of the Civil-Service Reformer declared: "Mr. Eaton shows
conclusively that the willing witnesses who hasten to the
front with their damaging testimony against Civil-Service
Reform, have got all their facts wrong and are themselves
discredited."

Eaton began with the history of administrative committees in Great Britain. "For more than sixty years there
has been a practice, on the part of the British Government,
of appointing from time to time, a committee of able ad-
herents of both parties, always, however, embracing persons
experienced in administration, whose duty it has been to
make investigations and report in regard to the economy,
efficiency, proper organization, and business methods of
the executive departments and offices." The author addressed
himself to two arguments raised by Blaine. The others he
dismissed as "misconceptions" or "willful misrepresentations."
One: "Our Civil-Service laws and rules are a substantial re-
production of the whole British system so that if any part
of that system shall be condemned in Great Britain, our new
system will be at the same time condemned." This shows a
"misconception of the facts" since the American system
adopted "non-partisan appointments on the basis of merits
as declared by examinations" but rejected three other essential parts of the British system, restricted removals,
promotions by seniority, and retirement pensions. Even the
examinations are not carbon copies of the British equivalent.
They are "made to respond to our educational system, to the
theory of our institutions, and to the spirit of our people."

Two: "that the examinations in Great Britain are so
recent and have been so limited, that it is only now that
their practical effects are being understood." Eaton dismissed the charge as "gross and stupid" because the British
introduced examinations some "sixty-six years ago." "From
that time to this, they have been steadily extended." This
is "time enough, one would think, to test the practical results of the system." Eaton reviewed the developments of
the 1853 commission, 1860 commission, and introduction of
competitive examinations in 1870. "This was a great triumph in Great Britain of the common people over the aristocracy. It was also a great victory of justice and liberty
over partisanship and favoritism." The climax of Eaton's
article resulted from his quoting Mr. Mann, Secretary of
the British Civil-Service Commission, who wrote:

> . . . there is no question as to the expediency
> of competition; that is taken for granted.
> The purpose, obviously, is to see if any new
> improvements, tending towards economy, can be
> effected in the organization of the force

313

selected by competition, etc. * * * There
is not the remotest idea of disturbing in
any way, the arrangements by which all persons to be appointed to the public service
are, before admission, subjected to examination.[22]

Similarities in the British
and American Systems

Most American officials in 1886 and subsequent historical scholars devoted considerable time emphasizing the
differences between the American civil service reform system and the British system. Analysis of the American Civil
Service Commission Annual Reports with the British Civil
Service Commission Annual Reports demonstrates the enormous
amount of similarity between the two systems. Differences
certainly existed, but most of them represented minor variations on a common theme. Major differences sometimes occurred in such areas as retirement, entrance age, literary
examinations versus practical examinations, and life tenure, but in time the American system incorporated the British methods into its organization.

An important concept embodied in the British and American system was the creation of a centralized Civil Service
Commission to provide a uniform control over the appointment system. Each commission included three commissioners
supported by a staff with similar duties. The British Commission used two permanent examiners, a secretary, and
several assistant examiners, while the American Commission
employed a chief examiner, secretary, and a series of examiners supplied by the agencies. Both found it necessary
to designate a chairman or first commissioner. The commissioners held office at the pleasure of the executive
branch of government while the legislature established their
salary. The duties of the commissioners were similar. Both
made and enforced rules and regulations pertaining to examinations. They kept minutes of their proceedings and issued
an annual report. Both countries established examination
facilities in various locations outlying from the seat of
government. They created rules to permit the commission to
control the activities of these examination boards and kept

---

[22]Dorman B. Eaton, "Civil-Service Reform in Great Britain,"
The Civil-Service Reformer (December 1886), pp. 100-109.

records of personnel actions taken by agency officials.
Both Civil Service Commissions used the services of an-
other government agency for their physical needs: the
Department of Interior supplied housing in the United
States, and the Treasury Department housed the British
Commission.

Coverage of the civil service system varied among the
two countries, but they employed similar techniques to expand that coverage. Policy making positions came outside
the purview of the classified system in both governments.
The difficulty came about in trying to draw the line between career positions and policy positions. The British
prepared a statutory list of exemptions on specific sched-
ules while the Americans established rules with similar
lists. At first both systems excluded employees on the
lowest level of employment. The American statutes excluded
laborers while British orders excluded temporary clerks
and boy writers. Both Commissions eventually extended control over these employees. The British created a new
classification they called the "Lower Division of the Civil
Service" in 1876 which allowed them to incorporate temporary
and boy employees into the classified system. Military
soldiers and sailors came outside the scope of the civil
service system. The American system began with ten per cent
of the government work force and adopted a British scheme
for expanding its coverage. The British used several methods of expanding the coverage of the civil service system,
but one was to "blanket-in" various segments of the work
force with an executive "order-in-council." The Americans
adopted the same method on a more extensive basis by expanding the coverage with "blanket-in" executive orders.
Both countries developed independent Foreign Service merit
systems.

Conducting examinations constituted the primary function
of the Civil Service Commissions in both England and the
United States. America benefited from the British experiment
with limited examinations and adopted open competitive examinations, which took England fifteen years to develop.
Each country incorporated provisions for non-competitive,
special, and supplementary examinations and waivers for
uniquely skilled employees. England and America offered
agencies an opportunity to use promotion examinations, but
they never acquired the success of entrance examinations.
The English Commission offered its examination facilities
to excepted agencies such as the police; the Americans did
the same at a later date. Reformers in the United States
stressed practical examinations, while British officials
placed their faith in literary examinations. Actually the

315

difference was one of degree for the results were not as
different as the names suggest. American examinations
contained questions on penmanship, arithmetic, accounting,
English, geography, history, and government. The English
examinations incorporated the same subjects in its "literary" examinations and used "practical" examinations for
the Lower Division employees. The two countries employed
written examination techniques, publishing a list of subjects,and testing procedures. They established similar
requirements for applications and gave public notice of
all open-competitive examinations. Failures in both
countries found it necessary to wait for several months
before reapplying.

Examinations were not the only requirement candidates
for government jobs had to meet. Eaton incorporated into
the Pendleton Act and Civil Service Commission rules similar collateral restrictions on prospective candidates that
the British employed. Both designated age and health requirements. They restricted the employment of handicapped
persons and established procedures to examine those who
appealed with Commission-approved doctors. The British
granted veterans preferential treatment in applying its age
regulations. This established a precedent for the Americans to incorporate a more extensive veterans' preference
clause in the Pendleton Act. The Americans followed the
English policy of denying employment to any persons "habitually using intoxicating beverages to excess." The two
Civil Service Commissions forbade acquiring information
on the political affiliation of candidates or using that
information if the political affiliation were known. The
British allowed women to take a separate examination if
the agencies requested, while the Americans allowed the
agencies to request certification by sex. One of the most
important techniques employed by both countries to augment
the examinations process was to designate a period of probation to allow the agency to observe the working habits
of new employees. The Americans adopted this provision
directly from the British.[23]

Candidates who passed the examinations and collateral
employment requirements received a certificate of qualification from the respective Civil Service Commission in each
country. The British and American systems explicitly forbade
recommendations from the Legislature and established penalties for acting on political influence. The British filled

---

[23]In theory this probationary period was the final "practical" part of the entrance examination.

vacancies from the top of the register of those passing
the examination, but the Americans adopted a Rule of Four
(later changed to Three) because of Constitutional restrictions. The Rule of Four allowed the Commission to
certify the top four candidates to the selecting officer
and permit him to choose one. The American Congress insisted on incorporating an apportionment provision in the
Pendleton Act to insure an equitable distribution of jobs
among the states, while the British kept close watch on
the distribution of jobs between England, Ireland, and
Scotland to insure that each country received its fair
proportion of positions. The two Commissions established
registers of the names of successful candidates in order
of their examination grades from which they certified
candidates to the agencies to fill vacancies.

The Civil Service Commissions on both sides of the
Atlantic established a number of restrictions and methods
of enforcing them. Americans followed the British example
in providing regulations for complaints and appeals, prohibitions against false statements, and examination cheating. Both created rules to regulate the transfer of employees from the exempt service to the classified service.
Both authorized removal of employees for violating civil
service rules. The Americans found it necessary to specify a series of prohibitions against political contributions and political assessments. The British funded
the examination system with a fee system, but the U.S.
Congress rejected a similar arrangement contained in the
original Jenckes bills. Spoilsmen successfully thwarted
the Grant Commission by withholding its financing and
did not want to lose another opportunity to deliver a
similar blow to the Pendleton Act commission.

The Civil Service Commission in the United States
followed the British Commission by imposing reporting requirements on participating agencies. It found it necessary to classify jobs and consider rudimentary moves to
preparing job descriptions. Employees who lost their jobs
through no fault of their own (reduction-in-force) received
the right of reemployment without examination.[24]

---

[24]U.S. Civil Service Commission, First Annual Report, pp. 45-56;
Second Annual Report, pp. 62-77; Third Annual Report, pp. 79-97;
Great Britain, Civil Service Commission, Sixteenth Report of Her
Majesty's Civil Service Commissioners, 1871, pp. 11-25; Seven-
teenth Report, 1872, pp. iii, 1-11; Eighteenth Report, 1873,
p. 48; Twentieth Report, 1875, pp. iii-xi; Twenty-sixth Report,
1881, pp. iii-xv; Twenty-seventh Report, 1882, pp. 21-31;
Thirtieth Report, 1885, pp. xvi-xxi.

The British Civil Service Commission recognized its assistance to the United States Civil Service Commission. In its Thirtieth Report the British Commissioners reported: "On several occasions we have had the honour of being consulted on behalf of the Government of the United States of America on this question, and we have had the pleasure in putting such experience as we have acquired in giving effect to Your Majesty's Orders at the disposal of those who have in view the establishment of similar rules of admission to the public service in that great country."[25]

Anglo-American Movement

The civil service reform movement in the United States should not be viewed exclusively as a phenomenon of America's political history, but should be seen in the context of Anglo-American developments. The British influence on the American administrative system was both general and specific. Charles Sumner modeled his 1864 bill after the British administrative system. Thomas A. Jenckes went much farther in studying several foreign systems and specifically adopting the British system for his bills. The culmination of Jenckes' campaign resulted in the passage of the 1871 Congressional law directing the President to establish rules and regulations for the admission of employees to the civil service. President Grant tried to carry out the mandate, but Congress forced him to suspend the attempt four years after it began.

The work of the Grant Commission, which established rules and regulations closely resembling the British system, continued far beyond its short existence. Nearly all the rules and regulations promulgated by the Grant Civil Service Commission were incorporated in the Pendleton Act of 1883 or in the rules and regulations of the present Civil Service Commission. Most of the concepts, structure, rules, regulations, and terminology still in use today followed closely the system used in Great Britain. Concepts such as (1) recruitment on the basis of ability, (2) administration belonging to the people and not the party, and (3) merit determined by competitive examinations, still sustain the public service. The structure included (a) a Commission, (b) a chief examiner (now called the Executive Director), (c) local examining boards, (d) civil service district system, (e) periods of probation, and (f) a classification of posi-

---

[25]Great Britain, Civil Service Commission, Thirtieth Report, p. xxi.

318

tions, all followed the English example. Rules and regulations requiring (1) qualifications such as citizenship,
character, and health, (2) restrictions on political activity, (3) promotional examinations, (4) temporary appointments, and most important (5) the principle of competitive
examination were adopted directly from the British administration. Terms and concepts taken from England still retain their use and original meaning. These include: merit,
rules, test, grade, eligible, register, position, classification, certificate, and hundreds more.

The long hard struggle, between progressive reformers
and professional politicians with vested interest in the
spoils system, finally culminated in the creation of a
Civil Service Commission modeled after the British example.
The system created by the Pendleton Act of 1883 incorporated
most of the elements found in the British administrative
system.

The close parallel between the British civil service
system and the system advocated by the American reform movement proved both an asset and liability to its proponents.
Both reform and spoils advocates recognized the British influence on the reform proposals. Reformers frequently
cited the British example as evidence that the system proposed would accomplish the objectives claimed of it. Spoilsmen attacked the proposals with appeals to anti-British sentiments. They charged that the reform was un-American and
un-Democratic. It would undermine the Republican form of
government and act as the first step in the establishment
of a monarchy in this country. Reformers denied these charges, arguing that the system proposed was actually more
democratic than the spoils system, since it allowed all citizens to compete for jobs in the Federal government without
regard to their political influence. It was not un-American
to borrow from Britain as the American political system contained many features taken from Great Britain and other
foreign governments. They dismissed as preposterous the
charge that civil service reform would create a bureaucratic
class. The two sides persisted in making such charges and
counter charges throughout the last quarter of the nineteenth century.

The civil service reform system, established permanently
by the Pendleton Act, is substantially the same today as it
was in 1883. It retains most of the structure and substance
of the British system from which it was modeled.

The Decline of British Influence

The influence of the British on the American civil service system did not evaporate in 1886 when Dorman B. Eaton
retired from the Commission. It did decline significantly
as his successors came to their jobs with very little knowledge of the British system. Reports of the Civil Service
Commission regularly contained a segment on "The Civil Service in Foreign Countries" with emphasis on the British system. The Commission examined the administration of British
and Dutch colonial possessions at the end of the nineteenth
century for information on the administration of American
territories. Dorman B. Eaton contributed a paper on the subject just before he died.[26] The government looked to the
British again when considering a retirement law, which did
not pass until 1920. Americans looked at England for wartime
precedents, and another expert on British civil service administration, Leonard D. White, Chairman of the Civil Service Commission under President Franklin D. Roosevelt, used
his knowledge of British examination practices to introduce
the beginnings of the Federal Service Entrance Examination,
a literary examination designed to test college graduates
for government employment. In recent years the influence
was reversed. Another of the British committees, formed to
review the government establishment, delivered a report to
Parliament in 1968. That Committee, led by Lord Fulton,
came to the United States and studied the American personnel
management system.[27]

---

[26]U.S. Civil Service Commission, Fifteenth Report of the United States Civil Service Commission, 1899, pp. 521-551; Dorman B. Eaton, The Need and Best Means of Providing a Competent
and Stable Civil Service for our New Dependencies, 1898, National Civil-Service Reform League Collection, U.S. Civil Service Commission Library.

[27]Great Britain, Lord Fulton Committee, The Civil Service:
Report of the Committee, 1966-68, 1968, 1:104-106; U.S.
Civil Service Commission, Tenth Report of the United States
Civil Service Commission, 1894, pp. 22-23; U.S. Civil Ser-
vice Commission, Eleventh Report of the United States Civil
Service Commission, 1895, pp. 326-395; National Civil-Ser-
vice Reform League, Superannuation in the Civil Service, 1901,
National Civil-Service Reform League Collection, U.S. Civil
Service Commission Library.

SELECTED BIBLIOGRAPHY

PRIMARY SOURCES

Public Documents

Great Britain

Chancellor of the Exchequer, The Civil Service, June
    1868, "Report of the Committee" 1966-1968, vol. 1,
    Cmnd. 3638.

Civil Service Commission, Reports of the Civil Service
    Commissioners, 1855 through 1886.

Parliament, Parliamentary Papers (Commons), 1847-48,
    vol. 18, "Minutes of Evidence of the Select Com-
    mittee on Miscellaneous Expenditures."

Parliament, Parliamentary Papers (Commons), 1854-55,
    vol. 20, "Papers Relating to the Re-Organization
    of the Civil Service."

Parliament, Parliamentary Papers (Commons), 1854, vol.
    27, "Report on the Organization of the Permanent
    Civil Service."

Parliament, Parliamentary Papers (Commons), 1875, vol.
    33, Cmnd. 113, "First Report of the Civil Service
    Inquiry Commission."

Parliament, Parliamentary Papers (Commons), 1875, vol.
    33, "Second Report of the Civil Service Inquiry
    Commission."

Parliament, Parliamentary Papers (Commons), 1860, "Se-
    lect Committee on Civil Service Appointments, Re-
    port . . . together with the Proceedings of the
    Committee: Minutes of Evidence: Appendix and Index."

Parliament, Parliamentary Papers (Commons), 1888, vol.
    72, Cmnd. 5545, "Second Report; Royal Commission
    Appointed to Inquire into Civil Establishments."

United States

Eaton, Dorman B., *Civil Service Reform in the New York City Post-Office and Custom-House*, 46th Cong., 3rd Sess., 1882, *House Executive Documents* No. 94.

Civil Service Commission (Grant), *The Civil Service of the United States: The Theory, Methods, and Results of the Reform Introduced by the President Pursuant to the Act of March 3, 1871, Stated by the Civil Service Commission in a Report to the President, 15 April 1874.*

Civil Service Commission, *Legislative History of the Civil Service Act: Pendleton Act; 47th Cong., 3rd Sess., January 16, 1883.*

Civil Service Commission (Grant), *Minutes of the Civil Service Commission, 1871-1875.*

Civil Service Commission (Grant), *Report of the Civil Service Commission, June 4, 1873.*

Civil Service Commission, *Reports of the United States Civil Service Commission, 1884 to 1899.*

Congress, *Commission to Examine Certain Custom-houses of the United States*, 45th Cong., 1st Sess., 1878, *House Executive Documents*, vol. 1, No. 8.

Congress, *Congressional Globe*, 1852 to 1876.

Congress, *Congressional Record*, 1876 to 1886.

Congress, House, *A Bill to Regulate the Civil Service of the United States*, H.R. 60, 39th Cong., 1st Sess., 1865.

Congress, House, *A Bill to Regulate the Civil Service of the United States, and Promote the Efficiency Thereof*, H.R. 673, 39th Cong., 1st Sess., 1866.

Congress, House, *A Bill to Regulate the Civil Service of the United States, and Promote the Efficiency Thereof*, H.R. 889, 39th Cong., 2nd Sess., 1866.

Congress, House, *A Bill to Regulate the Civil Service of the United States, and Promote the Efficiency Thereof*, H.R. 113, 40th Cong., 1st Sess., 1867.

Congress, House, A Bill to Regulate the Civil Service of the United States, and Promote the Efficiency Thereof, H.R. 948, 40th Cong., 2nd Sess., 1868.

Congress, House, A Bill to Regulate the Manner of Making Appointments in the Civil Service of the United States, H.R. 2633, 31st Cong., 3rd Sess., 1871.

Congress, House, House Document 13, 25th Cong., 3rd Sess., 1838.

Congress, House, House Report 313, 25th Cong., 3rd Sess., 1839.

Congress, House, House Reports, 27th Cong., 2nd Sess., 1842, vol. 4, No. 741.

Congress, Joint Select Committee on Retrenchment, Civil Service of the United States, 39th Cong., 2nd Sess., 1867. House Reports, vol. 1, No. 8.

Congress, Joint Select Committee on Retrenchment, Civil Service of the United States, 40th Cong., 2nd Sess., 1868. House Reports, vol. 2, No. 47.

Congress, Senate, Committee on Civil Service and Retrenchment, Report, Senate Bill 133 to Regulate and Improve the Civil Service of the United States, 47th Cong., 1st Sess., 1882.

Congress, Senate, Message of the President of the United States Transmitting the Report of the Commission Appointed to Devise Rules and Regulations for the Purpose of Reforming the Civil Service, 42nd Cong., 2nd Sess., 1871.

Congress, Senate, The Regulations and Improvement of the Civil Service, 46th Cong., 3rd Sess., 1881. Senate Report No. 872.

Congress, Senate, Select Committee to Examine the Several Branches of the Civil Service, Report No. 289, 44th Cong., 1st Sess., 1876.

Congress, Senate, Select Committee to Examine the Several Branches of the Civil Service, The Regulation and Improvement of the Civil Service, 46th Cong., 3rd Sess., 1881. Report No. 872.

Congress, Senate, Senate Documents, No. 88, 19th Cong.,
    1st Sess., 1826.

Congress, Senate, Senate Executive Document, No. 69, 32nd
    Cong., 1st Sess., 1852.

Congress, Senate, Senate Executive Document, No. 219, 49th
    Cong., 1st Sess., 1883.

Congress, Senate, Senate Journal, 31st Cong., 2nd Sess.,
    1851.

Department of Interior, 1870 Report of the Secretary of
    Interior, 1871.

Department of Interior, Patent Office, Special Order, 10
    April 1877.

Revenue Commission, Revenue System of the United States,
    30th Cong., 1st Sess., 1850. House Executive
    Documents, vol. 7, No. 34.

Private Papers

Chester Alan Arthur Papers, Library of Congress.

The Ismar Baruch Collection of Civil Service Papers,
    Civil Service Commission Library.

Charles J. Bonaparte Papers, Library of Congress.

John Bright Papers, British Museum.

Silas W. Burt Papers, New York Public Library.

Grover Cleveland Papers, Library of Congress.

George William Curtis Papers, Harvard University.

George W. Curtis Papers, New York Public Library.

Dorman Bridgman Eaton Papers, Vermont Historical Society.

E.B. Elliot Papers, Civil Service Commission Library.

James A. Garfield Papers, Library of Congress.

William E. Gladstone Papers, British Museum.

Edwin L. Godkin Papers, Harvard University.

Ulysses S. Grant Papers, Library of Congress.

Rutherford B. Hayes Papers, Library of Congress.

Thomas A. Jenckes Papers, Library of Congress.

Thomas A. Jenckes Papers, Civil Service Commission Library.

William L. Marcy Papers, Library of Congress.

National Civil Service League Collection, Civil Service
    Commission Library.

Charles Norton Papers, Harvard University.

Carl Schurz Papers, Library of Congress.

Goldwin Smith Papers, University of Toronto Library.

Charles Sumner Papers, Harvard University.

Lyman Trumbull Papers, Library of Congress.

Newspapers

Boston Daily Advertiser, 1 January 1885-31 December 1886.

The Civil Service Record (Boston), 1 January 1885-30
    June 1892.

The Civil Service Reformer (Baltimore), 8 January 1885-
    30 June 1892.

Evening Post (New York), 1 January 1865-31 December 1886.

Evening Star (Washington, D.C.), 1 January 1865-31 Decem-
    ber 1886.

Good Government (New York), 1 July 1892-31 December 1919.

Illustrated (New York), 1 January 1881-31 December 1881.

Milwaukee Sentinel, 1 January 1900-31 December 1900.

Nation (New York), 1 January 1866-31 December 1886.

325

The National Republican (Washington, D.C.), 1 January
    1881-31 December 1881.

New York Times, 1 January 1866-31 December 1886.

New York Tribune, 1 January 1868-31 December 1886.

New York World, 1 January 1867-31 December 1867.

The Times (London), 1 January 1854-31 December 1854.

                          Books

Abbott, Evelyn, and Campbell, Lewis, ed., The Life and
    Letters of Benjamin Jowett, 3 vols. (London: J.
    Murray, 1897).

Adams, John, The Works of John Adams, Second President
    of the United States: With a Life of the Author
    by Charles Francis Adams, edited by Charles Francis
    Adams, 4 vols. (Philadelphia: J.B. Lippincott &
    Co., 1850 to 1856).

Adams, John Quincy, The Memoirs of John Quincy Adams,
    Comprising Portions of His Diary from 1795 to
    1848, edited by Charles Francis Adams, 6 vols.
    (Philadelphia: J.B. Lippincott & Co., 1874-1877).

Adams, Henry, The Education of Henry Adams: An Auto-
    biography (New York: Houghton, 1931).

Armstrong, William H., ed., The Gilded Age Letters of
    E.L. Godkin (Albany, N.Y.: State University of
    New York Press, 1974).

Austin, James Trecothick, Life of Elbridge Gerry with
    Contemporary Letters, 2 vols. (Boston: Wells and
    Lilly, 1828-29).

Ball, J. Dyer, Things Chinese   (London: Sampson Low,
    Marston and Company, Ltd., 1893).

Benson, Arthur Christopher, and Esher, Viscount, ed.,
    The Letters of Queen Victoria: A Selection from
    Her Majesty's Correspondence Between the Years
    1837 and 1861, 3 vols. (New York: Longmans,
    Green and Co., 1907).

                          326

Cappon, Lester J., ed., The Adams-Jefferson Letters: The Complete Correspondence Between Thomas Jefferson and Abigail & John Adams (Chapel Hill: University of North Carolina Press, 1959).

Crowley, Julia M., Echoes from Niagara: Historical, Political, Personal (Buffalo: C.W. Moulton, 1890).

Curtis, George William, Address of George William Curtis to the National Civil Service Reform League Annual Meeting at Newport, Rhode Island, August 4, 1886 (New York: National Civil-Service Reform League, 1886).

Eaton, Dorman B., Civil Service in Great Britain: A History of Abuses and Reforms and Their Bearing Upon American Politics (New York: Harper & Bros., 1880).

_____, The Need and Best Means of Providing a Competent and Stable Civil Service for our New Dependencies (Baltimore: National Civil-Service Reform League, 1898).

Gladstone, William Ewart, The Gladstone Diaries, 4 vols., edited by M.R.D. Foot and H.C.G. Matthew (Oxford: Clarendon Press, 1974).

Godkin, Edwin Lawrence, The Gilded Age Letters of E.L. Godkin, edited by William M. Armstrong (Albany: State University of New York Press, 1974).

Gray, John Purdue, The United States vs. Charles J. Guiteau (Washington, D.C.: 1882, reprint ed., New York: Arno Press, 1973).

Hamilton, James Alexander, Reminiscences of James A. Hamilton: Men and Events, At Home and Abroad, During Three Quarters of a Century (New York: C. Scribner & Co., 1869).

Hayes, Rutherford Birchard, Diary and Letters of Rutherford Birchard Hayes: Nineteenth President of the United States, edited by Charles Richard Williams, 5 vols. (Columbus, Ohio: The Ohio State Archaeological and Historical Society, 1922-1926).

Hertslet, Sir Edward, Recollections of the Old Foreign Office (London: J. Murray, 1901).

327

Higgins, Matthew James [Jacob Omnium], Essays on Social
    Subjects by Matthew James Higgins: With a Memoir
    by Sir William Stirling Maxwell (London: Smith,
    Elder & Co., 1875).

Hinsdale, Mary L., ed., Garfield-Hinsdale Letters:
    Correspondence Between James Abram Garfield and
    Burke Aaron Hinsdale (Ann Arbor, Mich.: University
    of Michigan Press, 1949).

Holloran, Matthew F., The Romance of the Merit System:
    Forty-five Years' Reminiscences of the Civil Ser-
    vice (Washington, D.C.: Judd & Detweiler, Inc.,
    1928).

Howe, M.A. DeWolfe, The Life and Letters of George Ban-
    croft, 2 vols. (New York: Charles Scribner's
    Sons, 1908).

Jefferson, Thomas, The Works of Thomas Jefferson, edited
    by Paul Leicester Ford, 12 vols., Federal Edition.
    (New York: G.P. Putnam's Sons, 1904-1905).

_____, The Writings of Thomas Jefferson,
    Memorial Edition. (Washington, D.C.: Andrew A.
    Lipscomb, 1853).

Keith, A.B., ed., Speeches and Documents on Indian
    Policy (London: H. Milford, 1922).

Lamon, Ward Hill, Recollections of Abraham Lincoln:
    1847-1865 (Washington, D.C.: Dorothy Lamon
    Teillard, 1911).

Martin, Arthur Patchett, Life and Letters of Right Honour-
    able Robert Lowe, Viscount Sherbrooke. . . with a
    Memoir of Sir John Coape Sherbrooke, G.C.B. (London:
    Longmans, Green & Co., 1893).

Mill, John Stuart, Considerations on Representative Gov-
    ernment (New York: Harper & Bros., 1862).

National Civil Service Reform League, The Assassination
    of President Garfield: In Washington: July 2, 1881
    (New York: National Civil Service Reform League, 1881).

_____, Report of the Special Committee
    on the National Civil Service Reform League Upon the
    Present Condition of the National, State and Municipal
    Administrations (New York: National Civil Service
    Reform League, 1887).

National Civil Service Reform League, Report on the Ex-
    pediency of Asking Candidates for Public Office
    Their Views of Civil-Service Reform (New York;
    National Civil Service Reform League, 1882).

_____, Superannuation in the Civil Ser-
    vice (New York: National Civil Service Reform
    League, 1901).

Nevins, Allan, ed., Letters of Grover Cleveland: 1850-
    1908 (Boston: Houghton-Mifflin Co., 1933).

Norris, James D. and Shaffer, Arthur H., ed., Politics
    and Patronage in the Gilded Age: The Correspondence
    of James A. Garfield and Charles H. Henry (Madison,
    Wis.: State Historical Society of Wisconsin, 1970).

Norton, Charles Eliot, ed., Orations and Addresses by
    George William Curtis, 3 vols. (New York: Harper
    & Bros., 1894).

Ogden, Rollo, ed., Life and Letters of Edwin Lawrence
    Godkin, 2 vols. (New York: 1907).

Parker, C.S., Life and Letters of Sir James Graham:
    Second Baronet of Netherby, P.C., G.C.B., 1792-
    1821 (London: J. Murray, 1907).

Polk, James Knox, The Diary of James K. Polk: During His
    Presidency: 1845 to 1849 (Chicago: A.C. McClurg
    & Co., 1910).

Poore, Benjamin Perley, Perley's Reminiscences of Sixty
    Years in the National Metropolis, 2 vols. (Phila-
    delphia: Hubbard Bros., 1886).

Richardson, James Daniel, ed., A Compilation of the Mes-
    sages and Papers of the Presidents, 8 vols. (Wash-
    ington, D.C.: Government Printing Office, 1896-1899).

Schurz, Carl, The Autobiography of Carl Schurz (New York:
    Charles Scribner's Sons, 1961).

_____, Intimate Letters of Carl Schurz: 1841-1869,
    edited and translated by Joseph Schafer. (Madison,
    Wis.: State Historical Society of Wisconsin, 1928).

_____, Speeches, Correspondence, and Papers of Carl
    Schurz, 6 vols., edited by Frederic Bancroft. (New
    York: G.P. Putnam's Sons, 1913).

Severance, Frama H., ed., Millard Fillmore Papers (Buffalo: The Buffalo Historical Society, 1907).

Sherman, John, John Sherman's Recollections of Forty Years in the House, Senate and Cabinet: An Autobiography, 2 vols. (Chicago: The Werner Co., 1895).

Smith, Theodore Clarke, Life and Letters of James Abram Garfield, 2 vols. (New Haven: Yale University Press, 1925).

A Subordinate Therein. Administrative Reform: The Re-organization of the Civil Service (London: Smith, Elder & Co., 1855).

Sumner, Charles, Memoir and Letters of Charles Sumner, 4 vols., edited by Edward L. Pierce (Boston: Roberts Bros., 1877-1893).

Trevelyan, G. Otto, The Life and Letters of Lord Macaulay, 2 vols. (New York: Harper & Bros., 1904).

Trollope, Anthony, Anthony Trollope: Four Letters, edited by Morris L. Parrish (London: Constable & Co., Ltd., 1938).

_____, An Autobiography of Anthony Trollope (New York: G. Munro, 1883).

_____, The Three Clerks: A Novel (New York: Harper & Bros., 1874).

Washington, George, The Writings of George Washington from the Original Manuscript Sources: 1745-1799, edited by John C. Fitzpatrick, 39 vols. George Washington Bicentennial Commission (Washington, D.C.: Government Printing Office, 1944).

West, Algernon, Recollections: 1832-1886 (New York: Harper & Row, 1900).

Journals, Magazines, and Periodicals

Adams, Henry Brooks, "Civil Service Reform," North American Review (October 1869): 443-470.

Bing, Julius, "Civil Service of the United States," North American Review, 55 No. 217 (October 1867): 478-495.

"Mr. Blaine and English Civil Service," <u>Saturday Review</u>
62 (1886): 379.

Cox, Jacob D., "The Civil Service Reform," <u>North American
Review</u> 62 (1871): 101-104.

Eaton, Dorman B., "Assassination and the Spoils System in
the United States," <u>Princeton Review</u> (New Series) 8
(1881): 145.

_____, "Civil Service Reform in Great Britain,"
<u>The Civil-Service Reformer</u> (December 1886): 100-109.

_____, "Civil Service Reform in the United
States," <u>American Social Science Association</u> (May 1875).

_____, "The Experiment of Civil Service Reform
in the United States," <u>American Social Science Association Journal</u> 8 (May 1876): 54-78.

_____, "A New Phase of the Reform Movement,"
<u>North American Review</u> (June 1881): 546-558.

_____, "Political Assessments," <u>North American
Review</u> 135 (September 1882): 197-219.

_____, "Tenure of Office," <u>Lippincott's Maga-
zine</u> 27 (June 1881): 580-592.

_____, "Two Years of Civil Service Reform,"
<u>North American Review</u> 141 (July 1885): 15-24.

Lyman, Charles, "Ten Years of Civil Service Reform,"
<u>North American Review</u> 157 (1893): 575.

Marcy, William L., "Diary and Memoranda of William L.
Marcy, 1857," <u>American Historical Review</u> 24 (1918-
1919): 647.

Richardson, Lyon N. and Garrison, Curtis W., ed., "Notes
and Documents: George William Curtis, Rutherford B.
Hayes, and Civil Service Reform," <u>Mississippi Valley
Historical Review</u> 32 (June 1945): 235-250.

Reeves, Thomas C., "The President's Dwarf: The Letters
of Julia Sand to Chester A. Arthur," <u>New York His-
tory</u> 52 (July 1971): 73-83.

331

SECONDARY SOURCES

Books

Aronson, Sidney H., Status and Kinship in the Higher
Civil Service: Standards of Selection in the Administrations of John Adams, Thomas Jefferson,
and Andrew Jackson (Cambridge: Harvard University Press, 1964).

Auchanpaugh, Philip Gerald, James Buchanan and His Cabinet
on the Eve of Succession (Boston: J.S. Canner &
Co., Inc., 1926).

Aylmer, G.E., The King's Servants: The Civil Service of
Charles I: 1625-1642 (London: Routledge & Kegan
Paul, 1974).

_____, The State's Servants: The Civil Service
of the English Republic: 1649-1660 (London: Routledge & Kegan Paul, 1973).

Barker, Sir Ernest, The Development of Public Services in
Western Europe: 1600-1930 (Hamden, Ct.: Archon
Books, 1966).

Barrows, Chester L., William M. Evarts: Lawyer, Diplomat,
Statesman (Chapel Hill: The University of North
Carolina Press, 1941).

Baruch, Ismar, History of Position-Classification and
Salary Standardization in the Federal Service:
1789-1938 (Washington, D.C.: Farm Credit Administration, 1939).

Benedict, Michael Les, The Impeachment and Trial of Andrew Johnson (New York: W.W. Norton & Co., 1973).

Beveridge, Albert J., The Life of John Marshall, 4 vols.
(Boston: Houghton-Mifflin Co., 1919).

Bill, Edward Geoffrey Watson, University Reform in Nineteenth-Century Oxford: A Study of Henry Halford
Vaughan, 1811-1885 (Oxford: University Press, 1973).

_____, and Mason, J.F.A., Christ
Church and Reform: 1850-1867 (Oxford: At the
Clarendon Press, 1970).

Burn, William Laurence, The Age of Equipoise: A Study of Mid-Victorian Generation (New York: W.W. Norton & Co., 1964).

Burns, Sir Allen Cuthbert, Colonial Civil Service (London: George Allen & Unwin, Ltd., 1949).

Caldwell, Lynton K., The Administrative Theories of Hamilton & Jefferson: Their Contribution to Thought on Public Administration (Chicago: University of Chicago Press, 1944).

Carman, Henry J. & Luthin, Reinhard W., Lincoln and the Patronage (New York: Columbia University Press, 1943).

Carpenter, William Seal, Unfinished Business of Civil Service Reform (Princeton: Princeton University Press, 1952).

Cary, Edward, George William Curtis (Boston: Houghton, 1894).

Chitwood, Oliver Perry, John Tyler, Champion of the Old South (New York: D. Appleton-Century Co., 1939).

Clancy, Herbert J., The Presidential Election of 1880 (Chicago: Loyola University Press, 1958).

Clark, Dora Mae, The Rise of the British Treasury: Colonial Administration in the 18th Century (New Haven: Yale University Press, 1960).

Clarke, William Harrison, The Civil Service Law, 3rd ed., (New York: M.T. Richardson Co., 1897).

Clive, John, Macaulay: The Shaping of the Historian (New York: Alfred A. Knopf, 1973).

Cohen, Bernard S., "Recruitment and Training of British Civil Servants in India, 1600-1860," Asian Bureaucratic Systems Emergent from the British Imperial Tradition, edited by Ralph Braibanti. (Durham, N.C.: Duke University Press, 1966).

Cohen, Emmeline W., The Growth of the British Civil Service, 1780-1939 (London: George Allen & Unwin, Ltd., 1941).

Conkling, Alfred Ronald, The Life and Letters of Roscoe Conkling, Orator, Statesman, Advocate (New York: C.L. Webster & Co., 1899).
333

Cunningham, Noble E., Jr., The Jeffersonian Republicans: The Formation of Party Organizations, 1789-1801 (Chapel Hill: The University of North Carolina Press, 1957).

_____, ed., The Making of the American Party System: 1789-1809 (Englewood Cliffs, N.J.: Prentice-Hall, 1965).

Curtis, George Tickner, Life of James Buchanan, Fifteenth President of the United States, 2 vols. (New York: Harper Bros., 1883).

Davison, Kenneth E., The Presidency of Rutherford B. Hayes (Westport, Ct.: Greenwood Press, Inc., 1972).

Deming, William C., Application of the Merit System in the U.S. Civil Service System (Washington, D.C.: Government Printing Office, 1928).

DeWitt, David Miller, The Impeachment and Trial of Andrew Johnson: Seventeenth President of the United States: A History (New York: Macmillan, 1903).

Dimock, Marshall Edward, Congressional Investigating Committees (Baltimore: Johns Hopkins University Press, 1929).

Dobson, John M., Politics in the Gilded Age: A New Perspective on Reform (New York: Praeger, 1972).

Donald, David, Charles Sumner and the Coming of the Civil War (New York: Alfred A. Knopf, 1960).

_____, Charles Sumner and the Rights of Man (New York: Alfred A. Knopf, 1970).

Dunsire, A., Administration: The Word and the Science (New York: John Wiley & Sons, 1973).

Durant, Will, Our Oriental Heritage (New York: Simon & Schuster, 1935).

Easum, Chester Verne, The Americanization of Carl Schurz (Chicago: University of Chicago Press, 1929).

Eckenrode, H.J., Rutherford B. Hayes: Statesman of Reunion (New York: Dodd, Mead & Co., 1930; reprint ed., Port Washington, N.Y.: Kennikat Press, 1963).

334

Erickson, Arvel B., The Public Career of Sir James Graham (Oxford: Basil Blackwell & Mott, Ltd., 1952).

Finer, Herman, The British Civil Service (London: The
Fabian Society and Allen & Unwin, 1937).

Finer, Samuel Edward, A Primer of Public Administration
(London: Frederick Muller, Ltd., 1950).

Fish, Carl Russell, The Civil Service and the Patronage
(New York: 1904; reprint ed., New York: Russell
& Russell, Inc., 1963).

Foiney, John Wien, Anecdotes of Public Men (New York:
Harper & Bros).

Fuess, Claude Moore, Carl Schurz, Reformer (1829-1906)
(New York: Dodd, Mead & Co., 1932).

_____, Daniel Webster (Boston: Little,
Brown & Co., 1930).

George, Mary Karl, Zachariah Chandler: A Political Biography (East Lansing, Mich.: Michigan State University Press, 1969).

Gladden, Edgar Norman, Civil Service of the United King-
dom: 1855-1870 (New York: Augustus M. Kelley, 1967).

Goldsmith, William M., The Growth of Presidential Power:
Documented History (New York: Chelsea House Pub-
lisher in association with R.R. Bowker Co., 1974).

Gregoire, Roger, The French Civil Service (Brussels: International Institute of Administrative Sciences,
1964).

Gregory, Allene, John Milton Gregory: A Biography (Chicago: Covici-McGee Co., 1923).

Griffith, Wyn, The British Civil Service, 1854-1954 (London: Her Majesty's Stationery Office, 1954).

Hamilton, Holman, Zachary Taylor, 2 vols. (Hamden, Ct.:
Archon Books, 1966).

Hart, James, The American Presidency in Action: 1789: A
Study in Constitutional History (New York: Macmillan,
1948).

Hesseltine, William Best, Ulysses S. Grant: Politician (New York: Dodd, Mead & Co., 1935).

Hofstadter, Richard, The Idea of a Party System: The Rise of Legitimate Opposition in the United States, 1780-1840 (Berkeley: University of California Press, 1969).

Hoogenboom, Ari Arthur, Outlawing the Spoils: A History of the Civil Service Reform Movement: 1865-1883 (Urbana: University of Illinois Press, 1961).

Howe, J.A. DeWolfe, Portrait of an Independent: Moorfield Story: 1845-1929 (Boston: Houghton-Mifflin, 1932).

Hsieh, Pao Chao, The Government of China (1644-1911) (Baltimore: The Johns Hopkins Press, 1925).

Jeffries, Charles Joseph, The Colonial Empire and Its Civil Service (Cambridge: At the University Press, 1938).

Jordan, David M., Roscoe Conkling of New York: Voice in the Senate (Ithaca: Cornell University Press, 1971).

Kingsley, John Donald, Representative Bureaucracy: An Interpretation of the British Civil Service (Yellow Springs, Ohio: The Antioch Press, 1944).

Klein, Philip Shriver, President James Buchanan: A Biography (University Park, Pa.: The Pennsylvania State University Press, 1962).

Krug, Mark M., Lyman Trumbull: Conservative Radical (New York: A.S. Barnes & Co., 1965).

Lambie, Norris B., British Civil Service Personnel Administration (Washington, D.C.: Government Printing Office, 1929).

Lang, Andrew, Sir Stafford Northcote: First Earl of Iddesleigh, 2 vols. (Edinburgh: William Blackwood & Sons, 1890).

Latourette, Kenneth Scott, A Short History of the Far East (New York: Macmillan, 1951).

Lo, Koren Huang, The Civil Service System of China (Taipei: China Cultural Service, 1957).

Loewenstein, Karl, "Germany and Central Europe," Governments of Continental Europe, edited by James T.
Shotwell (New York: Macmillan, 1940).

Logsdon, Joseph, Horace White: Nineteenth Century Liberal (Westport, Ct.: Greenwood Publishing Corporation, 1971).

McBaine, Howard Lee, DeWitt Clinton and the Origin of
the Spoils System in New York (New York: Columbia
University Press, 1907).

McCormick, Richard P., The Second American Party System:
Party Formation in the Jacksonian Era (Chapel Hill:
The University of North Carolina Press, 1966).

McFarland, Gerald J., Mugwumps, Morals & Politics: 1884-
1920 (Amherst: The University of Massachusetts
Press, 1975).

Magnus, Philip, Gladstone (New York: E.P. Dutton & Co.,
1964).

Malone, Dumas, Jefferson the President: The First Term:
1801-1805 (Boston: Little, Brown & Co., 1970).

Mayers, Lewis, The Federal Service: A Study of the System of Personnel Administration of the United States
Government (New York: D. Appleton & Co., 1922).

Menzel, Johanna M., The Chinese Civil Service: Career
Open to Talent? (Boston: D.C. Heath & Co., 1963).

Milne, Gordon, George William Curtis & The Genteel Tradition (Bloomington: Indiana University Press,
1956).

Morgan, H. Wayne, From Hayes to McKinley: National Party
Politics: 1877-1886 (Syracuse: Syracuse University
Press, 1969).

Morley, John, The Life of William Ewart Gladstone, 3 vols.
(London: Macmillan, 1903).

Moses, Robert, The Civil Service of Great Britain (New
York: Columbia University Press, 1914).

Mustoe, Nelson E., The Law and Organization of the British
Civil Service (London: Sir Isaac Pitman & Sons, 1932).

Muzzey, David Saville, James G. Blaine: A Political Idol of Other Days (New York: 'Dodd, Mead & Co., 1934).

Nevins, Allan, Grover Cleveland: A Study in Courage (New York: Dodd, Mead & Co., 1932).

Nichols, Roy Franklin, Franklin Pierce: Young Hickory of the Granite Hills, 2nd ed. (Philadelphia: University of Pennsylvania Press, 1958).

Nourse, Mary A., A Short History of the Chinese (New York: Bobbs-Merrill Co., 1943).

Parris, Henry, Constitutional Bureaucracy: The Development of British Central Administration Since the Eighteenth Century (London: George Allen & Unwin, Ltd., 1969).

Pessen, Edward, Jacksonian America: Society, Personality, and Politics (Homewood, Ill.: The Dorsey Press, 1969).

Polakoff, Keith Ian, The Politics of Inertia: The Election of 1876 and the End of Reconstruction (Baton Rouge: Louisiana State University Press, 1973).

Pratt, Fletcher, Stanton: Lincoln's Secretary of War (Westport, Ct.: Greenwood Press, 1970).

Prince, Carl E., The Federalists and the Origins of the United States Civil Service (New York: New York University Press, 1977).

Raphael, Marios, Pensions and Public Servants: A Study of the Origins of the British System (Paris: Mouton & Co., 1964).

Reader, William Joseph, Professional Men: The Rise of the Professional Classes in Nineteenth-Century England (London: Weidenfeld & Nicolson, 1966).

Reeves, Thomas C., Gentleman Boss: The Life of Chester Alan Arthur (New York: Alfred A. Knopf, 1975).

Remini, Robert V., The Age of Jackson (Columbia: University of South Carolina Press, 1972).

_____, Martin Van Buren and the Making of the Democratic Party (New York: Columbia University Press, 1959).

Richards, Peter G., Patronage in British Government
(Toronto: University of Toronto Press, 1963).

Roach, John, Public Examinations in England: 1850-1900
(Cambridge: At the University Press, 1971).

Roberts, David, Victorian Origins of the British Welfare
State (New Haven: Yale University Press, 1960).

Robson, William A., ed., The Civil Service in Britain
and France (New York: Macmillan, 1956).

Rosenberg, Charles E., The Trial of the Assassin Guiteau:
Psychiatry and Law in the Gilded Age (Chicago:
University of Chicago Press, 1968).

Rosenberg, Hans, Bureaucracy, Aristocracy and Autocracy:
The Prussian Experience: 1660-1815 (Cambridge:
Harvard University Press, 1958).

Roseveare, Henry, The Treasury: The Evolution of a British Institution (New York: Columbia University
Press, 1969).

_____, The Treasury: 1660-1870: The Founda-
tions of Control (London: George Allen & Unwin,
Ltd., 1973).

Ross, Earle Dudley, The Liberal Republican Movement (New
York: 1919; reprint ed. New York: AMS Press, 1971).

Ross, Edmund G., History of the Impeachment of Andrew
Johnson: President of the United States by the
House of Representative and the Trial by the Sen-
ate for High Crimes and Misdemeanors in Office,
1868 (New York: Burt Franklin Research & Source
Works, 1896).

Rothblatt, Sheldon, The Revolution of the Dons: Cambridge and Society in Victorian England (London:
Faber, 1968).

Rothman, David J., Politics and Power: The United States
Senate: 1869-1901 (Cambridge: Harvard University
Press, 1966).

Royback, Robert J., Millard Fillmore: Biography of a
President (Buffalo: Buffalo Historical Society,
Henry Stewart Inc., 1959).

Sageser, Adelbert Bower, The First Two Decades of the Pendleton Act: A Study of Civil Service Reform (Lincoln, Neb.: University of Nebraska, 1935).

Sanderson, Michael, ed., The Universities in the Nineteenth Century (London: Routledge & Kegan Paul, 1975).

Schlesinger, Arthur M., Jr. and Burns, Roger, Congress Investigates: A Documented History, 5 vols. (New York: Chelsea House Publishers, 1975).

Seager, Robert, II., And Tyler Too: A Biography of John and Julia Gardiner Tyler (New York: McGraw-Hill, 1963).

Sellers, Charles, James K. Polk: Continentalist: 1843-1846 (Princeton: Princeton University Press, 1966).

Sharp, Walter Rice, The French Civil Service: Bureaucracy in Transition (New York: Macmillan, 1931).

Shores, Venila Lovina, The Hayes-Conkling Controversy: 1877-1879 (New York: Department of History of Smith College, 1919).

Spencer, Ivor Debenham, The Victor and the Spoils: A Life of William L. Marcy (Providence: Brown University Press, 1959).

Sproat, John G., "The Best Men:" Liberal Reformers in the Gilded Age (New York: Oxford University Press, 1968).

Stewart, Frank Mann, The National Civil Service Reform League (Austin: University of Texas Press, 1929).

Syrett, Harold C., Andrew Jackson: His Contribution to the American Tradition (Westport, Ct.: Greenwood Press, 1971).

Taylor, Martha Berris, History of the Federal Civil Service: 1789 to the Present (Washington, D.C.: Government Printing Office, 1941).

Thomas, Lately, The First President Johnson: The Three Lives of the Seventeenth President of the United States of America: A History (New York: Macmillan, 1903).

Van Riper, Paul P., History of the United States Civil Service (Evanston, Ill.: Row, Peterson & Co., 1958).

Ward, John Trevor, Sir James Graham (London: Macmillan, 1967).

Ward, William Reginald, Victorian Oxford (London: F. Cass, 1965).

Watson, Edward Geoffrey, and Mason, J.F.A., Christ Church and Reform, 1850-1867 (Oxford: Clarendon Press, 1970).

Webb, Ross A., Benjamin Helm Bristow: Border State Politician (Frankfort: The University Press of Kentucky, 1969).

Welch, Richard E., Jr., George Frisbie Hoar and the Half-Breed Republicans (Cambridge: Harvard University Press, 1971).

White, Leonard Dupee, The Federalists: A Study in Administrative History (New York: Macmillan, 1948).

_____, The Jacksonians: A Study in Administrative History: 1829-1861 (New York: Macmillan, 1954).

_____, The Jeffersonians: A Study in Administrative History: 1801-1829 (New York: Macmillan, 1951).

_____, The Republican Era: A Study in Administrative History: 1869-1901 (New York: Macmillan, 1958).

_____; Bland, Charles H.,; Sharp, Walter R.; Marx, Fritz Morstein, Civil Service Abroad: Great Britain, Canada, France, Germany (New York: McGraw-Hill, 1935).

Wilson, Woodrow, The Study of Public Administration: Annals of American Government (Washington, D.C.: Public Affairs Press, 1962).

Winter, James, Robert Lowe (Buffalo: University of Toronto Press, 1976).

Woodward, C. Van, Reunion and Reaction: The Compromise of 1877 and the End of Reconstruction (New York: Doubleday & Co., 1956).

341

Wright, Maurice, Treasury Control of the Civil Service: 1854-1874 (Oxford: Clarendon Press, 1969).

Journals, Magazines, and Periodicals

Adelman, Paul, "Gladstone and Education," History Today (July 1970): 496-503.

Armstrong, J.A., "Old-Regime Administrative Elites: Prelude to Modernization in France, Prussia and Russia," International Review of Administrative Sciences 38 (1972): 21-40.

Armstrong, Sir William, and Ugerson, Bernard, "The Largest Personnel Department of Them All," Personnel Management (June 1973): 18-22.

Clark, George Kitson, "'Statesmen in Disguise': Reflections on the History of the Neutrality of the Civil Service," Historical Journal 2 (1959): 19-39.

Compton, J.M., "Open Competition and the Indian Civil Service, 1854-1876," English Historical Review 33 (April 1968): 265-284.

Doyle, John T., "The Conquest of the Spoils System," Good Government (November 1937 to January 1939), run serially.

Eriksson, Erik McKinley, "The Federal Civil Service Under President Jackson," Mississippi Valley Historical Review 13 (June 1926 to March 1927): 517-540.

Finer, S.E., "Patronage and the Public Service: Jeffersonian Bureaucracy and the British Tradition," Public Administration 30 (Winter 1952): 329.

Formisano, Ronald P., "Toward a Reorientation of Jacksonian Politics: A Review of the Literature, 1959-1975," Journal of American History 63 (June 1976): 42-65.

Gerber, Richard Allan, "The Liberal Republicans of 1872 in Historiographical Perspective," Journal of American History 62 (June 1975): 40-73.

Graebner, Norman A., "James K. Polk: A Study in Federal
    Patronage," Mississippi Valley Historical Review 38
    (June 1951): 613-632.

Hart, Jenifer, "Sir Charles Trevelyan at the Treasury,"
    English Historical Review 65 (January 1960): 92-110.

Headey, B., "The Civil Service as an Elite in Britain and
    Germany," International Review of Administrative
    Sciences 38 (January 1972): 41-48.

Hogue, Arthur R., "Civil Service Reform, 1869," American-
    German Review (June 1952): 5-7 and 39-40.

Hoogenboom, Ari, "The Pendleton Act and the Civil Ser-
    vice," American Historical Review 64 (January 1959):
    312-318.

_____, "Thomas A. Jenckes and Civil Service Re-
    form," Mississippi Valley Historical Review 47 (March
    1961): 636-658.

Hsu, Francis L.K., "Social Mobility in China," American
    Sociological Review 14 (1949): 764-771.

Hughes, Edward, "Civil Service Reform: 1853-5," Public
    Administration 32 (1954): 17-51.

_____, "Postscript to the Civil Service Reform of
    1855," Public Administration 33 (Autumn 1955).

McFarland, Gerald W., "Partisan of Nonpartisanship: Dor-
    man B. Eaton and the Genteel Reform Tradition,"
    Journal of American History 54 (December 1967):
    806-822.

Moore, R.J., "The Abolition of Patronage in the Indian
    Civil Service and the Closure of Haileybury College,"
    The Historical Journal 7 (1964): 249-253.

Murphy, Lionel V., "The First Federal Civil Service Com-
    mission: 1871-1875," Public Personnel Review, No.
    1, 3, 4 (January, July, October 1942): 29-39; 218-
    231, and 299-323.

Nelson, Charles J., "The Press & Civil Service Reform,"
    Civil Service Journal 13 (April-June 1973).

Nigro, Felix A., "Two Civil Service Systems-- Alike Yet Different," Good Government 90 (Summer 1973): 8-11.

Prince, Carl E., "The Passing of the Aristocracy: Jefferson's Removal of the Federalists, 1801-1805," Journal of American History 57 (June 1970): 563-575.

Rader, Benjamin G., "Jacksonian Democracy: Myth or Reality?," Social Studies 65 (January 1974): 17-22.

Reeves, Thomas C., "Chester A. Arthur and Campaign Assessments in the Election of 1880," The Historian: A Journal of History 31 (August 1969): 573-582.

_____, "Chester A. Arthur and the Campaign of 1880," Political Science Quarterly 74 (December 1969): 628-637.

_____, "Silas Burt and Chester Arthur: A Reformer's View of the Twenty-first President," The New York Historical Society Quarterly 54 (October 1970): 319-337.

Rhodes, R.A.W., "Wilting in Limbo: Anthony Trollope and the Nineteenth Century Civil Service," Public Administration 51 (1973): 207-219.

Carl Schurz Memorial Foundation, Inc., "Carl Schurz," The American-German Review 18 (August 1952): Entire issue.

Smith, Brian C., "Reform and Change in British Central Administration," Political Studies 19 (1971): 213-226.

Unpublished Material

Berens, Ruth M., "Blueprint for Reform: Curtis, Eaton, and Schurz," Unpublished Master's Dissertation, University of Chicago, 1943.

Dyess, William J., "American Conception of the British Civil Service," Unpublished Ph.D. Dissertation, University of Alabama, 1951.

Wolfe, Arthur Vernon, "The United States Civil Service Employment System--To 1933," Unpublished Ph.D. Dissertation, University of Chicago, 1966.

U.S. Civil Service Comm., "The Story of the U.S. Civil Service," unpublished and undated (around 1960), U.S. Civil Service Commission Library.

Aberdeen, Prime Minister,
56, 70
Act of 1853 (Classification),
139-140
Act of Settlement, 25
Adams, Henry, 168-169, 179,
206-207
Adams, John, 108-109, 111-113,
116
Adams, John Quincy, 116-119
Administrative Reform Association, 74
Akerman, Amon Tappan, 213
American Social Science Association, 172, 178, 205
Arbuthnot, G., 67, 87
Aristocracy, 71, 86, 101, 173-
176, 196, 201, 206-208,
210, 238-239, 245, 302-
304, 308-310
Arthur, Chester A., 215, 218,
222, 227-230, 259, 262,
264, 270-287, 295-296,
301, 304, 307
Assassination, 1, 270-273,
279-280, 285, 289
Assessments, Political, 186,
279-281

Bentham, Jeremy, 28
Bigelow, John, 19-22, 142
Bill of Rights of 1689, 25
Bing, Julius, 159-160, 164,
166, 171, 177, 197, 200
Blaine, James G., 187, 223,
262-263, 281-282, 311,
312
British Civil Service, 23-100,
191-210, 233-256, 289-320
Brown, Joseph E., 302
Buchanan, James, 135-136, 140
Burke, Edmund, 25-27
Burt, Silas W., 221-222, 257,
269, 284, 306, 308
Butler, Benjamin F., 185, 281-
282

Cambridge University, 48-
51, 77
Chinese Civil Service, 3-8,
21-22, 160, 197
Civil Service, British,
32-39, 51-54, 60-67,
72-73, 75, 79, 81, 85-
88, 90, 94-97
Chinese, 3-8, 21-22
French, 13-22
German (Prussian), 8-
13, 21-22
Indian, 47-48, 53-59
United States, 101-320

Civil Service Commission,
British, 73-75, 78-84,
88-98
United States, 144, 148-
150, 165, 191, 193,
202, 209, 211-223,
231, 233, 235-237,
241-242, 248, 250-
251, 254, 256, 269,
274, 276, 278-279,
283-284, 293, 299-300,
305-309, 312-319

Civil Service Reform,
British, 10, 28-32,
36-100, 312-320
United States, 101-320
Competitive Examinations,
68, 70, 74, 80, 82-83,
86, 91, 96-97, 144,
148-149, 186, 193,
197-198, 201, 207, 212-
213, 215, 233, 257,
276-277, 282-285, 295-
297, 313, 315-316, 318-
319
Conkling, Roscoe, 185, 215,
218, 223, 226, 228-230,
259, 262-264, 271, 287
Cox, Jacob Dobson, 169,
186-187

Curtis, George William, 99, 168-
169, 177-178, 182-186,
202, 205-206, 211-215, 217-
218, 220, 224, 228, 233-237,
245-246, 248, 254-256, 260-
262, 267, 278, 280-281, 284,
289-290, 292, 297, 300, 303,
309-312

Dawes, Henry L., 190, 269-270,
277-278, 298
Disraeli, Sir Benjamin, 43, 70
Dissenters, 49, 77
Duane, William J., 129

Eaton, Dorman B., 99, 218-255,
258, 260-262, 278, 284,
290-299, 306, 309, 312-
313, 320
Equal Employment Opportunity, 267
Examinations, 3-7, 11-12, 15,
21, 57-58, 64-66, 68,
70-71, 73-74, 78-80, 82-
84, 86, 91-94, 96-97, 142-
144, 148-150, 191-197, 201-
243, 257, 267, 273-277, 282-
285, 291-300, 305-320

Fenton, Reuben, 215
Fillmore, Millard, 134, 139
Fulton Committee, 98
French Civil Service, 13-22, 68,
160, 197

Gale, Nathaniel, 161-164, 166,
171, 200
Garfield, James A., 158, 190,
216, 229, 257-275
German (Prussian) Civil Service, 8-13, 21-22, 160,
197
Gladstone, William, 43-46, 51-
96, 143, 200, 235-239,
246, 256, 310
Godkin, E.L., 99, 161, 186,
217, 246, 252, 267, 312

Gordon, John B., 243-244
Graham, Sir James, 37-38,
72
Grant, Ulysses S., 143,
153, 167-169, 171,
179-180, 185, 190,
211, 215, 217, 226,
229, 231, 233, 236-
237, 241, 248, 255,
257-258, 269-270, 274,
279, 284, 293, 296-
297, 299-300, 317-318
Grant Civil Service Com-
mission, 2, 218-223
Granville, Earl, 56, 89-90,
235
Great Britain, 1-2, 23-
100, 145, 151, 191-
192, 194-205, 210,
233-256, 289-298,
301-319
Guiteau, Charles, 270-272

Haldane Committee, 98
Hamilton, Alexander, 106-107,
110-111
Hamilton, Sir William, 49
Harrison, William H., 106,
132
Hayes, Rutherford B., 223-
231, 241, 248-259,
263, 267-271, 300
Hayter, Sir William, 82

India, 47-48, 53-60, 75,
252, 294, 299

Jackson, Andrew, 122-132,
138, 261
Jefferson, Thomas, 101,
110-111, 113-116, 118
Jenckes, Thomas A., 7, 99,
141-169, 171-177,
182-185, 187-190,
192-219, 234, 249,
255, 267, 300, 317-
318

Jeune, Dr. Francis, 68, 75-76
Job Descriptions, 317
Johnson, Andrew, 108, 149, 151-154, 166, 180, 191
Jowett, Benjamin, 39-40, 48-58, 60, 65, 68, 70, 78, 194, 235

Lefevre, J.G. Shaw, 52, 57, 66, 75
Lewis, Sir George Cornewall, 74
Lincoln, Abraham, 136-137, 140-141, 149, 173, 180, 219
Lingen, Ralph, 55, 67, 87-93
Logan, John Alexander, 173-177, 190, 200, 204, 216, 218, 264, 283, 285
Lowe, Sir Robert, 39, 44-45, 54, 56, 81, 85-87, 89, 91, 94, 96

Macaulay, Thomas Babington, 39, 41, 47-48, 53, 56-58, 72, 75, 193, 202
Macdonnell Commission, 98
Madison, James, 107, 111, 114-115, 118
Marcy, William L., 127, 133, 135
Merit, 73, 79, 104, 126, 205, 215, 249, 253, 268, 295, 307-308, 318-319
Monroe, James, 113, 116-118

Northcote, Sir Stafford, 42-44, 53, 55, 59, 61-68, 74, 81, 85, 92-97, 200, 234, 300
Northcote-Trevelyan Report, 61-81, 88, 200, 202

Oxford University, 48-51, 77
Order-in-Council, 1855, 74-75, 78-80, 85, 88, 91, 98, 164, 206

Order-in-Council, 1870, 88, 90-91, 95-98, 164, 188, 208-209, 315
1871, 94
1876, 97

Palmerston, Prime Minister, 79
Parliament, 25-28
Patronage, 1, 23-24, 32-36, 55-56, 68-69, 72-73, 79-81, 85-89, 94, 96, 98-99, 142, 147, 151-152, 210, 236, 246, 249, 265, 279, 285, 290, 293-297, 304, 309-311
Peel, Robert, 37
Pendleton, George, 266-270, 276-279, 283-286, 296-304
Pendleton Act of 1883, 2, 223, 257-304, 305, 307, 317, 319
Pensions, 65, 320
Pierce, Franklin, 135, 140
Pitt, William, 26-27
Playfair Commission, 59, 94-98, 252
Polk, James K., 133-134, 138
Position Classification, 318
Prestley Commission, 98
Probation, 316, 318
Promotions, 67, 96, 150, 188, 276-277, 297, 307, 313, 315, 319

Recruitment, 4-5, 9, 12, 61, 64, 318
Reform, 28-54, 57, 60, 67-68, 71-72, 74, 78, 81, 85-86, 90, 94-99, 142-144, 151, 154-166, 175, 192-194, 199, 201-225, 230-319
Reform Act of 1832, 32
Retirement, 19, 313-314, 320
Ridley Commission, 98, 311

Rosengarten, Joseph George, 155-158, 163-164, 171-175, 195, 197, 203, 208
Russell, Lord John, 50, 70-72, 76

Sand, Julia, 275, 280, 286
Schurz, Carl, 99, 141, 167-169, 177, 179-182, 186, 189, 217, 224, 225, 230, 244, 255, 260, 265, 269, 273, 291, 310
Seward, William, 19, 141-142, 145
Sinecures, 26-27, 30-31, 303
Smith, Sydney, 49
Snapp, Henry, 217, 241-243
Speer, Thomas J., 215, 241-242
Spoils System, 1, 35-36, 117-140, 141, 143, 157, 160, 165, 183-184, 190, 192, 194, 209-210, 223, 237, 241, 245, 271-272, 277-278, 286, 296, 300, 302-303, 309-310, 319
Sumner, Charles, 99, 141-145, 159, 185, 191, 318
Superannuation Act of 1859, 80-81, 84, 91
Swartwout, Samuel, 131

Taylor, Zachary, 134
Tenure, 117, 122, 128, 153, 274, 276, 277, 279, 271, 283, 295, 296, 309, 314
Tenure of Office Act of 1820, 117-119, 122
Tenure of Office Act of 1867, 159, 176
Tomlin Commission, 98
Trevelyan, Sir Charles Edward, 40-42, 47-53, 55-97, 145, 194, 200, 202-205, 234-235, 248-249, 300
Tripos, 48, 50
Trollope, Anthony, 27, 34-35, 42
Trumbull, Lyman, 189-190, 215
Tutors' Association, 75-77
Tyler, John, 132-133, 138

Van Buren, Martin, 126-127, 131-132

Vaughn, Henry, 55-56, 76-77
Veteran Preference, 105, 116, 279, 316
Victoria, Queen, 70-71
Villard, Henry, 163, 172-173, 175, 177-178, 219

Washington, George, 102-110
Wellesley, Lord Richard, 47
Wells, David, 151, 169, 185, 191, 195
White, Leonard D., 305
Wood, John, 34, 66, 68
Wood, Sir Charles, 53-58
Woodbridge, Frederick E., 158, 195-196, 210
Woodward, George E., 173-175, 177, 201, 202, 204

ABOUT THE AUTHOR

Richard Titlow holds a Ph.D. in History from the American University in Washington, D.C. He is a career civil servant who has worked for several federal agencies, including the U.S. Civil Service Commission. He has written articles on various aspects of the public service. He has taught courses in history and the federal personnel system. He has appeared on television to discuss the impact of current events on the federal government. He is a member of the American Society of Public Administration and the American Historical Association.